The Diari

Harriet Dunlop

1854-1914

a gentle life in Ireland and London

edited by Christina Casement

first published 2007 by Alauda Books
Dene Cottage, West Harting, Petersfield
Hampshire, GU31 5PA

ISBN 978-0-9555961-0-0

Typeset by Alauda Books

Printed and bound by RPM Print & Design

The Diaries of Harriet Dunlop 1854-1914

a gentle life

in Ireland and London

edited by Christina Casement

cover design by Elisabeth Howard

ALAUDA BOOKS

Christina Casement has written and illustrated four children's books and is a painter and designer of ceramic tiles.
She is married to one of Harriet Dunlop's many great-great-nephews.

She would like to thank the many friends and
relations who have helped to produce the
edited Diaries with family records and pictures, including:
the late Mrs E.K. Casement
Mrs Annette Firth
Sir Edward Greenwell
the late John Greenwell
Annabel Henderson-Stewart
Sir David Henderson-Stewart
Tom Howard
Viscount Massereene & Ferrard
Andrew McClintock
the late John McClintock
Mrs Nicholas McClintock
Christopher Miles
Mrs Josephine Ratcliff
Lord Rathdonnell
Mrs Peggy Wilks
Mrs Sylvia Wright
and for advice and technical help:
John Jones
Noel Osborne and
above all, the vastly patient
Michael Casement

The Diaries of Harriet Catherine Anna Dunlop, running with only a few gaps from **1854** to **1914**, lay unread, as far as anyone remembers, in the house in Co. Antrim bought by her nephew Jack in the 1920s. Harriet, or Haddie as she was universally known, was born on March 24, 1838, so she is not quite 16 when the first diary begins. She is the eldest child of Robert and Anna Delap, who live at Rohanna, near Ardee, Co. Louth. Robert's father, William D. Delap - the Grandpapa of the diaries - is very much alive, at 74. His first wife, Catherine, died in 1842, but he married a second time (Mary Gore Sankey) so there is also a Grandmama. Their home is Monasterboice, a fair-sized estate, between Dunleer and Drogheda, on the beautiful eastern coast. The family changed their name to Dunlop, the old Scottish form, but not till 1861, so the early diaries are headed: H.C.A. Delap.

Haddie's mother, Anna Delap, is the daughter of Viscount Ferrard and of Harriet, Viscountess Massereene: she is also her husband's second-cousin, both being descendants of Anthony Foster, Judge and "Chief Baron of the Exchequer" who settled in Collon, Co. Louth, in the time of the Commonwealth. Around them are a very large and confusing array of cousins - de Salis, Skeffington, Jeffreys, Gledstanes, Stawell, Vesey FitzGerald and

McClintock—Anglo-Irish families of the Ascendency; unflamboyant—mainly small landowners, Godfearing, protestant—Robert is grandson of William Foster, Bishop of Clogher. In the silhouettes we have of Robert and Anna, they are a good-looking couple, and happy in their occupations - he with a book and she playing with her two eldest little girls.

The early diaries are very small, each day contained in a space 1"x 2", often written in pencil. As girls were no doubt trained to do, Haddie confines herself to the Weather, and lists of those who came to the house - and went from it. And one is immediately struck by how these families were constantly on the move, coming for short or long visits, a ceaseless round of social and family events; Haddie's own family drive a clarence and a carriage, and several jaunting cars of various sizes. They seldom stay in the country in winter, migrating to Dublin or, often, abroad - we know that Grandpapa lived in Geneva, for instance, for long periods.

Next to Haddie in the family comes Annette, born in 1840, and their only brother, William J.S., born 1847. Three further girls - Blanche, followed by Helen and then Dora, at first referred to as "Baby", are often called "the children" in 1854.

Personal comments on people or events, at first, are scanty; a few examples of selected days are given here. She also left many days blank. Haddie uses special signs for when each of her parents goes to Dublin - and they go often! *Italics* show Haddie's own words, including some inconsistencies of spelling names and places.

The family have spent Christmas staying at Malahide, by the sea.

1854. *Jan 1 Fine, frost, intense cold, perished in church. Toasts at dinner for the New Year and all mankind.*

Jan 6 Miss Kennedy [governess?] *returned from Kingstown. Children dressed as kings and queens. Could not go out.*

Jan 13 ... colds better. Blanche in bed with hives, [afterwards proved to be nettle rash.]

Jan 14 Blanche in bed. Lady L[ouisa] *Kerr came at half past 5, dinner at 6. Annette, Willie and I took tea in the schoolroom. Tissie* [Haddie's cousin Letitia] *slept in the schoolroom. Mlle Samson from half past one to 3.*

Mlle Samson is the girls' music teacher. Considerable care seems to have been taken with their education: both Haddie and Annette write well, play the piano and speak French and German. It is not clear whether they had a governess living with them at this date, but in an earlier fragment we hear of Mlle. Ott and then Miss Harris. They learn French and English History with their mother.

Jan 22 Dark and showery; only Papa and Nettie to church. We all walked on the sea-shore with Mr Reilly. Intelligence received of a wreck last night at Lambay. 430 perished, 200 saved.

Jan 27 Very stormy ... Papa assisted at a coroner's inquest relative to the wreck at Lambay.

Feb 3 Mamma and I drove into Dublin to lodgings in Molesworth Street.

April 16 Easter Sunday. Lovely fine day; walked to church, drove back with Grandpapa. Had prayers with Lady Florence.

April 17 ... went to church [on Easter Monday!] *The little Balfours came.* [From Townley Hall, nearest large house] *Played killing games with them.* There is much visiting, to Antrim (Lord Massereene's home is Antrim Castle) to Dublin, a long spell with Dorcas Foster Skeffington, eldest daughter of Lord and Lady Massereene and Haddie's contemporary and first cousin. They go about together, under the care of Lady Florence (Balfour).Uncle and Aunt Massereene come on a visit In the summer there is much playing in the hayfield and once, *We walked and drove and pleasured ourselves, having great fun.* Cousin, Hungerford Skeffington, spends his birthday with them, and they have cake and punch in the evening; a German maid comes. And during a long visit, possibly at Antrim Castle, they visit Shanes Castle and Lord O'Neill. Whenever they are at Antrim they spend time on the loch, collecting pebbles and rowing. Later entries make it clear that Haddie can manage a boat.

July 12 Battle of the Boyne. Orange women and Protestant Boys. Went to the lake for pebbles.
July 19 Showery. Copied music and wrote poetry. Dorcas and I in deep thought.
Aug 21 Mrs Seller came in the evening.
Aug 22 Mrs Seller's day to herself. I walked out with her.
Aug 23 ... Dorcas and I did business with Mrs Seller.
[Probably this means learning to keep accounts.]

Willie 1854

People of significance include Mary Kirwan who cuts Papa's hair, and helps with shopping for Willie - a friend or cousin? The Kirwans were very much in the same circle.

Then there is Mysie Smith who often walks with Haddie, and seems to live in Dublin. Jane sounds like the nursemaid - she goes in the carriage with Haddie and Annette, and Willie, who apparently all attend the Monasterboice Ball on May 23rd, 9 to 5o'clock!

Mr and Mrs Singleton, living at Collon, are great family friends, and their son Mark often rides with the girls and joins in family excursions.
In September, with her parents in Dublin, Haddie "*has the charge of Willie*" as Jane is also away. We do not hear of Mark again, so he may have died young.

.

Haddie enjoys riding and her horse is Drummond. When Papa, on Topsy, and Annette ride in the morning, Haddie is able to have Drummond in the afternoon. Drummond is also Grandpapa's second name, and the name of one of the farms on the estate. At the back of this volume is the only drawing found in any diary - possibly by Haddie, titled "Clara Roquerbre, Robert

Allan's Sweetheart," The sketch is too faint to reproduce; facing it is a poem written out in pencil:

The jewels most on earth I prize
Sweet Clara, are thy sparkling eyes,
And when thus filled with liquid tears
Beside them dull as pearl appears.
Thy perfect symmetry of gaze
Equals alone thy matchless grace;
Thy soft and flowing raven hair,
Drawn meekly from thy face so fair,
Thy fairy footsteps, soft and light,
Thy noble and commanding height.

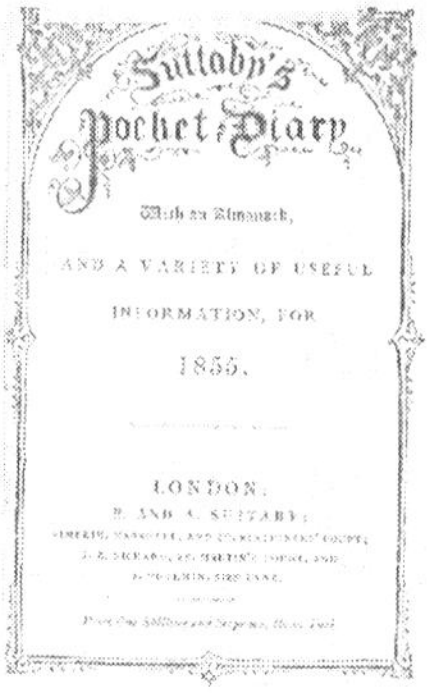

In September 1854 the Allied armies landed in Crimea, and the Siege of Sevastopol followed.

In **1855** many days are not filled in by Haddie. Although life in Ireland is peaceful at this time, war in the Crimea is going on and, whether or not it was compulsory, Robert Delap is called up to serve in the Louth Militia. His daughters evidently find the thought of him putting on uniform and being obliged to report for duty in Drogheda rather amusing, and call him "Little Captain". No sooner than he has his uniform and is summoned on "Muster Day", Haddie's Mama becomes unwell and three doctors are summoned in turn - one sleeps the night in the schoolroom. But Mama recovers, being first carried to her sofa, then to the spare room, then down to the drawing-room

Each entry, now and for the next 60 years, begins with a weather report, and all her life Haddie remains greatly affected by the weather, in her health and spirits. But the weather shows just as many extreme lows and highs as astonish us now, long before global warming was heard of, and always has its effect on daily life. For instance, women and girls were effectively confined indoors if it was wet - drying wet clothes was difficult, and even rubber boots had yet to be invented. But unless the day's events are directly affected, Haddie's weather reports have often been omitted in editing the diaries.

Jan 1 *None of us went to church. Mrs and Miss Filgate came to tea. Acted a Charade - Co-nun-drum ...*

Jan 27 *A little sleet. Mary K, Annette and I took a long walk. Papa shot one plover! Jan 29 Beautiful frosty day. Mary K, Annette and I walked to Ardee to shop. Papa rode in. Poor Captain's cold occasioned much sleep on the sofa in the drawing room! . ..*

Feb 6 Damp. Willie not very well. Played a Charade - Goose-steps.
Feb 10 Bright day. All of us out playing snow balls with the Captain. Got very wet.
Mar 26 Lovely day. Henry the man servant left us. Papa, Mama, Mary K, Annette, Willie and I to Monasterboice in G'papa's clarence. Papa rode.
Mar 27 Beautiful, cold day. Papa went to Drogheda early for his military duties. G'papa and Mary drove in phaeton. Mama and Annette in chariot.
Mar 28 Cold, with some sleet. Mama drove with G'papa to Mellifont. Poor Mary K. had a bad toothache. Papa in Drogheda. Dinner hour 5 o'clock....
Mar 30 Very fine. Annette, Willie, Jane and I walked to the source of the river. Mr Richardson of Prospect slept here, Papa also ...
April 4 Dull and foggy. G'papa, Mary, Annette Willie and I went to Drummond Farm, dined there, went on to Rohanna and brought back Baby.
April 5 Fine day. G'papa, G'mama and Mary drove to Townley Hall and brought back Mama, who was surprised to see Baby. Papa rode out here.
April 6 Good Friday. Captain had a holiday. Papa, Mary Annette and I walked to Church and came back in the carriage with Mama.
April 7 ... Jane and Baby to Rohanna on Johnny's little car. Jane returned.. Mama out driving.
April 10 ... very windy. Stopped at the Captain's lodgings in Drogheda. Had a lunch from the mess cook. Went to Dublin.
April 12 Mysie, Mrs Smith, Frank [Browne], Annette and I went to an amateur concert in the Rotunda in aid of the Crimean Fund..
April 21 Papa arrived unexpectedly on leave. Annette and I lunched with Aunt Dufferin.
April 22 Mysie, Annette and I went to Baggot Street Church.
April 24 Out shopping. Last day of Frank Browne's examination. Mamma, Annette and I took lunch with Aunt Dufferin [Lady Dufferin. A widow and childless - her husband's nephew was to be the heir.]
April 25 Very fine. Out shopping. Went to see Aunt Harriett
[Ross, Anna Delap's sister. She had married, as his second wife, David Ross of Bladensburg - and his first wife had been Robert Delap's sister. This sort of complication is typical, and it is hoped the Family Trees will help.]
Frank showed us the College Library. [Trinity?]

They go home to Rohanna on April 28, by way of Monasterboice.

June 26 Lovely day. Mama's birthday. G'papa, G'mama and Anna and Filgates came. Dined out of doors. .
July 3 G'papa's birthday. [His 75th] *Picnic at Drummond Farm. Numbers of*

people there. "Ockie's Pranks!" Great fun. Driving there and back in two phaetons.

Aug 24 We were prevented from going to England by very stormy weather.

Aug 25 Could not go as Sunday intervened. Out walking.

Aug 27 Rainy... I bathed. Left Malahide 4 for London. Went to Kingstown, sailed in the Iron Duke at 7. Rough passage. Burst a boiler.

Aug 28 Arrived at Birkenhead. 10 breakfasted, set off in train 12, slept at Leamington.. Very fine day.

Aug 29 Beautiful day. Left Leamington half past 10. Arrived at Paddington Station, London. Arrived at Long Ditton before 5 o'clock.

Aug 30 Beautiful warm day. Papa and I walked to Hampton Court. Went over the Ferry, on the Thames.

Aug 3 Very fine. Drove through Richmond Park. Mr and Mrs Vesey [FitzGerald] *came to tea.*

Sep 1 Not so fine. Out driving and paying visits. Saw Mrs Horstman's beautiful house ...

Sep 3 Set off in carriage at 9. Drove to Sydenham for the Crystal Palace, till after 5......

Sep 6 I did not go out. Mamma, Papa and Lady Li went to a flower show. Mr and Mrs Giffard dined here.

Sep 7 Breakfasted early and drove into London. Saw several sights and returned at 7 o'clock.

Sep 8 Very fine and warm; out driving ... Mr Francis Clements arrived unexpectedly at dinner time....

Sep 11 ...heard the news of The Fall of Sebastopol. Papa spent the day in London.. Mama and I walked to the station to meet him.

Sep 14 Damp day. Drove into London. Papa and Mamma out shopping. Went at 8 to Albert Smith's Ascent of Mont Blanc. Slept in town.

Sep 15 Fine. Mama seeing governesses. Lady Louisa Kerr came to spend the day. Returned to Long Ditton in the evening.

Lady Louisa is believed to be Lady Letitia Louisa Kerr, born 1800, daughter of Charlotte, Countess of Antrim and Lord Mark Kerr. She painted the charming portrait of Willie—see 1861. She probably died about 1870.

Sep 17 .... several people to dinner and company to tea.

Sep 18 Papa and I walked to Kingston to look at orange trees.

Sep 19 Fine, but close and heavy. Papa went to Aldershot. Mamma and Lady Li drove. I walked in the garden.

Sep 21 Lovely warm day. Papa and Mamma went off early to Greenwich. I walked with them .... at the school and out driving with Lady Li. Mr F Clements and 3 of his children came.

Sep 22 Walked to Surbiton with Anne and Caroline. Mrs Vesey came to dinner. Mrs Horstman and Miss Campbell to tea. A great deal of music.

Sept 23 Sunday. Very warm and close. Went to morning and evening service. Mr Clements preached both times. Papa and Mamma and I went up Cock Crow Hill and were caught in some rain.
Sep 24 ... Caroline and I went to see "The Old Woman in a Cart." Great packing. Put off going till Wednesday
Sep 25 Beautiful day. Caroline and I with G. Vesey and Helen Campbell made an excursion in the pony chaise. Papa and Mamma dined at Mr Coleraine's. We three went in the evening.
Sep 27 ... went by train to Bangor; 8 o'clock when we arrived at the Penrhyn Arms, as the train was late. Very tired and dirty
Sept 28 ... went by train to Carnaervon Castle, then to see Penrhyn Castle. Dined at Bangor ... arrived at Holyhead and went on board packet at 2 o'clock.
Sept 29 Arrived at Kingstown after a beautiful passage. Breakfasted at the hotel. Arrived at Malahide 10 trains, very tired and sleepy ...
Oct 1 ... Cattle and Fowl Show in Malahide to all appearances a failure. Annette and I out walking....
Oct 4 Papa, Mama, Annette, and Willie went into Dublin, to shop and see Sir Philip Crampton. Miss Harris came back with them and slept here....
Oct 6 ... Annette, Blanche, Helen, Baby and Jane to Monasterboice. Various packing going on in the house.
Oct 7 Sunday ... Day of thanksgiving for the taking of Sebastopol ...
- this heralds the end of the Crimean War.
Oct 8 ... very busy preparing to leave the house. out walking .... .
Oct 9 ... Left Malahide by 10 train. From Drogheda to M'boice in Major Burton's open carriage. Slept at M'boice while the servants went on to Rohanna.
Oct 10 ... we all left M'boice after an early dinner, in the chariot and brougham. G'papa and G'mama came with us but returned home immediately.
Oct 11 Very busy unpacking and settling things....
Oct 14 Sunday Annette, Willie and I to Church. Papa's 2 months leave out. He went off to Dundalk to join the Louth.
Oct 18. Blanche's birthday ... Children had a tea party and games in the evening.
Oct 22 ... Papa, Mamma and Willie went to M'boice, stopping on their way at Oriel Temple to see Aunt M(asserene).

Only the remains of Oriel Temple can be seen now, though there is a Monastery on the site. There used to be a famous shell grotto, built for his wife by one of the Foster family.

Oct 23 Mamma and Willie returned, and Miss Harris came.
Oct 25 ... Papa rode into Dundalk for the last time.
Oct 26 Much rain. Could not go out. Papa returned from Dundalk and was

out of the Louth [Militia].

Oct 27 Fine day. Out walking. Papa tried to fly Willie's kite.

Dec 10 Hard frost and snow. Papa, Annette, Willie and I walked to Ardee. Two arrows lost in the snow. Commenced preparing for the Christmas tree.

Dec 28 Wet day. Had the Christmas tree party; 49 strangers and 10 of ourselves

Dec 31 Windy and showery. Papa rode over to M'boice to inspect the progress of his oak cabinet ... Annette and I [are] getting up a charade ... the last day of poor 1855. What a happy, happy year it has been, rich in every blessing! May the coming year which will dawn tomorrow be as happy and prosperous.

There is always space for cash accounts at the back of the volumes—here on the credit side, Haddie notes 5/- from Grandmamma, and there is a shopping list, but without prices:

Bonnets. Belt buckles? Red velvet. Present Annette. Dutch dolls.
Diary. Riding Drawers. Gloves? Chamois. Drawing paper?

Early in **1856** Haddie and Annette go on a visit to CarraigBhan. She continues *Dressed rehearsal for the play. All in the house very busy, large party, acting and dancing.* She wheels Aunt Lizzie in her chair (Mama's youngest sister, Mrs William Poë, no children but two stepsons, Edward and Hutchinson Poë.) There are also walks up Cloghmore Mountain, Tableaux Vivants and dancing. Home on Jan 20. On the 26th she goes to Dublin for a long visit, which includes 12 singing lessons as well as many walks with Mysie or Dorcas, often accompanied by Miss Rainsford (a governess?) Dorcas and Haddie go to a teaparty and dancing at Mrs Grady's (Mama's brother, Lord Massereene, had married a Miss Grady or O'Grady.) With Mysie she goes to Lady Downshire's Amateur Opera. On Mar 15 she goes home to M'boice with Papa. Next day they go to Collon church for a charity sermon...
Haddie records starting several books - e.g. Waverley. (influence of Dorcas perhaps?).

In April Mamma usually stays behind from church and one of the older children stays with her. She is 4 or 5 months pregnant at this time; she goes out driving, however. She is staying at M'boice, and the younger children are brought over to see her. When Haddie goes back to Rohanna she is *very busy with the housekeeping.* They are all at home by the end of April. As always, there is constant driving about and visiting:

May 2 Annette and I drove to Ardee in the Curricle. Grandmama and Margaret (McCreight, orphan relative) *came. Drove to Lissrenny......*

May 3 Annette out riding. Drove the children into Ardee for their bonnets. Again to Ardee in Curricle to get Bread.

May 4 Went to church. Day of thanksgiving for the restoration of peace.

May 7 [To Dublin again] *Grandmama, Margaret and I to Dublin to lodgings, 27 Molesworth Street.... Mr Peyton drank tea with us.* There is much shopping every day - Margaret is soon to be married.

May 26 Aunt Lizzie and Annette out riding [so she is out of the bath chair now]...

June 3 Papa, Mamma, Annette and I to Ardee House and Red House in the phaeton

June 9 Margaret came to Rohanna, and drove back to M'boice with Mama, Annette, Willie and me; Papa rode.

June 10 Mr and Miss Peyton came. Dined at 6. Mary Hall came.

June 11 Making jams. Drove to Oriel Temple. Signing of Margaret's Settlement. Mr and Miss Browne came.

June 12 Margaret and Mr Peyton married at Mellifont Church. Gradually all the visitors leave - Papa and Willie fish at Drumcar - then:

June 17 G'papa and G'Mama to Rohanna to visit Mr and Mrs Peyton [the newly-weds]

June 24 The first very warm day. Mama's birthday. Dined outside. Grandpapa, the Filgates, Col. and Mrs Plunkett came.

July 3 Thursday. Annette and I confirmed at Ardee by the Bishop of Tuam.

July 4 Went to Lissrenny in the curricle; in the phaeton to South Hall, Glyde Court etc.

Glyde Court, near Ardee, is now a picturesque ruin; the house was built on the site of a much older one, then called Rosy Park and home of the Foster family.

Glyde Court, 2003

July 6 Papa, Miss Harris, Annette Willie and I went to Ardee Church as Charlestown was closed.

July 7 Papa to the Assizes at Dundalk. Mysie comes on a visit from Dublin and they go back there together. Aunt Ellen and Miss Butter drive in from Elm Park

July 27 Went to Mark's Church. Received the Sacrament for the first time. Haddie was to remain a life-long regular attender at Holy Communion, never shortening the term, e.g. to H.C. As was the Church of Ireland custom then, she attends Morning and Evening Prayer at Church every Sunday, and takes Communion not more than once a month.

July 28 Mr Brooks to dinner. I had champagne. Mysie and I had singing lesson in the evening.

July 29 Mysie, Aunt Bess and I drove to Elm Park in the phaeton and had lunch there. Saw Mr Handley...

July 30 Very warm day. Major Brown and Mr Handley lunched here. Dined at Elm Park at half past 8.

Aug 1 Mary Kirwan and I left Dublin. Saw dear Mama at M'boice. I went on to Rohanna.

Aug 4 Very hot. Mrs McLoughlin [wife of Dr McLoughlin] showed us how to use the still and remained all day.

Aug 8 Papa and Mama left M'boice and went to Drogheda.

Aug 9 Very hot day. Papa came in the Mail Car to see us and returned in the evening.

Aug 12 Baby born. Annette and I to M'boice. In the following days much visiting takes place between home and Drogheda, and Papa takes Haddie to two Balls.

Aug 30 Papa, Mama, Baby etc. left Drogheda and went to M'boice.

Sept 21. ... "Mary Rachel" always known later as May, is christened at evening service.

Oct 9 Drove in phaeton to Ardee. Chapter of accidents with Drummond.

Oct 27 ... in curricle to Ardee. Drummond misbehaved.

Oct 31 Heard of Aunt de Salis' death.

Nov 27 Baby vaccinated.

Dec 25 [at Monasterboice] *Went to Mellifont church. Sad ... because of Mr Balfour's death.* The Balfour family live at Townley Hall - near neighbours to Monasterboice.

Dec 27 *Papa and Grandpapa to Mr Balfour's funeral.*

Dec 30 [Back at Rohanna] *Commenced dressing the Christmas tree.*

1857 Blanche now sometimes joins the party for church.
May 10 After church at Melllifont they go to see "the old towers" in the ruins of Monasterboice Abbey [which are still well-preserved.] Most visitors to Monasterboice are taken to the ruins, either in a carriage, or on horseback, or walking, often for picnics.
May 16 Papa and Willie fish on the Drumcar river. Drumcar House is the home of John McClintock, who would be created Lord Rathdonnell in 1868. It was bought by his great-uncle Alexander McClintock in 1767. John's youngest brother, in a very large family, was Henry, father of Sir Leopold McClintock, who will feature large in Haddie's later diaries.

Henry McClintock 1810

May 27 Papa to M'boice to sit for his picture.
June 9 Papa, Mama, Aunt Lizzie [Poë], *and I out driving in the phaeton.....*
Sept 1 Grandpapa and Clara to Haddie Filgate's wedding. I went with them and saw the wedding from the gallery.
Sept 16 Walked to Lisrenny to see Col. De Salis's charger.. Saw the eclipse of the moon.
[Harriett Filgate marries her cousin, T.W. Filgate. Her mother had been a de Salis.]
.Sept 28 Crosses to Liverpool, with Papa and Annette, to see the Art Treasures Exhibition [in London?] which they have to leave early because of the crowds - 27,000 people having visited it! And returns on Oct 3.
Oct 7 Day of Prayer & Humiliation (sic) *for the Italian War.*
Oct 15 Grandpapa sent his carriage to take Annette, Willie and me to M'boice to meet Mrs and Anne Stawell.
Oct 19 Blanche's birthday kept.
Oct 26 To M'boice ... took a delightful walk. Disappointed Nettie by not returning to Rohanna.
Nov 3 Annette, Papa and I drove to Tullykirk to see the bride, Haddie Filgate.
Nov 4 Papa drove Annette and me over to M'boice for good..

It seems Rohanna is given up now: they go to Glendaragh for Christmas.
This is the year of the Indian Mutiny, and the Relief of Lucknow, not mentioned by Haddie.

1858 *Jan 28 Mr and Mrs McCausland lunched here. Willie to school for the first time to Mr Miller's* [this sentence crossed out] - *Put Off!!*

March, at Cloughsane. *Papa, Annette and I drove to see Dufferins'* [Lady Dufferin is an Aunt] ... *and Clandeboyes* [Castle] *& Helen's Tower.*

March 23 Shopped in Belfast. Went to Antrim Castle [home of Lord Massereene].
March 24 Drove through Antrim in Blanche [Skeffington, aged 14]'*s equipage with tandem donkeys.*
March 26 Went with Uncle Massereene to see the Poorhouses. Dorcas, A and I rowed to Shane's Castle.
March 27 Put the Donkey and Bathchair in the barge. Uncle M, Mr Otley, Dorcas and I rowed to the Main Water.
March 30....played games. Annette blew Harry McCausland in my face.
April 1 A and I made several very good April fools. Willie came for the Easter holidays.
April 3 Busy dyeing Easter eggs.
April 9 Papa, Mama and I to Mrs Mulholland's at Eglantine.
April 10 ... went to see Lord Downshire's palace at Hillsboro'. [Hillsborough Castle, later the seat of Government in Northern Ireland.]
April 15 (back at M'boice) A. and I to Mellifont Church to practise Seraphins! [Singing!]
May 12 Willie walked over from Ballymakinney and remained with us.
May 13 Ascension Day.... To church. Willie laid the foundation of the Tower on the Rocks.
July 9 To Ostend with Papa and Mama via Drogheda and Liverpool and London, where Aunt Liz joins them. Then by "La grande vitesse" to Liege; then to Frankfurt, then Hamburg; entries are very scanty. They have coffee out of doors at the Kirsaal, then *out walking and driving.*
Aug 27 Aunt Liz leaves for home via Ostend. On to Louvain, buys lace! All her life, Haddie loves lace!
Sept 2 to London and Storey's Hotel, train to Liverpool and across to Drogheda.
Sep 7 Willie returns to Ballymakenny to school.
No more entries, but Haddie lists some beautiful objects seen on her travels:
At Liege, beautiful carved oak pulpit, with white marble statues in the Cathedral; old house with 365 windows; at Ghent, old Hotel de Ville, Italian and florid Gothic; St Bavin dated 911, the Crypt, black and white marble, 4 candlesticks made for Edward VI Coronation, and used at Charles I's, sold by Cromwell; reclining statue of one of the Bishops' 24 chapels, little angels; fine pulpit, listening angels; fine pictures - St Bason by Raphael as a monk, all the faces portraits of Raphael's family. The Raising of Lazarus .... Maladie flamande - S. Nichol and S. Michel - Annunciation. Part of house where John of Gaunt and Charles V were born.
At Bruges, fine pictures in the Hopital. Notre Dame, fine church. A Crucifixion by Van Dyke. ... In the Palais de Justice beautiful with chimney piece with statues of Charles V, Charles the Bold, May of

Burgundy. In the Hotel de Ville, fine old ceiling made by the Spaniards... The Chapel du Saint Sang, 1100, restored. Beautiful chase of gold and precious stones ....

Haddie is now about to be 21., but she does not mention it on the day. They start the year **1859** in Dublin, at 102 Lower Baggot Street, and there are many balls and gaieties. Blanche and Helen come up for two days. Haddie helps at the Ragged Schools - the effects of the potato famine must have left much poverty. On March 2nd there is a County election, and Haddie lunches at Oriel Temple and drives in Dorcas' phaeton to hear the election news. By May they are at Glendhara, with walking, visits, much sea-bathing. Croquet and whist mentioned, and lots of prayer meetings. In October they return to Dublin, 14 Ely Place, seemingly to live there for the time being. The Kirwan family - Julie, Emma and Martin are often mentioned. Poor Baby - May - gets sore eyes, obviously quite serious: two doctors come to see her. Later we are told:

Dear little Baby able to distinguish objects after 7 weeks' blindness.

Willie about 1860, by Lady Louisa Kerr

1860 In Dublin (14 Ely Place) and again at the end of the year ... Twelfth Night is celebrated, and at Christmas there is always a tree and parties.

In March Mama, Annette, Blanche, Helen and Haddie go to the Continental Diorama at the Rotunda. Haddie goes to Belfast and Antrim on a visit; then, on June 11, with Uncle and Aunt Massereene and cousin Dorcas their eldest daughter, to England and via France to Hamburg where they spend several weeks. She and Dorcas are taken to concerts, balls, teaparties etc, and on excursions. There are no real excitements in the very short entries-cramped into a space one inch by two and a half on the page! There is just one reference to a

Sep 4 ...rencontre with ......D!!! young American student. She is escorted home, from Frankfurt, in September by Uncle Massereene - Dorcas remaining abroad with her mother - and they have a dreadful passage back to Malahide, at the seaside.

1861 Feb 5. Haddie observes: *Name changed to Dunlop!* [Annette, in her Recollections, says her branch of the family were reverting to the older, Scottish form of the name: none of their Delap cousins followed their example.] The family are spending the winter in Dublin, as was often the case. Willie goes to Winslow School - he is now 14.
Feb 5. Mamma and Annette go to Rathmines for a change of air after minor illness. Meanwhile Haddie is busy cutting up oranges for marmalade - and, next day, making it.
Feb 15 ...To Mrs Brabazon's from 4 to 6, practising the Imperial Quadrilles.
Mar 1 Heavy showers. Went to Lady Roche's to see the procession of Captain Boyd's Funeral.
Mar 21 Selling at Ragged School Bazaar in the Rotunda. Mary and Julie Kirwan, Tissie, Anne Garnett and Miss Ellen Filgate helped us.
Ap 5 Very fine. Went to Rostrevor to be near Aunt Lizzie ... Stopped at Fairy Hill with Lady Florence Balfour. Haddie comes back to Dublin with her aunt and helps to find her lodgings.
Ap 15 ...Papa, Annette and I, and Blanche and Olivia Skeffington, to a concert .., Went to Aunt Liz to let her see us dressed.
May 3 ... Dined at Aunt Liz's. Tissie Stawell, B and O Skeffington, Charles and Wade Garnett and I were there. Played Commerce after dinner.

In June they are at M'boice and Haddie takes a long walk with Grandpapa to see "the new road" etc. This road caused considerable local disapproval, and there is a story that a curse was put upon the family because of it. In a book of local legends, we read that old Mr Dunlop was contemplating the route of his new road one evening, when he met a local priest, walking along a footpath and reading his Office. Mr Dunlop intimated that soon the priest would no longer be able to follow the path, to which the Father retorted, "And neither will you or yours." Certainly, the family were to have their share of misfortune in the 40 and more years they were still to own Monasterboice.
In June Haddie has a visit to Tullykeel, near Ardee, to stay with Haddie Filgate. They play croquet at Red House (which years later would belong to Haddie's nephew Hal.)
Later that summer Haddie has a long, jolly visit to Glenshane. It is near Clandeboyes Gardens, and they drive there and have a *feast of strawberries*. Typical days:
July 31 Heavy showers. Uncle Chichester and his little boy came for a few hours. I dined at Groomsport House. Dance after dinner.
Aug 1 Bangor Castle. Dined there. Went a party of 14 to Mrs Hamilton's Ball at Craigdarragh. I went in omnibus with Lady Matilda Montgomery. Was not back till after 4 next morning. The Channel Fleet is sometimes to be seen in Belfast Lough and Haddie shows what will become a lifelong interest in ships and the sea.

Sep 9 ... to a dance at Groomsport House in honour of some of the officers of the Channel Fleet.

Sep 10 Lovely day. Went with the Crawfords in their yacht to see the Channel Fleet. Went on board the Conqueror and the Revenge, Flagships of the Admiral. ... Lieut Sanders so kind

Oct 26 Very fine. Out walking. Aunt and I drove to Bangor Castle and to Groomsport.
Met Lord Dufferin and Miss Hamilton and a large party of Maxwells on horseback.

[Back at Tullykeel] *Nov 8 Louth Hounds met at Churchtown. Hunting Breakfast. Haddie(Filgate) and I stood on a hill to watch the hunt.*
... She goes on to Belfast with an aunt and they stay at the Royal Hotel.

The whole family moves to France at end of 1861 - which is the year of the start of the American Civil War - and is there all through **1862.** They are near Montreux, at Veytaux, and then at Glion; also to Gingins, Nyon and finally Clarins; social life is rather thin, but all do plenty of walking, and fishing for papa, their party including the little ones. Willie goes to and fro to school and Papa to Geneva and to Ireland in August. Haddie's entries are very sparse, but there is no hint of illness. At the end of the tiny diary appears the only recipe we find:

LAKE OF GENEVA

Pudin aux Petits Pains: Butter a bowl and sprinkle it with toast crumbs. Then slice up 8,9 or 10 small sweet rolls, and place them in the bowl in layers, with a small breakfast cup of brown sugar, do. of currants and the grated rind of a lemon. Squeeze in some lemon juice, pour over it all milk enough to fill the bowl about three quarters. Place the bowl in a saucepan with very little water, and boil gently 2 hours. It is eaten with sirrup sauce.

The diaries for **1863, 1864** and **1865** are missing. We know that in 1863 Annette, Willie and their parents go on a trip to Switzerland - and write a journal about it, and when they come home they refer to "our dear invalid" being better - could this be Haddie? In **1866** we meet "James" or "Jim." He is James Bogle Delap, Haddie's second cousin. He and Haddie are clearly very close; they frequently go walking together, and apparently alone, so there must be, in the terms of those days, at least an understanding, though records suggest he is younger than Haddie. She begins the year with a visit to Monellan, his family's home in Donegal, and goes riding with James and his sister, Susan. Then Susan becomes ill, and is not much heard of till Palm Sunday when she is pushed in the Bath chair. The long visit ends with a return to Monasterboice on March 11. This year's diary has even smaller spaces for writing:

Apr 8 Sunday. Cold. To church. Walked to Collon with Jim
Apr 9 Fine. Rode and walked with Jim
Apr 11 Rain & cold. Mamma & Net to Dunany, not out
Apr 12 Damp. Out walking. Papa to Dublin and Dunany. Jim to Dublin and back, and got into Sackville Street Club.
Apr 13 Soft, showery and windy. Rode Constance with Jim and walked.
Apr 14 Papa, Mamma & Net returned from Dunany. Walked with Jim. Papa and James go to Dublin together. Jim later returns to Monellan - April 23rd.
May 29 The Halls, A and I spent the day in Dublin. Saw Jim at Monkstown on his way to London.
July 3 Papa to Dublin to see Aunt Liz. Papa very cross.
July 14 [after an absence] *James came from Arley Cottage.*
July 23 Dot, Willie and Jim to Port Ruth.
Nov 8 Papa to Carraigbhan for the funeral [whose?]
Nov 15 Helen and James came from Monellan.

The last entry about him is in December: *James Delap came.* The family are at Castle Bellingham for Christmas, and there are Theatricals at Dunany.
Dec 29 ... Willie and James shooting at Bragganstown.

Mamma

Papa

Dec 31 Sleet and frost. Had a cold. Remained indoors. Willie and James to Monellan. Was not out

Red House, Ardee, Co. Louth

There are no diaries for **1867, 1868** or **1869**.

In **1870** Haddie begins again, in a larger diary. Here, Haddie's writing is now very poor and weak, in wavering pencil, like someone who has had a stroke or perhaps is on strong painkillers (opium would have been commonly used then). Even the weather is hardly mentioned, and many days are left blank.

In the leather binding of the **1870** volume is found a letter of 1868 from some very kind person sympathising with Haddie, who is evidently suffering from some severe illness. This letter is almost certainly from Aunt Liz. [Poë] on a paper folded small, with "*For dear Haddie*" written on the outside.

Glen Ban, Abbeyleix, March 23 - Haddie has added *1868* in faint pencil.

Darling Haddie,

I received all your affectionate messages thro' dear Annette, for whose "jolly" letter with Blanche's I must commission you to present my thanks, as I shall not have time to write to more than you today. I often, often think of you my poor darling, as the dear child whom God in His great love willeth so heavily to chasten. My own long, long illness of 7 years standing last Xmas Day enables me in a degree to estimate your great Trial, but cheer up, child mine, take good courage. I long greatly to sit by your Bedside and should have done so sooner, dear Haddie, but for the weakness of my own health, which imprisons me during winter. But whenever I can I mean to go up to Dublin for the object of seeing you - for I know I shall not be too much for you. There is nothing like graduating in the same School for the full understanding of its Provisions! I am yr. ever fond Aunt. [probably monogram of] *E.P*

There is nothing in any later diary to tell us what has been wrong with poor Haddie. It could be a form of the modern M.E, or possibly rheumatic fever? It was some very debilitating complaint which leaves her with recurring headaches. The only illness, common among her relations, which does not seem indicated, is tuberculosis. We shall probably never know.

As 1870 ends there is a perceptible improvement - Haddie is taking drives sometimes, often with "Jessie", a superior maid or nurse or perhaps companion. She spends a long period at Castle Bellingham, February to May, and a Dr Smyley comes from Dublin to see her. During Haddie's long silence we have not been able to follow young Willie's growing up, but he has been away a good deal, now serving in the Royal Artillery..

Leo, about 1861, by Stephen Pearce
© National Portrait Gallery

She still writes very little, but records Annette's engagement to Leo (Sir Francis Leopold) McClintock on September 8 and their marriage on October 12: *wet and stormy*.

Leopold, always called Leo in the family, is aged 49 (Annette is 30) and has already had a distinguished career. After joining the Navy aged not quite 12, he had his first taste of Arctic exploration in 1838, as 2nd Lieut. of the "Enterprise", in an effort to find the ill-fated expedition of Sir John Franklin; and again in 1853 in command of the "Intrepid". In 1857, now promoted to Post-Captain, he commanded the yacht "Fox", commissioned by Lady Franklin to make one more effort to find her husband, the remains of whose expedition he did indeed find. Knighted on his return to England, he received many other honours and honorary degrees, and in 1868 served as A.D.C. to Queen Victoria.
In that year, too, he was persuaded to stand for election as M.P. for Drogheda, but his standing was strongly opposed by the local R.C. priesthood, who organised resistance and prevented his potential voters getting to the poll. There was some local disturbance, and William Dunlop (Haddie's grandfather) was slightly injured. The story goes that Leopold called at Monasterboice to enquire after him, saw Annette standing at the front of the house, and made up his mind there and then to marry her, achieving this two years later. The following year, 1871, he is promoted Rear-Admiral and goes as Admiral Superintendent of Portsmouth Dockyard. The house they lived in there is little

changed, to this day.
It almost goes without saying that Leo, through his grandmother is, like Annette, a descendant of the Foster family.

Haddie makes a packing list *"For Tassaggart: Brown petticoat, other Petties, LightBoots, Kid Gloves, Veils, Stays, Ribbons for Hair; & neck? Patchwork, Crochet cotton.*
Stationery. Cuffs & Frills; Dings(?)"
In a pocket at the back of this diary is a lock of blonde hair labelled: *Dora, June 1870* - Dora would have been 16 or 17. And another lock, labelled *"The Gosling's," Tassaggart, 1869.* This could be from a child - Haddie spends a good deal of time with the Verschoyles at Tassaggart. There are also instructions for making crocheted petticoats - thick and warm - and for elaborate indoor slippers.

1871 begins at Monasterboice with what seems to be a very quiet life (Communion taken at home once a month or so.) The handwriting gradually improves.
Aug 11 *Nettie's little boy born.* [Henry Foster McClintock.] Haddie and her parents are staying at Balbriggan. She goes to Dublin to stay with Annette and Leo at 1 Fitzgibbon St, where little Hal had been born, and sees Dr Smyley. Annette may well have gone to Dublin to have her baby, to be under the care of Leo's brother Alfred, a distinguished Dublin doctor. Haddie mentions that they dine with Alfred and his wife Fanny a few weeks later.
Sept 13 Leo, Nettie, Blanche and I to St George's Church; Annette was churched. [The short service to give thanks after childbirth, common in the Church of England, and Ireland, till well into the 20th century.]
Sept 15 Leo, A and Baby to M'boice. Blanche and I to Monkstown to stay with the Halls.
Sept 27 Rain & storm. Mrs Morton spent the evening.

Sept 28. Blank. But on the night of 27-28th poor brother Willie was killed on the railway as he took a short cut home.

Sept 29 Dr Kelly came to fetch B and me home. C & H. Hall went with us as far as Amiens St.
Sept 30 Aunt Harriett arrived. Jessie to Dublin and back.
Oct 1 (Sunday) All received the Holy Communion in the Oak Room.
Oct 8 Papa and Leo to church.
Nov 4 Leo, Annette and baby Harry leave to go back to England. It is clear from family letters that Leo has been of the utmost support to his parents-in-law during this terrible time.
Later, Papa takes Haddie to Bournemouth; Ellen Harris goes too. Haddie has

to say goodbye to Jessie, whose marriage takes place at the end of the year.

It must have been difficult for Papa, in his great grief, to know what to do with Haddie, whose diary, with an invalid's self-absorption, does not reflect the turmoil in the family. Notes in Nicky McClintock's family papers, (written by Marion, wife of Harry McClintock) describe finding some pencilled notes, made at the time of the Inquest on Willie by Papa, at which the account shows a clear verdict of accidental death; Willie left his luggage at the station to take a short cut along the railway, leaving orders to have it sent on next day; probably Willie did not hear the train coming because the night was exceptionally stormy. But there had been a broken romance, and he had been under pressure to leave the army and go as a civilian to India, so he certainly had a lot on his mind. There still exists a most touching letter, Willie to Nettie, agreeing gladly to stand Godfather to baby Harry, written just three weeks before his death. Willie is not mentioned again in Haddie's diaries for thirteen long years.

Towards the end of this eventful year Haddie, in Bournemouth, begins to pick up normal life again. There is a large list of books read at Bournemouth - including Jane Eyre, some Trollope, and religious works such as "State of the Blythe Dead," by Dean Abbott, "Ministry of Nature" etc. She is in lodgings near the Gardiners, and in December gives one of the Paget sons lessons in French and German. She does not quite manage a normal church service, but goes to the chapel in a Sanatorium. Bournemouth would have been chosen partly as a wellknown healthy spot, partly to be near Leo's sister Caroline: she is the widow of Captain Charles Paget, R.N, commanding officer of Leo's first ship.

[Leo first went to sea just before his twelfth birthday, under the protection of his father's nephew, William McClintock Bunbury, then a Lieutenant in the "Samarang." Though he did not see his parents again for more than three years, Leo was well-treated and taught, and seems to have thrived on his first, long voyage, writing home faithfully whenever he could. At first he was so small the sailors used to joke that he could not be found in his hammock. Captain Paget was very kind to him and once said that, if Leo had a sister at home with eyes like his he would like to marry her—and, in 1840 he did so and chose Caroline. Paget, son of an Vice-Admiral and related to the Marquess of Anglesey, had his naval career cut short by tuberculosis in 1845, leaving three sons, one posthumous. Later, Caroline married again, Colonel John Ballard Gardiner.]

1872 Distinct improvement in Haddie's health and handwriting begins. Mrs Gardiner, and her Paget sons, are very kind. Haddie stays in Bournemouth till June, by now attending services in church; then moves on to Portsmouth where

Annette and Leo are living in the Dockyard. They all go to Ireland on Nov 8th. Haddie visits Jessie in her new home. The anniversary of Willie's death goes unremarked by Haddie, as does his birthday, Nov 24. Leo has to go back to his duties before Christmas, which the rest spend at Monasterboice.

1873 Papa escorts Annette and Baby, also Blanche and Helen, as far as Holyhead on their way to Portsmouth. Still at Monasterboice, Haddie not only goes to Church, but plays the Harmonium there. Improvement in health is maintained, but she often suffers severe headaches which last a couple of days. She goes about almost as before, and walks. Her cousin Kathleen features a good deal; so does "Titie", another Harriet who marries her cousin William Ross on May 8th.
Jan 23 Dr Kelly calls to see Grandpapa's leg. We are told by Annette, in her Recollections written in 1915, that Grandpapa died just three months before his 93rd birthday, following a burn to his shin. Haddie does not record the death, but we know it was March 8th. Haddie is staying in Dublin then, and goes every day to see her step-grandmother, who is unwell, and living in 38 Lower Baggott Street. It looks as if Grandpapa died at Monasterboice.

Monasterboice House

Courtesy of Irish Architectural Archive

Annette, who remembered her grandfather as *a handsome, lively old man*, says he lived at Geneva a good deal. She wrote down some of the stories he had to tell from the past - his forbears had been in the Siege of Londonderry, (1688-9) and one of them could remember living on 7 figs for a week, and then crying when the head of a rat was stolen from his pocket ... His mother had been a Miss Mary Anne Bogle, corrupted from Bothwell, Claimant of the Menteith title, so commonly known as "the lady of Menteith". Her money came from West Indian property and she was widowed early when her husband died of yellow fever at sea, travelling to or from the West Indies. She always told of how, sleeping alone with her fourth son Neall (who died young), she became aware of the bed-curtains being drawn aside and seeing her husband there, gazing at her. The child also awoke: "There's a man in the room!" She believed this was at the very moment her husband had died, far away. Mary Anne brought up three other sons and is

said to have managed family affairs with *"judgement and success."*
Grandpapa had been devoted to both his mother and his grandmother. The latter had been a Miss Drummond and lived to be 93; he remembered being caught in the Rebellion of 1798, driving her over a bridge in Dublin through a howling mob, holding the carriage cushions against the windows as some sort of protection: it was the day when one of the Judges was killed, on the same bridge.

Grandpapa went to school at Dungannon - Annette comments that Irish schools had a higher reputation in those days, and were thought preferable to sending sons across to Eton and the like: her mother's father, Lord Ferrard, once spent the whole of his Christmas holidays at Holyhead, waiting for a wind, and at last went back to Eton without having crossed the sea at all.
Grandpapa, having married Miss Catherine Foster, whose family was prominent in Co. Louth, decided to settle there, *"bought land in 1819 and later enlarged Crosby's farmhouse near the ancient ruins of Monasterboice into a most pleasant family house in which I was born"* - says Annette - *"and from which I was married."*

We know.from a childhood diary of Haddie's, that she, Annette and their parents also lived at Geneva for two years, and were there when Willie was born. Mrs Dunlop, Haddie's stepgrandmother, survives four years more and is regularly visited by each of the family when they are in Dublin. She dies in 1877 and leaves Haddie £300, which seems to show compassion and fondness.
In May Mama leaves for England, and Aunt Liz comes to keep the girls company at Monasterboice.
June 3 Little Annie McClintock, Leo and Annette's second child, is born at Portsmouth [Anna Elizabeth].
June 6 Aunt Kitty's funeral at Collon. 10 gentlemen come to lunch.
June 21 Papa goes to Portsmouth for the Naval Review in honour of a visit from the Shah of Persia - Haddie sounds rather wistful: she would have liked to see this.
July 21 After a visit to Glen Ban May and Haddie return home and find Leo, Annette, Harry and Baby there. *Father better and in drawing-room.* In August he departs for Germany, on business perhaps?
Aug 11 Harry's second birthday; and Annette and Leo and the two children go back to Portsmouth. Haddie, remaining in Ireland, has a very busy, sociable period with many drives and picnics, families coming to stay (the Halls, Hungerford Skeffington, Clara Mowat etc.) with the younger sisters coming along on horseback. There are charades, croquet parties etc, every day. Papa

Annette c. 1874

returns from Hamburg.
Oct 1 Haddie is in Dublin and seems to have a recurrence of illness - Dr Smyly is constantly in attendance. Helen Verschoyle is her friend, often referred to with her sister-in-law Helen Verschoyle as *"the two Helens."* Ellen Harris, who looked after her three years before, often visits her. Christmas is spent at Tassaggart with the Verschoyles.

1874 The diaries now change to the edition she keeps up for the next 40 years and have the date of the year in gold on the spine, and a bit more room for writing.
The year begins at Tassaggart, near Dublin, with Haddie rather unwell. Helen V marries, Jan 15 1874, Moutray Gledstanes, Later, this Helen will become the mother of Marion, who marries Harry, though not until 1930. Back at M'boice, Henry West is mentioned with Helen - later, these two marry.

Feb 7 To Portsmouth. Epic sea journey with Mrs Hannan in S.S "Avocar". They travel by sea all the way, lying off Falmouth, then being met in a pinnace by Leo at Portsmouth. [Till Annette goes to live at Portsmouth the usual way of travel has been via Liverpool, then by train to London] Haddie stays with Leo and Nettie, later joined by Dora. They have a very sociable time, though Haddie is often kept confined by regular headaches. They drive to Mrs Thistlethwaite's at Southwick House to lunch, a prodigious pull over Portsdown Hill for carriage horses, and Haddie is often included in naval entertaining.
Mar 20 Went on board the Troopship that had brought the 23rd Regiment from Ashanti ... and next day, Sir Garnet Wolseley arrives at Spithead from Ashanti. [In David Murphy's biography "The Arctic Fox", 2004, he tells how Leo, noticing how the troops felt the cold on reaching Portsmouth, had an awning built on the quayside, and provided hot food and drinks for them. Later in his life, Leo would play a prominent part in many philanthropic concerns for seafarers, including the Royal Naval Scripture Readers' Society and the Royal Alfred Institute.]
Ap 23 Back to M'boice; *Harry and Baby so good on the journey.*
May 8 Helen, henceforward known as Dot, marries Rev. Henry West (of the Wests of White Park family) at St George's, Dublin. 30 people attend the wedding breakfast. The Wests go to Switzerland for their honeymoon - all her life Dot is very fond of hill walking, almost mountaineering.
May 10 James Delap called to see me.
May 28 Haddie goes to Portsmouth with Leo, Annette, children & Blanche.

Some typical entries:

June 10 ... Leo and A to London for Queen's Concert. Mrs Clement Lefroy came over from the Isle of Wight to see Elizabeth Lefroy and Baby who are staying; Elizabeth is a daughter of Dr Alfred McClintock, Leo's brother

June 14 Sunday. Blanche and I to church on board the "Excellent".

June 15 Cold wind. Colonel and Mrs Fortescue and Carrie Garstin spent the afternoon. Nettie had a large garden party.

Jun 17 ... Blanche to Ryde to go to Flower Show with Mrs Pare and Mrs Fortescue. A and I out in Brougham.

Jun 22 ... Henry and Dot arrived from London. Large garden party ...

Jun 24 ... B and I out walking in the Dockyard. A and Dot and the Halls drove to Portsdown Hills.

July 13 ... All our party went to hear Mrs Scott Simmons read. Did not think it quite so good as last time.

July 18 Parents, Dora and May arrive from Hamburg. So they still continue the younger ones' education by taking them abroad.

Jul 19 Sunday. All except Mother to morning service. Leo and May with Sir Rodney in "Fire Queen" to call on the Prussian Admiral off Cowes.

Jul 20 Fine and very warm. Father, Mother, A and I out driving. Dined early and went out in steam pinnace from 6 to 8.30. Very pleasant on the water ...

Jul 21 ... Took a little walk with May. Leo went over to Ryde to be present at a Ball given by Royal Yacht Club to the Crown Prince & Princess of Germany.

July 26 *Nettie's little boy born* - this is Jack - John William Leopold.

Jul 30 ... May and I left Portsmouth in S.S "County of Dublin" at 8 am. Father and Leo put us on board. Tolerably smooth. Reached Southampton, left at 3 pm. Cabin very full and company very mixed.

Jul 31 ... very rough all night.

Aug 1 ... Got calmer about 9.00. Reached Dublin and went to Dot's house, 25 Upper Gardiner Street.

Aug 15 ... Dot, May and I went to Kilbarrack to lunch with the Laws.

Aug 18 ...All down to Monasterboice by 5 train. Papa has returned, but Mama is still at Portsmouth with Annette. *Found everything looking so nice at home - papering and painting well done, and Jessie much better.* James and Minnie Delap are mentioned. Papa is not well at the end of the year - Dr Kelly is called to see him at home, and they go to Dublin to consult Dr Smyly. Most of the family go to Rostrevor for Christmas, when there is a hard frost. Frank and Kathleen Oldfield and some of their children are there often, and there is a Christening of their seventh, little Guy. *Everyone goes skating* at Christmas, except poor Haddie. She still has headaches often. Kathleen Oldfield is the only child of Papa's sister, Mary Anne, who married David Ross of Bladenburg. After her death David Ross married Mama's sister, Harriet.

1875 Jessie's first child born. [McClaggan]
Jan 22.... *auction of the land.* Haddie visits Jessie and baby. He is later baptised, at home, by a Presbyterian minister, and named Donald Robert - Robert possibly after Haddie's Papa.
Jan 26 ... Went to bed in afternoon, having bad headache and cough. Father went to Dublin, and to Sandymount to see Uncle Chichester who is very ill ...
Mar 2 Papa and H cross to England - the rest go to Rostrevor. Meanwhile *M'boice is lent to Charlie and Ella Garnett (who were married today) for their honeymoon.*
Mar 22 Papa leaves for Dublin with Harry (now 4).
Ap 9 Damp and very cold E. wind. Not out, headache etc. Leo and A out in boat to see the "Devastation" before she sailed. The Liddells, from Oxford, spent the afternoon. Leo dined with Sir Hastings Doyle, to meet Sir Rodney Mundy.
Ap 11 Dot's son born ... (William Robert West, known as Robin later; Haddie does not name him - was the name painful to her?)
Ap 15 ... Mr Parr and Mr Giffard, R.N, to tea, both going on the Arctic Expedition.
Ap 23 ... Mrs Ingle and Miss Browne, who had seen the Arctic Expedition of 1818 sail, came to see the preparations for the forthcoming one.
Ap 25 Sunday ... to Morning Service. Leo took A and me all over the two Arctic ships, "Alert" and "Discovery", very tired.
Ap 29 ... Miss Cockburn spent forenoon and lunched, and taught A to embroider the Arctic flag.... Dinner party of 16, Arctic Officers, Lady and Miss Giffard, Mr and Mrs Coneybeare, the Clements Markhams etc.
May 1 ... A and I very busy finishing 2 copies in MSS of Leo's speech on Arctic Work for the Geographical Society
May 15 ... Adml. and Mr Cooke (Marine Artist) to lunch.
May 17 Whit Monday ... Dockyard crowded with excursionists to see the Arctic ships.
May 18-19 James Delap comes to stay at Portsmouth, from London.
May 21 Dark and rather heavy. A and I out in Dockyard, to see the Prince of Wales, who came to see the Arctic Museum and ships. He was not very genial. Leo lunched at Sir Hastings Doyle's to meet him ...
May 22 ... Leo and A lunched at Admiralty House to meet the Empress Eugenie who came to see the Arctic ships ... she was charming.
May 26 ... Lady Montgomery & daughter, Mr and Mrs Hutton, Purefoy FitzGerald wife and party to luncheon ... Father, Mother, Dora and Harry arrived from Ireland.
May 29 Dark and cold, E. wind. Nettie went early to open the sluices of new Docks. All except Leo and me to Review for Queen's Birthday on the Common. At 4 o'c we all went with the Elliots on "Firequeen" steam

yacht to see the Arctic ships start. We never witnessed such a sight of immense crowds cheering. Leo dined at Admiralty House. A. and Dora went in the evening.

Jun 3 Fine and warm. Mother, Father, A and I out driving ... Little Annie 2 years old.

Jun 5 Fine, warm and breezy. Father, Mother, A and D to Ryde to the Laws and Garriots. Harry and I went with them in Pinnace and back. Later, Leo and the 3 children and Hayes went to fetch them home. House unpleasant with plumbers at work [on the drains!]

June 12 ... Baby Jack's wet nurse, Mrs Elliott, left.

June14 ... I had two teeth drawn, with gas.

July 25 ... All to morning service, except me. Sat on the water jetty and King's Stairs ...

July 26 ... A's baby boy 1 year old, such a darling jolly fat boy! [Jack]

They are all kept very busy for some days preparing for a Bazaar in aid of the Sailors' Orphans Home. Mrs de Salis, Louisa Law, Miss Ponsonby and the Jeffreys girls all come to help. Haddie is only on the stall for short periods, but still becomes very tired.

Aug 13 Damp and chilly. Leo, Henry and Dot to Dublin and back. Most of the party played Lawn Tennis in the afternoon.

Aug 17 20 people to afternoon party. R. McClintock and Capt. Hayland, Mrs Balfour and Miss O'Brien. Supples, Hannans, Coddingtons, Mrs Nicholson, Florence Massereene, Mr F.Foster, and Mr C.McClintock ...

Haddie's cousin, Clotworthy Skeffington, had succeeded his father as Viscount Massereene in 1863 and married Florence, only daughter of the writer G.J.Whyte-Melville, in 1870. They have two sons, Oriel and Algy, at this date, a daughter Nora, and are to have several more daughters.

Aug 18 ... Leo, A and children to Dublin by early train to see Leo's people and G'mama. Sat out of doors watching lawn tennis and croquet ... they returned by 5 train from Dublin after a most successful expedition.

Aug 19 Fine and bright. Father, Mother, Siggenny, Leo, A, Blanche, May and Henry went to Pic Nic given by Mrs Murphy at Castletown, Dundalk, and were not home till 9 o'clock.

Aug 30 Very wet most of day. Mother, Leo, A and I to Red House to lunch ...

Sept 9 and 10 Leo A, and children left us for Portsmouth, via Greenore. Heard of fatal accident to Greenmore boat "Edith" by collision, last Tuesday. Father not well. Mother took Blanche and May to bathe at Termonfechen. I was out in the place.

Sept 11 Heard of safe arrival of Portsmouth party.

Sept 17 ... Father to Malahide and back to take lodgings for us there.

Sept 20 B, May and I to Malahide by 2.30 train to lodgings ... Father and Mother drove with us to Drogheda.

Sept 21 ... went to Longford to stay with Dot who was alone as Henry was at

Bray, not well.

At Longford Haddie observes and joins in the busy Parish life of Henry and Dot - he has a curate, Mr Little, but still runs congregational practising, Young Men's Christian Association, prayer meetings, concerts at the Protestant Hall, etc. Their immediate neighbours are the Edgeworths of Kilshrewley, Col. and Mrs Mauleverer, Bessie Moore and her brother Charlie Wale. As usual, Dot is very active, walking and often riding everywhere.

Oct 19 Mother, Dora and I left Longford by train., very late in Dublin. Father met us, and took Mother and Dora to the Hannans. I went to the Halls at Monkstown ... very tired indeed.

At Monkstown Haddie walks with her cousin Henrietta to visit Sydney and Clementina Skeffington. Sydney had married, in 1872, Miss Campbell Denniston.

Oct 25 Wild rain and storm ... Minnie Delap to afternoon tea. Dreadful accounts in the papers, of floods and shipwrecks in England.

Nov 2 ... went into Dublin to 20 Ely Place to our Father and Mother and Dora, who had come up from M'boice that morning . Saw Cissie Garstin who was up for shopping. Dora and I out for a little shopping.

Nov 7 ... all to Church except Helen V who had to stay with a sick servant ...

Nov 12 Blank. But the day before, Nov 11th, is the day of Papa's death.

Nov 13 ... left Tassaggart in afternoon. Minnie and William drove with me to town, where I met Jessie. Found the sisters at home, and Leo and A and Harry. Henry, Dot and Baby, and the darling Mother better than we could have hoped.

Nov 14 Henry administered the Holy Communion to us all in the drawing room.

Siggenny came from Collon to join us.

Nov 16 Heavy showers. Our loved Father laid to rest till "He comes". Nettie and Dora followed him to the last. We all saw several of the kind friends who came. Uncle Poë left..

A week or so later, Haddie leaves with the McClintocks to return to Portsmouth. Harry is left behind with his grandmother, possibly as company for her. They lead a quiet life till Christmas, because of mourning; one of the few activities recorded is when the two sisters take Annette's contribution to a Sale of Poor Clothes for the Industrial Society at Portsea, also a visit to a Ragged School; and Annette is unwell over Christmas. We begin to hear of Haddie taking care of Annie and Jack occasionally, when Nana Hayes is out. At the end of this diary comes an impressive list of things Haddie has made during the year:

2 caps - Kathleen. Handscreens - Nettie, half-finished. Couvrette. Poor

Orphans, half-finished.
Sewed lace couvrette for Mother (2). Cap (copied from Ella's bridesmaids), 2 frills for each and habit ...
2 caps for Mother. 1pr. lace handscreens. 2 caps for A and altered bonnet. Beaded bt. Cochinese Tablier and body.
2 Hats trimmed Annie and Baby. 1 bonnet made - self. Made tablier etc. brocaded silk.
1 bonnet made (Dot), black tulle and jet. The same for Nettie and self, remade.
2 sashes and shoulder knots for Annie and Baby. Embroidered Roman work apron (S.Vitt. Bazaar) Beaded lace on Coche... Mantle. 1 cap - Nettie. Beaded lace on Mantle - A. Mounted lace screens - A. 2 veils made - A and self. Dot. Made ... Tulle bonnet for Dora, Mother, Nettie and self.
3 caps, S.V.H Bazaar. Trimmed hat - Dora. Made up shawl - Dora,
2 caps - Mother. 1 tulle bonnet - Blanche. 2 caps - Nettie.
Altered brown holland dress.
2 frock bodies - Dot. 2 caps - Nettie.
2 bonnets trimmed - Blanche and Dot. 2 hats for Dot. White muslin tablier and body altered. Yellow ... dress altered. Cap - C. Hall. Medieval cushion - Nettie. Trimmed 7 hats. Made crepe Bonnet - self. 1 cap - A.
A good deal of the above must have been for (rather hurried) mourning. Haddie usually remarks "not out" when the weather has been too bad for exercise - and we see that she had plenty to occupy her indoors. We know that Annette was a good pianist, but though Haddie sang and always enjoyed good music, she seldom mentions playing the piano, though she can do so well enough to play the harmonium in church, very occasionally.

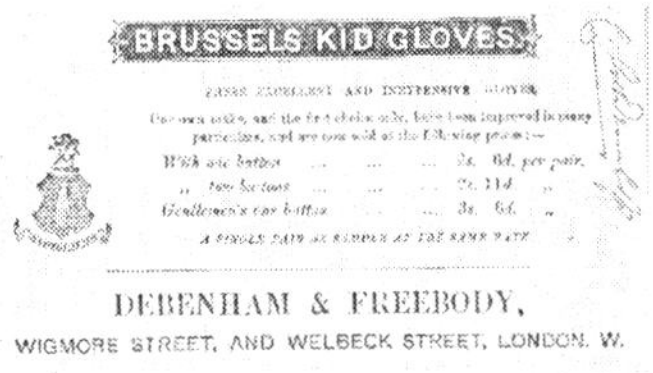

1876. On Jan 14 Leo goes to Chester to meet Our Mother, Blanche, Dora and May who are on their way from Ireland to Bath. He escorts them as far as Birmingham, and brings home Harry. Annette is not well early in the year - a threatened miscarriage probably; and while she is laid up H seems to have fewer headaches. She may not be part of all the social happenings in the dockyard, but she knows all that goes on and is interested in the ships and naval grandees as they come through. Queen Victoria embarks for Hamburg in March and Leo dines more than once on the Trinity Yacht. Meanwhile "the Mother" and younger sisters continue at Bath. Little Jack is unwell and has his two middle lower teeth extracted. A fragment of a Diary by Annette mentions a fall in which his teeth were pushed back into his gum.

Feb 10 Very cold, but fine. Out in open carriage with A. Quite too cold for me. Mrs Bunbury called...... Heard of Sydney Skeffington's death at Madeira on the 6th. [Haddie's first cousin, brother of Lord Massereene.]

Feb 14 ... Heard the sad news of Bammie Ross's Apostasy. Blanche or Bammie, a few years younger than Haddie, married to John Foster Ross of Bladenburg, is sister of the above Sydney. Some relatives may have deplored Bammie's conversion to Roman Catholicism, but family closeness continues.

Mar 7 ... Leo to London to attend "Grocers'" dinner.

Mar 24 ... My birthday. A and I and the 3 children and Hayes drove in open carriage and went over the new building for the Royal Seamen and Marines' Orphans Home. There are many committee meetings on behalf of various charities - the Soldiers' Hospital is another.

In April, Blanche and Dora go back to Dublin (to the Verschoyles), while Mother and May come to Portsmouth. All are assisted in their journeys by Leo. Haddie and Harry go to London on June 2, meet up with Mother and May there (met by Siggenny). They all go back to Monasterboice ... *where were found Blanche and Dora, - but! .... Poor Mother had a bad bad headache.*

This first homecoming after Papa's death must have been very sad, and all the usual neighbours and cousins are constantly visiting or being visited, in the succeeding weeks. Some sample days:

Jun 5 Whit Monday. Fine, but chilly. Mr Wynne [man of business] *to lunch. Out walking to see the garden and greenhouses, all so nice & promising despite the cold backward season. Dot returned to Longford from Dublin.*

Jun 10 Fine & mild and sunny ... The Mother, May, Harry and I drove on the car to Mellifont and through Townley Hall demesne.

Jun 18 Fine and mild. but stormy. Kathleen, Dora, May and I to Church (my first time there since.) Mother not well enough to go; Blanche staid with her.

Jun 24 ... The Oldfields and sisters drove to the old Tower and played croquet afterwards. Siggenny came from Dublin ...

There are many excursions in the jaunting car, with Blanche and May often on horseback.

Kathleen Oldfield [Papa's only niece] comes on a visit. Mamma is finding life difficult in her widowhood, as a letter of hers to Nettie shows:

June 26th [1876] - deep black edge round the paper. *My darling, Another worry has cropped up ... are not Lawyers too bad in always leaving a loophole for future litigation in all their deeds. I shall have to name a nominator after me or perhaps two or three and I intend to put Leo's name first and who else shall I put?.......Now I am obliged to look for a Butler. Johnny has kicked at the work, put up by the last man I had. I cannot go on here. It is too much for me, so I feel getting worse .....You see, unfortunately there is not a half head among all the girls, very willing and anxious to do all for me but utterly useless except as hands. Haddie has some head but so often laid up and suffering that I cannot lean on her. I have given her Harry's lessons which she seems to like and is very regular at ....A broiling day. We have still some influenza in the stables. Fortunately the Carriage horses have escaped as yet. Rain much wanted. Coals now to be laid in. I have just bought a ship load. Love to Leo and from all, Your own Mother, A.E.D.* [P.S] *Harry very well.*

We can imagine the recently-widowed Mother and four daughters (though they were all coming and going on various visits) and the small boy, sent here to run wild, while Nettie is awaiting another baby. In another letter, to Leo, Mamma says:

July 1...Harry is getting such a Boy that I fear Nettie will find his Clothes and Boots in a very sad state when he returns, sliding down the slopes on his Thighs and slipping into the brook in a vain attempt to catch fish, but this is all as it should be, Ever yr. affecte. Mother.

July 11 ... Mother, Mea Bernard [visitor] *May and I drove along the Boyne and called at Townley Hall - no one at home. Had afternoon tea out of doors.*

July 14 Fine and very warm. Florence Massereene's 3 children and Mrs Wynne and her children spent the afternoon here and played with Harry.

July 15 In the evening the Mother, Blanche, Dora, Harry and I drove on the Car along the Boyne Towing Path. Mea Bernard and May rode.

July 17 Lovely fresh warm day ... The Mother, Mea, Blanche, May and Harry to Termonfeckin and sat by the shore for some hours and had coffee there.

July 22 Dark and threatening, fine and bright later. Siggeny, and Dora, May and Mea to Castle Bellingham to enquire for Mabel Bellingham who is very ill from consumption.

Jul 23 Sunday. All to church. Mr Hannan stopped the service, because Capt. Nicholson was faint ...

July 26 Heard by telegram of the birth of Nettie's 4th child, this morning, at Portsmouth Dockyard (Robert Singleton)... and on the 31st - Nettie's birthday - ... *excellent accounts of her and the Baby.* [Singleton is after "Siggenny" who became Bob's godfather,]

The following letters were written by three of the sisters on Bob's birth - they are perhaps worth giving as they show something of the character of each:

July 27, 1876 Monasterboice House. My dearest Leo, I must send you at all events a line of congratulation on yr new possession ... it will really be quite an imposing sight to see you and yr three sons swaggering along through life. I got a bitter disappointment at yr second telegram. I had quite made up my mind that it was to announce the birth of Mary Patience ... you know this long expected and clearly female infant must come sooner or later, I hope as head of yr house you will see to it. ...If this little fellow turns out something like his brothers he will set to work at once by enlarging our hearts to hold them all. Give dear Nettie my love and a kiss, I think I shall wait to send a kiss to the Baby until Nettie is able to give it, you might be afraid of breaking it, I mean the Baby, in the administration, and if you really did succeed in so doing I should never forgive myself for being the cause. ... Much love dear Leo from your affect sister Blanche S. Dunlop. May will write to you tomorrow and sends her love in the mean time.

July 27, 1876 Temple Michael. My dearest Leo, I heard this morning from Dora that Nettie had another little son, and I must send you a line to tell you how glad I am to hear it. ... I wonder if you were a wee bit sorry it was not a little girl, however I suppose whatever comes is equally welcomed as a precious gift from God. I fear Bammie Ross is not with you. I hope she will be allowed to go to Nettie. I know you have a lot of writing to do and now more than ever, but could you ask Hayes to let us have a line to tell us how Nettie goes on. Give darling Nettie much love from us both and from Hungerford, and with the same to yourself and best wishes from us both for little Robert Singleton. Believe me, dear Leo, Ever your affec. sister, Dottie. [Dot West already has a baby of her own, William or Robin]

July 27 1876 Monasterboice My dear Leo, I cannot tell you how rejoiced and thankful we all are at the good news of darling Nettie. The Mother has just received yr and Nettie's letters which have cheered us as she had such an easy time of it. But Leo, alas for poor little "Mary Patience", when is she to come?

Annette & children, c. 1876

We have however (as McLagan says) always hope left. All yesterday when we spoke to Harry of his new little brother all we could get out of him was a grunt and a grin, today he is more curious on the subject, got very red and looked pleased when the Mother read him yr message. The other day he informed us with the greatest delight that he was going to see a sheep killed! and added, "Those are the kinds of things I like seeing" however, when the day came he fortunately forgot all about it, and so had not to be forbidden to go ... Give darling Nettie my fond love and kisses, Ever dear Leo, Yr affec'ate sister, Dora R. Dunlop.

Aug 10 The Mother, Blanche, Mea and I on car to Slane Castle, and went in to see the pictures. Mr and Miss Adair and Dora rode in Oriel Demesne. He had a fall, but very little hurt.

Aug 11 Fine and very warm. Harry's 5th Birthday. B,D, M, Miss Adair and Mea spent the afternoon with Mrs Nicholson, boating on the Boyne, and were not home till 9.

Aug 15 Fine and warm. Blanche and May took Mea on Car to Drumcar, and left her there. Dora and Mr and Miss Adair rode to Collon and Mellifont Abbey.

Aug 16 ... Dot and her Baby arrived from Longford. Blanche drove into Drogheda to meet them.

Sep 7 Showers and wind. Blanche and Dot drove to Spencer Hill to see Cissie Garstin, who is going to be married to Mr McNaghton. Henry and Julia Jeffreys [visitors staying] *rode.*

Sep 19 Lovely bright warm day. Mr Jeffreys and Letitia left us early, and Frank and Kathleen and Allen arrived from Rostrevor. Out blackberry picking with Mother, B and Harry.

Jack

Sep 28 ... Out in the place. Heard of the death of Dorcas FitzGerald. This is Haddie's early friend and cousin, who had married Percy FitzGerald in 1869, during Haddie's long illness.

Oct 6 Haddie and Harry travel to England ... *with the Garstins, 2nd Class, passage rather rough.* She and Harry have breakfast at Siggenny's house 3 Grosvenor Mansions, Victoria Street; Leo comes to meet and take them down to Portsmouth, where they find everyone well. They resume busy dockyard life - Annette now has an "At Home afternoon on Wednesdays, which we know she keeps up for most of the next forty years. At the end of October the "Arctic Ships" come home and Haddie goes out in the pinnace with Leo and Nettie to come into harbour on board the Discovery. Lots of officers from her and from the Pandora come to visit, and on Nov 4 Mother and Blanche and May arrive on their way to Italy, where they are going to pass the winter. In early Dec she goes with Leo and Nettie to London, partly to help with househunting.

Dec 19 A. and I out in brougham, shopping and visiting, and took "Pretty Jack" to have his hair cut short."

Dec 27 Leo thinks he has found a house to rent in London - 29 Kensington Park.

1877 Portsmouth. Fitzclarence Paget comes to stay.

Jan 24 *Heard of Jessie McLaggan's 2nd boy born at Monasterboice* (Haddie's nurse/companion in her illness.)

Feb 7 Mr Stanley McClintock's two daughters and their brother Frank come to stay. [Another brother, Charlie, will later marry Blanche.] Stanley and his children seem to have been very musical - the eldest, Freddie, is a good violinist and collects old violins, and is known as "Freddy the Fiddler." In later years he and his wife Antonia entertain a good deal with highbrow musical parties, in their Chelsea house, 7 Ormonde Gate. The brother of today's entry, Frank, becomes a clergyman, a quiet and spiritual man, we are told, a wonderful pianist who becomes Dean of Armagh eventually.

Feb 12 A better and up. The Clemengers and their party for the concert dined with us at 6.30 All to Amateur Concert in the R.N.College, where A played and also accompanied some of the singers. Very good concert, and all went off as well as possible, excepting accident to the steam pinnace, taking the Clemengers home to Gosport.

Feb 16 Very fine. Leo, A and I after lunch out in boat with Capt. Herbert to see the Whitehead Fish Torpedo at work., Went on board one of the 4 gunboats for the Chinese Government, made in England, and each carrying one 38 ton Armstrong gun. Mr Ching, the English officer in charge, most politely showed us the gun working etc. After dinner, Leo and A went to one of the Protestant Educational Services .

Haddie does love this sort of thing, but alas, next day she is in bed all day with a *bad cold and cough.*

Feb 26 James and Minnie Delap come to stay. Minnie is no doubt James's wife - he had married, in 1872, Miss Marian Prothero-Smith. At this time Haddie seems to be included in many more evening occasions than formerly; it appears she is getting stronger.

Mar 1 Lovely bright mild day. Leo, A and I and the Delaps went out to Spithead to see the "Alexandra", the new Flag Ship for the Mediterranean, which is to take out Admiral Hornby. Afterwards went on board the Victory and the Royal Yacht ... James and Minnie left for London.

Mar 2 ... The Bishop of Winchester came to stay. Dinner party of 16 ... pleasant evening.

Mar 3 ... Went to Confirmation in Dockyard Chapel. Numbers of sailor boys from the St Vincent. Good address from the Bishop, Dr Rutherford, DD and Mrs Williams to lunch

Mar 15 ... I walked in Dockyard with Harry. Leo and A returned from London. We 3 dined at the Maitlands.

Ap 2 ... A and I in open carriage, drove over the Portsdown Hills to Waterloo [ville] *to call on Capt and Mrs A. Gordon.*

April 14 A and I to dentist early, and then lunched at Dover Court with the Maines. Leo, A and I dined at Government House with Sir Hastings Doyle. Pleasant evening ... I heard from Blanche in San Remo giving a much better account of herself.

April 24 Harry and I by train to Bosham to spend a few hours with Capt. and Mrs Hobson. Visited Chichester Cathedral, very beautiful and interesting. A not well enough to accompany us. [W.R.Hobson had been a Lieutenant in the "Fox" on Leo's Arctic expedition.]

April 30 Leo's flag comes down after five years as Superintendent of the Dockyard. ...

May 3 ... and the Admiralty men come to go over the Inventory.

May 18 ... Packing first van of furniture ...Capt and Mrs Swainson brought 4 Chinese Naval Officers to take tea with us. They speak English well, and are intelligent; and have come to study in England. They wear full Chinese dress.

May 19 ... Leo to London and back, taking the Coxwain to help to settle the house ...

May 25 They leave the dockyard *with much regret*, for London - to 29 Kensington Gate. Next day, Hayes (Nana) and the *four darling children* are brought up.

May 30 Mother, Blanche and May arrive from the Continent. Lodgings have been found for Mother but she changes them before long. From now on Mother spends the summers in London, and finding the right lodgings for her is not always easy.

Jun 3 They attend Christ Church in Victoria Road.

Jun 4 Leo to Ireland for Lady Elizabeth McClintock's funeral. [Widow of his uncle, John McClintock]

Jun 9 Hayes had a holiday, so we minded the chicks.

Jun 24 Haddie, Blanche, May and Mother start for Ireland, to be joined two days later by Dora, who has spent the winter at Longford with Dot.

June 28 Mother and we four drove in Waggonette to see the rhododendrons in flower at Oriel [Temple]. But the weather is dull, rainy and depressing. Haddie often has a headache and appears to be missing her nephews and niece.

July 14 Very mild, with showers. Mother and I and the Halls drove on Car to Collon and Oriel. B and May rode. Kathleen Balfour rode over from

Townley Hall.

July 15 Sunday. St Swithun, and such pours of rain that we could not go to church.

Haddie and Dora go on a little visit to Fardross, to the Gledstanes.

Jul 20 ... Mr Gledstanes took Dora and me in a pony carriage to call on Mrs McCartney at the old Palace at Clogher.

Jul 21 ... All our party drove to Favour Royal to lunch and spend the afternoon. It is a very fine place, with splendid old trees, belonging to an uncle of Mr Gledstanes - Mr Moutray.

Back at Monasterboice, Haddie is ill with headache for several days.

Aug 1 Heavy showers. Mother, Mary McCartney, Dora and I took a drive on the car, and it rained all the time but cleared afterwards. B and May rode to Castlebellingham, and spent the day with the R.McClintocks and Miss Stubbs. B sprained her leg in the stirrup.

Aug 23 Very chilly, some showers. B, Dora and Henry (West) rode to Rokeby. ... saw the Eclipse of the Moon.

Aug 30 Leo arrives with the four children, and Nana Hayes. Annette is not well enough to come over.

Aug 31 ... Leo rode over to Collon to see Dr McClintock (his brother) who was spending a night with the Wynnes. Mother, May, Harry, Annie and Jack took a short drive on the Car. I walked in the place.

Leo returns to London next day.

Sep 4 Very fine, and not cold, we 4, and 5 children and 2 nurses drove (2 sisters rode) to Termonfeckin and spent some hours on the Strand and had tea there. The children were so happy, and all spent a pleasant time.

Dot's little boy, now aged two, is of the party, but Haddie still does not give William his name.

Sept 6 Cold, and very wet all afternoon. Mrs Balfour called. Hayes in bed with rheumatic attack. Played with the children indoors.

Sept 17 ... Mother, Kathleen and I to Mellifont to see the school children's tea, which Mother is giving.

Oct 10. Haddie goes to Monkstown to see Grandmama who is very ill with "paralysis". Aunt Liz is also ill, at Baggot Street. Then she meets Hayes and the children at the Packet to travel back to London. She finds Nettie better, and Mrs Alfred McC and her little girl Caroline are staying with her.

Oct 21 Dr and Mrs Alloway arrive from Sydney (Leo's sister Florence.) Leo goes to East India Dock to meet them.

Oct 27 Fitz Paget dined.

Nov 8 .... Leo took Dr Alloway to a Hydropathic establishment at Richmond.

Nov 13 Grandmama passes away at her home in Dublin.

Nov 20 ... Leo and I by train to Portnall Park, [Sunningdale] *to stay with the H.de Salis's. Freda and Ethel Law and Captain Law went down with us. Dinner party, including amongst others, Mr Flint, a clergyman, who is*

half brother to Lady Castlestuart.
Nov 21 ... Mr, Mrs and Miss Palgrave came to stop at Portnall. He is Clerk of the House of Commons; also Charlie Filgate.
Nov 22 ... lunched at 12.30, and afterwards drove through the Park to Windsor Castle and saw the beautiful Albert Memorial Chapel ...
All through December Annette is quite unwell and if she does go out it is in a bath chair
Dec 19 Mrs De Salis came and took A and me in her carriage to Dawley [near Sunningdale] . *Poor A was sadly tired. Leo followed with the luggage by train, and had to wait for two hours at Hayes Station for a fly.*
Dec 20 Foggy and damp. A. so tired that she was in bed most of the day. Sir Rawson Rawson and his sister Mrs Parry, also Admiral and Mrs Cochrane, to dinner.
Dec 21 Damp but mild. Not out. A a little better and out in Bath Chair. Mrs de Salis out riding. She and I very busy preparing things for a Xmas tree.
Dec 22 Fine. Hayes and the nursery maid, and the four children, arrived from London. Mary Hayes, generally known to them all as Nana, is an important person to the family, valued and looked after by them to the end of her life.
Dec 23 Fine. Mrs de Salis, Leo, Harry and I to Church. Annette drove in open carriage to meet us coming back.
Dec 24 General and Mrs de Salis arrived from London. A's 4 children and 4 little Garrats and Mr Thomas' little girl had a teaparty, and Xmas tree afterwards and games. Colonel and Mrs Garratt, and Captain Garratt, dined here. A out in Bath Chair.
Dec 25 Fine, bright and frosty. To Church in open carriage. A. came to meet us. I walked in garden with Harry. He and Annie and Jack sat up late, and came in to dessert. Snow at night.
Dec 27 Heard of the birth (by Telegram) of Dot's Twins at Longford this morning. [One of these is Alexander H.D., always known as Alick, and the other Annie E.B., henceforth called Daisy.]

1878. The family are in London all year, except for a long summer holiday at Walmer.
Jan 8 *Harry went for the first time to the kindergarten at the Albert Hall. A Schoolboy!!* But he does not remain there long, possibly because Leo is on half-pay. It must have been an anxious time for him, with a wife ailing and 4 young children.
Feb 1 A out in Bath Chair before lunch. I went with her to shop for Mother, and to see the Monument Mr FitzGerald is erecting to Dorcas's memory.

Feb 11 ... Heard that the North American Command, for which Leo was a candidate, has been given to Adm. Sir Edward Inglefield..

Feb 16 ... went with Leo and Harry to the South Kensington Museum to see the Trojan Treasure discovered by Dr Schleiman ...

Feb 23 ... Went with A to her Dr. Leo took Harry and Annie to the Westminster Aquarium.

Feb 27 Mea Bernard called, also Bammie Ross and Pussy Drummond and Maria McC. Capt. Jim Gambin called, and gave us interesting accounts of events in Turkey, where he has just been Times Correspondent at the Turkish Headquarters. Haddie's interest in world affairs is just beginning to show itself.

Because Annette is still unwell, Haddie goes about a good deal, helping Leo with the children and sometimes dining out with him. Mother and Dora arrive to stay from Ireland. They are getting reports that Mother's sister, Aunt Lizzie (Poë) is gravely ill. It has seemed that Haddie was particularly fond of this aunt

Mar 16 ... I lunched with Lady Carmichael at 1 Sussex Place, and went with her and Louisa Storey to a Saturday Popular concert at St James's Hall. Joachim on the Violin, and Barth on the piano were first rate ...

Mar 21 ... Clara Mowat, Dora and I to the Albert Hall to hear the "Creation" Most enjoyable. Anna Williams has a charming clear soprano voice ...

Mar 24 ... HMS Eurydice lost off Ventnor, with 320 souls!... Mother lunched with John and Bammie.

Mar 25 ... Heard of John Ross's Perversion [sic]. This follows his wife, Blanche or Bammie's, conversion to Roman Catholicism two years before. They are both Haddie's first cousins, and the news must have come as a shock to their Protestant relations, but family closeness is hardly affected.

Ap 2 ... Heard the dreadful news of Lord Leitrim's assassination, which made the Mother decide to remain another day in town.

Ap 4 ... Mother left us for Bath; Dora also joined her from Clara Monat's.

Ap 12 ... Leo and I to an evening party at Lady O'Neill's, 117 Piccadilly.

Ap 15 ... I went with A to the Dr. I began teaching my darling Harry again ...

Ap 19 Good Friday. Harry and I to Church in Victoria Road - A. walked round Kensington Gate!

May 11 ... Leo took Harry to Bath to stay with the Mother at 7 St James's Square.

May 12 ... I went to Victoria Road church and missed Harry so! A and I sat a long time on Balcony ...

May 18 ... Leo dined with Titi to meet Eddy Ross's intended, Miss Lindsay, and her people.

Jun 19 ... Mother, Leo and A, Annie and Jack to Ramsgate. May and I drove with Mr Mowat in his brougham to the Civil Service Co-operative Stores, and to see the Russell Club, which has just been opened in Regent St for

Ladies and Gentlemen.

Jun 20 May, Harry and I out walking in the Park, and visited the School of Art Needlework, Kensington. Heard that dear Aunt Lizzie had passed away yesterday..

Jun 30 Sunday ... Helen Verschoyle spent some hours with me. Titi and Aunt Harriet called, and took May to see Eddy's and Nina's wedding presents

Jul 4 ... Mother, A, May and I lunched at Titi's, and afterwards ate ices at Gunters

Jul 11 ... Agnes Skeffington came to lunch and spent the afternoon, and told us much about dear Aunt Liz. [Agnes, 21, daughter of Haddie's uncle Rev. Thomas Skeffington.]

July 19 ... Left London, a party of 12, by "Granville Express" for Walmer. Very rough, hot, dusty journey. Found the house, 1 Strand Terrace, very nice and comfortable

July 25 ... Went after breakfast to see the children bathe on the beach. In afternoon all went to see Deal Castle, built in 16th century, and now inhabited by Lord Clanwilliam.

Jul 26 Fine and warm. Jack's and Bob's birthday - 4 and 2, dear little men!

July 27 ... Mother, Leo, A, May and I drove to Walmer Castle, where Lord Granville is now Lord Warden, and saw the room where the Duke of Wellington died. The grounds round the castle are very pretty ...

Aug 1 ... Drove in open carriage to see Bettshanger, Sir Walter James's place. It is very lovely, with beautiful trees, flowers and greenhouses ... The house is Elizabethan and large.

Aug 2 Fine, but stormy, causing high waves, one of which broke over the Mother, A, and May and wet them through, though they were a considerable distance from the sea, on the shingle. Leo went to Sandwich, and saw some fine old churches, and much to interest him.

Aug 3 ... Leo, Mother, May, A, Harry and I drove in open carriage to St Margaret's Bay, half way to Dover. It is a lovely little secluded spot with a Coast Guard Station and apparatus for saving life at sea with rockets. We had tea in the Inn garden, and enjoyed our afternoon much

Aug 11 Sunday ... Dear A to church in evening for the first time since more than a year ago ... Darling Harry, 7 years old today..

Aug 12 Bob very ill, and alarmed us greatly, being quite unconscious, but got better as the day went on. It is thought to be an attack of heat apoplexy. Sat up with him till 2 am, then Hayes watched till 6, when the Mother got up.

Aug 13 Dear little Bob nearly quite well again, thank God ...Dr McClintock came to stay.

[Leo's brother Alfred, distinguished Dublin physician]

Aug 15 Fine and bright. Mother, May, Leo, Dr McC and I by train to

Canterbury, where we visited the splendid Cathedral. The town contains many quaint old houses. We lunched at the Rose Inn and got back to Walmer having spent a most enjoyable day....

Aug 24 ... We ALL went to the Pier at Deal - A in a Bath chair and the children in a Goat carriage.

Aug 28 Mother and May have now left for Ireland, and the Ruxtons [old friends from Ardee] have taken a house nearby ... *Leo to Portsmouth to appear as witness at the "Eurydice" Court Martial ...*

Aug 29 ... Elizabeth Lefroy [daughter of Dr McClintock] *and her 3 eldest boys came to stay in a lodging close by. A and I sat on the beach enjoying the lovely evening ...*

Aug 31 ... Elizabeth and I walked to Deal ... Leo made an expedition on a 4-wheeled Velocipede, and came back rather the worse for the wear!

Sep 2 Lovely mild still day ... Leo, A. Elizabeth and I out in a rowing boat, very enjoyable and everything so pretty. Boatman told us much about the Deal fishermen etc. His boat is named the 9 Brothers, after his 9 sons. Hayes took Harry and Annie on a Donkey to spend the afternoon with friends of hers in a Windmill.

Sep 5 Elizabeth, Leo, A and I drove to Dover Castle, to see Major and Mrs Trench, and Gen. and Mrs and Miss Lefroy who are staying with them. Visited the underground passages, cut in the chalk, and the Garrison Church, built by the Britons in the 4th Century, and believed to be the oldest Xtian Place of Worship still used as such. It is very curious and interesting, as is also the old Roman Pharos, in the enclosure of the Castle.

Sep 6 ... Saw the children bathe in the morning. In the evening Leo, A, Harry and I out rowing, which was very enjoyable. Harry made his first attempt at rowing ... Elizabeth came to dinner with her husband and his cousin, Miss Boyle, who arrived today.

Sep 12 ... Leo took Harry & Annie to Sangers Circus ...

Sep 13 ... We all left Deal and reached London after a prosperous journey, thank God, and found the house looking so nice and comfortable.

About this time Leo begins a long and sometimes contentious correspondence with brother-in-law Rev Henry West about misunderstandings which had arisen between the sisters, especially Blanche and Nettie. It looks as if both sides had been a little over-sensitive, and between them all the chief sufferer was Mama, who could not bear any sort of coolness. Perhaps at the root of the trouble was some resentment by the other sisters of their parents' fondness of, and reliance on, Leo and Annette. At the time of Willie's death, Papa had wanted to make Leo his heir (with Harry to follow) and though Leo had persuaded him not to do this, he seems to have left Harry an equal share, with his mother and the other daughters. Not long before his death he felt aware that he had not been quite fair, and of course the younger sisters soon started their own families. Whatever the rights of it, family feeling runs high at the time, so much so that they do not go to Monasterboice at all in this year. In one letter Leo refers to Annette's very sensitive nature, and she certainly seems to have been made ill by it all. Henry and Dot West try to act as peacemakers throughout, but Leo clearly finds Henry's long letters irritating.

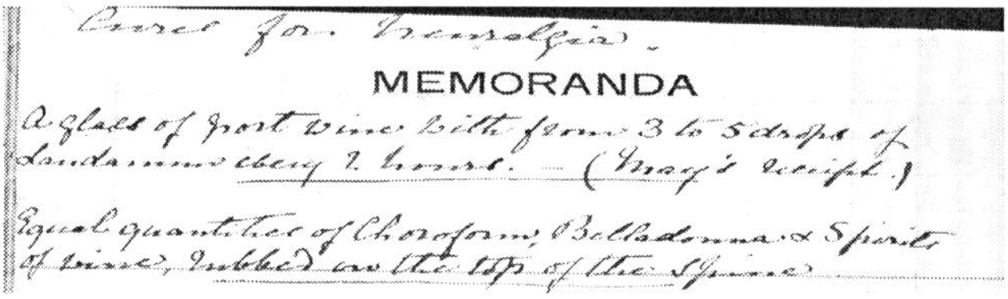
Cure for Neuralgia.
MEMORANDA
A glass of port wine with from 3 to 5 drops of Laudanum every 2 hours. (May's receipt.)
Equal quantities of Chloroform, Belladonna & Spirit of wine, rubbed on the top of the Spine.

Part of May's Recipe for Neuralgia

1879. They are in London, and Haddie goes about a good deal, including evening engagements, and seems better in health.

Jan 15 Annette and I drove to London & Westminster Bank to lodge my £300 left to me by Grandmamma.

Feb 8. Leo hurts his left eye and *Nettie got a great fright* about it - the doctor says he was lucky not to lose his sight, and he stays in a dark room for some days. Mama is expected for a visit and they find lodgings for her -16 St George's Terrace, Gloucester Road, and on Feb 20 Haddie goes to make sure all is ready for her.

Bob and Annie 1879

Feb 21 Mama, Blanche and Dora arrived early, but were two hours driving from Euston as their cab twice got stuck in a snowdrift.

Feb 22 Harry breakfasted with Mother, Leo, A and I went over to see her after breakfast, She, B and D spent afternoon with us. Titi and Bammie called, also Mr Maurice Beauford. Leo's eye much better.

Feb 23 Snow. A and Leo to Parish Church, Harry to Christ Church, also the Mother and B and D. Afterwards Mother spent the day with us. I went to St James's Palace to see Mrs H.Ward, and brought her back to Mother, who has headache. I saw Lady Dufferin, who with her husband our Ambassador, starts for St Petersburg tomorrow.

Feb 24 ...Annie breakfasted with Mother. Mother, A and I to L.D.A (Ladies Dress Agency) before lunch about A's court dress and Mother's things.......Captain Beaumont called, just returned from the Flag ship, Bellerephon, in West Indies.

March 21 Leo and A take the four children to be photographed at Fall's in

Baker Street [see picture on previous page.]
April 30 L and A dine with Admiral Wellesley, 1st Sea Lord.
May 19 Old Lord Rathdonnell dies and Leo goes to Drumcar for the funeral. May comes from the Hospital, where she appears to have been doing some training.
June 10 Mother and May go to Ireland.
June 13 Blanche and Dora arrive from abroad and go to Ireland.
June 12 All the chicks to Richmond for change of air.
June 19 ... and now all four have unmistakably whooping cough.
June 25 Saw a telephone at work.
Aug 14 *Heard unofficially that Leo is to get the North America and West Indies Command.*

In August Haddie is clearly very well, paying visits, going out everywhere, taking children to dentist, visiting Westminster Abbey for the first time. Weeks go by without her being laid up. The whole family are to go to Bermuda with Leo!
Aug 29 Annette goes to see Hayes' parents - perhaps to see if Nana can come to the West Indies with them.
Sept 11 Leo purchases a landau.
Sept 12. Leo's appointment is now official. May and her friend, Miss Temple, come to call. May seems to have a succession of female friends, some from the Hospital. As time goes by, we see that May is often at hand to help with family illness: perhaps, in a later age, she would have liked to train professionally, rather than accepting her role as companion to her mother.

Sept 16 Fine. Leo, A, Harry, Annie and I by the night mail to Dublin, via Holyhead and Kingstown. Beautiful smooth passage.
Sept 17 ... Breakfasted and lunched in Dublin at Dr McClintock's, 21 Merrion Square N. Several of Leo's sisters, and Ellen Harris, called. The children and I by 5 o'c train to M'boice, where we found the Mother and Blanche and Dora well.
Sept 24 Dot and her baby boy came from Bray. [This one is probably Harry]
Sept 25 Mother, Leo and A by an afternoon train to Rostrevor to spend 2 nights with Aunt Harriet ... Leo and A were to go on to Hillsborough.
Sept 26 Dick Quin called [he later marries Dora.]
Sept 30 Very fine. Mother, Dot and I drove to Oriel Temple and Collon. Dined at 6, after which Mother and I to Townley Hall to see a Play got up for the Tenants. Miss O'Brien, Kathleen and Mary Balfour, and Blanche and Dora acted very well. Leo and A to Stephenstown.
Oct 5 All, including Harry & Annie, to Church.

Oct 7 Back to London - and farewell to Ireland for the next three years.
Oct 23 They choose a piano to take out to Bermuda.

Oct 29 May brings her friend Miss Henry to 5 o'c tea.
Nov 4 *May and Mother to Ireland.* This was goodbye for perhaps a long time. From now on they are all very busy, visiting dentists and doctors and generally preparing for their departure for Bermuda. Much packing. At some point it must have been discussed and decided that Haddie would go too. She is very active and seldom ill.
Nov 28 Leo hoists his Flag on the Northampton.
Dec 10 Nana Hayes and three children to Southsea early, followed later by Haddie and Harry.

Dec 11 Beautiful sunny day. Harry and I went on board the Northampton, with Francis Poë, and lunched in the Ward Room with Edmund Poë. Saw Mrs Fisher and Mrs Coote and party, and Fitz Paget. Leo and A arrived in the evening from London, very tired.
Dec16 Northampton is coaling all day

H.M.S.Northampton—here seen dressed overall, Spithead, 28 June,1897.

On this voyage she is commanded by Captain Jacky Fisher (later Admiral of the Fleet Lord Fisher)

Dec 18 Lovely bright day. We all went on board the Northampton after breakfast. Started at 12.30. Saw the Queen leaving Gosport for Osborne. Remained at Spithead, swinging to adjust Compass, and taking in Powder till 10pm. Anchored for the night. Beautiful clear, still night.
Dec 20 Fine, and became bright and lovely later. Wind S.E and much warmer. Spent most of the day on deck. Hayes and the children sick off and on but better on deck. A pretty well, and I am very well indeed; but in evening felt sick and wretched. Edward Poë, Captain Northcote R.M.A and the Paymaster to dinner.
Dec 21 Very fine and bright, but wind against us so that we got on but slowly. Attended morning service. Harry still sick enough, and so A. and I felt too..
Dec 22 Sick and headachy, and not up till 11. Fine, sunny and breezy and rough enough. Sat a great deal on deck.

Dec 23 A great swell, but very fine and bright. A good many sails were set and the steam diminished. Felt quite well again. Captain Coles (the Staff Commander). Mr Pretyman, some of the Lieutenants and Mr Cox, assistant surgeon, to dinner. Went on deck after dinner to look at the moon and hear the band.

Dec 24 Very mild and fine, but dark. Sun came out at 1.30. Great swell, and ship rolling a good deal. Mrs Riddel, Lieut. and Mrs Wells, Sub Lieut and Mr ... chief engineer, to dinner. Very rough, and the glasses etc sliding about.

Dec 25 Xmas Day. Swell continues, but the temperature getting quite warm. Attended morning service on Battery Deck. Afterwards, went all round the men's Messes, and visited the Ward Room and Gun Room. On deck after dinner to see the men dance and sing.

Dec 26 Lovely bright warm day .. Enjoyed the day, much on deck ..."

Sadly, diaries for the next period, **1880, 81** and **1882** are missing. During this time, Gladstone succeeded Disraeli for his second time as Prime Minister. Lord Frederick Cavendish was murdered in Phoenix Park, Dublin, and Parnell had begun his affair with Mrs Kitty O'Shea.

There exist a few letters written home by Haddie; and three, written by the children to their Father while he was away in H.M.S Northampton have survived, and are reproduced here to give some idea of what their lives in Bermuda were like:

Feb 11th 1882, My dear Father, I have got to write with pencil because I have sprained my ankle a little. Fly caught a cat and Harry skinned it, without making any hole in it. Mr van Haughuick's puppy killed a rat and then had a tug of war with Fly to see which should have it. One day Fly caught a rat and a cat and a mouse. Last Saturday Johnny and I went out in the boat with Jolliffe and Harry and Bob went to the sports, and we found a buoy in one of the caves but Jolliffe could not get it out. Jolliffe says that he will have a job to keep his cat down at the cottage because it is so fond of him. We had all such pretty valentines and Johnny's and mine were the prettiest. My foot is better and I can hop on one foot. ... Last night I played cricket laying on the sofa on the veranda and the ball fell off the veranda. Harry found your name in a lesson book and we all think it is wrong and a great shame to turn you into a lesson. Mother has had a lot of tea-parties since you went away and they are very horrible only we get cake. Mother is going to let me walk a little today on both feet and as soon as I am quite well we are going to have tea on the rocks. There is a well near here with maiden-hair in it. I send lots of love and kisses, Your own little child, Tommy Round Head [this is Annie, aged 8 and a half]

Feb 11th 1882. My dear Father, Toby Bols puppy had to be given away because we did not want to pay the tax for him. We went last Wednesday to Mrs Ponsonby's and we rode by turns on the pony and the ponys name is Bob, and Annie rode like a boy because there was no side saddle and we saw two guinea pigs and we saw some cotton growing wild and we brought some home, and Harry sowed some in a pot. We went yesterday in the dingy to Mount Langton and when we were coming back we saw a dead horse in the sea, and a boy said it tumbled in yesterday. Annie and I slept together last night, and we awoke at half past six to jabber and tell stories. Mother has had a letter from Gaga, and she is quite well. We all send loves and kisses, Your own little boy, John. The muddle about Toby was Miss Jolly's fault. [This is from Jack, aged 7 ½]

Haddie in Halifax

Feb 12th, 1882. Dear Father, The Wye and the New York mail both came in this morning. Fly caught two wild cats that live on birds, one she chased so hard that it fell over the cliffs into the sea but it scrambled into the cave and Fly caught it there. Yesterday Fly caught a mouse as Johnny was going to the cove to get some water for Annie's foot; she only frightened it, so Johnny picked it up alive, but it bit his hand so he dropped it and Fly killed it. There were six rats caught at the stables and one monstrous fellow in the kitchen, Bascomb says it measured 16 ins. long from the tip of his tail to the tip of his nose ... we saw a crayfish thing alive but we could not catch him because he ran under a stone, but we saw another and Jolliffe stuck the oar into him and we fished him up with a boathook. I had some of him for breakfast and on Monday we made a lobster salad of him he measured nearly a foot and a half long ... We rode on the pony to get some butter, at the house we got the butter from there was a cotton plant it had rather cut out leaves I brought some pods home ... We all send lots of love and kisses ...
Your own little boy, Harry. [aged 10 ½].

We know that Bessie, the youngest McClintock child, (Elizabeth Foster Mary) was born in August, 1882, in Halifax, Nova Scotia, also part of Leo's command. Bessie is the much-adored five-months baby when they come home, in January, **1883.**

They all arrive at Portsmouth in the Transport "Nepaul", seeing many naval friends there before going on to London where they find Mother, May - and Harry, home from a school at Crowthorne, where he evidently started while his family were still overseas. " Our Mother " has taken a house opposite Leo's - 4 Kensington Gate. Haddie lives there with Mother and May (who goes off to Guy's Hospital on Sunday afternoons) but Haddie soon takes ill, and is in bed for some weeks. But by the end of February she is getting back to normal, enjoying her first carriage drive, and worrying about Baby Bessie's vaccination arm, sore eye and teething. She obviously adores the baby, and often "minds" her when Nana Hayes has her rare times off.

Leo and Annette resume their usual round of social and charitable events; they see Nina Ross dressed for the Queen's Drawing Room. Nina, formerly a Miss Lindsay, is the wife of Edmond Ross of Rostrevor, second son of Mother's sister, Aunt Harriet. Nina is presented from her sister-in-law's house in Curzon Street: sister believed to be Titi (short for Harriet) Aunt Harriet's daughter and married to another Ross: William. Leo and Annette also go to a Drawing Room on March 12: *I dressed A ... who looked so well in Black and pink - Fraise Ecrasie. Several people to 5 o'c tea to see her.*

Leo's niece, Helen Crozier (daughter of his sister Emily) comes on a visit) and she goes with Leo and Annette to see the Oxford and Cambridge Boat Race in Mr Baden-Powell's steam yacht. Mother and May give up their house and go to stay with Titi at 27 Curzon Street. Haddie goes across the road to Leo (No. 29 Kensington Gate).

March 10 Leo and A to evening party at Lord Northbrook's to meet Lord Alcester and the Prince and Princess of Wales .....Bammie Ross came to see us - just over from Dublin.

Bammie it will be remembered, is Blanche, formerly Skeffington, Haddie's first cousin and married to another first cousin, Sir John Ross of Bladensburg, eldest son of Aunt Harriet. They have no children, according to Harry's Family Tree. [This is a large, elegant parchment, handwritten in 1910 and invaluable to the editor.]

Mar 27 ... Walked to Barkers and returned by Omnibus. Helen Crozier and I were to have dined at Titi's but got a put off.

Harry gets mumps and then Jack, chicken-pox. Poor Harry will be in quarantine for some time, though *he has it so favourably.*

All children, including Baby, get chickenpox. *Second anniversary of the death of Lord Beaconsfield* (Disraeli) *-Many primroses worn.*

Mother and May, after a stay in Bath, leave for Ireland. Leo and all of them take the children on frequent educational visits - Kew Gardens, the Kensington Museum, and to a Gallery to see Millais' "The Stowaway."

May 19 Hayes left for Portsmouth on four days' leave. A new housemaid is come, and Alice, the former one, minds Baby. A, the three children and I by underground to see poor Miss Jolly, who is still ill and on her sofa. This day year we left Clarence Hill and slept in Grassy Bay on board Northampton. Miss Jolly is a governess, with the family in Bermuda.

This sounds as if Haddie was looking at diaries for the period abroad - but where are they now?

June 2 Lovely day. The Chicks have a holiday in honour of Annie's birthday. Hayes took them to the Fisheries Exhibition, A. and I minded darling Baby ...

June 12 ... A. and I to Meeting of Ladies' Working Guild in Kensington Vestry. Mrs Raby and her son to afternoon tea. I was to have gone over to Ireland tonight, but put it off till Friday, not being quite well. Thus I have three days more with my darlings!

June 15 To Ireland. Travelled all by myself in a Ladies' Carriage. Rough passage, from Holyhead, but I was not ill.

Mother and May are at Monasterboice, and they all pass a quiet time there, with not many visitors, perhaps because the weather is consistently cold and wet. She does not see Dora, now married to Dick Quin, until July 2nd; she also sees their boys, Aylmer and Robert, for the first time. Next day, Charlie McClintock, first-cousin-once-removed to Leo, and now married to Blanche, both arrive, with their baby boy, Stanley. *An immense fine boy, only 14 months old...* And another day: *Dick and Dora drove over with their children - a great baby show!*

The rain continues, unremitting... *When will this wretched weather improve?*

July 19 Dear Jessie McLaggan died today Jessie, nurse/companion to Haddie in her long illness. She is buried, with her baby, two days later. Mother, May and Haddie attend the funeral in Mellifont churchyard, a significant act of affection and respect, as in general most Irish funerals seem to be attended by men only. Dot calls one of her daughters Jessie, which may or may not be a coincidence.

July 21 They hear that Nettie has gone by train to Liverpool to see Aunt Harriet, who is ill there, but gets better soon.

At Monkstown they see many Dublin friends and relations. Haddie puts off going to Tassaggart till she has seen Nettie and ... *the Five Darlings. My sweet Bessie knew me again I think.*

During this visit, to Monkstown, at the back of the diary, Haddie notes some cash expenditure:

Telegram to Nettie: 1s. Train into Dublin: 8d.
For Housemaid at Tassaggart: 2s.
Gave Harry: 2s. Sir W. Jenner's mixture: 1s.6d.
Church: 1s. Train to Drogheda: 5s.6d. Wool & ribbon (baby): 11d.

When Leo and family arrive at Monasterboice they bring with them a Cook for Mother.

Aug 16 Mother, Leo, A and I drove to call at Drumcar, then to Greenmount where we saw the Quin children and had tea, Dick and Dora being out.

There are references in family letters to some feeling that a rather poor welcome home was afforded to Leo, Nettie and family after their long absence abroad. Two marriages and several births, in Nettie and Haddie's immediate family, had taken place in the interim.

Aug 18 Sweet little Bessie's first birthday. She weighs 21 lb.

Sept 4 A large party go to Malahyde, at the Royal Hotel. They are joined by Dot and Henry West and their little girl, Daisy, from Bray.

Sept 11 Leo and his family leave for London. Life sounds rather unsettled for Haddie, and she mentions feeling lonely when left at Monasterboice by herself. The weather has improved, but it must have been a gloomy summer after the West Indies. Mother is trying to decide whether to let or sell Monasterboice and rent a house in England - and nearly settles for one in Herefordshire, in fact she flits across to see it. However she changes her mind because her sister, Aunt Harriet Ross, is now obviously seriously ill and she plans to look after her at Monasterboice the whole winter.

Sept 27 Mother sent her carriage to Greenmount to fetch Aunt Harriet to spend the winter here. Poor thing, she looks sadly ill and changed and worn. She sits stooped forwards all day, and cannot occupy herself in any way. Florence Massereene called, also Mr Wynne.

Sept 28 ... May had a most distressing account of Dot from Henry - and in consequence will start for Longford tomorrow.

Sept 29 ... May left early for Longford - and Mother for Greenmount, having heard that Dora's eldest child, Aylmer, is very ill with convulsions. Mother came back with a much better report of the child ...

Sept 30 ... quite chilly, autumnal. Mr Wynne called about Mother's cook, who is so violent she has to be turned out of the house tomorrow.

Oct 2 ... Dr Kelly came to see Aunt H. and gave, I grieve to say, a very poor opinion of her state.

Oct 6 ... Dr Kelly saw Aunt H, who is somewhat better; just a rally, he says...

Oct 9 ... I walked in the place. John Ross came to see his Mother, and spend a day or two.

Oct 14 Wet, so we did not go to church. Poor Aunt H. seems very suffering today.

Oct 20 Haddie starts for London - glad, no doubt, to be going back.
Oct 26 ...to L.D.A [Ladies' Dress Agency] to help Bammie to choose her Court dress....
Oct 29 ... was not out having a little cold....
Richard Smith, Leo's steward when abroad, called. ... Hayes out with friends all afternoon, so I had much of darling little Bessie's company.
Oct 30. ... A bad account of poor Aunt H. Her children have been telegraphed for ...
Oct 31 ... Mr Price, R.N., called. He is called "Jonah" having been shipwrecked in "Phoenix" and "Lively" within a few months.

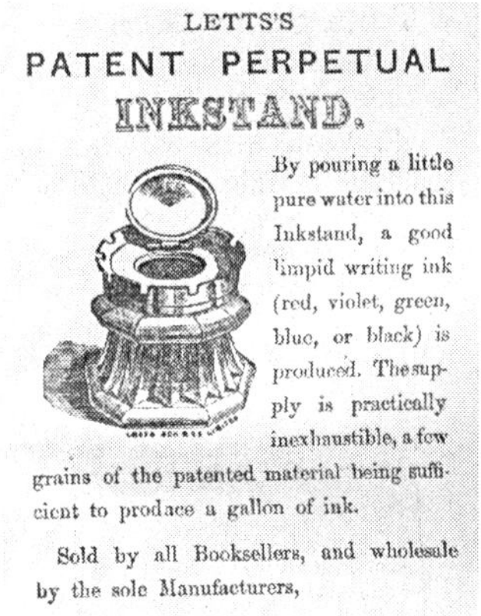

Nov 2 ... heard that Aunt H. had entered into rest ...
Nov 3 Out shopping. Nettie was to have been "At Home" today but, of course, she could not see anyone.
Nov 5 Aunt H. was laid to rest today at Rosstrevor.
Nov 10 ... Edith McC (daughter of Dr Alfred, who is staying*) and I to choral concert at Albert Hall, to commemorate the birth of Luther, and in aid of a Home for little boys.*
Nov 11 ... we elders to a 3 o'c service at Westminster Abbey, where the Archbishop of York preached about Luther. Great crowds, and beautiful music.
As the year closes, they try to prepare lodgings for Mother in Westbourne Place, but can do nothing *owing to a tipsy woman being in charge of the house. Leo came with a policeman to turn her out ... Poor little John has the mumps, and has to be isolated from the others.*
Annie and Bob get mumps, too, and Christmas is spent in London.
Dec 31 *... After lunch we went to an afternoon tea at Lady Gore Browne's, where her daughter's wedding presents were being exhibited. She is to be married to Mr Locker- King on the 3rd January.*

1884. Leo is unaminously elected an Elder Brother of Trinity House, causing great rejoicing. *Most flattering to him. The Prince of Wales, Duke of Edinburgh, Lord Lorne and others MOST kind about it.* Mumps again, and Bessie is very unwell with bronchial trouble. In February she is said to be weak after a heavy cold, and is to have 2 drops of brandy, 3 times a day.
Jan 11 Leo takes Annie and Bob to the Westminster Aquarium - the children are frequently taken to see such places of interest as the British Museum: also

to a Pantomime - Cinderella.

Jan 17 Haddie goes to buy *things for* [Leo's nephew] *Leopold McClintock's poor little baby girls expected daily from India* [his first wife having died].

Some of Leo's many interests, reported by Haddie:

The French Huguenot Hospital (his Mother, Bessie, was daughter of Archdeacon Fleury, of Huguenot descent)
Royal Naval Scripture Readers
Orange Club
Member of the Worshipful Company
Of Grocers, and attending functions
Of other City Guilds
Fellow, Royal Society
United Service Institute (helping judge
Prize Essay)
Dines with Coldstream Guards at
Windsor to meet Prince Christian
Royal Geographic Society
Agnes Weston Home for Sailors

Apr 1 Lay on my bed. A has a heavy cold and loss of voice. Leo out all day. Mrs Fane de Salis and Nancy Stowell lunched with A, who was ill able to entertain them! Dot's twin girls born today. She is very ill [Dot gets better, and Jessie survives, but the other, Helen, dies at 6 months of age. These are the second set of twins for Dot we have heard of.]

May 31st. Haddie goes with Annette and Leo to stay at New Lodge, Hawkhurst, with the Hardcastles. Also of the party are Mr, Mrs and Miss Houldsworth and a Mr Howarth, the last *a most amusing, agreeable and well-informed man.*

June 2 (Whit Monday) Mrs Houldsworth drove us to see Mr Beresford Hope's fine place, where there are curious Dutch cattle, black with a white streak on their backs. Some people to afternoon tennis, and a dinner party. Lovely flowers on the table. Roses, Rhododendrons, Clematis and Wisteria are beautiful here.

June 3 ... went to see Mrs Crumb's Cottage, date 1290, belonging to Mr Hardcastle. Drove to Scotney Castle, Mr Hussey's beautiful place. He is father to our young R.E. friend at Bermuda. The azaleas there are the most magnificent possible, the house fine, and ruins of the old moated house standing among the ruins of a much older Norman Castle..

June 7 Leo, A and I to British Museum where Mr Howarth met us and showed us ancient glass, pottery, gems and ancient jewellery. The old Greek gold work, most found in tombs, was exquisite. Saw old Mexican masks covered with turquoise, mosaic etc. Went to an At Home at Lady Plunket's, but she did not appear. Lady Lefroy drove A and me home in her carriage.

June 9 A and I, with Miss Nisbet, to St. Olave's Church for Trinity Monday Service, at which all the Trinity House Brethren were present. All so old world and interesting. Then to Trinity House, where the gentlemen had a great luncheon and the ladies lunched with the Housekeeper, Miss Dyer. The loving cup was sent in to us, and we drank their health. We were shown the beautiful rooms and fine pictures afterwards....

June 24 Leo and Jack started in Trinity Yacht "Galatea" for a cruise to inspect lighthouses on the South Coast.

June 25 A and I to French Huguenot Hospice with Morris Beauford. Miss Layard and Mr Leonard were also of the party. First we had a French Divine Service. Canon Duckworth preached beautifully in French. We had a great champagne luncheon, with speeches, toasts and Loving Cup. About 200 people, walking about the pretty grounds and greenhouses. It is near Victoria Park in the E. End. 40 old gentlemen and 20 old women are maintained, all of Huguenot Descent. We got home at 9.30, very tired, but much interested.

July 8 Intensely hot. ...Today Leo must retire from the Navy, but unfortunately only as Vice-Admiral, not having been promoted yet! Letters, telegrams etc. flying, on the subject.

July 10 ... Leo received his Promotion to Full Admiral by the retirement in his favour, of Adm. Sir Reginald Macdonald.

In August the family goes to St Margaret's, Cliffe in Kent. *Our lodgings are clean and comfortable, and the people most obliging.*

Aug 4 ... the chicks so happy on the beach, paddling in the sea, up to their knees.

Aug 18 Our darling Bessie's birthday, two years old. Truly she is a blessing to us! Leo, A and I drove to Kingsdown Coastguard Station as he wanted to speak about the observation of the Lights: we had a walk over the Downs.

Sept 5 Back to London. *Found the house so nice and clean, 8 rooms having been papered and painted during our absence.*

Sept 13 Mr Kimball Cook called. Leo is thinking of sending Jack to his school at Brighton. Jack's health has caused some concern, he was said to be weak and wanting muscle!

Sept 12 Bob to Mr Wilkes school in Hereford Square. He is to dine at home every day.

Leo took dear John by 1.50 train to Mr Kimball Cook's school at Brighton, where he left him in good spirits on the cricket ground.

The house is so quiet and lonely without the dear boys!

Oct 5 Sunday ... Hayes out, and I put my darling to sleep both morning and evening.

Haddie often does this on Sundays, and is obviously very happy in the task

Oct 31 Poor little Bessie unwell all day.

Nov 1 Dear Bessy worse. Dr Merriman came to see her and says it is cold on her liver. She was in bed all day, sweet pet, so sick and weak but as good as an angel...

Nov 2 ... Bessie got worse and so weak that we sent for the Dr. again. Nettie sat up with her till 2 am, May the rest of the night. I came at 6 a.m. ...

Nov 3 Bessie continues ill but there is some bettering and the Dr says no cause for alarm.

Nov 15 ... dear Little Me begins to be like her old self.

Nov 24 Went to see Mother, who has headache. - Our dear Willie's birthday, 37 years since. -

This is the very first mention of Willie since his death in 1871. One may wonder if the emotion, called up by her strong anxiety for the beloved Bessy in her illness, somehow enables Haddie to make this small comment.

Dec 18 ... Jack came home from his school at Brighton looking very pale and thin, he has done so well, and got a Prize ...

Christmas is spent in London, though they go down to Portnall Park (to their cousins the de Salises) for New Year. No party though, as Minnie de Salis has just lost her father, Mr Henley.

It will have been noticed that the Diary entries are becoming fuller and that Haddie is taking greater interest in many things - including all Service and military matters and, especially, anything to do with her beloved nephews and nieces. She is also using larger books, so there is more room for comment! She gives a list of Books Read, from March: Story of Chinese Gordon, Life of Professor Palmer, All Sorts & Conditions of Men, Queen's Journal in the Highlands, The Pharoahs and their People, Court Life Below Stairs (4 vol.), and 20 or more others, including books on the Indian Mutiny and on the Jesuits.

There is also a list of Clothes for Annie (now nearly 12) - perhaps Haddie had been put in charge of these? The long list includes material bought for dresses, and £1.3s to Miss Reed for making them up. Two pairs of gloves cost 2s.9d., beach shoes 4s.11d, seaside hat 1s.6d., Leghorn hat 3s., and two pairs of stays cost 8s.6d. The total is £13.11.5., and seems to cover everything.

1885 Haddie is anxious about the campaign in Egypt and Sudan, and very scornful of Gladstone and his Government. The large, hospitable home of the senior members of the De Salis family is now Portnall Park, near Sunningdale. The hosts are Harry and Minnie De Salis.

Jan 1 We, ie Nettie, 5 children, Hayes and I, came here on the 29th. Leo followed, being detained in town by business. Harry and Minnie De Salis, their 4 sons, and Georgie: also Rodolph's wife and child, and a young friend, Miss Waller, are here. Cold, and sufficient frost to prevent the young men hunting, and not enough for skating. Minnie left to go to her sister's in Oxfordshire. The young people played a farce called "My Uncle's Will" and, assisted by our Harry, Annie & Jack, a little play called "Little Toddlekins" very nicely. Audience: the party in the house, and the servants etc., also Lady Stepney and her little girl.

Jan 2 Still cold. Harry De Salis took Leo, Nettie and me a drive to see Princess Mary's Homes for Girls at Addlestone, which interested us much.

Jan 4 Sunday ...Hayes went off to Portsmouth for a few days' holiday. Poor little Bessie will miss her ...

Jan 5 ... Leo took the 4 children to a Circus at Covent Garden Theatre. Dear Little Me is very good, and wonderfully happy with Mrs Arnold, Hayes' sister.

The 4 elder children have a great many parties and dances, at Mrs Brandreth's, Lady Culme Seymour's, the Plunkets, Lady Theresa Boyle's, etc. and Annette gives a children's party in return, *with a good Magic Lantern from the A & N Stores.*

Jan 22 ... Heard of the Battle of Abu Klea, fought by Sir Herbert Stewart in the Soudan. Our forces victorious though only 1400, against 10,000 - but many casualties.

Jan 31 ... Leo, A, Annie and I lunched with the Clanwilliams in Belgrave Square, and we 3 dined with our Mother ... Mr Wynne came in at Dessert. He is in town on business consequent on the death of Col. Burnaby, who was killed at the battle of Abu Kila in the Soudan.

Feb 5 ... Heard the sad news of the fall of Khartoum and probable death of the great General Gordon - and extreme peril of our small army! ...

Feb 4 Saw Titi, who is very happy at having succeeded in being admitted to a Sacre Coeur Convent in France, where she is to go after Easter.

As reported earlier, many of the Ross family had converted to Roman Catholicism.

There is a large Mission on in the local Parish - or perhaps wider. Sermons at church are about the Mission, and on Feb 10 A and Haddie go to Mission Instruction and dinner is moved to 6.30, to let the servants out to evening

Mission services.. General Gordon's death is confirmed - *all, ALL the fault of this miserable, wicked Government!*

Feb 12 Robert Ross has a week's holiday from the Jesuits in Wales.

Feb 14 Some of the family attend the wedding of Clementina Skeffington (widow of Stanley and mother of Florence and Mabel) to Colonel Craig.

March 22 Many fear that war with Russia is inevitable.

March - April. Harry has an English prize from his school at Crowthorne and John comes home from Brighton looking much stronger.

Ap 8 ... May and I to National Gallery, and to lunch at Charing X Dining Rooms. ... I saw the new Raphael, purchased by the Nation from the Duke of Marlborough for £70,000. It is very fine - but that is an enormous sum!

April 23 Leo and Harry go to Winchester to meet Mr Morshead and are *much pleased with all they have seen and heard.*

April 24 A. and I paid 14 visits, ending by going to tea at Lady Montgomery's. Captain Van Kaughuick...[whom they knew in Bermuda] *turned up here while we were out. Leo saw him. He is just back from the Soudan where he was wounded in the steamer with Lord Charles Beresford, going to rescue Sir C. Wilson. He has been promoted. Dear Harry went back to school at Crowthorne, for the last time.*

April 28 A and I paid 15 visits in a Brougham. ... Leo dined with Ironmongers. Cap. Van Kaughuick dined with A and me. He managed to get up and down stairs with 2 sticks. He looks weak.

April 29 ... Leo left in Trinity Yacht Galatea for Flushing, to escort back the Queen. A. has not been at all well lately; she saw Mr Merryman today, who says she is weak.

May 9. A and H go for a night to Dawley for one night, to stay with the Garratts. Sir Wm. Stawell and Nancy are fellow-guests. *Fires in all rooms and stoves in the passages, so cold is it!*

May 16 ... A and I to Harley St in forenoon to see Dr Barnes. Little Violet Clarke came to tea with the children. Our troops are coming home from the Soudan, which it appears, Gladstone is going to abandon after all the loss of life and treasure, and for what!

May 22 A and Leo go for a three-day break, to the Wellington Hotel at Crowthorne, because she has been weak and ailing, and they will see Harry at the same time - and she comes back looking much improved by the change.

May 28 *A and I paid a number of visits and went finally to Mrs Hood's At Home. She had hoped to have had the Japanese Villagers to entertain us, but they have been sent for to Berlin. We met many acquaintances there.*

May 29 ... several visitors, Gertrude Plunket, Maria Cole etc. Leo dined with the Grocers, this being "Restoration Feast", and brought back a beautiful box of bonbons.

June 3 Dear Annie 12 today. A and I to Parish Church to see the Confirmation there, Anne our housemaid being one of the candidates. ...

to tea at Lady Carnwarth's.
June 5 Leo and A went to stay with the Le Blancs at Northaw House, Potter's Bar. I went with Lady Carnwarth to a large afternoon party at Mrs Drummond's, where they had Grossmith to amuse the company.
June 10 Julia Jeffreys came to stay here for a few days ...
June 13 ... and went to Sandown races with her uncle.
June 19 ... I went with Mrs Kennedy to Albert Hall to hear Strauss's Band. Leo and A to an evening party (theatricals) at Lady Tarleton's.
June 20 ... Leo, A and I to Hurlingham Club to dine with Mr and Mrs Tyler, a party of 12. Sir R and Lady Montgomery, Sir Howard Elphinstone, Mrs Morrison etc. Such a pretty place and all so nice and novel. A and I drove both ways in a hansom. Rain prevented the illuminations and band in the gardens.* [* In course of time, Sir Howard's daughter, Mary, marries Bob.]
July 4 Leo and A to an afternoon party of Knights and Dames of the Primrose League, at Kensington Town Hall
July 6 Leo, A and I by 2.15 train from Waterloo to Winchester, where we met Harry from Crowthorne, took him to Mr Morshead's house, where we had tea. Liked Mr Morshead so much. Harry stays with them during his Exam for the Scholarship. The rest stay with the Shipleys at Twyford.
July 7th ... drove to Longwood, Lord Northesk's place, where there was a cricket match. Met several acquaintances. Tea and strawberries in a tent. Drove to Winchester Town Hall, where the boys were coming out from their Exams. Saw dear Harry, who thinks he has done well so far. Mr Crofton, a parson, Mrs Shipley's nephew came from Bristol to dine and sleep. Queer, very high and very Radical!
July 10 ... heard in Winchester that Harry has not won a scholarship, but is among the ... best, most creditable to him.
July 31 ... saw the announcement of Robert Delap's death, aged ?83/93
[Probably Rev. Robert Delap, father of James.]

The Family go to stay at Grantham Hall, on the Sussex/Kent border for the holidays. The house and garden are found *very nice and everything so comfortably arranged for us by the Grants, from whom Leo has taken the house for 8 weeks, at 4 guineas a week*
Aug 5 Leo had to leave us for London, thence to Cowes, to join the Galatea and go right round Great Britain. Mr Morland, the chief landowner here, called, also Mrs Hussey. Both so kind.
Aug 6 We are so pleased with this place. The neighbourhood is all so rich and pretty. The Grants have left us their very nice cook.
Aug 7 I walked into Lamberhurst to get some things wanted. A and I and 4 children drove by a hired Waggonette to Knowle House, to spend the afternoon with Lady Cottenham, whose little girl's birthday it was.

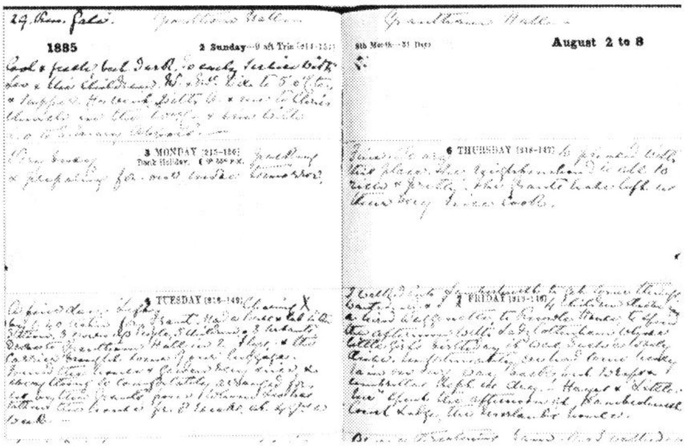

Aug 9 Sunday. Nettie and Annie drove to Church. The boys and I walked. The church is old, but not beautiful. A 3-decker pulpit and a clergyman aged 80, who preached prosily ...

Aug 15 John left early for Bayham Abbey, where he lunched and went on with little Lord Camden. and other boys to join Lady Cottenham's cricket 11, who played the Frant Band of Hope boys, and won by 9 wickets. We drove over in a fly in the afternoon, and did not get home till 8 o,clock' It is a long drive to Knole. There was a lady's match against the victorious 11, which was great fun. The boys played with cricket stumps instead of bats, and the ladies won. Some of the girls played well.

Aug 18 Dear "Little Me" 3 years old today. SUCH a good and lovely little creature....

Aug 19 A and I lunched with the Morlands. Afterwards children joined us and we went, a large party, to Bayham Abbey, where Captain Green and Lady Camden entertained all the neighbouring Primrose Habitations. A most "popular" entertainment. I went in a Merry Go Round worked by steam! There was also Aunt Sally, swings, Cricket, Races etc. and tea on a large scale in tents. Lord Curzon, Mrs Hussey, Mr Morland and Cap. Green made speeches out of a Waggon, but had to be very careful what they said, for fear of being hit by the Corrupt Practices Bill. We all marched under banners. Two Primrose songs, and God save the Queen, were sung under difficulties as the accompanying band was out of tune ...

Aug 21 A and the children and I went in afternoon to the Village School, to see the children do Musical Drill. The clergyman, Mr Hawkins and his wife called. He is 80 years of age, but looks much less.

Aug 27 ... Nettie and Harry drove to meet Leo at Frant Station, and he came back looking well after his absence of over 3 weeks.

Sept 2 ... we all went into a Hop Garden to pick hops.

Sep 3 ... Mrs Hussey called and brought Partridges and Peaches.

Sep 4 Children and Hayes took their dinner out to the Hop Garden ... Mrs Morland took Nettie, Harry and me for a lovely drive.

Sept 8 Leo to London early. A and I in a Fly paid some visits, and then went to Wadhurst Station to meet Leo, who however was not in the train. Soon we heard by Telegram that he was in the wrong train, and had been carried on to Etchingham., so we had a long wait at the Station for the next up train ...

Sept 9 Leo, A and I started in a Fly for Glassonbury Park, where we lunched with Major and Mrs Atkin Roberts. It is an old (400 years about) red brick moated house, with splendid trees, and a beautiful Lime Avenue, fine wainscoted and tapestried rooms, and old oak furniture. We then called on Lady Jessel, a Jewess, and then visited Goudhurst Church, where there are some very curious old monuments, of the very beginning of 17th Century.

Sept 10 ... dined with the Morlands at Court Lodge, a party of 12. Mrs Thornycroft and her married son and his wife, and some gentlemen staying in the house for shooting, amongst others a Mr Harbord, who met our Mother at Tangier a few years ago ...

Sept 14 ... Leo A and I went with Mr Hawkins, the Vicar, to see Lamberhurst Church, part of which dates from Edward 1st. In afternoon we all, Bessie included, went to Scotney Castle, where they had a children's party out of doors - cricket, rounders, running races for prizes, etc. and tea. Such a merry party and enjoyable to all. The day was perfect.

Sept 16 ... dear Harry left for his first term at Winchester. Leo drove with him to the station at Wadhurst ...

Sept 17 ... walked to the Village and called on the Hopes and on Mrs Croft. We also went to see a cottage with a Smugglers' hide carved out in the solid rock underneath.

Sept 19 ... Leo and A dined at Lady Jessel's. She lives near Goudhurst, and is a Jewess, by race and religion, and is the widow of Sir G.Jessel, late Master of the Rolls.

Sept 23 ... drove to call on the Goschens ... went at 7 o'c to see the hops being packed in the "Pockets" in Mr Morland's Oast House.

Sept 29 ... we had several farewell visits and notes, everyone so kind, and regretting our departure, and hoping we may return to Grantham Hall next year. Certainly we have had a most pleasant and happy 8 weeks here, all have enjoyed it, elders, children and servants.

Back to London. Bob returns to Mr Wilkes in Hereford Square. The house is found nice and clean with new papers and paint in the dining room. Bammie Ross and her husband John are in London, as he is on duty with the Coldstream Guards.

Oct 7 ... I joined the South Kensington Habitations of Primrose League, as a Dame.

Oct 12 ... the 15th Anniversary of dear Leo and A's Wedding Day. Thank God! ... Leo, A and I to an evening lecture in Houston St Chapel, by a Mr

Pericles Green, who spent many years in the Soudan. We cd. not help laughing, it was so grotesque, and Mr P.G, although evidently very pious, put it often in a ridiculous and irreverent manner. We never heard anything like it before!

Oct 15 Walked with Nana and children to Whiteleys to shop for Little Me. Leo ... to political meeting of Sir Algernon Borthwick's Committee. He is Conservative candidate for South Kensington.

Oct 17 Leo, A and I to Primrose Demonstration at Albert Palace, Battersea Park. We heard some excellent speeches from Capt W. Cook, Mr Marriott, M.P. Brighton, and Judge Advocate, formerly a Liberal! and others. Also, out of doors, an excellent address from a working man, Farquharson, the son of a Scotch crofter. A good concert of patriotic songs. Charming Lady Folkestone sang Rule Britannia and Auld Lang Syne, the audience singing chorus, and all joined in God save the Queen. We were much interested and impressed with our own GOOD cause and the necessity of all doing what they can before the elections.

Oct 18 ... Admiral Murton called, also Cap Van K., who has not yet recovered from the effects of his wound in the Soudan.

Oct 22 ... to Kensington Town Hall to attend Sir A.B's meeting. ... The Radicals made some disturbance, but on the whole it was a good humoured crowd.

Oct 23 ...Mr James's (clergyman in Bermuda) boy Philip arrived from Bermuda to compete for the Navy. Poor boy, his Mother died 3 days before he left. Leo and A are taking him in till his exams are over. Major Philips, who brought him over from Bermuda, brought him here today. A took him to Whiteley's for clothes. Mr Wilkes called to arrange about reading with him.

Oct 24 ... Philip James began his work with Mr Wilkes. Annie and Bob took him to the South Kensington Museum.

Oct 27 ... Alick [West] *and our Mother's Servants arrived at 56 Queen's Gate Terrace.*

Oct29 ... Mrs Crozier [Emily] *Leo's sister arrived from Dublin.*

Oct 30 Our Mother and May arrived early this morning from Ireland ...

At some point it must have been decided that Haddie would make her home permanently with Leo and Annette. May takes on the role of companion to their Mother.

Oct 31 ... Leo took Mrs Crozier and Phil James to the "Inventions".

Nov 4 ... went to see Mrs Binney (wife of the Bishop of Nova Scotia) and her daughter Fanny, and poor Mrs Belfield's baby girl ... Phil James has unfortunately sprained his leg.

Nov 5 ... Phil will have to keep his leg up for some days, and Mr Wilkes says he will come here to teach him.

Nov 6 ... took dear Little Me out walking in Kensington Gardens.

Nov 7 ... Leo, A and I to 3o'c representation of "The Private Secretary" at Globe Theatre. We went by Underground and then walked down the Strand to Charing Cross and thence home by underground. After dinner, Leo took Mrs Crozier to the Inventions to see the gardens and fountains lighted up

Nov 13 ... Mr and Mrs Dillon (Constance Crozier) to tea.

Nov 20 ... went to Battersea to Mrs Cooke's (Conservative Candidates) Committee rooms to help to address papers, but unfortunately they were not ready. Went canvassing with Mrs Cooke. After dinner Leo went out to a meeting at the Town Hall. Sir Algernon Borthwick made a capital speech.

Nov 21 ... Emily Crozier left by the night mail for Ireland, to travel with her daughter and son-in-law.

Nov 23 Leo took Phil James to Admiralty for his Medical Exam. A and I busy canvassing and distributing leaflets ...

Nov 24 ... We 3 dined with Sir Robert and Lady Montgomery. The elections have begun and there is already a Conservative gain.

Nov 25 ... The Conservatives still gaining seats, thank God. Phil went up for his Navy exams.

Nov 26 ... Our member Sir Algernon Borthwick returned 2 to 1. ... Leo out in the Mewses getting the men out to vote.

Nov 27 ... A and I went with Leo to the American Legation in Lowndes Square. Mr and Mrs Phelps are very nice people.

Nov 28... the Elections going on, the Conservatives, and Radicals and Liberals combined about equal so far, and this is a great Conservative gain

Dec 1 [Our Mother had felt faint in the Army & Navy Stores the day before]. *Mother saw doctor, who gives a very good opinion of her general health, but she is suffering from her nerves.*

Dec 4 ... Alas! the Liberals are getting a majority in the more distant counties, owing to the LIES told to the ignorant Agricultural Labourers by the leading Liberals! It is a shame, and a sin!

Dec 5 ... and I paid several visits in Belgravia, taking dear Little Me with us. She was so good. Heard that Phil James has failed for the Navy, poor Boy. A very pleasant dinner party of 8 - Mr and Mrs Frank Gore Brown, Miss Kate Hardcastle, Capt Markham and Capt Beaumont R.N. We talked of little else but the Elections!

Dec 8 Hard frost. Very cold. Leo, A and I to an afternoon Reception of the Primrose League at Lady Borthwick's. Annie with Gaga to Private Theatricals at the Brompton Hospital. I called to see Miss Henry and May at our Mother's. Leo and A dined with the United States Minister and Mrs Phelps.

Dec 12 ... Leo, A and I dined with Sir G and Lady Richards. Gresly the American Arctic traveller was there, also Sir G and Lady Nares - Miss

Cracroft, Mrs Scott, and Sir James and Lady Anderson. I went down with Sir James, a kindly agreeable man, many years in Merchant Navy. ...

Dec 22 ... Miss Cracroft dined with us and then we went to meeting of Geographical Society to hear Major Greely speak. As there were many people there we knew, it was a pleasant evening.

Dec 23 ... Harry arrived from Winchester. After lunch the whole party and Nana went to Portnall. Found Edith, Cecil and Willy there.

Dec 24 ... Mr and Mrs Fane de Salis came from Dawley.

Dec 25 All to Church. Xmas tree in the evening. The Curate to dinner

Dec 28 ... Mrs White, a cousin of Minnie's, came. She is to be Mrs Jarley at the Wax Works She is most amusing. Charlie de Salis came from Coventry.

Dec 29 ... we had The Waxworks in the evening. Very amusing. Afterwards we danced till nearly 12 o'c. It froze so hard that Lady Stepney could not get home, and had to sleep here.

Dec 31 Rather cold. We all came home in time for lunch. 2 of the Portnal sons travelled up with us. The colds are better. Went to see our Mother

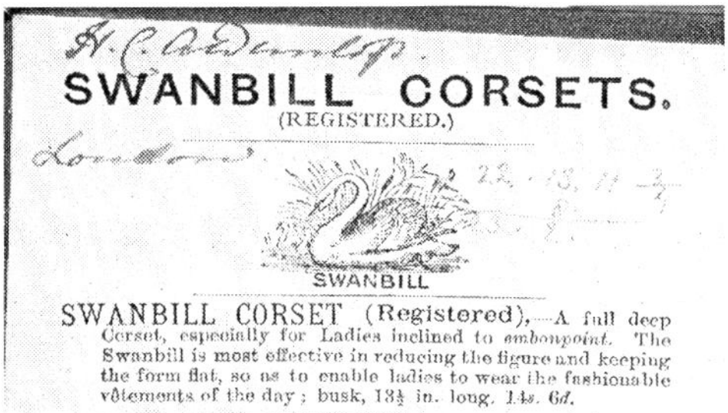

1886 *Jan 4 A took Annie to shop in Jermyn St, and then took Harry and Bob to their 1st Dancing Lesson ...*

Jan 6 Heavy snow, not out. Mr James (clergyman from Bermuda) and his boy Phil to dinner. Expected Mrs Fane de Salis to lunch here and dress for a wedding, but the weather prevented her coming.

Jan 8 ... Froze again in the evening. Very cold. Leo and A dined at Lady Rathdonnell's. Weather so bad they cd. only get a Hansom to go in, and had to come back by Underground and walk.

Jan 9 A rather the worse for yesterday's adventure. She took the children to a party at Lady Cottenham's, where they had children's theatricals.

Jan 12 Frozen again ... Henry & Dot [West] arrived this morning at Mother's house from Ireland. Leo A and Harry to Canterbury to stay with the Bishop of Dover. Annie and Jack to a children's party at Lady Montgomery's ... Parliament met today to elect a Speaker.

Jan 13 ... Mother and I to Musical Afternoon at Mrs Green's, Grove House. Heard the 2 Miss Ellneys and Mrs ...? (harp). Annie and Jack to children's dance at Mrs Butters'. Not home till near 11. I minded Bessy.

Bessy has a bad cold, has to stay in bed and have a kettle steaming on the fire. One of our Mother's servants has the measles so they all keep away from her house.

Jan 21 Leo, A and I to All Saints, Margaret St and then to 70 Portland Place, to Hutchinson Poë's and Miss Dornville's wedding. Very cold. We went in a brougham - Our Mother, Henry and Dot and Uncle Poë and Mrs G. Poë dined here. A dull evening.

Jan 26 I do not think I ever had a worse cold. Our Mother came to see me. This night, Gladstone & Parnell (a nice pair!!) turned out Lord Salisbury, who has been 7 months only in office! ...

Feb 1 ... to see Bob's last dancing lesson.

Feb 3 A took Annie to 1st lesson on Elocution at Lady Cottenham's.

Feb 5 Went to our Mother's to say goodbye to the Wests, who leave tonight for Ireland, and to see May, who is in bed with a cold. Frank & Emily McClintock, George Macan and one of his sisters, and Mr Woodhouse (Curate of Christ Church) dined with us.

A great deal of work is done towards fighting an election at South Hackney, but this is lost on Feb 11.

Feb 13 Damp & sloppy. Leo, A and I to Grosvenor Gallery to see Millais's paintings ... Leo dined at Mansion House, a Dinner to Trinity House. Lord Salisbury was much cheered.

Feb 21 Sunday. Very cold. All except Annie to early service. Our Mother spent afternoon. Leo and A to Congregational Service. There was another larger meeting of unemployed and roughs today. The latter smashed some windows etc. but nothing so bad as last time ... We had a gleam of sunshine today, the first we have seen for many days.

Feb 24 ... Annie better, and able to do some lessons.

Feb 23 ... Annie went with Hayes to Lady Cottenham's, where she figured in a

Tableau as one of the ... children. She looked so pretty, in a sky blue tunic, and her masses of beautiful fair hair round her shoulders.

Feb 24 ... I went to needlework party at Mrs George Pepys', At 3 pm we were shocked to hear of the death of Frederica Plunket, of inflammation of the lungs, after a week's illness. Kate sent for Leo, who went off at once to them ...

Feb 25 ... Leo to Kensal Green Cemetery on business for the poor Plunkets. Miss Ferrier, Annie's daily governess, is ill. We went to see her and A sent her beef tea etc. Annie went for her last appearance in the Tableau. Her cold is still heavy ... Dear little Bessy has been in the house for nearly 3 weeks. She is quite well, but the weather is too cold to let a small child go out without running a risk.

Feb 26 ... We are trying to induce Miss Ferrier to go to stay with our Mother, who has kindly asked her, but so far without success ... [But she does go there, next day]

March 2. ... dear little Bessy has an attack like mild croup, but it yielded to linsed poultice ...

March 5 ... Poor Annie had fresh cold, and was feverish at night. A went upstairs to sleep with her. Hayes still in bed.

March 7 Sunday. Very cold and dark. We are all a poor lot with our colds (Leo too) and none of us are going out today. When will this long cold winter come to an end? ...

Almost all the family suffer more than two weeks with "the prevalent influenza".

March 20 ... Nettie's first "Afternoon at Home" at which she could not appear, so Leo and I had to receive for her. Only about 40 people came. Nettie better but still in bed. The little girls much better, thank God.

April 3 Nettie's At Home 4 to 6.30. She was able to receive her company. About 60 people. Very pleasant. Cap. Schroeder, German Naval Attache came - we knew him at Bermuda and Halifax.

April 8 A and I to afternoon party at Admiral Mayne's where Clifford Harrison recited beautifully.

April 9 A and I to John Verschoyle's lodging to see Katie Shaw who has just returned from India ...

April 15 John came home for his Easter holidays, looking so bright and well.

May 12 Harry left for Winchester. Leo A and I called at the Mitchells, and then drove to the Criterion where we dined with Morris Beauford, and then attended a Huguenot Meeting in another room.

Annie cannot get over a bad cold and cough and is sent to Portnall for a change. By May 14 she is still so unwell that Nana Hayes is sent down to take care of her, and they come back after a few days.

May 25 Breezy, dark, threatening rain. A and I paid a number of visits in a 4-wheel cab, ending with tea at Mrs Stopford's (wife of the High

Commissioner for Canada) where we met many Canadians, also a Parsee Lady and Gentleman. The flowers in the rooms were beautiful.

June 7 Leo and A drove to Camberley to look at Eddy Ross' house which they have decided on taking for the summer holidays ...We are all very anxious about Gladstone's wicked Home Rule Bill which comes on tonight. The Division took place at 6 o'c and 30 against Gladstone, thank God. 93 Unionist Liberals voted with our 250 Conservatives. We hear the scene in and near the House was wonderful.

June 8 ... Sir R. Montgomery came to rejoice with us about the throwing out of the Home Rule Bill.

June 10 ...A and I to the Drummonds to tea. They attacked me over politics! ... all to an evening party at Lady Victoria Preston's, where we were all among the Unionist Liberals, who seem (justly) very proud of themselves.

They are kept busy filling in Lodgers' Claims for voting.

June 15 ... we paid many visits near the Regents Park in a brougham, taking dear little Bessie, who was charming and so pretty in her new summer bonnet, white with white and pink daisies.

June 17 ...went to the Irish Loyal & Patriotic Office to get leaflets ...

June 19 ... all to Primrose meeting, to go through the form of dissolving our Habitations during the Elections, to avoid Corrupt Practices!

June 20 Sunday. All to 9.30 service at Parish Church. We sang God save the Queen and had part of the Accession Service, this being the 49th Anniversary of our dear Queen's accession to the throne. Sunday & all, no end of election work came to us today - & Nettie wrote a leaflet, and sent it off to the Printer.

June 21 Leo took A and me to Trinity House [for a Service at St Olave's and ladies' luncheon] *Afterwards we saw the Prince & Princess of Wales and other Royalties drive past in state to lay the foundation of the Tower Bridge.*

June 23 ...Nana went with me early to Dentist - Mr Webb in New Bond St. A and I to new Hospital for Women in Marylebone Rd. It is very nice - all the Drs. etc. are women. .....Leo went alone to Queen's concert, because A had not got a black gown fit to go in, and there is a Court Mourning for the poor King of Bavaria, who committed suicide.

June 26 ... all to Lady Mary Glyn's Garden Party in the charming Vicarage Gardens.

June 29 Northaw House, Potters Bar. Leo, A and I to the Le Blancs ...

June 30 Miss Brotherton left, and Miss Anderson, very nice, and who spends much time with Mr Ruskin, came ...

July 1 A lovely warm day. Mrs Le Blanc drove us through Hatfield, Lord Salisbury's place, and we visited Emily Ewington, who was so pleased to see us.

July 2 A still more lovely day, if possible. Mrs Le Blanc had a garden party. The Elections have begun - may God bless our efforts, and give us success!

July 3 ... returned to town ... found the dear children well. At the 11th hour a Gladstonian, one Major Speed, has started for this Borough in opposition to Sir Algernon Borthwick - so we are to have a contest in South Kensington, after all.

July 5 ... I had a tooth drawn under gas ... we got but little sleep, the excitement about the elections is so great, and crowds were cheering in the streets and singing patriotic songs.

July 6 A, Annie and I to the High St to hear the Declaration of the Poll. Sir A. Borthwick is in by a majority of 4 to 1. Also Mr Whitmore for Chelsea, putting out Sir C. Dilke!!...

July 8 The Dentist called to see Nettie ... She and I to Mrs Law's to hear Mr Watts Russell recite. In the evening to Mrs Francis, where some Tyrolese sang and played on various instruments. A little girl of 5, a prodigy, sang and played wonderfully. Many Conservative gains, but Edinburgh has rejected Mr Goschen.

July 10 ... Nothing but politics are spoken or thought of in this crisis!

July 11 ... We hear that Lord Hartington is in with a majority of 1400 for Rossendale. We had been very anxious about him.

July 17 Dear little John came home from Brighton because we hear that he must join at Mr Littlejohn's on the 3rd August, which gives him but short holidays. He looks so well.

July 19 ... A, with Annie, Jack, Bessie, Nana and the cook went down to take possession of Eddie's house at Camberley. Leo left for Liverpool on Life Boat duty. I remain in town for a day or two. Very busy indoors. Miss Wishart came to look at our house, but we did not come to any definite agreement about it.

July 20 Very hot. A. came back from Camberley much disgusted at the dirt and disorder down there. Miss Wishart came and took this house for 6 weeks at only 4 gns a week but it is better than nothing. All the carpets are taken up, and we are very busy, and find this heat very trying.

July 21 Very very hot. Working hard all day, preparing the house. A and I with the Maids Harriet and Anne, came down to Camberley in the evening. Found the children well and happy, but the poor servants in despair at all the disorder in this house.

July 24 Leo and Bob arrived from London. Bob has won 2 swimming prizes - and has got a cricket bat.

July 26 Leo took the boys out in a boat - and arranged about cricket, fishing and bathing for them. Today John is 12 and Bob is 10.

July 28 Harry came at 11 o'c. He is much grown, and is very thin and looks a good deal older, but he looks well otherwise.

July 31 Dear Nettie's birthday. God bless her!

Aug 1 Sunday All to morning service at (Camberley) Parish Church. A and I remained for Holy Communion . Annie, John and Bob to Litany and Children's Service at 3 ...

Aug 2 Damp and chilly. This is a cold damp draughty house..... We sat in the woods, and A and I to tea at Mrs Pillean's (one of the officers' wives in the Terrace. We knew them at Bermuda.) Poor little John has a heavy feverish cold, which is too bad, in his short holidays. He slept with Nettie.

Aug 5 A and I called on Mrs Cameron, wife of the Commandant of R.M.College. Had tea out in their pretty grounds. Met there Mrs Johnstone, wife of Cap. J of HMS Volage, and who distinguished himself at Madagascar - also 2 Bermudan ladies, Mrs Clegg and Miss Harvey ....

Aug 7 A to London early with Harry and John. Shopped for them. Then down to Greenwich, where she left John at Mr Littlejohn's, to be prepared for the Navy. Jack's future has been decided.

Aug 10 ...A and I, with Bessie and Hayes, drove to call on Mrs Fitzroy Somerset (he was C.R.E at Bermuda before our time, and was the owner of the horse "Coloured Elizabeth.") We had tea with Mrs Johnstone, and had a very nice drive.

Aug 11 Dear Harry's birthday. He is 15 today. This house looks and smells much cleaner now - but it will never be really clean or nice in our time!!

Aug 12 A and I walked with all the children and Hayes to a farm whence we get milk. Bessie in a hired perambulator. We sat in a cornfield. May's birthday.

Aug 13 No news from Leo for some days, but he walked in at 2 o'c, looking well, and having finished his cruise of inspection ...He, A, Annie and I drove in Mrs Cameron's waggonette to tea at the Miss Majendies', The Warren, Sandhurst.

Aug 14 Fine. I went out in the boat on the lake, with Leo and all the children.

Aug 18 Darling Little Me is 4 today. Such a sweet bright little Pet! She was very happy with her presents etc. The "Alice" was rigged, and sailed on the lake, and Leo took all the children out in the boat. A flying column of Cavalry, Infantry and Artillery marched past this house, to Bessie's great delight...

Aug 21 Fine & warm. Leo, A and I took a lovely drive to Wellington College, and then back to tea at the Miss Majendies', where we saw some very good tennis playing ... A. felt sick and unwell in the evening.

Aug 23 Leo, A and I lunched with the Dyer Edwardes, who afterwards took us a most delightful drive of 18 or 20 miles. We went to see Eversley Church, and visited Charles Kingsley's grave ... We then drove past Bramshill Park, a grand old mansion built by James Ist for his son. The Copes, who now own it, are too poor to keep it up. We had tea at Harford Bridge

Ville..., a charming old house where George III used to stay, also Queen Victoria when a girl.

Aug 30 A very hot day. Harry played in a boys' cricket match on the Sandhurst Cadets' ground. We went to look on from a tent. Harry's side was much the weakest and was beaten ...

Sept 1 ... Eddy Ross came to stay here for his duty. Leo took Bob out riding. Leo and A dined with Gen. and Mrs Clive at Staff College.

Sept 14 Very hot indeed. A and I went early to the Riding School of R.M. College to see Harry and Bob riding. It is surprising how much they have learned in 8 lessons. Bob is a born rider. .... Got home safely before 5.30. Leo met us at Waterloo. Oh! how hot it was. Miss Wishart (the Tenant) has left the house clean and tidy.

Sept 15 Quite cool. Unpacking. Harry left for Winchester.... A and I went to see Katie Shaw at 21 Half Moon St, on her way out to India ...

Sept 17 A and I and Little Me to Paddington Baths to see Annie swim. Then A and I to Whiteley's, and home in a hansom. We had an accident by collision in our Hansom, the wheel of which was smashed. We had a very narrow escape; A only trifling bruises and I was unhurt - thank God.

Sept 18 A very lovely day. Leo, A and I after lunch to Greenwich. Jack met us at the station, looking so well and bright and happy. We saw the Museum and Painted Hall. Had tea at the Littlejohns', who gave an excellent report of dear Jack, and came home in time for dinner, tired but much pleased ...

Sept 21 ... Annie went to the High School at Nottinghill for the first time. The Martin W... girls called for her in a brougham.

Sept 23 ... A and I ... spent some time in our Mother's house, looking after things for her.

Sept 25 Hayes left early for 3 days holiday. A and I took Annie and Bessie to the Paddington Baths. Bessy sleeps with me and I mind and dress her etc. dear little Pet.

Oct 1 ... Leo, A and I down to Northaw House, Potters Bar, to spend a few days with the Le Blancs. Found that their kitchen maid had been taken ill and it looked sufficiently like scarlatina; so by the Dr's advice, we left after dinner and reached home again at 11 o'c pm.

Jack comes home for a brief, happy exeat. Annette experiments with taking Annie to and fro from school in a *buss*. Florence Alloway, Leo's sister, comes for a short visit en route for Dublin, from Bath. Soon after, Agnes Skeffington comes to stay, and Leo's nieces, Sarah and Georgina Richardson come to tea; these two are staying in Beaufort Gardens with Mrs Fitzroy. A little dinner party is given for Agnes (Mr and Mrs Borrer, Mr Harvey, R.M and Mr Bruen RM)... and they take Agnes to the Tower ...

Oct 29 ... We saw very well, as, having an order from Trinity House, we had a Warden all to ourselves. Such a nice man, late R.E, who had served with General Gordon in China and Crimea and knew him well..

Oct 31 Sunday ... Leo, Agnes and I to Temple Church; as usual, lovely music and good sermon. Cap. May, late R.N, now Artist, called with his son-in-law. None of our party to evening service, which we read at home.

Captain May had done many of the illustrations for Leo's book—see "The Fox leaving the Pack." p. 189.

Nov 24 Frosty, and so foggy that the carriage did not come to take Annie to school, so she did not go ... Bessie Emerson, our Mother's maid arrived from Ireland to take possession of the house

Dec 4 ... Dear John came from Greenwich for an Exeat, looking so bright and well ... At dinner we had fun - John sang some good songs and Bob recited.

Bessie ails for some days, mumps suspected but pronounced to be just a cold. Mr Merriman sees her and says she is weak and wants red blood: they are to keep her warm and quiet and feed her, so that her throat may get well. Dottie (Haddie's younger sister Helen West), arrives in town with two children and stays at the Grosvenor Hotel. Haddie remarks that though she has spent two days and nights in London, they have never seen her, though her boy Robin called for a few minutes. Our Mother leaves for Switzerland, probably accompanied by May and the Wests.

Dec 21 ... Leo out after dinner to a lecture on Cromwell. Sir Charles Russell in the Chair! An Irish R.C Home Ruler!!

All to Portnall to spend Christmas with the de Salis's. There is a bit of skating and Harry de Salis goes in the evening to Windsor Chapel to sing "Messiah."

Dec 25 A perfect day, frosty and bright and not very cold. All to morning service and Holy Communion. All the young people skated after lunch. Had Christmas tree. All the children (except the babies) dined late and we played round games till bedtime. The Curate, Mr Hamilton, came to dinner.

Dec 28 Snow lying, and made bad for driving. Leo started for Dublin, as the accounts of Mrs Dix (his eldest sister, Marian) *were no better.*

Several of Leo's siblings are still living in and around Dublin. Although he had left home for the first time before he was 12, and some of the younger ones were not even born then, he retains a close relationship with them all, as some surviving letters between them clearly show.

Dec 31 ... Thank God for all His very great Mercies all through this closing year!! Grant us the same throughout 1887 - Amen.

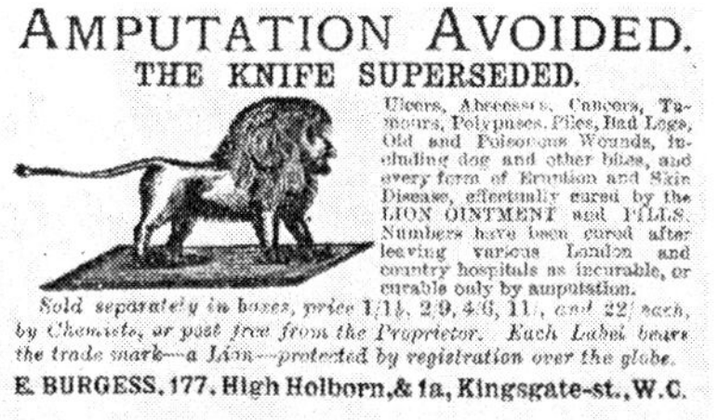

1887

Jan 1 The serious illness of Mrs Dix has damped the pleasure of our visit here (to Portnal). We have had heavy snow, and very severe frost; and the young people have had capital skating.

Jan 3 Back to Kensington Gate ... the house is very cold, from having been some days, uninhabited.

Jan 5 Cold. Snow still lying. We all, except poor wee Bessie, to an Xmas tree and games and dancing at Mrs Ruxton's in Cornwall Gardens. A and I drove to enquire for poor Captain Nisbet, one of the Trinity Brethren who is quite broken down since his daughter's death.

Jan 6 .... Leo is extra busy, being put on the Life Boat Committee. He is also made Chairman of the Royal Alfred Home for aged Seamen.

Jan 8 ... Leo, A and I to see Harry and Annie learning Drill and Dancing from Sergeant Major Macpherson ... then to L.D.A to order an evening gown for Annie ...

Jan 13 ... Nettie took the four children to a Juvenile Dance at Lady Clanwilliam's from 5 to 10 o'clock.

Jan 19 ... I went with A to Kingsley & Northcott's where she was photographed to be put in an Album to be presented to the Queen for her Jubilee ... Robert Ross called, and spoke a lot of nonsense about the Bishops & Priests (R.C) in Ireland, the Pope - a Legate etc. etc.

Jan 26 ... A. went to open a Bazaar at Hammersmith for Mr Eden. Harry accompanied her. The dear boy went back to Winchester. He has been so very <u>*dear*</u> *these holidays ...*

Jan 27 Damp and foggy, and colder. Poor wee Bessie is not thriving, never having got over the ulcerated throat she had in Nov. A took her to see Dr Dickinson, who has ordered her to the sea side.

Bessie goes with Hayes to lodgings in Hastings, and they get good accounts of her, gaining one and a half pounds in the first week, but miss "*our Sunbeam*" badly. Meanwhile Annie and Annette are both unwell, and Leo takes Annette to see Sir William Gull, who *"expects she will yet be much stronger."* Haddie takes Annie to join Bessie for a week at Hastings, and they both return, rosy and strong, by early March. [Sir W. Gull is a very distinguished physician, and in 1876 had given evidence at the inquest in the notorious Bravo case.]

March 15 Leo heard from the Admiralty that he has been awarded the Flag Officer's Good Service pension ... by the death of Sir Michael Seymour on

Feb 23. This was worth £300 per annum, according to a contemporary biographical note.

March 16 ... Leo, A and I to an evening reception at Lady Salisbury's. A great crowd. Hard frost. We had to walk up to Piccadilly to get a cab.

March 18 Cold, and occasional snow falling. We started for the Queen's Drawing Room at 12.30, 2 hours in the line. A large and pretty Drawingroom. We much enjoyed it. Just in time to see the Queen. I was presented. A. wore black velvet, grey satin and black lace with coloured roses. I wore Heliotrope and white lace and A's amethysts. Home soon after 5. Many people congratulated Leo on the G.S.P. Mr and Mrs Luard, Mrs Ware & daughters and Mrs Ruxton to tea to see our dresses.

April 2 ... A and I paid visits in a Hansom and then to tea at Mrs Fitzroy's, where we heard a Mrs Millar Rossiter play beautifully on the Piano and Concertina. She does it for her support. Met Miss Petrie, Annie's teacher at the Sunday School. She praised her much.

April 6 ... Harry arrived ... so well and bright. He has got his remove into the Upper School at Winchester, and a good report. Bob has got 2 prizes, and an excellent report. He is not going back to Mr Browne's School. Annie has won 3 honours, and has a good report. Jack arrived from Greenwich, looking so well. He has passed 1st in Mr Littlejohn's exam (bracketed with another boy).

April 11 Easter Mon. ... had tea with Lady Inglefield. Sir E. showed us a small Alligator he brought from Florida. The horrid little thing ran about the room.

April 16 ... A and I ... to Brompton Consumptive Hospital to see a young man patient there, whom Fitz Paget asked A to visit. He is such a nice gentle young man, a grocer's assistant from Yorkshire. He seems very ill, poor fellow.

April 20 Leo, A, Harry and I to an evening Primrose Entertainment at ... Mrs Vansittart's Habitation. It was very crowded, and they had the Toy Symphony, much too loud, and out of tune! but some things were pretty good.

April 29 ... dear Bob ...left for Crowthorne, where Leo took him ... Harry left for Winchester. How sad and lonely we feel without darling Bob! No boy in the house now.

April 30 ... Leo and A to meet our Mother on her return from Switzerland. Henry met Dot and his children and took them to an Hotel at Euston. May went to Miss Renshaw at her Club. Mother came to us. All are well, but tired

May 5 A and I to House of Commons by Mr Howorth's order. Arrived before 3.15, but almost too late. An interesting Debate on Proposal of Ministers to prosecute the Times for (possible?!!!) libel against Mr Dillon. Heard Gladstone make a most wicked speech in favour of Home Rulers, by whom he was much applauded. Heard ... Lord R.Churchill and the Attorney General. Had tea by Mr Howorth's kind orders. ... came home at 9, much interested but very tired..

May 10 ... A and I to the Bishop of Derry's house in Cadogan Place to see Mrs and Miss Alexander and Lady Montgomery in their Court dresses. Sir Robert Montgomery, also, in his uniform and decorations. He looked grand. [Mrs Cecil Alexander, whose husband is a cousin of the Delaps and of the McClintocks, is the author of many famous hymns, including "Once in Royal David's City" etc.]

May 12 ... our Mother has most fortunately let her house for 6 or 7 weeks for £100.

May 13 ... A and I to tea at Miss Hampton's in Cadogan Place to see Gertrude Plunket, who is staying there. Found them in trouble about an eccentric man, who is always coming about the house. The Police came and took him away. He is off his head, poor man.

May 16 Leo, A and I to Annual Meeting of R.N.Scripture Readers at Exeter Hall. The Bishop of Sodor and Man, who was to have taken the chair, was not well enough to come so Leo took his place and did it very well, a nice meeting. He then went off on board the Trinity Yacht, to inspect Light Ships in the Thames. We had several friends to tea: O'Neills, Clarkes, Pussy Drummond, Lady Carnworth etc. etc.

May 19 Ascension Day. Mother, A and I to a Flower Service at Parish Church at 5 o'c. Took Annie and sweet Little Me who both presented flowers, the latter a pot of Forget me nots. She looked charming. Turned to wet. We came home in a Buss.

May 21 Mother, A and I lunched with Mrs Tighe and Mrs Wanderforthe. Then to New Bond St to see Captain May's sketches in Madeira. That funny woman, Leonora Hope to tea ...

May 25 ... Blanche (our sister) spent the forenoon with Mother ... Leo and I to an evening Conversazione given by the Institute of Civil Engineers at S . Kensington Museum. It was a beautiful sight. The band of the Royal Artillery played beautifully.

May 26 ... A and I in afternoon selling the work of Distressed Irish Ladies at Kent House. Unfortunately so many other sales etc. were going on that we sold but very little. Mother lunched with Blanche and went with her to American Exhibition to see Buffalo Bill [later, Leo takes Annie to see him]

May 31 Blanche called again on our Mother, with May, who has come up from Westgate where she was staying with Miss Renshaw ... and go on by night mail to Ireland.

Jun 5 Sunday Leo and Annie to early service. A and I were ailing, and staid at home and had prayers. Charley & Blanche came by appointment to tea.

June 8 A lovely day. John's exam for the Navy begins today in town, but we are not to see him till it is all over.

June 16 Called at Lady Carnwarth's. Leo and A dined with the Martin Wares, and they and I to evening party at Lady Montgomery's, where we saw the Rao of Kutch and other Indian Princes, and some of the native officers commanding the Indian troops come over for the Jubilee. Such fine big men. Very crowded and oh! so hot.

June 19 Still very fine and warm, but a change in the weather is feared. All hope it may keep fair until after the Jubilee. The High Street is beautifully decorated with flags, flowers ... gas and electric lights, Chinese lanterns and a Triumphal arch. We have put up several small flags and Leo's Admiral's flag, also Chinese lanterns, Japanese parasols, and a row of fairy lights.

June 20 Lovely warm sunshine. Miss Jolly to lunch. Annie has 2 jubilee holidays. A and Leo, Annie and I all to Liverpool St, where after vainly trying for a Buss, we got places in a long open Waggonette and drove all through the City to see the Decorations and preparations for Illumination. Very beautiful they are and some of the Mottoes hung up in the streets are most touching. John has passed no. 2 for the Navy!! He came up from Greenwich for the Jubilee.

June 21 The great Jubilee Day! A lovely day. Started at 7.45 am in brougham. Two hours in the streets from the block, but what a sight! Annie and I to seats at Leo's Club, John to Capt. Fisher's window at the Admiralty. Leo and A to Westminster Abbey. We saw the procession beautifully. How the Queen and Prince of Wales were cheered! A sight ever to be remembered! What crowds! 7 million people said to be in London. Home about 3 o'c. Out at night to see illuminations in neighbourhood. Afraid to go far, because of the crowds.

June 25 ... Leo and A to Portnall, to look at houses near Ascot. I was tired, and did not go out. Annie, with the Stapletons to see some sports in Kensington, for the Soldiers and others, got up by our Vicar Mr Glyn. A man, one of the churchwardens died there suddenly a few minutes after pulling in a tug of war. A dreadful occurrence, after wh. of course, the party at once broke up.

June 26 Annie to early service with the parlourmaid ... a special service of praise which was to have followed, did not take place because of the sad event of yesterday.

June 29 ... the little girls and servants went out to see the Queen drive through Kensington, which was beautifully decorated. Leo and A to Queen's Garden Party at Buckingham Palace. Could not get an invitation for me, alas!

June 30 ... Leo, A and I to an afternoon party at Mrs Tyler's, to meet the Prince of Siam and the Rao of Kutch. The former came so late, owing to a mishap with his carriage ...

July 15 Still hot enough [following a long drought] *Mr and Mrs Le Blanc, Fitz and little Charlie Paget called. A and I called on Goschens and Mrs Moulton, an American Poetess. Thunderstorms and heavy rain came on. A fine night. Leo, A and I to the Queen's Concert at Buckingham Palace. Very enjoyable, and such a beautiful sight.*

July 17 Sunday ... all to early service. Dear John wearing his uniform for the first time. A went to see Lady Hood about SSAFA....[First mention of the Charity by this name.]

July 19 ... Leo and I after a somewhat early dinner by train to Strand, to annual Meeting of Victoria Institute. We heard Professor Stables, President of the Royal Society, speak, and were rather disappointed that there was so little in the Paper he read.

July 21 A gloriously fine day. Leo started before lunch for a cruise in Trinity Yacht "Vestal" taking the Duke of Argyll and other guests to Portsmouth for Naval Review. A and John left for St Clare's Ryde, to spend a few days with Mr Vernon Harcourt, who is filling his house with guests for N.R. ... Harry de Salis and Miss Drake came to dine and sleep here, so as to start quite early in morning for N.R..

July 23 A perfect day, so fine and bright with light breezes. Started at 8.15 with Admiral and Mrs Ruxton and their boy. Left Waterloo in special train. Walked through Dockyard to H.M.S Serapis for which we had tickets. She steamed out to Spithead and took up her position for the Review. We, and some hundreds of guests had a capital lunch on board. At 3.30, the Queen came, salutes were fired, yards and rigging manned and cheers. It was truly a great and glorious sight! Such a fleet, 134 ships of all kinds, 20,200 officers and men, and as far as the eye could reach, the sea was covered with crafts of all sorts, ships, steamers, yachts etc. Mr and Mrs Williams most kindly asked me to stay with them till Monday, but I had come unprepared and could not. We landed in a tug, caught a special train and got home before 11 o'c - very tired, but a day ever to be remembered.

John has a chill, overdone, and Bob comes home from Crowthorne with a prize: He actually won three, but *they only give one to a boy at a time.*

All go to Portnall Park, lent to the family till end August by the de Salis's. They are joined by Mlle Gregory, a French holiday governess.

Aug 3 ... A and I in Break to Sunningdale Station to meet seven little children from East End of London (Lambeth) sent by Charity Organisation Soc. for a fortnight to the country. We took them to the Cottages where they were taken in.

Annie has her first riding lesson from the Coachman. They like Mademoiselle greatly. It is too hot to do anything but sit on the grass. Little Me goes to Church for almost the first time. Sunningdale church is being enlarged so they worship in an *Iron church, which is very hot when the sun shines on it,* and

Portnall Park—from a postcard c. 1904

Reproduced by permission of Surrey History Service
Copyright of Surrey History Service

[The house still stands (2007) and forms the Club House of a local Golf Club]

which gives Haddie headache.

On Harry's 16th birthday they all go by Break to Windsor to Bammie and John Ross and are shown around. They go in a pony carriage to visit the London children on holiday.

Aug 18 Dear Little Me's birthday. 5 years old. So happy, till alas! her new Doll was broken! Leo, A and I and the four eldest children to Tennis party at Mrs Noble Taylor's. Mlle well again (after face and toothache)

Haddie takes the London children to catch their train home, and three days later another batch arrive.s

Aug 24 ... A and I to garden party at Mr and Mrs Parsons' house near Winkfield. Fitz Paget, who is related to them, was to have been there, but had been called away to Bournemouth in consequence of the serious illness of his little nephew. We met at the Parsons', Agnes Kirwan whom we had known when we were all young girls in Dublin ...

Aug 25... A to London about wedding present for Cap. Van K ....[He who was badly wounded, now apparently recovered] *The four eldest children to Ouseley Lodge to spend the day with the Butters. They boated and fished in the Thames. Little Me and I drove over in afternoon to fetch them. We had tea out of doors with the Butters and a lovely drive home.*

The family moves on to Fair View. The boys and Annie spend the day at the Miss Hardymans at Silkwood Cottage, and the rest dine there *which was a great convenience to us.*

The Clanwilliams take Tytness Park nearby for the summer and many activities take place between the Meade children (of whom the eldest daughter, Lady Elizabeth Meade, is said to play the piano very well;) also the de Salises, now back in their own house. Georgie de Salis has a phaeton and there are many drives in Windsor Park etc. Leo takes John to Dartmouth to start in the Britannia - he is reported to sleep well, his first night in a hammock. Captain Trench, the Commander, was one of Leo's midshipmen in the Aurora.

Sept 17 More or less rain all day. A, Bessie and I in Miss Hardyman's Brougham to lunch at Portnall where were Minnie, Georgie, Edith and little Margery.

Sept 20 ... A and I to the Clanwilliams, met Princess Victor of Hohenlohe and

her girls there ...

Sept 27 ... Mlle Gregory left us ... we like her much, and A has engaged her as walking governess for Annie in town.

Sept 29 We all ... returned to town ... Found the house at home so beautifully clean - but the drains have been tested, and found defective and we shall have to turn out of the house and have them put to rights.

October 3 We all had to turn into our Mother's house ... as Scarlatina is prevalent in town it was thought necessary to put the drains right at once. It is annoying! We found this house very dirty and much knocked about by tenants. Annie went to Kensington High School in Cromwell Road for the first time.

Oct 28 ... Nettie sat for her portrait, a Photo painted on china ...

Oct 29 ... A and I to Popular Concert at St James's Hall. Halle S... and Norman Neruda, quite delightful ...

Mlle. Moffay, a well-recommended Parisian, takes over from Mlle Gregory. Haddie and Annie go to tea at Mrs H. Hildyard's to meet Lady Harman's two girls, at the same school as Annie. Our Mother comes back from Ireland on Nov 18 and will stay with Leo and Annette till her own house is ready. May goes to Miss Renshaw, at her club. Harry gets measles at Winchester, and though he recovers well, he has to miss his Confirmation on 26 Nov - but the Bishop holds another in December, and his parents go down to Winchester for it.

Annie gets a prize for Geography at her school, where the prizes are presented by Dr Mary Garrett Anderson. They get the glad news that the Queen has consented to be Patroness of the Irish Distressed Ladies fund.

Annie is fitted for her bridesmaid's dress - [Georgie de Salis and Revd. Hamilton, formerly a curate at Portnall, are married early the following year. Leo and A go to the wedding, but not Haddie.]

Christmas at Portnall includes the tree, skating, and all the children except Bessie and Margery stay up for dinner.

Haddie concludes the year: *Thank God for this happy, prosperous year. How good He is!*

This year **(1888)** as a whole is a rather quiet one for Haddie. There are even more family colds and ailments than usual, and much house-hunting goes on.

Mar 8 ... N took Annie to hear Mrs Barker recite in Queen's Gate Hall. I went to Primrose Party at Mrs Vansittart's alone, as N would not leave Leo, whose cough is still bad. Lady Randolph Churchill presented honours to some of the Primrose party. She also played a piece on the Piano. A large gathering of Paddington Primroses and many Associates.

Mar 17 ... A and I to tea with Mother to meet Lady Maude Hooper, and two of her nieces, the children of Charlie and Ella Garnett....

Mar 20 Very cold indeed, and snow so deep, that Annie did not go to school... and no visitors were foolish enough to call in this bitter weather ...

Mar 24 ... Annie and I went with Mother, May and Miss Renshaw to Mme. Tussaud's. Spent a long time there and had tea. It is worth seeing. My Birthday. [Haddie is 50]

Ap 11 Mother's new tenants, the Lidbetters, come into her house today. Only 8 gns a week for the Season! ... Mother and May to Dublin...

Ap 18 Annie & Bessy with Hayes went down to Bognor, to lodgings ... How we shall miss them! Dear Harry left for Winchester - he has been quite charming these holidays ...

May 1 ... Heard of the sad death of Admiral Ryder. Poor Nettie got a shock, as she saw the Posters: "An Admiral drowned in the Thames."...

May 2 ... N and I to Charity Concert at Queen's Gate Hall. Miss Alice Gomez (coloured, we think) has a glorious voice - on to Lady Salisbury's, a crush, but many people we knew.

May 23 ... Leo and N to Banquet at the Criterion for Royal Alfred Asylum for Aged Seamen. £2,100 subscribed for the Charity.

May 24 ... Accounts of Bob are good, but meagre, and really we do not know very much about the child. It is truly annoying! ... Leo, A and I by Buss to strand, to a meeting of Anglo-Israelites. 3 clergymen spoke, also Philo Israel, and a Congregational Minister. It was deeply interesting ...

Annie is attending a High School, and has a French governess to walk there and back with her - presumably with conversation! Princess Louise presents the prizes at end of term, but poor Annie is very often away from school with colds and bad cough.

Jun 8 ... Leo, N and Annie started for Dartmouth in Trinity yacht (Galatea), the Duke of Argyll and Mr Glyn, our Vicar being also on board. Hayes left for a holiday in the country. I went to afternoon party at Mrs Drummond's, and Mr Grossmith was very amusing ... I am alone with sweet little Bessie, and very happy.

Jun 11 ... to Bammie's lodging for lunch, then she, Lady Caroline Howard and I to Terry's Theatre where we saw "Little Lord Fauntleroy", such a pretty play ... B wanted me to stay for dinner, but I had too much to do at home.

Jun 15 ... Emperor Frederick of Germany died today, of cancer in the throat, much lamented and honoured. He only reigned 90 days and was ill and suffering all the time.... Nettie and Annie home.

Jun 17 Sunday. Heard that a general mourning for a fortnight is ordered for the late German Emperor.

Jun 18 ... I had to do some necessary shopping for our mourning, which we put on today. A and I paid visits, and left names at German Embassy and at Marlborough House.
Jun 19 ... A and I to evening party at Mrs Blanc's. Excellent music and acting. Only two ladies appeared in colours ...

After many reverses and indecisions the whole family moves from 29 Kensington Gate to 8 Atherstone Terrace, in November, and Haddie and Annette are both worn out from the work of many weeks. Nothing has gone smoothly, and the worst thing is that the kitchen range in the new house is found to be faulty, and eventually has to be replaced. Haddie frets that at this busiest of times, she has a really bad cold and bronchitis and cannot help as she wishes. Of the children, Harry's future is under discussion between his father and housemaster, Mr Morshead. Harry is bitten by an adder in the New Forest, not too much anxiety being expressed, though four days later his arm is still black and blue and swollen!

Annie, now 15, has to have a brace to straighten her teeth. We know that she is, and remained a gifted artist, and for the first time her art is mentioned - she goes for a lesson, from cousin Bammie Ross. Bob is removed from Crowthorne, his headmaster having given his opinion that he is unlikely to get a scholarship to Winchester - because, he opines, *of mistakes made in his early education.* So he is sent at short notice to East Sheen School - later referred to as Temple Grove, where all seems to go well. (The school much later moves to Herons Ghyll, East Sussex.) Annie continues at Kensington High School, and has two changes of "walking governess", the second a German lady.

For the summer, the family go to a house called Bur Lea, Walton-on-Thames, and have the usual pleasant and sociable stay, with the bonus of a donkey-cart at their disposal. Mr Atkinson, a local curate, gives Bob some extra coaching. Annie goes to friends in Wales - the Coles - for a three-week visit.

Our Mother and May go to Ireland, to Blanche at Glendarragh. One wonders if Monasterboice is let? It is several years since Haddie or Annette went to Ireland, but family correspondence shows that lively dispute was going on between Blanche's husband, Charlie McClintock, and Leo on money matters. Leo tells his mother-in-law that Annette becomes so upset about family disagreements that he thinks it better if visits to Ireland are given up for the present. Charlie is, of course, Leo's first cousin, once removed, but having married Leo's younger sister-in-law, he seems to have concerned himself greatly with the aftermath of the Will of their father-in-law, Robert Foster Dunlop.

At the end of each diary, Haddie lists her monthly expenditure, which is almost all on haberdashery to help make clothes and bonnets. etc. for herself and the others - she must have spent much of each daylight hour on needlework. It averages about £15 per month, and we know from family letters that though she was left money under her Father's Will, she only gets £50 per year regularly, and in spite of frequent reminders from Leo to Our Mother, more is seldom forthcoming. She makes a note in November 1888, that Leo gives her £20 *"owing to me"* but Leo must have subsidised her considerably - a difficult position for her, though not unique in that day and age.

From this date, Annette is usually referred to as "N" for Nettie, rather than "A" - which is much less to be confused with daughter Annie's name.
This year, for the first time, they stay in London for Christmas, not going to Portnall, though no reason is given. They have just about settled into the new house, all are weary and Haddie barely recovered from bronchitis. Her remarks as the year ends are decidedly muted.

1889

Jan 7 Now, the whole family does go on a visit to Portnall, finding the young married Georgie Hamilton, and having the usual winter fun with skating, etc. Home on Jan 12.

Jan 18 The dining-room floor was polished for a children's dance: *We had a most pleasant and successful children's dance from 6 to 10 o'clock. About 50 young ones and a few grownups - Mother, May, Miss Renshaw, Bammie, Mrs Fisher etc. A Mrs Underwood played the Piano well. We had several nice Britannia boys in uniform. How dear wee Bessie did enjoy herself!*

Jan 25 Nettie and I from 10.30 to 3 in the Law Courts, hearing the "Times" and Parnell trial. Unfortunately it was a dull day - no witnesses examined, only reading out inflammatory speeches made in Ireland by the Land Leaguers since 1880 ... ["The Times" had published a letter said to be by Parnell, implicating him in the murder of Lord Frederick Cavendish and Mr Bourke in Phoenix Park, Dublin. This was shown in Court to be a forgery and Parnell was cleared, on this occasion, to rapturous acclaim. However, Captain O'Shea's divorce action the following year began the decline of Parnell's career.]

Jan 27 Sunday. All except me to 9.30 service at Parish Church. I went to 11o'c at S. Stephen's. Mother spent the afternoon. N to afternoon tea with H.R.H. Princess Louise at Kensington Palace, to talk about Irish Distressed Fund etc. Leo forgot to give Jack his Health Certificate, and a telegram from the Britannia, says he is isolated in consequence.

Feb 12 ... Henry West called. He has brought his little Alick over to school after the Hooping Cough [sic]

Feb 15... May called and gave account of the Parnell trial, at which she, Mother and Miss Renshaw have been today, and where there were exciting scenes ...

Feb 19 ... Leo & N dined with the Edgars at Temple Grove. They very kindly sent their brougham both ways to fetch them. They saw dear Bob, looking well.

Feb 20... Leo & N dined at the Gillilans, where N got faint at dinner. She has not been feeling well for some days past. Henry West and I dined at our Mother's ...

Feb 25 ... We were alarmed about darling Bessie, who had a lump on her stomach which could not be accounted for. Sent for Dr Reid. She is to stay in bed and be poulticed and steeped. Leo has ricked his leg, and is to keep quiet. Bessie and Hayes are in my room. I slept in Hayes's.

A tubercular gland, perhaps?

Feb 26 Dear Bessie much better, but was kept in bed. I went with May and Miss Renshaw to Theatricals at St George's Hall, by the Romany Amateur Club, in aid of Royal Albert Institute for Aged Seamen. The performance was excellent - Old Cronies, and The Silver Shield. N gave hers and Leo's tickets to May and Miss R, as Leo had better keep his leg quiet.

Feb 28 Bessie all right again thank God .. Leo, N and I to Primrose entertainment of our Habitation 219 - "Darkie Minstrels" and rather good political address.

Mar 18 Leo, N, our Mother and I to St Mary Abbotts for dear Annie's Confirmation by Dr Earle, Bishop of M... I was in a good place and saw her well. She looked so sweet and pretty. We had a drawing-room meeting here at 4 o'c - about 100 people to hear the Bishop of Caledonia, and Mr Glyn in the chair. It went off very well and there was a good collection of money. We were tired, very, after such a busy and emoting day. Leo and N dined at Miss Towers' in Ken. Gate.

Mar 20 ... Leo and I to evening party at Lady Hood's in Queen Anne's Gate. N was quite too tired to go.

Mar 21 I went out in forenoon to buy fruit and flowers for dinner ... Home Dinner of 10 - Captain and Mrs Fisher, Cap and Mrs Douglas, Mr and Mrs Ponsonby Moore, Cap Younghusband and ourselves.

April 1 ... dear wee Bessie very happy, making April Fools of everybody!

Ap 2 ... Major McClintock to lunch. and was to have dressed here for the Levee, but unfortunately his bootmaker never sent his boots, so could not go!! [Leo's nephew, known sometimes as the "Mud Major."

Ap 13 Leo and N went down to Dartmouth for dear Jack's Confirmation ... Bessie was seized with a hard ringing cough at night, and had to be poulticed.

Ap 17 ... Harry arrived from Winchester very well, and having won Lord Selbourne's prize for Natural Science.

The family's busy life goes on, punctuated by the usual colds and ailments. A children's dance is given, for about 50, got up at a few days' notice. Jack passes No. 19 from Britannia, and spends nearly a whole day with his mother at the Army & Navy getting his uniform. Bob takes a scholarship exam for Charterhouse - several hours of examination - and gets the 6th Scholarship, to everyone's joy. Bessie is actually recorded as being "very naughty" one day! She takes a great fancy to Leopold McClintock, Leo's nephew, whom she calls "The Captain" - and he likes her company, as he has little girls of similar age and has not seen them for five years! He departs for India, but it is not clear where his children are at this time.

An unfortunate workwoman, Miss Watts, staying in the house, is unable to work for several days with bad head and face ache. N and Haddie are concerned about her, and get a doctor, who says she has cancer, and arranges for her to go to the Brompton Cancer Hospital. N and Haddie both visit her regularly, but her recovery or death is not recorded.

Leo has to go to sea unexpectedly owing to someone else's illness, and has a very stormy passage, up at 4, 5 and 6 am, but has obviously enjoyed it greatly! Nettie's sisters, Blanche (McClintock) and Helen or Dot (West, with her little girl Daisy) are in London and visit occasionally. Haddie notes that Helen accompanies Hayes to a *Baptist Church!!!* one Sunday.

Haddie records a red-letter day, on ...

Aug 2 (from Bognor, where all are staying) *A glorious day, and to be long remembered. Six of us, all but Bessie, to Portsmouth, thence in a steam launch on board the "Anson", flagship of Adm. Darcy Irvine. She is a grand new ship. Had some lunch on board. Then to the "Monarch" where we saw dear Jack, in full dress! The Emperor of Germany arrived with 12 ships (we have 112). Ours saluted and manned yards! Oh, what a sight our fleet is! Our train was late, so we did not get home till 9 o'c.*

They have a pleasant stay at Bognor, the boys walking to Pagham; all watch the German Emperor's Review of the Fleet, a magnicent sight from the beach. They visit Chichester and admire the Market Cross and the walls built from the old Roman walls. They take a waggonette to Goodwood, and enjoy the house and the pictures there. A hawk (possibly a pet) escapes "again" and is finally caught after 5 hours by Nana in a butterfly net out of an upstairs window! They visit Arundel Castle, with a special order from the Duke of Norfolk. Everyone bathes in the sea as often as possible (though Haddie only paddles) and Bessie (between colds) is said to benefit greatly from it, and can swim with an air cushion. They go on the pier to hear the band and Bessie has a drive in a goat carriage.

September sees them all back in London, sad at the imminent departure for sea of Jack - whose spell in the "Monarch" left him very tired and thin. Bob starts at Charterhouse, (Jack and he were 14 and 12 in July) and Harry goes back to Winchester for the last time.

Oct 20 ... This is darling Jack's last day with us. It is hard to part with him for so long - and yet, we would not have it otherwise, for it is best for him, dear boy.

Jack is 3 years older than his Father was when he first went to sea.

Oct 21 Leo and Annie took dear Jack down to Portsmouth where they found lovely weather. They left him on board the troopship Himalaya, and he sailed at 4.30, first for Plymouth, then Madeira and Bermuda. Many kind friends turned up, and cheered them, but it was very trying ...

Nov 13 ... Home Dinner. Miss Dutton, Fanny Carmichael, Capt. and Mrs Bedford, late of the Britannia, Admiral and Mrs Ruxton, Mr Parry and Mrs Macleod - Lady Fremantle and Cicely Macleod had to disappoint us, and we had to go out to look for a lady - and by accident got 2, so that I did not come in to dinner. All went well, though we had 2 new servants.

Dec 13 ... a letter from Jack from Bermuda....N and I by train to D'Almaines, where we chose a practising piano for the schoolroom for 14 gns... Leo, N, Annie and I to Primrose entertainment .... excellent wax works. A thick fog had come on, and we could not get a cab to go home. Good Nana came to meet us, with a lantern and warm wraps which were most acceptable, as we had a walk home.

Dec 16 ... Dinner party at home. Capt Beaumont and his lovely bride, Sir Charles Tupper (High Commissioner for Canada) Capt and Mrs Fisher, Admiral and Lady Edith Adeane, Francis Poë came after dinner. Annie dressed up as a Parlourmaid, and came into dinner!!!

The year ends with everyone ill or just recovering: however, Haddie's final words are *"Thank God for all His Mercies, Amen."*

1890 After the usual New Year visit to Portnall Haddie unluckily sprains her hand badly, falling over a footstool in her bedroom. Her handwriting is affected and on at least one day a child fills in the news for her. Bessie is now 7 so it may be her:

Mar 2 Bitterly cold. Frost & E.Wind. I started to go to Church with the others, but was advised to go back as the cold is so bad for my hand.

Mar 10 Dr Haran has put my hand on a splint, and bandaged it so tightly as to be quite immoveable ...

Four weeks are completely blank. She has a great deal of pain and many agonising treatments are tried, including manipulation under ether. At last, in June, she suddenly announces it is better, and her activities go on as usual.

One wonders how she managed to sew, and in fact her expenditure on haberdashery sundries is dramatically down till May. Bessie has started singing lessons. They all anxiously wait for letters from Jack, which sometimes arrive several together - he certainly writes regularly.
Bob is happy at Charterhouse and Harry goes to a crammer before taking Smalls, preparing for going up to Oxford. Annie, now 17, is having gowns made and starting to go to more grownup parties.
Leo's sister, Emily Crozier, comes to London in July to meet her son Alfred, who has been 2 years in Australia for his health. Alas, they are all shocked at his looks when he arrives: they summon a doctor, who says he is "in Consumption" and cannot recover, though he may live some time. In fact, he dies in Ireland in October, and Leo goes over for the funeral.
Nettie has her purse stolen at the Ladies Dress Agency, with £1.11.0 in it.
Leo goes to the July 12th wedding of his cousin Stanley, at which *Stanley was so unwell, that he was under the influence of morphia, and had to sit down during the service.*
[This is possibly Leo's first cousin, Stanley McClintock, now aged 78, and perhaps marrying again, as a widower, but not verified for certain.]

Annette gives Mr Yates several sittings for her portrait. They are preparing to go away as usual for the summer.

Aug 13 Harry and Bob started for Ireland. They are going first to stay with the Gledstanes at Fardross.

Bathing from a machine

Aug 14 Annie, Carter the Cook and I left ... to take up the house at Alverstoke [5 Anglesey Crescent]...*The house seems comfortable and faces the sea. It is clean upstairs, but not so in the kitchen regions.*
Aug 18 Dear wee Bessie's birthday (8). All except me to bathe with Mrs Holland in her box. Bessie spent afternoon with the Holland children and they dressed up and had great fun. ... we sat on the pier till late - lovely day.
Aug 20 A beautiful day. Leo, Nettie, Annie and I by 11.40 boat to Ryde. On by train to Newport, drove to Carisbrooke Castle, then to see the Roman

Villa in the Rectory grounds. Back to Newport, where we visited the church and admired the lovely recumbent statue by Marochetti erected by the Queen to Princess Elizabeth. By train to Cowes, thence to Ryde by steamer and by another boat to Stokes Bay, arriving home by 7 o'c after a most pleasant day.

Aug 21 A doubtful morning, but we risked it and Mrs Holland joined us 4. Steamer to Ryde, train to Ventnor, then in an open carriage, a most beautiful drive along the south coast to St Catherine's Lighthouse, shown to us by Mr Miller, the Engineer; he and his wife were most kind and gave us cake and ginger beer. This is the most powerful light in the world - between 6 and 7 million candles. It was lighted up for us - and the syren sounded. Drove on to Black Gang Chine, then back to Ventnor, train to Ryde and back to Stokes Bay. We much enjoyed our day.

Aug 24 Sunday A fine bright day. All to church twice, but we only heard Curates preach, very indifferently.

Aug 25 Windy and showery. ... Annie, Bessie and I bathed. I had not been in the sea for many many years. We walked and met Leo and Nettie at Stokes Pier.

Aug 26 Dreadful weather, high wind and pelts of rain. Leo, N, Annie and I drove to Gosport, saw the Biscuit making for the Navy in Clarence Victualling Yard. Crossed the harbour in Capt. Markham's steam launch, lunched with him, where we met the new German naval attache. Called on the Commerells and Gordons, who gave us tea and showed us over the dockyard House [where Annie, Jack and Bob had been born]. *Then on board the St Vincent where we had 2nd tea with Capt and Mrs Conybeare - home by steam launch and carriage.*

Aug 27 Leo to London and back on business. N, Annie and I lunched with Sir Allen Young on board his fine steam yacht, Stella, which he brought over to Stokes Bay for us. Lord Alcester was the only other guest on board. We steamed off to Cowes to get shelter and went on board the new Trinity yacht Irene.... Allen Young landed us at Stokes Bay. We were sorry not to have Leo with us.

Allen Young had been an officer of the Merchant Marine on Leo's expedition to the Arctic.

Aug 29 We all crossed in Duke of Wellington's boat, called on Mrs Cole, then walked through Queen Street to Anglesey Barracks, where we had tea with Major McClintock, then by tram and walking to call on 2 or 3 people, and home by a public launch and carriage.

Aug 30 We all bathed. General and Mrs Gordon and Mrs Heneage drove over and had tea with us ...

Sept 1 Leo to Portsmouth on Scripture Readers business. We took a walk together, and had tea with Captain and Mrs Churchill. He commands the Indian Trooper "Crocodile".

Sept 2 We all went to Gosport to see the sports of the St Vincent boys. They were very good, and we met many acquaintances there. We walked there and back, and were very tired.

Sep 3 I had headache all day and did not go out. Leo, N and Annie to Portsmouth to see Miss [Agnes] *Weston's Sailors' Rest. Harry and Bob* [visiting in Ireland] *left Fardross and went to Monasterboice.*

Sep 4 ... all went on board the "Galatea" and lunched with Captain and Mrs Holland. We were shown over the ship. She is a fine swift Cruiser and has only been commissioned for the Manoeuvres this year and last. Capt Holland sailed us across the harbour, which was most pleasant.

Sep 5 We bathed, and it was delightful. We all went to the Children's Sports at Alverstoke. Bessie won 2 prizes and Annie one. Nettie pulled in the Tug o' War, married women against spinsters...Each side won once.

Sep 8 The young ones bathed. We all went to Fareham by train, where General Gordon's Victoria met us, and we spent a pleasant day at St Margaret's, Titchfield, the Gordons' place. We lunched and had tea. Mrs Heneage and her dear little boy were there. ... Annie went in to the Hollands after dinner, and danced!! A party of 5, all told.

Sep 9 Very fine and sunny. We all bathed and liked it much. Leo, N and I went out in a boat to assist Mrs Holland and Annie in a long swim.

Sep 11 ... Annie and I with the Hollands and a whole lot of people (about 60) in a large steam launch after dinner to see the Fireworks at Southsea. We enjoyed ourselves greatly. We had food on board. We saw the Howe and the Camperdown lying at Spithead - they looked very grand lighted up at night. It was about 11.30 when we got home.

Sep 12 ... Leo N and I after lunch to Fareham by train and drove to Uplands Park, to dine and sleep with Mrs Gordon of Fyvie. Her sister Mrs Belman and her husband were there, also Miss Duff Gordon, a pretty young girl but a R.C. We had a dinner party in a fine banqueting hall hung with old arms and armour. There are old cabinets which belonged to Mary, Queen of Scots, and many other curious things. We played croquet before dinner.

Sep 16 ... Harry and Bob arrived from Ireland, where they spent a very pleasant time from Aug 13.

Sep 18 ... We all left Alverstoke with much regret and travelled by Portsmouth, Brighton (where we changed) and Eastbourne to St Leonards. Found this house [Holme Lea] *kindly lent us by Mrs Tyler, comfortable and roomy.*

Sep 20 We went to explore old Hastings, where we saw some very quaint old houses. Mr and Mrs Marlow called. He was Leo's secretary in N.America and is now Paymaster to the Coastguard here...

Sep 25 ... All except Bessie by train to see the old towns of Rye and Winchelsea, an old Church and old houses and gateways. The sea has retreated from both 2 or 3 miles. Winchelsea is more decayed than Rye.

Both stand high with flat plains around. We had tea at Winchelsea, served by a most original woman and we drove back to the Station.

Sep 27 Nana, Bessie and I bathed. Rough sea. Leo and Harry to Lamberhurst Court Lodge to stay with the Morlands ...

Oct 5 Sunday ... all except Bessie to morning service at the old Parish Church of St Leonard's. Very low.

Oct 6 Leo, N, little Bessie and I drove to Sir Robert and Lady Heads about 3 miles off and lunched there. Then Leo and N went to see Battle Abbey, by special permission of the Duchess of Cleveland ... Bessie and I staid with the Heads till 5 o'c. They sent us in their carriage to Hollingston, and thence we got home by 2 busses.

Oct 9 .... Harry left for New College, Oxford, at 11. Later in the day, we all went home to London, where we found the house nice and fresh and clean, all but the Drawing room, which is not finished yet.

Oct 18 ... Bessie has a feverish cold and is in bed. The Canadian Mail is in, but no letter from dear Jack. This is the 3rd mail without hearing from him. It makes us all anxious ...

Oct 19 Sunday... Leo went early to the Admiralty and heard there was an undelivered Canadian mail in London. Mrs Tyler is going to St Leonards tomorrow, and promises to telegraph if there are letters from Jack there ..

Oct 20 ... In the evening came Mrs Tyler's telegram that she found 2 letters from Jack in the empty house at St Leonards, dropped in by the Postman

[they came next day with nothing but good news]

Oct 22 ... N went early with Leo to Dr Forbes, the Aurist ...

Oct 24... Nettie sat for Mr Yates ...

Oct 26 Sunday ... Rain coming out of Church and we had no umbrellas! came part of way in a bus .. John and Blanche Ross called, also Miss Lloyd Williams and Edmund Poë [stepson of Haddie's Aunt]

Nov 1 ... Out shopping. Nettie, Annie, Bessie and I at L.D.A, Bessie and I on to Regent St to hunt for the McClintock Tartar, as she calls it. Bob came for his exeat from Charterhouse, looking well and happy.

They go on with their usual termtime habits. A Governess called Mlle Forstermann comes to teach Annie and Bessie, so Annie's education is not yet considered complete. Bessie goes for her singing lessons and Annie has a special gown made. Haddie is busy with sewing parties for a charity called "Helping Hands".

Nettie and Annie go to St Albans for a Sale of Irish Work which is most successful - they stay with Lord Verulam.

Nov 13 Heard the sad news of the wreck of H.M.S. Serpent in which poor Cicely Macleod lost her Brother, Torquil ... dined with the Kennedys in Kensington Gate, a party of 10, Annie's first dinner party, but we were SO sad!

Nov 14 Leo has sprained his right arm, near the shoulder. Our Mother arrived at her house in town. All except Leo went to meet her and May, at 56 Queens Gate Terrace.

Nov 16 Sunday ... N sent for Mr Merriman who says Leo must stay in bed, and have liniment kept perpetually on his arm. Nettie staid with him all day. Our Mother and May came to early dinner.

Nov 17 Leo in bed, and very good and patient. Merriman saw him again. N took our Mother and May to the Kensington Stores and gave them tea. I staid with Leo, and read to him.

Nov 22 ... N to SSAFA about the relief to be given to the families of the poor men lost in the Serpent. N and I paid a round of visits in a "Wheel and Tyre" Cab ...

Dec 3 ... Leo and N dined with Major and Mrs Clarke, to meet the E. Poës. He is just starting for the China Station, as Flag Captain to Admiral Nicholson.

Dec 5 Heard of Mrs Alfred McClintock's death. [Fanny, widow of Leo's younger brother, Alfred Henry, distinguished doctor in Dublin, Master of the Rotunda Hospital; he had died in 1881, while Leo and family were abroad. Leo goes to Ireland for her funeral.]

Dec 7 ... our Mother to lunch and spent the afternoon. Kathleen and her two boys Harry and Lewis to 5o'c tea. All this week has been going on the exciting squabble among the Parnellite MPs about Parnell retaining the leadership or no - Gladstone is in a fix!!

The Irish M.Ps vote, after an acrimonious debate in which Mrs O'Shea's name is very nearly mentioned, by 45 to 29 to depose Parnell as leader of the Irish party. It is the beginning of the end for him and he dies in October the following year.

Harry returns from his first term at Oxford, and Bob comes from Charterhouse with the 2nd (Junior) cup for rifle shooting; there is skating on the Round Pond. It is a white Christmas, and they celebrate on Christmas Day with a Loving Cup in Bob's cup, and round games of cards. Our Mother, May, Miss Renshaw and Miss Poynter the novelist are of the party. On December 29th the family go to Portnall to join the large party there: the three married sons and 2 children, Georgie Hamilton and her husband, Charlie de Salis and Beatrice Fisher. Much skating. Letters from Jack are always a great relief to his family.

Haddie ends the year with this prayer: *So ends this year, so full of mercies and blessings, for which I give thanks from the bottom of my heart - to the Blessed Giver of all - and oh! may He make me somewhat less unworthy of these Gifts and Blessings, Amen.*

1891

As usual at Portnall, there are many homemade entertainments - Willy de Salis and his wife act a little play called Cups and Saucers, Rodolph recites and Charlie sings. *Our young ones have greatly improved at skating.* About 30 people come for a dance, at which Nettie and others help with the music. Back in London, there is a dance at Lady Hamilton's (wife of the First Sea Lord) which they all attend, coming back in two hansoms, the boys by underground. On 14 Jan, though half the family is ailing, they hold a Young People's dinner. Guests are Mrs and Miss Tyler, Ella Harman, Mr Bluen R.N, Mr Wentworth. *We played merry noisy games, and the young ones seemed to enjoy themselves.* There are children's parties for Bessie, often at the Thesigers, and a visit to the theatre, *much amused by "The Cabinet Minister."*

Jan 20 Leo, N and I dined with Capt. and Mrs Durrant, a party of 11. I went in with Dr Russell, formerly Times correspondent, very amusing. Prince Lesingen(?) was there, so nice, and Captain Beaumont and others. We had a most recherché dinner.

Jan 22 N and I to d'Almaines about a piano ... to Onslow Gardens to fetch Bessie from her Dancing lesson. N's 2nd At Home (now on regular Thursdays) *A good many people came, many of whom I missed, by being out with Bessie.*

Jan 24 ... Mr Merriman saw Annie, who has been feeling faint occasionally of late. He says it is Anaemia, and orders iron and wine ...

Feb 1 Sunday ... the Fishers called. C and O Macleod spent the evening and had supper here, and we had prayers together; they start tomorrow for Italy. Often when bad weather means no one goes to Evening Service, they say prayers at home. Nana is called away to the deathbed of her brother-in-law Fletcher. Afterwards she comes home quite worn out and has to be looked after for a few days. Annie is able to go to the Albert Hall to hear Gounod's "Redemption" in place of Our Mother, who has headache. Nettie's portrait is finished at last and they go to the studio to see it and are *much pleased.*

Some time in this year, Nettie makes an attempt to straighten out her sister's finances. We have a copy of a letter she writes to Our Mother, though Haddie probably knows nothing about it. It is undated:

My own Mother, I am more distressed than I can say at these rubs and annoyances between us on the subject of whatever care Haddie's not very strong health may from time to time require. My own desire all through the 20 years of my married life as regards my own family has been to serve them all round and keep love and unity unbroken. Now I have a proposal to put to you. Will you accept it, or else hereafter not ...... Haddie or me with anger when Haddie happens not to be well. Leo and I leave annually in your hands £70 of

our money. Will you give Haddie out of this annually £25, to meet some of her expenses, which cause a scene when we propose to you to pay them, her limited means being insufficient to cover nearly all the expenses of life. If you agree to this, we will never ask you for any of her expenses, and these causes of annoyance will be at an end. Why should love and ?union be interfered with when so easy a remedy lies in our own hands. You and I know perfectly well that it would not add to your happiness if Haddie were living with you, and in mere £.s.ds it would cost you much more than what I propose. If you refuse it, I feel certain you will comply with the alternative which is to meet willingly and cheerfully the occasional calls for a Dr or Dentist's fee. From something you said I am quite prepared to find that you may say that you regard it as a question of respect and not of money, but here you must be mistaken, because one year ago when Dr Heram unpaid attended Haddie you were not in the least annoyed, though he came at first without your consent and attended her sprained hands twice and sometimes three times a week for nearly 3 months.
.....[No ending to this copy]

1891 is a terrible year for sister Helen (or Dot) and Henry West. On 27 Feb their eldest son, William, named by Haddie as Robin, dies at Haileybury, of pleurisy and inflammation of the lungs, aged 15. Only May is recorded as going to his funeral at Sacombe, near Ware, Herts, his Father's parish. Nettie and Haddie cancel most engagements, but Haddie is a "prisoner" anyway due to bad cold and cough. Then, on May 23, another West son, little Harry, at his preparatory school, also dies. This time, Leo and Nettie go down to Sacombe for the funeral, and then meet Mother and May at Euston, to give them an account of it, before these two depart for Ireland. If there had been any coolness between Leo and Henry West, it is laid aside. The Wests had moved from Ireland two years earlier, to the pleasant living of Sacombe, where St Catherine's Church sits on high ground surrounded by parkland. There is a touching memorial to the two brothers; a Celtic cross, no doubt to mark their Irish roots, inscribed "William Robert and Henry Erskine, loving and beloved sons of Henry and Helen West, of Sacombe Rectory ...", and the guide-book in church refers to the family tragedy.

Work goes on all the time for "Helping Hands", also "Irish Waifs & Strays".

When Leo is laid up with a cold and inflamed eye Haddie does a good deal of writing for him. The cook, Mrs Mower, is not well and goes home for a week - the charwoman comes in her place. Harry, home from Oxford, goes to the Lyric Club to see the Boat Race (which Oxford wins by half a boat's length.)

April 1 Dear little Bessie very happy making April Fools of everybody all day!!

Harry is photographed by Van Dyck. Bob passes his Preliminary exam for Woolwich; though not yet 15 he does well.

April 11 ... N and Annie to tea with the Hanbury-Tracys. Miss Lloyd Williams called, and told us all about Mr Tyler's end.

April 22 N, Annie and I drove to L.D.A and back to fit on our gowns. We 3 to afternoon party at Mrs Bright's where we had Corney Grain, as amusing as ever.

April 24 ... Drove with N to Naval Exhibition where she and Leo were labelling the Franklin Relics. Later Nettie is very busy writing a pamphlet about the Franklin Search, to be sold at the Exhibition.

April 25 ... Surely there never was such a winter for colds. I wish I could get rid of mine.

April 29... There is a Sale at Devonshire House in aid of Irish Distressed Ladies at which N has a Dorcas Stall. They are very busy for two days ... *We sold rather well, considering we had only Poor clothes ...*

May 2 Annie is fitted for her Court dress and train, preparing to be presented at Court.. The Naval Exhibition goes off *splendidly, all but the heavy rain just as the Royalties came. The P. of Wales opened it, the Princess was there, Duke of Albany, Prince Edward etc.etc. It is a very fine and interesting Exhibition . The Arctic section is very good.*

May 13 Nettie presented dear Annie at the Drawing-room held by the Princess of Wales. Leo went too. Annie looked so sweet and pretty, and N looked particularly well. They had bouquets given by the Plunkets. Between 50 and 60 friends came to tea afterwards to see them. Harry came up from Oxford to see Annie and slept here.

May 14 Leo, N & Annie to Oxford to stay with the Turners for the Eights ... spent the evening after dinner at our Mother's where were Charlie and Blanche McClintock [the third sister] *who have been staying there for a few days but leave tomorrow for Belgium.*

May 26 ... Leo and N dined at the Houldsworths, and then took Annie to an evening party at Lady Victoria Buxton's. Her first grownup party! dear child she looked so nice in a pretty pink crepe gown.

May 30 Leo and N and Annie to Dawley till Monday. Queen's Birthday kept and Leo is made a K.C.B. Tardy justice indeed!! ... many congratulations already on Leo's honours.

June 5 ... Leo, N and Annie to R.N. Dance at Greenwich, driving there and back in an Omnibus, shared by the Columbs, not home till next morning.

Leo, c. 1891

Annie's first Ball, which she well enjoyed ...
June 18 ... to afternoon party at Lady O'Neill's. Leo & N dined with the Hoods, and I dined with the Ruxtons. Morris Beauford walked home with me.
June 22 ...N, Harry and Annie to Florence Massereene's Ball, given in a house in Cadogan Square, hired for the occasion as hers in Park Street is too small.

June 24 Leo, N, Annie and I to Lady Salisbury's Evening Party at the Foreign Office. Very pleasant, and as ever, a beautiful sight.
June 26 ... N, Annie and I paid visits and went to the Miss Nepeans' Afternoon party ...

Annie, after parties and dances every day, develops a rash and Mr Merriman pronounces her needing a little care and attention. A few days later she goes to a Ball at Buckingham Palace in honour of the German Emperor and Empress, but is too tired next day to go to the Fireworks at the Naval Exhibition, which greatly delights Bessie, however. Annie must have relapsed, because on 15 July she and Bessie, with Nana, go on Doctor's orders to lodgings at Broadstairs. Haddie has a few days with the Plunkets at Wimbledon and has a jolly time, but finds the house sadly quiet when she gets back. Harry has gone to join a reading party with Oxford friends.
July 5 Sunday Capt Guise, just home from Bermuda. called and gave us a delightful account of dear Jack, how nice and remarkably popular he is!
Watched by Leo, Bob shoots for Charterhouse at Bisley, and helps them win a Shield; he is much the youngest, still not 15.
Aug 2 Sunday ... also to congregational service at Christ Church, where we heard a remarkable and most unprofitable sermon from a Curate, a "vision" of a Cave with chained Prisoners inside!

They get the house ready for workmen, before going away for the summer. They join the girls and Nana at Broadstairs, having taken a small house there. (Sydney Cottage, Stone Road.) Annie meets them at the station, looking much better.
Aug 9 Sunday ... to church at St Mary's Convalescent Home (Kilburn Sisters)

VERY high! Leo and Bob to afternoon service at St Peter's more than a mile away.

Aug 10 ... all drove to North Foreland Lighthouse where all was well explained to us - and on to Kingsgate, a pretty little place with ruins, some supposed to date 500 AD.

Aug 14 Leo went off to London ... being summoned to Osborne to be invested with the K.C.B. by the Queen, and he must get his uniform etc. Harry arrived just after late dinner, having much enjoyed his visit in Staffordshire to the Dawsons.

Aug 18 ... Dear Bessie's 9th birthday. She was to have had a drive in a Donkey Chaise, but it rained ...

Aug 19 ... Leo arrived back again and the 4 young ones went to the Station to meet him.

Aug 22 All, by open Omnibus and train, to Ramsgate Minster and Sandwich. Unfortunately I was neuralgic and afraid to go, though I very much wished to do so. The others greatly enjoyed themselves.

Aug 24 ... all except Bessie to a Tennis party at Mrs Whitehead's at Bleak House, where Dickens used to live, and where he wrote the book of that name. We met Lady and Miss Tancred there ...

Aug 30 ... N, Annie, Bessie and I drove to St Peter's Church, where the Rector, Mr Whitehead, preached well... had evening prayers at home as we find the services in the Church here, too tremendously high for us.

Sep 1 ... heard today that Helen [sister] *West has again had twin girls, born at Portrush.* What a year for that family! These are believed to be their third set of twins, and we are told later the girls are named Kathleen and Eileen.

Sep 11 ... all, except Bessie, to Canterbury, by train to Margate, then early train to Canterbury. Saw the Cathedral, and walked about the Precincts and the dear old town. Had bread, cheese and Beer at an Inn. We greatly enjoyed our day, and came back to Broadstairs for tea. Bessie had Sybil Thesiger and Honour Vansittart to tea with her.

Though they have to give up the lodgings before they wished, all enjoy Broadstairs with its excursions, donkey rides and congenial neighbours. Leo and Nettie leave to go and stay with Maria Cole at Llys Murchian in Wales (she is the remarried widow of a cousin of Leo's). Haddie and Harry go back to London to open up the house, but the girls stay on at new lodgings. Later, Nana and Bessie come back to London and Haddie goes down to keep Annie company. They have rather a pleasant, quiet time with a good deal of sketching by Annie (who had several sessions painting with Mrs Thesiger) We know that Annie was a gifted artist, but the teaching she receives is, at best, spasmodic.

They are back in London to a warm welcome, glad to be home, though almost at once Nettie comes down with a mild attack of shingles. The Naval Exhibition closes, to general regret, on Oct 24. Miss Wyatt, Bessie's schoolmistress, gives a good account of her, and evidently *likes her much.* Jack sends photographs of himself, from Halifax, Nova Scotia.

On 8 November Bessie develops a rash, and Mr Merriman pronounces it to be Scarlatina. From the tremendous quarantine precautions which then come into force, we would call it Scarlet Fever. They particularly fear Annie catching it, and she and Haddie at once move into lodgings in St George's Terrace close by, very sad at leaving home. (Later, they move into Gaga's house) From then on, neither of them see poor Bessie for 40 days - she is confined at the top of the house, and when at last she begins to "peel", everything has to be fumigated, the walls scraped down and re-papered, and of course Harry and Bob are not allowed home. Nettie seems to share the nursing with Nana, but Leo frequently visits Haddie and Annie and gives them news of Bessie - who evidently has a mild attack.

Dec 7 Annie is packed off to stay with the Wests (and their new baby girls) at Sacombe. She travels down with their new governess. She then goes on a week later to stay with Capt and Lady Jane Van Kaughuit at Lythenhanger Park, St Albans. [It is understood from references in family letters that Annie first met Bernard Greenwell at the Van Kaughuits' house, but it may have happened later than this visit.]

They are not all finally at home again together, with Bessie free of quarantine, till December 30th. They manage a small Christmas Tree for Bessie, and she makes her first trip downstairs to see it:

Dear child, I never saw anything like her delight!

Dec 25 The fog still and dreadfully slippery. Quite dangerous to walk .. to church. We had what is called a silver thaw but fog was too thick to see the icicles. We all (except Bessie) dined with Gaga and had great difficulty in walking there and back. Leo led Nettie, and Bob took care of me both ways. I was wonderfully muffled up, because of my cough.

1892

Jan 3 Dear little Bessie came down freely among us, for the first time, having completed the fortnight of ... quarantine, in addition to the 6 weeks of complete isolation. We can now kiss her, and be with her as usual.

Jan 7 Nettie and Annie to tea with Mrs Storr, and met Mr Storr, vicar of St Peter's, Eaton Square, who had been out on a visit to the Bellerephon and met Jack, of whom he gave a charming account ...

Jan 9 Extremely cold. Harry and I lunched with the Plunkets, and went with G. Plunket as her guests to see "The Match Girl" at the Savoy Theatre. Leo, N and Annie to Miss Beynon and Mr Monier Williams' wedding. Bob skated a little with Penell at Putney but the ice was bad.

Jan 12 The young Duke of Clarence, eldest son of the Prince and Princess of Wales, is struck down with influenza.

Jan 14 Alas! the Prince passed away this morning. His poor parents and Princess May of Teck, to whom he was to have been married on Feb 27. The greatest sympathy is felt for them all, and Prince Edward is indeed a loss to the Nation, so good and Kind and amiable, and so devoted to duty!

Jan 15 ... Annie and I shopped in the High St - of course, everyone is going into mourning ...We can be sure Haddie is kept busy applying black crepe for everyone.

Jan 17 Sunday Raining and freezing and very slippery and cold. Leo, Annie and Bob to early service. Harry has a cold and did not go out. ... I went to St Stephen's where the Bishop of Bedford preached, and spoke most feelingly about the Royal Family, and also about the Pestilence among us, and the Bishop of London's prayers for both these were read. It was all very solemn.

Jan 20 Leo (in uniform) by personal invitation of the P. of Wales, to Windsor for the funeral. He said he never saw a more grief-stricken party of mourners than the Royal Family. Our Mother came to see N. in our darkened house with all the blinds down.

Annie and I to a Memorial funeral service at St Mary Abbotts. A very, very sad day! There was snow on the ground at Windsor, but not here ... Oxford is not to meet for another fortnight as this terrible Influenza is raging there. Deaths risen to 59! ...

Jan 22 ... heard that Leo's sister, Mrs Gardiner [Caroline] *is very alarmingly weak after influenza ...*

Jan 23 The Dr called and says Harry is as weak as water and has had a slight attack of influenza and has ordered him ammoniate Feri... and Port Wine. N rather better. All the household are to take Quinine and Feraxicum, and keep oil of eucalyptus about the house ...

Feb 6 Harry just fit enough to go back to Oxford ... *we watched the planets Jupiter and Venus which are in close proximity to each other.*

Feb 7 Sunday All to 11o'c service at St Jude's, occupying the sittings Leo has taken ...a pew rental system was quite usual at this date; St Jude's is to become the family's regular church for many years.

Feb 9 ... Annie and I to House of Commons for meeting of Parliament. We were there from 3.30 and remained until almost 10.30, having tea there. Heard the opening speeches, making address to the Queen. With touching allusion to Prince Edward's death. A fine speech from Mr Balfour, and a shameful attack on Lord Salisbury from Sir W. Harcourt and Sir Charles Russell.

Feb 18 Heard that Uncle Poë passed away last Sunday at GlenBan aged 81.

N's At Home, about 35 visitors. May and Miss Renshaw came, but not our Mother. Annie went away at 5.30 with the Tatton Browns, to spend a week with them near Guildford. Leo to P.L.Entertainment. N and I did not go because of this morning's news.

Feb 26 ... heard that Jack came out at last June's Exams 43rd Midshipman in the service. He was 148th last year. This is excellent.

March 4 Very, very cold. Came down to Oxford to stay at 36 St Giles with the Turners. Had to wait at Paddington for one and a half hours, as the train I meant to go by had ceased running. Harry met me at Oxford Station and came with me to the Turners. He also came to dinner. He looks so bright and well.

Mar 5 ... Harry came at 11 and took me out to see St John's, Trinity and Balliol. He lunched here, and then took me to see the "Torpids" rowed at 3o'c., after which I parted with him and went by tram to call on the Burrows! She was too unwell to see me but I saw Cap. Burrows. The famous Mrs Bustle came to tea here.

Mar 6 Sunday Harry and I to Cathedral at Trinity College [does she mean Christ Church?] *at 9.30 . He took me at 3o'c to New College where he showed me the grounds, the Hall and the Chapel. I had tea with him in his rooms, and then went to Chapel with him at New College, where the music was excellent, particularly the "Final Amens". I came back to the Turners alone, as Harry had to dine in College.*

Mar 7 ... Harry took me out for an hour in the morning. We saw Brasenose Chapel and other places. He took me to 6 o'c service at Magdalen, where the chanting was quite perfect ...

Mar 8 Very cold indeed. Mr Turner took me out in the forenoon to see Keble and Exeter, then to the Bodleian Library and Ashmoleum Museum. All so deeply interesting. Oriel Skeffington to lunch. [cousin] *At dinner we had Mr Godley, Dean of Magdalen, Mr Stacey, tutor of Keble, Mr Bustle, fellow of Brasenose (most original), Miss Harbottle, pupil at ....* (Haddie evidently cannot remember the name of her College, but Miss H. may have been one of the early female undergraduates) *and Harry.*

Mar 9 ... Harry came and saw me off to Bath. A bad train and long wait at Didcot and Swindon. Reached Bath before 6o'c to stay with the Jeffreys at 9 Cavendish Place. Found Julia and Tissy there: Mary is abroad.

Mar 11 Hard frost: very cold but fine and sunny. Out walking with Julia in forenoon. Saw the Roman Baths and Pump Room. After lunch Tissy took me out driving.

Mar 12 ... out with Julia in the town. The Jeffreys' had an afternoon party. I knew no one except Mrs Keating.

Mar 14 ... drove with Tissy in a Victoria, a lovely drive in the sunshine, with flakes of snow falling frequently!

Mar 15 ... had a small dinner party, inc. 3 gentlemen in addition to the house party of 5.

Back to London:

Mar 19 ... Annie and Bessie lunched with the Macleods and went with them to Maskeline and Cook's. N and I paid visits and went to Mrs Trotter's and Marion Keating's At Home, where we heard good professional music. Annie joined us there. Leo went across to Cherbourg with the Queen today.

Mar 22 Cold and wet. Our Mother, N, Annie and I to Mrs de Pomeroy's (15 Cavendish St) about our summer gowns. ... Annie drove home in a Hansom, open, and got a chill and increased her cold.

Mar 23 Annie in bed all day ... Leo and N to Lady Salisbury's with Annie, but of course as she was in bed, she could not go.

Mar 31 N's At Home. About 25 people. Annie and I went to the Grosvenor Club At Home, where there was good music. Mrs Tyler gave us the tickets and sent us there in her carriage.

April 12 ... Leo and N to Charterhouse for dear Bob's Confirmation

Ap 14 ... went early to Mrs de Pomeroy's to fit on. Dear Jack arrived from Plymouth at 10 pm.. Harry and Bob went to the station to meet him. He looks tired and dazed and perished with cold. We hope to have him until the end of May. Gaga remained here after dinner to see him. We waited until 8.30 for dinner.

Ap 15 Good Friday We all except Bessie, who still has a bad cough, to service at 10.30 at St Jude's. It is so delightful to have dear Jack again! ...

Ap 21 ... Gaga spent the day here till 9.30 pm as Miss Renshaw and May had gone down to Bristol for Miss Edwardes' (the Egyptologist's) funeral.

Ap 22 ... Dear Harry left us for Oxford, and thus our happy family party is already broken up!

*Ap 25 ... Mr Merriman saw Bessie and says she is thoroughly relaxed after her various illnesses, and ought to go to Bournemouth for a fortnight ...*She leaves, with Hayes, on the 28th, in hope of doing her cough good.

May 3 ... I chaperoned Annie at a dance at the Gillilans, mixed children and grownups, but it was very dull.

May 6 ... N, Annie, Jack and I to Grand Habitation Primrose League at Covent Garden Theatre, where we had a box, where Henry West joined us. A grand night and a fine speech from Lord Salisbury. Jack dined with Commodore and Mrs Beaumont and went to the Court Theatre with them.

May 12 ... Bob left for Charterhouse. How Jack will miss him!...

May 18 ... N, Annie and I to Ebury St to see Maria Cole and Violet dressed for the Drawing Room, before they went. Princess Christian held it ...Nettie and Annie to Lady Robinson and Mrs Kinahan's Drawing Room Teas.

May 19 ... Cicely and Olivia Macleod to lunch. They are going to Nanheim for the waters for Olivia ... Leo and N dined with Lord Justice and Miss Kay.

May 20.... Mr Merriman saw me again. I lunched with our Mother to see Helen Verschoyle who is spending a few days with her. Leo, N, Annie and Jack to the British Museum where Dr Kirens took them over the Egyptian and Assyrian galleries and explained all: so very interesting. Mr Gledstanes and Helen spent about 3 hours here. They are both much better. I was quite tired out and lost my voice from being obliged to talk so much...

May 21 ... N took Annie again to see Dr Broadbent, who says she is much better and need not go to Switzerland! Good news indeed!...

This is the first time Haddie has mentioned Switzerland for Annie. Perhaps it would have been a good idea.

May 25 ... Helen Verschoyle came to stay. She is very unwell and needs care ... saw Mr Merriman. He also saw Jack, and says he will be all right, but has been overworked and overstrained ... Jack spent the afternoon at Charterhouse with Bob.

May 26 Helen ... left us after dinner to sleep at Buckingham Palace Hotel so as to start with her brother Judge Foster and his party for Ireland.

May 28 ... N, Annie, Jack and I to Portnall ... found Cecil and his wife and Baby, Lady Chesney and 2 children, Col. Filgate Henley, and Margery de Salis and her governess there. Most of the party drove to Ousley after lunch and went in a boat on the river ...

May 31 ... Jack left to go to Portsmouth to join the "Royal Sovereign" ... Annie and I to two evening parties, Mrs Wingfield and Mrs Corder.

June 1 ... Our sister Blanche and her eldest boy (Stanley) to tea ....

June 2 ... Our Mother and May left for Ireland in the evening... Nana got something in her eye, and went to have it taken out at the Ophthalmic Hospital. Annie went with her.

June 3 ... Annie's 19th birthday ... Mrs Kay, Emily Drummond, my sister Blanche and her husband and boy to tea. Dear Jack arrived from Portsmouth, having been given two days leave ... he looks so much better.

June 4 Mr Merriman saw Jack and me, says I am much better but my chest not yet quite free. Went out with Bessie to get her a hat. Leo, N and Annie left for Charterhouse to stay till Monday with the Haig Browns; provoking to go when Jack is at home ...

Allan Oldfield comes to stay to attend a Medical Board at the India House to get an extension of sick leave. Haddie dines with him at the Ross's and meets Mr and Mrs Tyrell, a daughter of the late David Urquhart, also Mr and Mrs Moores, *all R.C.s.* Nettie is having her portrait done again, this time by a Miss Merritt. Haddie goes to Miss Shute's afternoon party, where there is good professional music. The London season gets into full swing with many parties at all times of day, also exhibitions, concerts and the Royal Academy. "Helping Hands" gets dissolved, no reason given. The Ross's have taken Our

Mother's house and May stays there before going abroad with Miss Renshaw. Parliament is dissolved, *after 8 years good government under Lord Salisbury.*

3rd Marquess of Salisbury

W.E.Gladstone

June 29 Harry arrives from Oxford, having rowed down the Thames with two friends to Reading. His luggage gets lost, so that when Annie goes to Mrs Haigh's Ball, he cannot go with her. Major McClintock comes to lunch with Miss Poynder, his fiancee. There is an Election at which (conservative?) seats are lost, to Haddie's sorrow, and Gladstone's gain. There is an afternoon party with the Bishop of Derry and Mrs Alexander (hymnwriter)

Dr Richardson (Leo's nephew) dines, on his way to a Children's Hospital at Birmingham. Haddie spends a few days at Wimbledon with the Plunkets. Harry comes down from Oxford and goes to France to learn French, and later his place is taken by Bob, who comes home from Charterhouse having grown greatly, and just missed a senior scholarship through being ill.

July 21 Gertrude Plunket and I out walking, and drove to tea with the Miss Plunkets, sisters of the Archbishop of Dublin, who live down here with their Brother, Mr David Plunket, MP, who is secretary for the Board of Works in Lord Salisbury's Government.

July 22 Gertrude and I out walking. We drove from 3 to 5 through Richmond Park to East Sheen. An American, a Miss Washington Jackson and her pretty niece to tea. Gladstone has a majority of 42 - alas! I wonder how he will contrive to drive his unruly team made up out of 5 or 6 different cliques! ... Hayes is away on a holiday, and a new housemaid has just come, so there is a good deal to be done in the Household.

July 26 ... Annie and I to the Hopes' wedding. The eldest girl Nora marrying a clergyman, Mr Arnold. It was very funny and rowdy. We did laugh so!

July 29 ... Hayes came home (she has been 10 days away) *to Bessie's great delight; indeed we are all very glad to have her back again.*

Aug 9 They leave from Kings Cross to quite a new area -16 Abbey Terrace, Whitby, via York. ... *We are greatly pleased with the lodgings and our landlord, Collingwood. All the appointments are as nice as at home - real silver, good linen etc. and excellent cooking...*

Aug 14 Sunday Leo, Harry, Annie, Bessie and I to service at St Hilda's, close by. A very handsome new church, not quite finished. A nice service. Leo left at 5.30 to sleep at York and join the other members of the Royal Commission on C... Communication tomorrow at Liverpool. ... the Collingwoods make us most comfortable.

Nettie, who arrives very tired, remains in bed most of the time. They have friends in The Crescent, the Wares, and there is much toing and froing between the families, Annie and Harry playing tennis every day with the young Wares. They visit Whitby Abbey, and Haddie goes with Mrs Ware to visit the several old furniture and Curiosity shops. Nettie goes out in a donkey chair with Bessie and enjoys it, but still not well. Bessie has her tenth birthday.

In between local excursions and walks on the moors, Harry goes to London to consult with his father about whether to compete for a Clerkship in the House of Commons - this would have meant leaving Oxford but he decides against it. The party is joined by Jack and Bob. There is much rowing up the river - and down to just outside the harbour. Haddie of course had done a good deal of rowing at Antrim Castle in her youth. When they go to Mulrose Castle, Harry photographs them all in a group, so cameras are beginning to be in general use. On the way home (having left Whitby regretfully) they stop at York and are taken over the Minster by Canon Fleming.

Dick Quin, husband of the fourth sister, Dora, calls: he has just left his oldest boy, Aylmer, at Mr Edgar's School where Bob was. Jack joins a new ship, the "Active".

Dr Broadbent sees Nettie, and pronounces she is suffering from "nervous breakdown" and needs care; she is to take a short walk, and also a drive, every day. Bessie goes back to school - Miss Wyatt's in Queens Gate.

Nina Ross calls to say goodbye, as they are going to Mauritius.. Annie, after several visits to watch, starts riding lessons. Jack is back and forth, evidently always enlivening and amusing.

Oct 15 Foggy and damp. I went with Mrs Tyler to Drury Lane Theatre to see The Prodigal Daughter which pleased us much; it is so realistic. ..

Oct 17 ... N drove me to Sussex Place and left me there to see poor Louisa Luard and Agnes Bean, who have lost their good kind sister Fanny Carmichael. She died in Italy on Sep 1st and we never heard of it until today

Oct 22 ... Annie returned from visiting the Macleods. Olivia came with her and staid to lunch. Leo took N again to see Dr Broadbent. There is as yet no tangible improvement in her. The "Active" sails for Portland today on her way to Madeira, Las Palmas, Sierra Leone and the West Indies, and we hope they will be home again in April.

Nov 10 Fog all forenoon and all day, very bad as evening came on. Annie and I to 1st Choral meeting at the Davisons at 9o'c, the fog so thick that the horse in our cab had to be led by a man with a lantern. No cab would take us coming home, so we had to walk. A gentleman kindly accompanied us.

Nov 14 ... Leo dined at Geographical Soc. Annie and I went to meeting to hear Nansen read a Paper about his proposed attempt to reach the Pole next year.

Nov 17 Much colder and dark. I went with N to an Invalid Communion Service at 12o'c at St Jude's Annie had her last riding lesson. Annie and I to Bessie's school to watch the Drill class.

Nov 19 Cold and misty. Annie and I to tea at Mrs Pickering's in Bryanston Square. On our way home by train, she got left behind, and I had a long and weary search for her, and got home quite late, finding she had wisely driven home in a cab! ... they were quite alarmed at my not turning up - and Leo was enquiring about me at the Railway Station!

Nov 21 ... I took Annie to the first of a series of Dances at Queens Gate Hall. Mrs and Miss Cave, Major Gambier, Mr Alderson and Mr J. Burges were our guests. Annie danced a great deal. It was all nice and well done. We got home before 2o'c.

Nov 26 Dr Broadbent pronounces Nettie is better, but not much. Our Mother and May come back to London from Ireland; Bessie has a fall, cuts her knee and sprains her arm. It is cold enough to start fires in the bedrooms. Bessie performs in a French play at Miss Wyatt's. A new cook comes but, two days later, they are disappointed in her *who was so highly recommended.*

Christmas Day. ... We find the new cook has been drinking ever since she came into the house. We had most uncomfortable meals today and altogether it was not a pleasant Xmas Day. Harry has a cold and no one went to Evening Service. The housemaid Parfitt went home today on 2 days' leave.

Not surprisingly, they all dine at Our Mother's next day.

Dec 30 Very cold and very thick fog. Heard that dear Lady Plunket is passing peacefully away. (She dies a fortnight later)

Haddie all her life had been familiar with the problems of getting—and keeping—good servants. Bob relates that when in the mood Haddie could be very amusing about life at Monasterboice in her youth. There was a Butler named Dropes who was a great character. Once at a lunch party Dropes handed round potatoes with his thumb firmly in the dish. Haddie's Mama asked him, first quietly and then more sharply, to remove his thumb—which he finally did, revealing a crack in the dish, and remarking in a loud and mournful voice, "For the honour of the family I was trying to hide it." On another occasion, he had been sent to the cellar to see how much remained of a certain wine and, on his return, he flung open the door and announced in a stentorian voice, "Ma'am, there's corn in Egypt!"

They used to be very proud of their glass at Monasterboice, especially of some delicate wine glasses with very slender stems; once on a festive occasion a young fellow was pressed into service in the pantry to help wash up, and Dropes found him enthusiastically twisting off the heads of these glasses, and remarking, "D'ye ever see the like of that now? By gum, they unscrew!"

Sacombe former Rectory, 2007

1893

Annie starts the year with a bad cough. The boys go to skate at Portnall, and on Jan 7 Haddie takes Bessie to spend a few days with the Macleods at The Yews, Bengeo, Herts, where Haddie comments she never was in a house as cold as this! Her sister, Helen (Dot) West sends her dogcart to fetch them over to lunch at Sacombe, where they see all the children. She finds Atherston Terrace so warm and comfortable when they get home, after the cold of The Yews! Annie gets gradually better and goes off on a visit to Hadley with Mrs Kay and Emily Drummond. The family go into mourning for Caroline Gardiner, Leo's sister, next to him in age and always a favourite.

Jan 25 ... Annie drove with N in the Plunkets' carriage. They paid visits and went to the Ladies Dress Agency. Dear little Bessie went back to Miss Wyatt's school in Queens Gate today. How she will be missed in the house, the bright little creature! Leo calls her his "little Joy Ball."

There is constant searching and re-searching for servants. Annie goes to Ambulance classes and continues the part-singing course at Lady Denison's. Mr Merriman is now attending Nettie, and Haddie finds her decidedly better because of it.

Feb 13 ... this afternoon, Gladstone introduces his Home Rule Bill in the House!! "Confound their Politics,
Frustrate their Knavish Tricks" - Amen.

Feb 15 ... Leo is very unwell with a Choleric and sick attack; still he went about his business, but came back worse so Merriman was called in, and sent him to bed. N and I are both ailing, and we think that a rabbit we ate on Sunday disagreed with us 3!

Feb 18 ... Lady Mary Glyn's children (3) and a boy of Lady Blanche Balfour's came to tea. The boys were much interested in seeing Leo's Arctic things.

March 6 Nettie in bed till noon. ... Annie and I to Westminster, and to nearly all the Political Associations to get political leaflets. We even went into the Home Rule Office, to see what our enemies were doing! Saw poor little Fitz[clarence] Paget, who looks wretched since losing his Mother ... [Caroline Gardiner's son by her first marriage].

Mar 7 ... met Gaga and brought her in here. She gave me a lovely little diamond brooch! She begged N to give up her intended visits to Helen West and the Macleods, as she does not seem to be strong enough for the journey. This is disheartening, after so many months of care - since July!

March 9 ... out early, getting signatures to a Petition against Home Rule.

March 14 ... Gladstone in bed with only a cold! He has been obliged to postpone the 2nd Reading of the Home Rule until after Easter Recess!

March 22 ... Harry to the O and C Boat Race with Mr Hankey and Leopold Dix. Oxford won ... so sorry I could not go to the Primrose League Meeting, nor take Annie to Lady Victoria Buxton's party, but my cold is still too bad

Mar 25 ...Leo, N and Annie to Dawley for a few days. I went to 5o'c tea to the Mitchells. Beatrice Mitchell's Intended, Mr Majendie was there ...

April 1 ... little George Richardson came to Dinner and afterwards played to us on the violin, Leopold Dix accompanying him.[both nephews of Leo].

April 3 (Easter Monday) ... Annie, Harry and I down to Portnall ... crowds of trippers at the Station. We travelled 2nd Class and were quite comfortable ... Annie rode with Harry de Salis. Harry and the gentlemen shot at clays ?tin pigeons. A little girl of 18 months, child of one of the gardeners, died just after Minnie and I had seen it. Rodolph came over from Windsor where he now lives, on his Bicycle for the day. Bessie's school broke up today unexpectedly, on account of the illness of Miss Wyatt's Mother; so she might perhaps have come here had we only known in time. She will be dull and lonely, poor child, with so many of our party away from her.

April 7 A very lovely day, and the wind much milder. Miss Lambert, who is engaged to be married to Mr de Salis, came to lunch ... I drove with Edith de Salis in open landau to call on the Butters at Ouseley; we had a lovely drive round by Runnymede.

April 12 ... N and Bessie took Gaga out driving in the Plunkets' carriage. Annie and I to wedding at Sir Beauchamp Walker's. His granddaughter Hilde von Alversleben marrying Mr Chetwynd; a great crowd ...

April 15 ... N and I went early in Plunkets' carriage to see Dr C. Harley, in Harley St [no details given]...

April 22 The Great Irish Unionist Meeting took place in the Albert Hall. 1200 Irish delegates, half from Ulster and half from the rest of Ireland. Duke of Abercorn in Chair, Bishop of Derry, Alexander, made a splendid speech. Great enthusiasm and a great success. God grant it may do good.....

Ap 23 Sunday All to St Jude's; Nettie left before the sermon. Gaga could only come to us after lunch as she could not leave her Delegate, who is old and infirm, a Mr Godley ...

Ap 28 ...N and I before lunch to see Dr Harley in the Plunkets' brougham, and had it again for a few visits taking Bessie to jump in and out for us [to leave cards]. *This is the last day of the Plunkets' carriage ... Dear Jack went back to the "Active" after only 10 days leave. The Midshipmen in the other ships of the Training Squadron have all had 3 weeks leave. We feel very cross with the Commodore.*

May 3 ... Annie and I to afternoon party at Lady Keyes and Mrs de Boode, her American friend. ... in early afternoon I went shopping with our Mother, and she bought me a pretty "plush" mantle.

May 4 ... Annie had a painting lesson ... went to Sale of Work for Distressed Irish Ladies at Mrs Davison's. Julia Jeffreys came to spend a few days. I went out, I forget about what!

Yes, I remember, I was hunting all forenoon for lodgings and hotels for the Dix's, and after all they are coming to this house on the 11th.

May 5 ... N and I drove in Hansom to leave our names at Marlborough House, on the Prince of Wales and Prince George Prince George has just announced his engagement to Princess May of Teck, fiancee of his dead brother.

May 6 ... Mrs Tyler lent her open carriage and N, Julia Jeffreys and I drove in the Park, and to Buckingham Palace to ask where we could leave our names on the Duchess of Teck, but heard she had no Book. Leo and Annie went to Cambridge to stay with Mr and Mrs Austen Leigh - he is Provost of King's College.

May 9 ... Annie, Julia J and I went in a Hansom ... to Lady Palgrave and to two "Plain Teas" as the Queen's 3rd Drawing-Room takes place today. Julia J took Bob to the Lyceum Theatre, to see "Becket" (Irving and Ellen Terry).

May 10 Queen's Weather! Opening of the Imperial Institute by the Queen ... she and all the Royal Family (except the Princess of Wales and her daughters and Princess Louise, who are abroad,) went in full state. Princess May, who is engaged to Prince George, was much cheered ... It was a grand sight. Poor Nettie, who is not yet strong enough, did not go (to watch) After lunch, Julia, Annie and I went to a R.E.Band Concert at St James' Hall, which was excellent. The crowds in the streets were great! Lord Salisbury I hear was given an ovation inside the Institute. The bad old man did not go - it is said, that he would be hissed!!! ....[Gladstone]

*May 11 ... Emma Dix (*one of Leopold's sisters, aged 63 at this date) *and her daughter Eva arrived from Dublin ... Emma is in bad health and wants to consult Sir Prescott Hewitt ...*

May 12 ... I went with Julia J as her guest to see "Diplomacy" at the Garrick

Theatre and enjoyed it much. Mr and Mrs Bancroft, Lady Monckton and other good actors ...

May 15 ... Annie had some girl friends to tea. Sir Spencer Wills saw Emma again, and gave an excellent opinion of her ...

May 16 Heavy showers. N, Emma and Eva Dix and I drove in open carriage in the Park and to see the carriages returning from the Drawing Room. I went in at the Lord Chamberlain's Office to speak about getting Annie asked to the Palace parties, and we paid a few visits.

May 17 ... Annie and I to Admiral and Mrs de Kentgau's afternoon party where there was bad music (a band). Leo took Eliz. Lefroy to the S... garden at the Imperial Institute. The Prince of Wales and several other Royalties were there, and Gladstone, who was well hissed and booed!!! There were tremendous crowds and strings and ... of carriages and cabs. Annie and I to a very nice dance at Mrs Campbell's in Lancaster Gate. They kept up the dancing a long time, and we had to wait so long for a cab that we did not get home until 4o'c in the morning, in broad daylight.

May 18 ..... Annie and I to Mrs Vansittart's afternoon party, which was most pleasant ... very good music and singing, and an amusing Comediette acted.

May 19 ... Annie and I to Lady Simmon's party at the Albert Hall, where we had excellent private theatricals, a piece called "Cyril's Success." Leo dined with the Duke of Argyll .. Sir Spencer Wells gave a final opinion of Emma Dix, even better than the former one.

After all this chaperoning of Annie, in the height of the London Season, we are not surprised that Haddie spends 22 May in bed all day with a headache! But it is clear, Haddie loves a party! Dr Harley of Harley St is said to be pleased with Nettie, but she must continue keeping quiet and doing nothing! Our Mother has let her house, and then goes down to visit daughter Helen West at Sacombe. May, Miss Renshawe, Blanche and Charlie McClintock have perforce to go to the South Kensington Hotel.

May 30 ... Gaga came from Sacombe to spend 2 days here. Mr Beaufort dined with us; he wanted to talk to Leo about the "row" at the Geographical Soc. touching the admission of women as "Fellows."

Haddie is laid up for a while with a cold and has to miss Trooping the Colour, but by 6 June is able to take Annie to an afternoon party, and then a Ball at Mrs Gillilans, where Annie has a good many partners.. She calls on the Oswalds, only to find that Mr Oswald had died a few days before. At Lady Hood of Avalon's, Corney Grain is again performing. Kate and Gertrude Plunket return from the South of France, looking very much better, and bringing pretty presents for Annie, Bessie and Haddie.

The weather is very hot, and when Nettie and Bessie go to Portnall, Minnie de Salis writes to ask Haddie to join them, which she is very glad to do. Bessie particularly is happy to be in the country, where however the drought is quite serious, and the hay and corn scarcely worth gathering. Meanwhile, Annie and her father are in Oxford for Commemoration.

June 23 Heard of the terrible catastrophe in the Mediterranean yesterday, of the sinking of the Flagship H.M.S. Victoria with Admiral Sir George Tryon and over 400 officers and men. Alas! - We know some of the lost midshipmen (7) and some of the saved officers. Leo and I were to have gone to the Comedie Francaise, with tickets given us by Morris Beauford, but we could not go, with such sad hearts.

Bob comes from Charterhouse to take his exam for Woolwich, and Harry leaves Oxford

...where his career is now ended! I am sorry for him, that this bright happy part of his life is over! He starts work at once with a tutor to prepare for his exam for Clerkship in the House of Commons. At last Nettie is a little better, and goes out to dinner with Leo at Mrs Tyler's, the first appearance for about a year.

July 1 ... N and I drove with Miss Lloyd Williams to Edgar's School at East Sheen, where we had tea and sat under the trees, and talked to Stanley McClintock and Aylmer Quin, our nephews. Little Robert Quin could not be found.

July 2 Sunday ... at St Jude's [the vicar] *Mr Eardley Wilmot spoke feelingly about the loss of the Victoria, and had an offertory for widows and orphans.*

July 3 ... Admiral Markham's Despatches regarding the loss of the Victoria are published today, and make it all more sad than ever! Rear-Admiral Albert Markham, and his cousin Clements, 11 years older, would have been well known to Leo: both had been involved in planning and taking part in Arctic expeditions.

H.M.S. "Victoria"

July 5 ...N, Annie and I to Marlborough House Garden Party, where we soon

found Leo. Our cab got into the string and we were a long time making our way. It was pleasant as ever, and we met lots of friends. Unfortunately we never came across the Queen, but we saw the Princess of Wales, looking young and lovely still; her charming graceful daughters, the P of W looking old and worn, and the Princess May of Teck, most attractive. Cap. Burrows came from Oxford to stay here, and went with Leo to the Navy Club dinner. Nettie is less tired than I could have believed after the Garden Party, but she went to bed at once.

July 6 A glorious day for the wedding, but very hot ... Leo, N and Annie to the United Services Club to see the procession. Such crowds and such enthusiasm, and the streets decorated so beautifully. Truly loyalty to the Royal Family is not dying out in dear old England ...
Leo leaves for Ireland for 3 weeks, about his Royal Commission on Coastal Communication. Harry and I to Drury Lane Theatre to the Comedie Francaise where we saw Hermani. Wonderful and very French acting, but they gabbled so, we could not understand the half.

July 15 ... N and I to Primrose Fete given by Lady Ilchester at Holland Park. It is such a beautiful place, and the grounds quite large; like a show country place! We were late for the political speeches.

Haddie is laid up unwell, so it is Nettie who gets dressed to take Annie out to dinner at the G.Campbells, but they have to come home again as they had been asked for the wrong evening!

July 24. Miss Towers has kindly lent her carriage (victoria, brougham and pair of horses) to Nettie for the remainder of the time we are in town, so it is delightful. We drove out in victoria this afternoon ... and they make the most of it, paying many calls.

On 31 July Annie goes by night mail to Ireland, to spend time with Gaga there.

They go to Harrogate for the summer holidays - Montague House, Devonshire Place, High Harrogate, in lodgings found for them by Lady Dodsworth.

Aug 6 Sunday Chilly, but fine. Bessie and I to Christ Church at 11o'c, but owing to the Yorkshire Yeomanry and the crowds of people who came to see them and hear their band, we could not get seats, and so came away ... Lady Montgomery and her sister Miss Lambart came home with us. They are staying at the Granby Hotel. We were out a great deal. The air here feels strong, fresh and bracing, and is already doing us good

Bessie makes friends with the Fawkes children at Christ Church Vicarage. Bob appears from Charterhouse, having passed into Woolwich (44th out of 50), so that now *We have no Schoolboy left!* His medical exam shows up a small varicose vein which has to be removed in the Pay ward of St Thomas' Hospital. Leo stays in London with him, and manages to dissuade Nettie from going there in a great heat wave. It is very hot in Harrogate, too, but there is a field where they can sit out. Bessie rides a pony with the Fawkes', who also have a donkey, and celebrates her eleventh birthday. The two curates and Harry (newly arrived) play games with them. They all join Sir Matthew and Lady Dodsworth and some other friends for a visit to Fountains Abbey (belonging to Lord Ripon) in a Wagonette, to Haddie's great enjoyment.

Aug 25 ... The heat is quite gone; one cannot sit out of doors for more than a short time, unless in a sheltered spot. Leo, N, Bessie and I by train to Knaresboro', Harry walking both ways. We saw the ruined remains of the old castle, the cradle of the De Burgh family ... The old town is interesting, and the church with its fine oak carving, dating from the Reformation. Cromwell stabled his horses in the Lady Chapel, and afterwards set fire to the church, but it escaped. Two fine recumbent figures of the Slingsby family, one early 17C and the other quite modern, the last of the family.

Aug 26 .... with Mr and Mrs Fawkes by train and carriage to Farnley Hall where [they] gave a large musical party. Very good music ... It is a most beautiful old house. Oak carvings 3 hundred years old. They have Cromwell's hat, watch etc. Also a large collection of Turners (who was a great friend of the family). One of them is better than many in the National Gallery .. on coming home, found Hayes and the dear Chip (family nickname for Bob) *who is well, but thin and weak, requiring care and rest for a little time. He is very glad to be out of hospital, poor boy.*

There are many little expeditions and walks on "The Stray". Bob gradually gains strength but Nettie is back in a bath chair for a while.

Sept 2 ... the rest of our party to tea at the Vicarage. Bessie and the 2 little Fawkes girls rode a piebald pony and two donkeys. They took the saddles off the donkeys and rode astride, to their great delight, and to our great amusement!

Sept 9 ... N and I to the Vicarage to get flowers, which Mrs Fawkes kindly asked us to do in her absence. After lunch, N went in Bath Chair pushed by a little girl, and Bessie and I walked. Bob walked home from Bolton Abbey all the way, a long walk. He seems to be getting quite strong ... Last night, the House of Lords threw out the Home Rule Bill by an immense majority!!!

Bob goes back to London, to do some extra mathematics with Scoones before Woolwich. Jack comes on leave, and joins the Harrogate party. By a feat of planning, Leo and Jack meet up at Chester, with Annie, from Ireland, and go on to visit the Coles at Llys Meirchion.

By 28 Sept all are back in London, Bessie back at school. Cecily Macleod is staying with them and Haddie says: *Had a little fire as Cicely has a cold, but as coal is 36/- a ton in consequence of the strikes, one must be saving of it ... N, Annie and I out in a carriage sent on approval by Bayleys but it will not do ... This day, 22 years ago, my dear Brother was taken from us - and from the Service!* [only the second mention of Willie in 22 years.]

Jack gets a First Class in his Seamanship exam so is now an acting sub-lieutenant. Bob is apparently happy at Woolwich. Leo takes Haddie to dine at the Mansion House - *I had never seen a Lord Mayor's dinner before - the speeches were rather dull.*

Sept 23 ... Nettie had her carriage for the first time, a small pretty one horse Landau. May she have many a happy drive in it!

Perhaps the end of school fees for the boys means the carriage is now possible. Harry, with his friend, Mr Wentworth, goes to Oxford to receive their degrees; we are not told what class he gets.

They go to Thyrcle's in Denmark St, Soho, to choose a sword for Jack. He is having some coaching in French, before going to Greenwich. Annie goes to stay with the Hamiltons there, for two dances.

Nov 10 ... The dreadful coal strike still continues. Coals very expensive, £2 a ton, and very scarce, difficult to get at any price. We have very little fire in the house though it is so cold: how bad it must be for the Poor!

Nov 16 ... Major L.McClintock arrived here early from Paris and went on to Northamptonshire to fetch his 2 little girls, to take them to live with him and his new wife in Paris. He has just left the Army.

Nov 17 ... L. McC and his children arrived and dined and went off by night mail to Paris. N wanted them to stay the night here as it blew so hard, but they preferred going on. I took Annie to a Cinderella Dance at Queens Gate Hall, where we were Mrs Kennedy's guests. We did not much like it, as the company was not select.

Nov 18 ... It is well that L.McC and his children went yesterday; for the gale is much worse today, so bad, that the Dover & Calais and North Wall boats could not get across!!

Nov 22 ... out in close carriage to pay visits on At Home days. We ended at Mrs Ware's ... the Coachman wore his new livery for the first time, so we felt very grand!!!

Dec 14 ... to a Musical At Home at the Campbells. Kate Plunket dined here and went with N, Annie and me to P.L. Entertainment at Queens Gate Hall. Sir Algernon Borthwick made a good speech and there was a Lecture on the British Empire, illustrated by a Magic Lantern.

Christmas is somewhat muted due to Nettie having a heavy cold, though they do play Snapdragon and have a little dancing on Xmas Day. All three boys go down to Hampshire to stay with Admiral and Mrs Ruxton, but are reported as having had *a heavy time of it* when they come home, three days later.

Dec 31 Sunday Very cold and a little fog. Only Leo, Harry Annie and Jack to Church, the rest of the party have more or less cold. Col. Lloyd Evans, Mr Tyler and the Vesey Fitzgeralds called ... only Leo and Jack to evening service.

1894 starts with plenty of parties for all, and Jack and Bob are generally at home every weekend. Harry, after a good deal of hard work, unfortunately is unsuccessful in getting the clerkship in the House of Commons. The whole family are much cast down, and Harry and Annie go off to a dance at Mrs Bosanquet's, and do not much enjoy it. He is soon at work again with Scoones, the crammer, to prepare for the Civil Service exam. Emma Dix, Leo's sister, dies and Haddie has to find a workwoman to help with mourning clothes for Nettie, Annie and Bessie. Cousin Agnes Skeffington visits, before going to learn nursing at a Hospital at Winchester.

Feb 14 Colder, bright and frosty. Gaga came to lunch, and then she, N, Annie and I drove down to Greenwich where Jack and Bob met us, both in uniform. We saw the Painted Hall, and the Arctic Relics, called on Lady Hamilton (out) and had tea in the Guest Room with Jack. We did so enjoy ourselves. We found that dear Jack has lost all pain thank God, but he looks pale and thin He has had very bad toothache, for two weeks or more.

Feb 17 ... Bessie had 5 little friends to tea, and they acted tableaux vivants and amused us much ...

Feb 22 ... Leo took Annie, Miss Sutcliffe and me down to Belvedere (beyond Woolwich) to see the Royal Alfred Institution for Merchant Seamen. We were very much interested in seeing the old men, and how well they are cared for. We lunched with Cap. and Mrs Alderton (he manages the Institution) - rather a dreadful affair, and Annie and I came back to Charing X, where the carriage met us. Leo and Miss S home by a later train. We had a most glorious sunshiny day in the country.

Feb 27 ... Annie and I to Francis Stapleton's wedding party (Mrs Lush) and then to a Drawing Room Tea at Mrs Wells', where we saw 6 Trains from the Queen's Drawing Room. The P of Wales received when the Queen left. "Trains" evidently means the court dresses and trains of those who are to be presented.

Bob goes to Germany to study the language, and they hear that Jack has passed an important exam, 7th out of 40 boys.

Feb 28 ... There have been for some time past persistent rumours about Gladstone's retirement from the Premiership. So far these are denied by his party, but we hope it is coming, and that right soon!!!

March 3 Another beautiful day ... Harry and Jack took Annie and Bessie down To Richmond to boat on the Thames ... Today Mr Gladstone placed his resignation in the Queen's hands, and Lord Rosebery is to be Premier. How long will this disorganized and discredited party hang together without the figurehead of the G.O.M?

April 4 ... Dear Bessie went for her musical Exam for girls under 16, and she is only 11!! She passed, making 91 out of a possible 100 marks!

Nettie and Haddie take some trouble to inspect the Samaritan Hospital, to get a place there for an Emily Ewington (possibly a former servant) and Hayes meets her and settles her there, but on 5 April the doctors tell them nothing can be done for her, so she goes home to Hatfield a few days later.

May 1 ... Leo heard of the death of his sister, Mrs Dix This must be Leo's eldest sister, Marian, b. 1812, whose second husband was E. Spencer Dix: probably related to H.Torrens Dix who married Emma - her death having occurred a few months earlier as recorded above. As usual, Leo [now aged nearly 75] goes over to Ireland for the funeral, and back two days later.

May 12 Annie and I to evening party at the Mitchells where we had music and a pretty little piece acted by the two daughters.

The whole family spend a few days at Portnall [with the de Salis's] and Haddie revels in the spring shrubs in flower and a perfect concert of birds. They also have a delightful drive to Windsor, to the Sports Day of the Middlesex and Berks Yeomanry.

May 20 ... Leo and Nettie to afternoon service and were present at Kate the Parlourmaid's Baptism ..

May 22 ... after being up till 2.30 at the Bishop of Marlborough and Mrs Earles' dance, *...Annie and I to a large afternoon party at Mrs de Kentgouw's, where we met numbers of friends, mostly naval, and where a band was playing. Then on to Mrs Marcus Hare's, small and dull. The cold day did not improve Annie's and my coughs..*

June 1 ... Blanche McClintock's 2nd boy Willy, aged 10, in his first term at Templegrove School, has had Whooping Cough for about 4 weeks. It has taken a bad turn and his temperature is alarmingly high at night. It is well that Charlie and B. are staying here in town with Gaga, so that they can see their boy every day ...

June 2 ... dear Annie is 21 today - her cold is rather better, but she cannot come downstairs yet.

June 4 & 5 A bad account of Blanche's boy. Congestion of the lungs and very high temperature ... accounts still worse. Inflammation of both lungs, and they fear tubercular mischief. They are calling in another Dr. and getting a nurse, at last.

June 11 ... accounts of Willy McClintock better in some respects; but the Dr says a soft spot has appeared on one lung.

June 16 ... my cough is bad. I saw Dr Kingston Barton: he says it is severe Bronchial irritation, complicated with stomach derangement and a little gout. He allowed me to go for a few minutes walk in this lovely weather.

June 18 Dr Douglas Powell, the best Chest specialist, went down to Templegrove to see the boy and says he is very ill, but not hopelessly so. The school Dr maintains that he is, and has tuberculosis of one lung: the specialist says no.

June 19 ... N and Annie drove down to Templegrove and saw Blanche and Charlie who are a good deal cheered by Dr Powell's opinion ...

June 25 ... still bad and alarming accounts of poor little Willy McClintock. Stanley, his elder brother, has taken whooping cough, and has some congestion and a spot of pneumonia on one lung.

Meanwhile Haddie too is laid up in bed with, her doctor says, gouty bronchitis - *a tedious affair!*

June 26 ... Helen came early from Sacombe bringing lovely roses with her. She drove down to Templegrove with N, to see Blanche. Both boys continue very ill; of course Willy, who has been ill so long, is worst.

June 30 ... excellent accounts of B's boys. Willy was to sit up for half an hour ...

Meanwhile, due to Haddie's illness, Nettie is taking Annie about ... *N. is much stronger, to be able to do so much.*

Blanche is eventually able to bring her boys to London, to Gaga's house. Haddie begins to go out in a bath chair, and there is talk of a drive for her and young Willie - but it is judged too damp. Jack misses a 1st class in Gunnery by a very few marks ... *such is the luck of exams! He and we all are sadly disappointed.* Competition is extremely fierce in all naval training.

July 21 This is the last day of the carriage. Nettie has had it for 9 months from Bailey's Hotel, and it has been a success in every sense of the word.

July 29 ... Blanche and Charlie took their boys down to lodgings at Broadstairs ...The Chancel our Mother has added to Mellifont Church, was consecrated today by the Primate of Ireland, Dr Gregg.

In modern times Mellifont Church has been deconsecrated and is now a private house, though the graveyard is still in church hands and is supposed to be accessible.

Aug 2 They all go to Malvern - to a cottage in West Malvern, St Mary's, comfortable and standing high. The young ones find plenty to amuse them, but Haddie is still half an invalid and goes for little drives in a donkey cart.

Aug 9 Harry has been offered a vacant Clerkship in Secretary's Office, General Post Office, which he gladly accepts. Thus ends his long grind ... which bore fruit even though he was not among the successful 10; at last Civil Service Exams he passed 14th, which was very good. We are SO thankful!

Sept 3 Harry leaves Malvern to take up his new work ... *he has had a nice holiday of over 4 weeks, and looks all the better for it.*

Meanwhile, the others seem to have an enjoyable time, with tennis with the Nevills, Cobbetts, and Packingtons and others and trips to Worcester, Hereford etc, though Haddie is restricted to the donkey chair. She enjoys a drive with N and Leo to Eastnor Castle and to Ledbury; also *by the Wyche and Malvern Wells, round by old Colwall, where we saw the old Norman Church, and monuments of 16th century ... and a fine old timbered house (now a farm) all that remains of the Hunting Lodge of the Bishops of Hereford, and the ruins of some of the splendid old oaks, 800 years old.*

They go back to London on 18 Sept and Haddie is mortified not to have regained more strength. Harry, cheerful about his job, is very pleased to see them all back as he has been alone. Bessie, now 12, starts at a new school, Miss McDowell's.

Oct 8 I went to Holy Communion at St Stephen's and was shocked to see how far they had gone UP there, even since Mr Waldoe's time. Haddie sees Dr Maclagan, who says she has never recovered from influenza back in June and must rest more.

Oct 9 N and Annie go to an afternoon At Home at the Gervers', before the marriage of their daughter Dora (aged 19) to Admiral Markham (54). [Albert Markham had been involved, the year before, in the notorious "Admirals in Collision" incident, and his career, though not cut short, never totally recovered. The marriage seems to have been happy, with the pretty young Dora doing much to cheer and encourage her Admiral. They had a single daughter, Joy, who sadly died aged 20. One of Dora's sisters, Annie Gervers, married John Moore Casement, and their sons, John, Roddie and Roy all served in the Royal Navy. F.T.Gervers, having made money in South Africa, bought a delightful, large lodge on the River Carron, at Amat, Ardgay, Easter Ross. Much loved by the whole family, the estate was eventually sold in the 1930s.]

Oct 18 ... nearly all the residents are back in town and a good many people call here; unfortunately I cannot see them when the others are out - for my voice is very weak, and talking makes me cough!

Annie goes on visits to Lincoln (the Sub Dean's family, the Clements'), and to Guildford (Tatton Browns) and Helen West (Dot) comes to stay, with her daughter Jessie: she and Bessie have *great games* together. Jack gets a First Class for Pilotage and is given leave till the end of the month - he and Annie go

to a dance at the Brights.
On 17 Nov, Harry is gazetted as 2nd Lieut, 24th Middlesex Rifle Volunteers (P.O. Corps). There are great floods in the Thames Valley, and all the boys are sent home from Eton. The family is much interested in an election to do with the Board Schools in London - and their party, the Moderates, *who believe in Religion*, got in by a narrow and reduced majority. Jack, now a Sub-Lieutenant, leaves to join "Royal Sovereign" at Gibraltar. Bob puts on a frock coat for the first time *and looks lovely in it.* He is at Woolwich, and has two weeks holiday for Christmas, while Harry gets only three days from the Post Office. Christmas is rather quiet, as Haddie is not going out much, except for occasional drives in the carriage, which Nettie has again. She mentions heart trouble, and on Boxing Day she is ordered a Belladonna poultice over her heart. ... *N's nice housemaid, Anne, left to be married. She will be a great loss!*

Dec 29 ...A sad day in the household. Annie's uvula was cut by Dr Maunsell, and Bob was put under chloroform and ether, in order to stretch a tendon in his toe, which had become contracted. Both operations succeeded well ... 130 days indoors this year. I have been so very unwell.

Nevertheless, Haddie does not cease to take active interest in her clothes, and does a good deal of making-up herself, though often paying shillings to a "workwoman" to help. Her cash account for May includes:

Bonnet shape (vieux rose); roses; green wreath; velvet strings; mignonette; drab serge gown (Harvey & Nicholls); 1 yd. yellow silk for front; tape & belting; 1 yd. mauve silk for front; stocking suspenders. black moire belting; dress preservers; gold shakers for bonnet; 4/6d for Miss Small (workwoman) total: £5.6.0

H.M.S. Royal Sovereign

1895 A year dominated by illness - even more than usual! Nephew Alick West comes up to cram for Woolwich - a *nice gentlemanlike boy - but looks very delicate.* Another, Robert Quin, (second son of Dora and Dick) comes over from Ireland to prepare for the Navy. At the end of January extreme cold sets in - we hear of ice on the Thames. There is an influenza epidemic, many die - one of the victims is the comedian Corney Grain. "Our Mother" is taken seriously ill with influenza in mid-February and they continue very anxious about her for some weeks. She has to have nurses in the house. Blanche comes over, and Dot visits often. Gaga does recover, eventually, having her first outing in a bath chair in May. Daughter May does not think she will ever get back her old strength, and there is weakness down one side.

May becomes exhausted, takes her mother to Blanche at Glendarragh and goes off for a tour of Cornwall with Miss Renshaw. Meanwhile, Haddie is ill herself, with real or fancied concerns about her heart and many doctor's visits. Worst of all, Annie and Bessie are ill on and off, Annie especially worrying with loss of weight, terrible cough and a rise of temperature at night. Nana goes with the girls and Haddie to Bournemouth at the end of March, which does them good. The Paget son who still lives there with his wife, is kind to them. While they are away, Henrietta Skeffington, their cousin, gets married (to Major Arthur D.D.Kelly, or the O'Kelly) from Leo and Nettie's house; she is a daughter of Uncle Chichester and his wife Amelia, but both parents are dead. Back in London, Haddie lets Annie have her bedroom, as the doctor wants a larger room for her till she is better.

Haddie has a short visit, in June, to Cheltenham with Helen Verschoyle and Katie Shaw. As usual, the interest she takes in all sightseeing does her good, but she is not equal to much. Among many other remedies, she has been put on a strict diet - no bread! All the family are delighted when Jack is appointed as one of the sub-lieutenants on the Royal Yacht.

Annie is by now well enough to take part in some of the Season's activities. We hear of the Greenwells for the first time, on 8 July - a Ball at their home in Portman Square. Annie by now is just 22, and Bernie Greenwell, eldest of his large family, is 20 or 21. His youngest brother, (of the family of 13) was only born the previous year! Annie goes off to Aberdovey to join a sketching party. This lasts more than two weeks and must have been a great experience for her. She joins the rest of the family at Ryde, Isle of Wight, where they have taken lodgings for the summer holidays - too tired to go to a dance, just as well as her evening gowns have inadvertently been left in London! Bob passes out (4th) from Woolwich into the Royal Engineers.

Aug 16 Jack and the two other Sub-Lieuts. Mr Raikes and Mr Hodges dined at Osborne with the Queen's household, and joined her circle after dinner, and were presented to the Queen, who asked Jack how Leo was. Princess

Louise, the P. of Wales and Prince George, Duke of York, all sent for Jack and spoke most kindly to him. ... I am feeling so much better and stronger too, thank God. This place seems to suit me well, but I wish I could get about a little more. I can walk but very little at a time, and carriages are so expensive. ... we find that Bob is the youngest officer in the British Army, so we have good cause to be proud of him!...

Aug 25 ... I slept better last night than I have done for many months (without an opiate).

The boys now have bicycles - and use them for many long rides. Annie and Bessie are said to be learning!

Sept 5 Leo and N and their 5 children were photographed in a group at Debenham's in Ryde - for the Silver Wedding. It seems certain that this is the group picture we have. Bessie has just turned 13, which looks about right.

Leo and N. have endorsed a Cabin at Miss Weston's Sailors' Rest with 30 gns, as a thankoffering for their Silver Wedding ...

Aggie Weston's is still going strong, 110 years later!

Sept 14 A lovely day, sunny and still, but more autumnal. At 3 o'c we all - 7 in number - in a boat to Wootton Creek, between this and Cowes, where we lit a fire and had Picnic tea, and picked Blackberries. The two boys rowed us each way. The tide was low, and the boys had some trouble in landing us. They got planks of wood and laid them over the mud for us to walk on. We did so enjoy ourselves, but we missed Harry. Got home at 7o'c, landing close to our lodgings. I did nothing but this all day, and was very tired after it - but I did so enjoy myself!

Back in London, Bessie goes back to school at Miss MacDowalls, having missed almost all the summer term, as she had rather outgrown her strength: but is now quite well again.

Oct 4 .... Annie dined with the Greenwells and went to the Indian Exhibition with them ...

Oct 7 Haddie helps Jack and Annie to choose a Silver Wedding present for their parents - a pretty Marquise Diamond and Ruby ring.

Oct 12 Dear Leo and Nettie's Silver Wedding Day. Henry, Helen and Alick West to lunch. Afterwards an afternoon tea of old friends and relations, 75 came - and Leo and N had 51 presents, and such numbers of kind letters and congratulations so it was a very happy day! and having the 5 dear children all present, all good and well and happy, was most happy.

In November, Jack leaves with his ship the Immortality (Captain Chichester) for the China Station.

Dec 24 ...The American scare about war with England is cooling down, I am thankful to say. President Cleveland has made a great mistake!

Dec 25 Cold, raw and damp. Bessy and I staid indoors. All the rest to S.Jude's. Gaga, May and Miss Renshaw dined here. We played cards after dinner ...

Dec 30 ... Harry, Bob and Annie to the Savoy Theatre to see the "Mikado".

Dec 31 Annie, Bob and Bessy to a dance (grown up and children) at the Mitchells, which they much enjoyed.

1896

opens damp, dull and foggy. Bessie takes part, as Princess Rosalie, in the play "Prince Pigenano" with her friends the Scotts. There are at least three performances.

Jan 4... Everyone is very anxious about affairs in the Transvaal. We hear that Dr Jamieson's party has been defeated by the Boers, and he and a few other officers are prisoners of President Kruger, as well as 500 men - a good many killed and some wounded.

Jan 6 ... We are all so angry with the German Emperor for his gratuitous insult to England, in telegraphing his congratulations to the Boers for beating Jamieson's handful of men! What business has he to interfere?

Jan 8 ... Harry took Bessy and Helen Lacy (!!) to a Juvenile Fancy Dress Ball at Mrs Eardley-Wilmot's. Harry in his Volunteer Rifle uniform, Bessy as an Alsatian peasant. She looked very pretty and enjoyed herself much. The American row is quieting a little. Also affairs in the Transvaal ...

Jan 13 Harry has a bad attack of influenza.... *(Annie) and Leo had to go alone to the Hares in Devonshire, as Harry cannot go, and N. will not leave him ...* Later he is reported as taking a carbolic bath.

Jan 22 Bessie starts at yet another new school - Miss Geach's, in Thurloe Place.

Feb 5 ... "At Home", 17 visitors. We wore mourning today for Prince Henry of Battenburg. As it is the day of his funeral at Osborne ...

Feb 21 Much family illness. *... Dr Harley came to see N. and says she has had "Hybrid Influenza" and must stay indoors for a few days longer and eat light food. Dr Evan Smith saw Harry and says this last attack has been feverish cold coming after Influenza; that he is run down and unfit for work and must go to the country for change of air...* Later he goes to Bournemouth to stay with the Pagets.

March 5 ... Leo presented Bob (on getting his commission in the R.E.) at the Levee. Bob looked beautiful ...

March 19 A lovely sunny day. N. saw Dr. E.Smith .. I dove in cab to see Dr Philpot, who thinks me better in 2 or 3 respects, but I must be careful of this cough in the large bronchial tube, but go out when fine and dry and not cold, and I must on no account overdo my strength, else I shall suffer for it. I may try a very little farinacious food...... Men came to move the pianos for the party on Saturday ...

March 21 ... N had large Musical "At Home", about 150 present. Quite a success, I think. Miss Hedingham recited beautifully, and Miss Simons played the piano, and her sister, Miss Hilda, sang.

Daisy West comes on a visit, goes on several expeditions with Annie, and is pronounced, *a nice, dear girl.*

April 15 Bessie has measles, fortunately fairly lightly. Leo consults Dr (Mrs Clare) Bishop about his eyes. She hopes to do him some good after treatment.. He goes daily, for a time.

April 23 ... Bessy going on well. We were asked to several Drawing Room teas, but did not go because of the Measles. Harry and Annie to theatricals and Dance at the Staples Hawkins', who are not afraid of them, as they have never been into the sick room, but did not wish to have N., who has been seeing Bessy.

Haddie has a long spell of illness, congestion of the lungs, etc. and remarks on 3 June that she has been indoors 72 days running.

June 11 ... Leo, N and Annie to Portnall for Ascot ... Leo and N have been very unfortunate in not getting Enclosure tickets for Ascot. We believe they were too late in applying for them .. but subsequently get them by applying to Lord Coventry direct ...

June 17 Went to see Dr Philpot, who says that the bad cough I have had lately has weakened me, and made my heart, and the gout rather worse. My left lung is delicate, and I must be very careful not to take cold ..

June 18 ... went at 11 oclock to say goodbye to my dear Mother, who drove to Euston in N's carriage and with May went to Chester to sleep ...[en route to Dublin].

June 27 Dr Clara Bishop says that Leo's eyes are so much better, that he may use them a little every day to read and write ...

July 2 ... there were 5 invitations for evening parties today ... Annie and Harry are attending many events of the London season, and generally enjoy themselves - though, on *July 3 ... Annie knew but few of the men there, and consequently got little or no dancing ...*

July 9 Leo, N and Annie lunched at Trinity Ho. to meet the Duke and Duchess of York, Leo, Annie and I to Lady O'Neill's afternoon At Home, where we heard good glee singing.. Leo and N had a House Dinner Party - Col. and Miss Burges, Mrs and Miss Hare, Mr and Mrs S. Parry, Major Hussey, John Ross of B, and Annie & Harry. I did not come down, as I was tired, and it was hot, and the game not worth the candle!

July 13 ... The Queen's Garden Party at Buckingham Palace. Leo, N and Annie not asked - and Leo has not received very courteous replies from the Lord Chamberlain's office about it. Several other naval men in good position not asked ...we drove out.

July 21 Charlie de Salis marries Lady Mary Parker at St Paul's, Knightsbridge, but reception is much restricted due to the illness of her father, Lord Macclesfield.

The carriage goes back - it was hired only for the season - and now they go away - to 13 Paragon, Ramsgate, this time, on 24 July. *It is delightful to be out of the heat and noise, dust and bustle of London ... It blew hard at night and there was a lovely moon which rose out of the sea. The lodgings are clean and comfortable (3gns a week inclusive) close to the sea, and the sitting room and my room face it.*

July 27 ... much shocked to see in the Papers that Mrs Fane de Salis died at Dawley on Saturday and is to be buried today! and she was at Charlie's wedding this day week! [and her husband dies 9 days later.] Harry goes to camp with his Volunteers regiment, Bob on duty at Chatham. Haddie much enjoys watching the little paddle ship Triton, always busy in the harbour.

Aug 3 ... many trippers down from London etc. for Bank Holiday, but we were not annoyed by them. A and B bathed (and Haddie too has been trying a Seaweed or Ozone bath, as ordered by Dr Philpot.) Annie goes to London to join her parents, and they all set off for Ireland and Monasterboice. They don't spend long there, going on to Sir Charles and Lady Burton's in Carlow, and thence to the Bruens at Oak Park, Carlow. Haddie and Bessie feel rather lonely, but the latter often joins the Scott family nearby for expeditions.

Aug 21 A very lovely day. Bessie and Hayes bathed, but found it very rough. After lunch I drove into the town in 3rd Drag, and Nana and I took B to hairdresser, to cut her hair which is falling sadly since the Measles. Then we went and sat on the sands, and found it very amusing watching the people!

Aug 24 ... Bessie to tea with the Scotts, where she fell down and sprained her right ankle, poor child. Mrs S sent one of her sons to tell me, and Nana brought her home in one of the public Breaks, and put Bran & Vinegar poultice on.

Aug 25 Poor Bessie has to lie on a sofa. She hopped down and lay on a seat in front of the house. Mrs Scott and her children came to enquire for her. Hayes got seaweed and sea water to bath the ankle.

They hire a wicker bath chair for a week for Bessie.

Meanwhile, in Ireland, her parents and Annie stay with Helen Verschoyle and then with Leopold Dix, at Farndale. Then on to Drumcar, Co. Louth, home of Leo's cousins, and birthplace of his Father, Henry; then to the Leslies at Ballybay.

Drumcar in 1900

[In her Recollections Annette tells that Ballybay was a house full of treasures, including some very fine old books annotated by Catherine de Medici, with an inscription to the Lord Rothes of the day, an ancestor of Mr Leslie. Several Scottish nobles went to France to take Mary, Queen of Scots to be married to Catherine de Medici's son, Francis II. Next day, the nobles were asked to declare Francis King of Scotland. Lord Arran consented and was given a dukedom, but Rothes and others refused: they died of poisoning at Dieppe next day. However, the treasures they had been given had been sent on ahead, and so reached Scotland safely—and some to Ballybay eventually.]

The Irish party go on to the Ross's at Rostrevor, and in September, to Armagh Palace to stay with the Bishop and Miss Alexander. [Mrs C.F.Alexander, the hymn-writer, died in 1895] Haddie records their progress, but there is no hint that she would like to be in Ireland herself, and she and Bessie are good company for each other. When they go home, on 24 Sept, she says ... *I much enjoyed my 9 weeks at Ramsgate, where the perfect rest and freedom and lovely air* [and 29 seaweed baths!] *have done me much good. I am a great deal stronger, and can generally now come down to breakfast. Bessy, Hayes and I were very happy together. Bessy has grown and developped* [sic] *and is a nice dear good little girl. Had a fire in Dining-room in afternoon, it was so chilly.*

May and Miss Renshaw, (Lucy), just back from Italy and Switzerland, search for and take a house for our Mother for the winter (23 Cornwall Gardens) and then go to Ireland themselves. Meanwhile Leo and Nettie are home, Harry having joined Annie in Ireland., where they stay with the Gledstanes', at Rostrevor and at Glendaragh with Blanche and Charlie McC. In London, sister Helen West (Dot) brings her 5-year-old twins, Kathleen and Eileen, on a visit.

Oct 17 ... Helen and her Babes were to have gone back to Sacombe today, but Henry telegraphed saying that the Church music for tomorrow was provided for, and that they could stay here, as Nettie wished them to ... they went to the Indian Exhibition, where they got a gold bangle for Bessy, to her great delight.

Oct 24 ... went to see Dr Philpot, who says I am a good deal better, but my heart is not well yet, and I have a good deal of gout. He advises me not to be up early except every 2nd day, to walk a little every day I can, to lie down every day when tired. To drive out all I can in fine weather. To continue the restrictions in diet, and to be very careful about taking cold. Not to go out yet at night and to remember that my strength is small and my "tether a very short one". He wishes to speak to Mother about me, when she comes to town.

Nov 23 ... Heard from Katie Shaw wanting hats, gloves etc. sent out at once to India. As I cannot go out [she has had a bad cold] *poor N. had to rush about all day shopping ...*

Nov 24 ... sent off a box, insured to Katie Shaw, with 1 hat, 6 veils and 8 gloves ...

Nov 25 ... 8 or 9 people to our At Home, amongst others our kinsman Purefoy FitzGerald who is very nice and knew Jack at Kiel in the Royal Sovereign ...

Haddie, on doctor's advice, goes to stay with her mother so as to receive a series of treatments called the Schott Movements, which seem to be exercises and baths administered by a nurse and which contain 5 lb common salt and half a bottle of Mannheim salts (chloride of calcium). The treatments sounds most rigorous and Haddie's pulse keeps dropping alarmingly! A dull Christmas, though the family visit her. Haddie is exhausted from the treatments. Little Edwy McClintock (third son of Blanche) visits - he has just had scarlatina at East Sheen School and is spending a week in lodgings in town before going over to Ireland. His old nurse Ray is taking care of him.

Dec 31 ... my cough is better, partly owing to mild weather, and partly, let us hope, to the effects of the treatment. I have been, as nearly as I can make out, 150 days in the house this year ...

In the accounts for July, we find: *cloth mantle, £2.9.6; umbrella 16/6d. 12 pearl pins 6d. chiffon rosettes 1/-; gauze veil 10d.*

The year begins depressingly for Haddie; she is still living with her mother at 23 Cornwall Gardens, and most of her time is taken up with the treatments and exercises, which the doctor says are having an excellent effect, her heart being soon "almost the normal size" but she is still much troubled by cough, and does not get out in the open air till March, and then it is usually to be driven with Nettie in a closed carriage. Her nieces, and Harry and Bob, visit her often, which she much appreciates. Meanwhile, Harry goes away on a tour of inspection for the Post Office; he will be mainly out of town, for 6 months or so. Annie still goes the social round, and a visit out of London to the Greenwells is mentioned. Time hangs heavy, because Haddie's eyes are very weak ... *My life is very dull at present as my eyes get worse and worse and I can use them but little.*

When one thinks of the prodigious amount of needlework she used to do one can imagine the frustration. Books are seldom or never mentioned so perhaps she never was a great reader, though it is clear she is a thorough peruser of daily newspapers. In April, Nana, Annie and Bessie go to Ramsgate again to recover from recent bad colds, but Haddie is still ailing, in London, hardly stirring outside. Friends and relations make frequent calls, and in May she goes to see a court dress fitted on Annie

... *Very pretty, cream brocade train, trimmed gold, lined pale green, cream gauze skirt and bodice ... pink roses and pink satin trimmings. ... all to the Drawing Room and remained for the Train Tea - 5 Trains - Nettie, Annie, Julia Jefferys, whom Nettie presented, Mrs Riddell and Lady Walker. Princess Christian held the Drawing Room.*

Haddie takes advice about her eyes and gets stronger glasses: later we hear of her trimming a hat for Annie so perhaps things are better. She goes back to *dear Atherstone Terrace* on 10 May, and soon after, our Mother and May leave for Ireland: *Mother is so very well and strong!* Poor Haddie is now 59 and Mother is about 20 years older. Bessy and Annie are both often ailing, and Dr Evan Smith shows concern about them. Bessy is not to go to school for the present, and Annie must be allowed to sleep on in the mornings, when she has been out in the evening.

On June 10 Haddie goes down to Sacombe to stay with the Wests - owing to her own mistakes, she is not met at Ware, the carriage having gone to Hertford, so she takes a fly and gets there at last - *Henry and Helen very kind.*
Haddie feels better and stronger from the change of air and fine, warm weather, but poor Dot, Daisy and Jessie are overcome with the heat! She has a very pleasant visit, gets back on 18 June in time for a dinner with Mr Thesiger and Mr Greenwell, who go on with Nettie, Harry and Annie to Mrs Marcus Hare's dance. The Queen's Jubilee on June 22 is a great affair with everyone finding places from which to watch the processions, but Haddie is not up to going. There is also a great Naval Review on June 26 about which Haddie is wistfully glad that the day is fine - just what she loves most!

Victoria & Albert (Royal Yacht) at the Naval Review

July 15 Harry, Annie, Bessy, Mildred Greenwell and her brother and Ambrose Gledstanes left at 8.30 for Henley, where a boat was awaiting them. Went for a very short walk ... all the boating party came in to supper here at 10 o'c. Haddie is definitely doing more, and usually gets to church on Sundays.

July 24 Norah Skeffington was married today to the Rev. Charles Johnston, from Mrs Chetwynd's house, where she has been spending the Season. A stranger gave her away. Both Norah's parents are alive - where are they on this day?

July 29 ... Oriel and Ethel Skeffington dined here. We are much distressed to learn that he is determined shortly to join the Romish Church [like some of his Ross cousins] *She is still living with her grandmother, Mrs Duncan, in Brook Street.*

Aug 4 All go to Sheringham, near Cromer, and near their kinsmen the

Fardells. Much fun for the young, with tennis, bicycling, bathing. Mr Greenwell (Bernie) turns up for tea. He is, officially, looking for lodgings for his little brothers and sisters.

Aug 28 The young people have a very good time of it here: bathing, tennis, golf, rounders, hockey, bicycling etc. etc. Haddie herself sits out in the open air almost all day, and one can feel her getting stronger. She notes (Sept 4) that Bob, at 21, is now a man, and fairly launched in his profession, as he leaves for Aldershot.

Sept 6 Miss M. Allanson Winn and her brother came over to see us from Cromer, and she brought the lovely brooch the Queen gave her when she sang before her at Osborne, to show us.

Sept 7 The two little Greenwell girls from next door came in here to tea. Came down to breakfast, 1st time for many months; but I am now really so much better, and feel stronger than I have done for more than 3 years.

Sept 11 B. out all day with the Fardells. They had a children's Picnic at Sheringham Hall. The Upchers joined the Greenwell and Pigott children, etc. and Margery Lubbock. They much enjoyed themselves.

Annie manages to do a little sketching here and there - the church at Sheringham, St Peter's is new and was only opened in June. Harry gets a long-deferred leave, and he and his father make several long walks.

Haddie leaves Sheringham very reluctantly, to go back to London, rejoicing in her improved health, which is soon severely taxed by an enormous Sale of Work which they hold at home in aid of the Royal Navy Scripture Readers Society. All the family help in preparations ... *I do not know what we should do without Bob, who is so useful and dear! all the furniture has to go out of the drawingroom to make way for the stalls.* Friends and relations send parcels - *lots of country produce, chickens, pheasants, cream cheeses, butter, crysanthemums, violets, grapes, apples, etc, sold by Nana and Mrs Hadingham.* All this naturally results in several days' recuperation and exhaustion, in the midst of which she has to get yet another box off to Katie Shaw in India. *Staid in bed half the day, and then got up (quite unfit to do so) as the servants and everyone are tired too.* Harry and Bob (thankfully, no doubt) escape to the country with the Fardells to play golf.

Profits made at our sale are now quite £145!

Earlier in October, Annie goes with her parents on a visit to the Greenwells at Marden Park. [Marden, originally the seat of the Clayton family, in a beautiful Surrey landscape— lived in briefly by William Wilberforce, some say- had been mostly destroyed by fire in 1879. The Victorian Gothic mansion built in its place was rented, and then bought by, Bernie's father, Walpole Lloyd Greenwell, a stockbroker. The Greenwells came from County Durham originally.]

They also have a congenial visit from Leopold McClintock and his *two sweet daughters,* Patience and Bunny.

Haddie does not always make it to church these days, but most of the family attend faithfully each Sunday, often twice. The family is always At Home on Sundays (Wednesdays, too) and Mr Thesiger, R.N. is a frequent visitor.

Bessy is often ailing during this autumn, and at least once, when she cannot attend her music lesson, Annie goes in her stead. Bessie hardly seems to get to school at all. Annie on Dec 15 goes with Mrs Wallace to the Gillilans' dance in the country, and home by Special train. Meanwhile, it is Nana's turn to be ill and she is quite unwell for several days: the doctor attends and the family seem to give her every care - as well they might.

Dec 18 ... I drove with Leo after lunch to the Rev. Commander Roberts at Streatham, three quarter hour's drive. He showed us very ancient maps and drawings of coins, illustrative of very early English history, and as such of the Identity. Fog thick, driving became not easy for Coachman to find the way!

Dec 25 Christmas Day. The only one reported as unwell today is May! The Fardell girls come to tea and games, and Bob turns up unexpectedly from Aldershot, *looking so well and so handsome!*

1898

This opening new year finds us thus: Leo, Nettie and Annie down in Devonshire with the Hares. Bob at Aldershot in Telegraph Battalion of R.E, Jack in Japan in HMS Immutable. Our Mother and May at 4 Southwell Gardens - Harry, Bessy and me here; I am much better and stronger thank God; the others all well: our Mother remarkably so ...

Jessie West is spending a week here with Bessy.

Bessy, despite precarious health, takes part in a French play at the Lubbocks, and Hayes and Reeves, the daily ladiesmaid, go to see the Dress Rehearsal. Her cold and cough are still troublesome for the performance, but she is said to look *so nice in her Spanish dress (wonderfully white and fair); she spoke very good French.*

Jan 12 Alick West has failed to pass out of Woolwich, and though Nettie writes to Sir C.Wilson on his behalf, he can do nothing for him*; but he can have an extra term, and another chance at Woolwich. He forfeits the* *riding prize he had won, poor boy.*

Bessy goes back to Miss Geach's school, at Roland House.

Feb 5 Ambrose Gledstanes (young cousin*) left early for Southampton, on his way to Mandalay. He looked very nice in his uniform. Poor boy, he felt it all very much.*

Feb 17 Blanche arrives at their Mother's house with her second son, Willie, who has been very ill at home with influenza. Dr Philpot orders the Mannheim treatments for him, his heart pronounced to be "dilated", and the poor fellow starts the "movements" and baths at his grandmother's house.

Mar 5 ... Bessy to tea with Maroussia Grigorovitch (daughter of the Russian Naval Attache.) Mother took me to the theatre to see Julius Caesar. It was beautiful; I did so enjoy it, but I was miserably tired after it!

Perhaps this was an early birthday treat - Haddie's 60th birthday passes on 24 March with only a brief comment, and no special celebrations.

Mar 9 ... the Queen has put off going to France - cause slight ailment and rough weather - but it may be caused by the state of foreign affairs, as our relations with France are very strained!

Mar 10 ... drove in cab to see Dr Philpot. He says my cough comes from the same cause as last year, at base of left lung ... I must put on mustard leaves ... as my heart is rather affected by the cough and violent sneezing from the constant catarrh, for which latter, I am to spray with Cocaine - and to let him know how I am in a month's time. N and Annie out shopping and visiting. I am so sorry to have to stay indoors. I do so enjoy driving out, but there is no doubt that the least cold air makes me cough and feel unwell.

Our Mother is, unusually, stricken with mild influenza. Haddie is kept from visiting her and on 16 March reports, ... *Bailiffs came to Mother's house, for rates and taxes overdue by Mrs Conolly, the owner of the house. (She owes money all round!!) One man spent this night in the house, and he had to be paid to get rid of him. It is most annoying, and of course Mother must know nothing about it, till she is well again.*

Mar 17 Dinner Party of 14 - Sir Clements and Lady Markham, Adl. and Mrs (?)Donbile, Mrs Penrose FitzGerald, Adm Wilson, Miss Mackenzie, Ethel Skeffington, Mrs Cator, Mr Weller, Leo, N. Harry and Annie. I dined in the schoolroom.

Mar 18 ... Charlie and Blanche McC and their boy still staying at Mother's house, but I scarcely ever see them or even May - as they do not come here, and I cannot go out. We know from family correspondence that a coolness had arisen between Nettie and Blanche, because Leo and Charlie had had disagreements about the financial affairs of their father-in-law—and now of their mother-in-law. Matters are to deteriorate further, but in later years, normal family warmth is restored.

Mar 21 Storm, snow and rain. The Oxford & Cambridge Boat Race in terrible weather - the C. boat filled with water and O had an easy victory - it is wondered why they did not put it off in such weather. Very anxious about Foreign Affairs - our relations with Russia, Germany and France are not pleasant!

Ap 5 ... Bessy dined at Gaga's to play games with Willie McClintock as his mother, May and Miss Renshaw were out ...

Eventually, Willie seems to recover and they all go back to Ireland - these McClintock boys are Stanley, Willie and Edwy.

On Sundays now Haddie often goes to St Stephen's, while the others mostly attend St Jude's, where the Rector, Prebendary Eardley -Wilmot, is preparing Bessy for Confirmation.

Ap 18 ... May went with me to consult Dr Macdonald, of 85 Harley Street, specialist for throat and nose, for the constant catarrh and irritation I suffer from. He seemed confident to cure me at once, but his remedies (very disagreeable) did me little or no good.

May 14 ...with Annie by cab to see the Skeffington girls dressed for the Drawing Room in Dover St - Coachman drunk; and N and I had to follow by cab ...

May 25 ...cold wind and overcast, like a blight. N, Annie and I to the Miss Bowers' At Home, then to Mrs Bacon's Music and Acting, and finally to Oriel Skeffington's little tea, where we met his 2 youngest sisters, Winifred and Violet. [Oriel is Lord Massereene's elder son, but in poor health.]

At this time Annie is playing a good deal of golf outside London, often with the Fardell girls and Mr Cator, and her health seems better. Gaga leaves as usual for Ireland, Leo is made a vice-president of the Geographic Society, and they hear Jack has got his wish of becoming a Gunnery Officer. Gladstone's death and State funeral are reported, without comment.

June 21 ... then met me at Mrs Hardinge Tyler's evening party, where I went for a short time. Then N took Annie to Mrs Cator's Ball, at the Watercolour Gallery, while Leo put in an appearance at Mrs Gascott's evening party ... I do not think I have been at an evening party for 3 years! I was talking to a very nice little Bombay Parsee Lady, who speaks beautiful English.

Jun 22 ... N, A and I to Lady Bowden-Smith's afternoon on the terrace at Imperial Institute, where we met many friends and acquaintances. Leo and N dined with Adm and Lady Bedford, then came home early to receive dear Jack, who arrived from Plymouth at 10.30, looking wonderfully well considering he has only just recovered from Influenza. It was a happy meeting! At 12 o'c N took Annie to Mrs Cave's Dance, and left her there, with Mrs J. Campbell as a Chaperone, and we went to bed ...

Jun 23 Darling Bessy was Confirmed today at St Jude's by the Bishop of London (Creighton) She looked so sweet and pretty. Leo, N, Annie, Jack, Nana, and Leopold McC her godfather, and I her Godmother, were with her. [Harry is away in Ireland]

Leo, N and A to an evening party at the Duke of Hamilton's.

July 13 Dark and threatening, but it kept dry, which was fortunate, as N and Annie went down to Strawbverry Hill to Mrs de Stern's Garden Party. N. left A there under Miss Dutton's care, and she returned to town at 7.30 and dressed in a great hurry, as she and Leo dined with Mrs Ruxton. I drove twice to Waterloo Station, to leave N and Annie and to fetch N ...

July 16 Harry and Annie with a party of young people to Taplow and spent all the day on the river. Leo, N and I to Bessy's school to see her act in the French play "Le Sentier de Cremone" She did her long and difficult part very well, indeed, it all went off very well. The Duchess of Albany and Princess Alice were present.

July 18 ... N and Annie to Marden Park for a cricket match at the Greenwells. The Prince of Wales met with an accident today, slipping, and breaking his knee cap. He is a bad subject for such a thing, being so stout and heavy.

Aug 4 Off to Sheringham again (Frogmore, Augusta Street) and the Fardells have a house just opposite. Also not far away are the Greenwells in a house called Elcot, with the clutch of younger children and, occasionally, Bernie. Jack has to study mathematics every morning (before going to Greenwich) but the young people have much fun, bicycling (often to the Roman Camp for picnics) tennis, golf, cricket and rounders. There are at least two cricket matches between Gentlemen and Ladies, when the men play lefthanded, and with clubs (golfclubs?). Haddie sits and walks in the open air nearly all day, and is much better in health as a result. They hire a boat on the Broads, and the Fardells won't let their girls go unless Jack is in command of it!

Harry joins the Post Office department of the Army and will serve under Sir Redvers Buller. *He is so glad to get out of London and go soldiering.* Later, they learn that Bob is to go out to the Niger to lay telegraph wires in the Interior for the Niger Co. *He is to have the rank of Captain and £600 a year. It has come so suddenly, but it is good for him professionally.*

They are joined at Sheringham for a time by H. Dix and his daughter Eva, for whom Nettie takes lodging nearby. He was husband of Leo's late sister, Emma. Annie goes off for a visit to the Bakers in Dorset, and while she is away Bessy spends a good deal of time with the younger Greenwells. Haddie and Mrs Greenwell see a lot of each other, too, especially when Leo and Nettie go away and leave Haddie in charge. Harry and Annie then go off for a round of visits in Ireland. Nettie goes back to London early with Jack as he has to do some intensive studying before Greenwich.

Haddie and Bessie return at the end of September, and Haddie then goes to Brighton for a short visit with Kate Williams. They go in a bus to see the *beautiful Metropole Hotel* and on the pier to hear the band. Back to London, then off again to Bungeo to stay with the Macleods. Sister Dot comes over to see her and persuades her to come on to Sacombe, sending her brougham to fetch her. She enjoys her time there, and on getting back to London, goes to Harvey & Nichols to order an evening gown for Dot.

Bunny McClintock gets typhoid fever, so the other daughter, Patience, a few months older than Bessie, spends several weeks in Atherstone Terrace to avoid the sickness and give room for nursing. Bunny eventually recovers, but is said to be very weak and still in bed, after what seems a long time.
Whenever the boys turn up at home there are parties and excursions - after dinner one evening they play *"the Feather game"* and *"Are you there?"* (possibly a forerunner of "are you there, Moriarty?") Haddie is often anxious about the world political situation, fearing war with France and mentioning the Dreyfus affair. Christmas is quiet, our Mother having arrived back in London less well than usual.

1899

Finds at 8 *Atherstone Terrace, Leo, Nettie, Harry, Annie, Bessy and me, all well! Bob left us on 29 December to sail from Liverpool for the interior of the Niger Territory to which he is seconded for one year by the R.E. to put up telegraph wires. He has the temporary rank of Captain. Jack has been at the R.N. College at Greenwich since Oct, studying hard for gunnery. He always comes up to us on Sat. afternoon till Sunday evening, and generally for an hour or two on Wednesdays. Harry has long hours at the General Post Office. Annie has a bright and happy life of it - and Bessy (aged 16) is working well at Miss Geach's School, and turning into a charming girl. Leo and N. are well. I am thankful to say, I am better in health than I have been for years past, but have not much strength to boast of, and have to be careful of cold and cough, which obliges me to keep indoors. Mother and May and Miss Renshawe at 23 Cornwall Gardens for this winter. Mother not so well as usual, suffering from indigestion, but Dr Philpot is hopeful of doing her health good. Altogether we have all to make us most thankful.*

Jan 5 ... Bessy with Leo to the British Museum to see Sir E. Maude Thompson about an old manuscript book of Leo's ... we are lonely without a boy all day, till Harry comes in to dinner!

Jan 11 ... Annie to Sheringham Hall to stay with the Upchers for a dance and a concert ... B to a children's dance at the Gervers'.

Jan 14 ... Harry de Salis called; the first time we had seen him since he lost dear Minnie ... Harry took Bessy out for a bicycle ride.

Jan 18 ... Jack's temperature still too high, the Dr saw him. His loss of time at Greenwich is rather serious for him, but it can't be helped! He is in Hayes' room and she sleeps in Annie's. N. had a Committee of Soldiers and Sailors Families here (SSAFA)

Annie, having missed a Hunt Ball in Worcs which she should have gone to with Harry, is now well and goes to Marden Park for a dance in the house. Harry meets her there.

Feb 14 ... Mr Hamilton and Georgie called [de Salis cousin] *They have asked us to try and get votes among our friends for his admission to the Athenaeum Club....*

Feb 22 ... Reeves, our workwoman, down to Sacombe for a fortnight to work for Dot ...

Annie we have been told, goes "modelling"with Lady Baker - at first this seems to be posing to be drawn or painted. But it may well have been for lessons in sculpture, because, on 8 March, Lady Baker comes to lunch, and helps Annie to set up the clay for a bust of Leo. This may be the start of the work for the eventual finished fine bronze head by Annie, now in the Royal Naval Church in Portsmouth Dockyard. Sadly, this is believed to be the only sculpture she ever did, though later we hear of her beginning on one of Bessy.

Mar 17... Annie now spends most of her time making a bust of Leo. Daisy West comes on a visit, and the house is often full of girls and young men, with a busy round of work parties, shopping, teas and evening parties. Bessy goes back to Sacombe with Daisy, *and the dear child's delight was charming.*

Mar 30 Maundy Thursday ... after breakfast N, Annie and I drove to Westminster Abbey, having tickets given by Lord Alwyn Compton, Bishop of Ely, the Queen's High Almoner, to see the ceremony of distributing the Queen's Maundy. It was most quaint and interesting, over 500 years old. The Almoners etc. etc. all carried bouquets of white flowers, and were girt with towels. The Beefeaters looked splendid, the Coronation anthem was sung. Going in, we were mistaken (by Dean and Mrs Bradley) for the Grand Duchess of Mecklenberg and her party, to our great amusement! On leaving the Abbey, we drove to Waterloo Station where there was a great crowd of people and carriages. N left Annie there in Harry's charge as he and she are going down to the Oldfields in Wiltshire for their Easter holidays ...

Ap 4 Blanche has been very ill in Ireland, now said to be better. *Her eldest boy Stanley, is off to Paris, to speak French!* Haddie finds life *very dull and quiet without any children.* Later, the usual round of concerts, exhibitions, plays, meetings for charities, shopping and paying calls, has them in a whirl, but Haddie still remarks that Bessy is having very dull holidays. Of course life is duller for the girls when no boys are at home, as they lack the freedom that their brothers, as available and willing escorts, enable them to have. On 25 April we hear that Harry and Annie go to an evening Whist Tournament, the first time this pastime has been mentioned.

May 5 First appearance of a kinsman, Mr R. Lyle McClintock, R.E. He has been in the Niger, where he saw Bob. He is thought to look very much like both Jack and Bob - and subsequently, he and Bob are often mistaken for each other. Annie spends much time practising for a performance of the Toy Symphony, but we are not told what instrument she plays. We know both she and Bessy were good pianists.

May 10 ... N and Annie to the Drawing Room, held by Princess Christian. N Presented Mrs ...... and Miss Tagore went with her. Dot and her Twins came up to see the Trains ... We had about 160 to 180 people at this Drawing Room tea. Jack came up for an hour from Greenwich. Bessy did not go to school, in order to help me - and truly we were busy, setting the tea tables, flowers etc., and all looked so nice. [Utterly tired out next day!]

May 20 They all go on a short visit to Portnall, where Harry de Salis seems to be assisted by Miss Mary Drake as hostess : doubtless a cousin or niece—Harry's mother had been a Miss Drake, descendant of Sir Francis Drake. Haddie finds it *sad and strange without dear Minnie.* As usual, she loves being in the country in beautiful surroundings.

May 25 ... The most wonderful rejoicings and keeping of the Queen's 89th Birthday, all over the Country and in the Colonies and in America.

Jun 13 Jack comes top in Gunnery, to everyone's deep satisfaction.

Jun 23 Reeves, our working dressmaker, was confirmed today at St Jude's. N, Annie and Bessy went with her.

July 5 Mr Mullins, the Sculptor, came to look at Annie's bust of her Father.

July 10 Jack left for Chatham to join H.M.S Andromache ...Captain Pelham, for the Naval Manoeuvres ... And Jly 11 - as his lst Lieut. did not turn up in time, it fell to him to do all the work of commissioning the Andromache, which he did to the Captain's complete satisfaction.

July17 ... Leo, N, Annie and I by train down to Marden Park (Mr Greenwell's beautiful place,) to see a cricket match. Had lunch and tea there; many people. Back at 8 o'clock. [Haddie's first visit to Marden.]

Bessie is taken ill, with what is said to be "Remittant Fever" due to the very hot weather and to her having been unwell for some time. Dr Euan Smith sees her, and lances a sore gum with an incipient wisdom tooth. They all feel the heat, but are busy packing to go to the country.

This is to be their first visit to Shirrell House, at Shedfield, a house probably belonging to the Phillimores, living, then and now, at Shedfield House. *We are so agreeably surprised to find how nice and pretty this house and grounds and gardens are! as N had led us to expect something very different. We ought to be very happy and comfortable here.*

They are soon joined by Harry, *who bicycled all the way from Chislehurst, about 40 miles - he was so hot, poor boy.*

Meanwhile, Bessy is said to be picking up fast. The days pass pleasantly with walks to Wickham, tennis, visits to neighbours, church twice on Sundays as it is just across the road. Bob, out in Niger, is not yet getting any mail , and kind Sir George Goldie gets a telegram to him to tell him all is well at home. Everything is parched from a long drought, but Haddie is revelling in the beauty of their surroundings, sitting out in the garden nearly all day, and in the evenings to watch the falling stars. It is a friendly neighbourhood, with outings for the girls nearly every day. Annie goes with her parents to the wedding of Miss Culme Seymour, the commander-in-chief's daughter, in Portsmouth dockyard. Ethel Skeffington comes to stay, and Jack and Annie begin to teach her and Haddie to ride a bicycle! Haddie greatly enjoys an expedition to Netley Abbey, where the foundation stones above ground show the cyphers of Henry III and his Queen.

Sept 6 ... At 2 o'c we all started in landau and a small trap, picked up Col. McClintock at Fareham and drove on to Gosport. Crossed the sea to Whale Island in one of the Excellent's launches - Jack received us and gave us tea, and he and Mr Duff and Mr Thesiger showed us over the place. Such wonderful guns and their ammunition - 1200 men live there, officers and men, and 1 woman!! horses and several beautiful and gorgeous India pheasants in Aviaries. The Mess Rooms and officers' rooms, and all the appointments are so nice. We were much interested, and all agreed it was one of the pleasantest days we had ever spent ...

Sept 9. ... It is much feared that War is inevitable in the Transvaal - President Kruger is so unreasonable ... The trial of the unfortunate Capt. Dreyfus is drawing to a close in France. It has been conducted in the most shamefully onesided way, and it is feared he will not be acquitted ...[Soon after, he receives a pardon]

More fears of war, and, back in London, Haddie has to find material for, and then make, a lampshade to replace one that was accidentally burned at Shedfield. So her hands and eyes, cause of much concern in the past, are in working order at this time. And her haberdashery lists and accounts at the end of her diaries show a great variety of work that she undertakes.

Harry has a riding lesson, in view of possibly going to the Boer War.

Oct 2 ... What we have known (strictly privately) for some time is now announced, that a P.O corps is to be sent out to the Transvaal for the war, and Harry is the junior of 3 officers going ...

Oct 21 Hal leaves for the Transvaal with the P.O Corps, on a dreary, dark day: Haddie feels it very much ... *News of our Victory at Glencoe: but alas! 11 officers killed, and 22 wounded ... and our General Symons mortally wounded. A great victory, dearly bought!*

Oct 24 ... Bessy [17 in August] *is beginning to put up her hair. Of course it must be, but her long loose hair was so lovely!*

Oct 30 Much confusion, as Robert Lyle McClintock, R.E (Bob's "double") is reported slightly wounded at Kimberley, and letters and telegrams of sympathy start to arrive ... *Went to the War Office, but there was no news there, save that fighting was believed to be going on all day at Ladysmith.*

Oct 31 Sad news from Natal. 2000 British troops and 40 officers capitulated to the Boers at Ladysmith. A Naval Brigade from the "Powerful" under Cap. Lambton arrived at Ladysmith with their big 45-pounder guns and did splendid work - also some from the "Philomel".

Nov 1 ... very little news in today. The mules with all the ammunition stampeded, and the 2 regiments, Gloucesters and Irish Rifles and artillery being left without guns or ammunition, had to surrender.

Nov 3 ...we 3 paid visits in a brougham. Every house we went to had a husband or son either gone, or going out to the War.

Nov 6 ... today's news is that we are holding our own at Ladysmith, Kimberley and Mafeking, but poor Mr Egerton of the "Powerful" has succumbed to his terrible wounds...

Nov 9 ... Nettie took Daisy West, Annie and Bessy to Dr Robertson's Terrace at Somerset House to see the Lord Mayor's Show ...

Haddie is on a visit to Dot at Sacombe Rectory: ... *In the afternoon, several ladies came and we all read part of Schiller's "Neffe als Oncle" in parts, in German, and Dot's foreign governess helped us.*

Nov 13 ... very anxious about Ladysmith, lest they may not be able to hold out until relieved by Sir Redvers Buller ... the Transports with troops etc. are now arriving in rapid succession at the Cape, some being sent on to Durban.

Nov 15 ... Dot rode, and I drove with the 2 little ones, Eileen and Kathleen, for the latter to be measured for a habit between them.

Dot, active as ever, takes Haddie for pleasant drives in the dogcart, including to shop at Ware, where they have to take shelter from heavy rain, and to tea with the Macleods at The Yews, Bengeo.

Nov 27 [back in London] Bessy sees the doctor again; *she needs iron tonic, wine and care ... Lord Methuen has won one more victory on his march to Kimberley at ?Graspan, but alas, many casualties - 105 in the Naval Brigade alone, including 5 officers killed.*

Nov 30 ... to the Norfolk Hotel, Harrington Road, to hear Miss Weston speak - interesting as ever, but sad, because of the war! [This may be Agnes Weston, of the Sailors' Refuge?]

Alas! poor young Leslie of 2nd Battalion, Grenadier Guard, has had to suffer amputation of the right leg. A heavy list of casualities at Lord Methuen's last battle at Madder River.

Many fundraising events are now being held to raise money for Soldiers & Sailors'Families - the beginning of SSAFA? - and Nettie frequently visits soldiers' wives. In one evening, at Queen's Hall, over £700 is raised, which seems a good deal in the terms of those days.

Dec15 Our Mother, with May and Miss Renshaw, returns to 23 Cornwall Gardens ... *This morning heard the sad news of the defeat of Sir R. Buller and great loss among the Connaught Rangers and other Regiments. Nettie went to see Mrs Brooke, wife of the Col. of C.Rangers who is dangerously wounded. She, poor thing, badly burnt her arm in railway accident to Irish Mail.*

Dec 18 ... a letter from dear Harry from Petermaritzburg ... Lord Roberts to go to Cape as Commander in Chief. Lord Kitchener as Head of his Staff. Another (8th) Division of troops to be sent out, also Volunteers and Yeomanry. Colonies sending extra contingents - any amount of Spirit & Patriotism in the country.

Dec 20 ... not many visitors; Mr and Mrs Ingilby were here, looking so sad and anxious. Their 2 sons in the Scots Guards and Gordon Highlanders, both with Lord Methuen, the eldest has already been in 4 fights ... Alick West is going out to the front, with an Ammunition column ...

Dec 22 ... Alick came (with his Father) to say goodbye to Gaga and to us. He leaves for Newcastle tomorrow and expects to sail ;for the Cape from Liverpool ... He looked so nice and handsome, God preserve him!

Most of the family spend Christmas at Portnall (though Nettie and Annie cannot go due to bad colds)

Dec 26 ....No news from the seat of war. Our 3 armies, under Sir R. Buller, Lord Methuen and Sir Wim. Gathacre are facing the Boer armies, and doing nothing.

1900

This New Year opens sadly, gloomily and anxiously, because of the War with the Boers. So far, we have not been successful alas! & Sir Redvers Buller and the others have all been defeated. We have had some small successes, but not much. Ladysmith, Kimberley and Mafeking are all besieged by the Boers, and pretty hard pressed. Lord Roberts and Lord Kitchener are on their way out, and so are troops of all sorts ...the Spirit of the Country and Colonies is splendid. ...Bob is still in Nigeria, laying telegraph wires along the River Benin. We are all well except for some ordinary colds, and have so far escaped Influenza which is so prevalent everywhere, and carrying off so many people

Jan 4 ... John Foster Vesey FitzGerald died at his house in London from pneumonia following influenza; he was first cousin to my father.

Jan 6 ... a letter from Hal, from Pietermaritzburg. He had seen the Battle of the Tugela, on Dec 15, from a distance, where Sir R. Buller was repulsed by the Boers. He was well and very busy.

Jan 8 A sad, sad, anxious day as we were awaiting news from Ladysmith, which was assaulted on Sat. by the Boers. Fighting lasted 15 hours. At last came the news that the garrison gallantly repulsed attack after attack, and was safe, thank God.

Jan 10 ... to War Service at Westminster Abbey. Special prayer was asked for Lord Roberts (who is due at the Cape today) who sacrificed his own grief at death of his only son, to go out and take command of our armies.

We have Annie's diary for this period and she records that their "up and down [stairs]" girl, Hilda, saw the death in the papers of her brother in Ladysmith of enteric. *Poor girl, she has two more brothers still out at the war ...*

Jan 20 ... Mr Larken, R.N, a friend of Jack's, dined here ... and he and Jack, Annie and Bessy to theatre to see "A Message from Mars" very good and amusing.

Jan 21 ... There is a coals famine, nobody knows why - it is 30/- a ton and almost impossible to get.

War news is mostly bad - *Warren's Division has had to recross the Tugela. Ladysmith cannot be relieved in that direction as the Boers occupy Koppy after Koppy, impregnably entrenched. What next?*

There are also rumours, later confirmed, that Bob had been involved in fighting in Nigeria, with "Minchie Savages".

Feb 1 The Opposition, in the most unpatriotic manner, are trying to bring a Vote of Want of Confidence against the Government for not being better prepared for the war! A General Election, or change of Ministers, would be most disastrous at this juncture!

Feb 3 A letter from dear Hal, from Pietermaritzburg, where he is very well, but intensely busy. He was just going up to Frere with mails - he seems depressed about the war.

Feb 15 Today came the welcome news that Lord Roberts has invaded the Orange Free State, and crossed the rivers Riet and Madder, and captured several Boer(....... ...s)

Feb 16 Kimberley was relieved late yesterday evening, by French, with Cavalry, Horse Artillery and Mounted Infantry - such good news ...

Feb 17 More good news from Lords Roberts and Kitchener. We have taken Jacobsdal in the O.F.State. Kruger's army is retreating, and we are bombarding his L... and have taken 78 of his Waggons with food, ammunitions etc.

Feb 20 ... Roberts fighting Kronje on the way to Blomfontein ... Heard that Lord Rathdonnell's eldest son, [Billy] *in the Scots Greys, and Gen. Stubbs' eldest son in the Worcs Regiment, have been killed.* [Lord Rathdonnell, formerly Thomas McClintock Bunbury, is the head of Leo's family.]

Meanwhile, the usual social round of the family goes on, as well as much visiting of soldiers' families, but Bessy is ailing again and Dr Evan Smith says she needs great care, and is not to go out in the evenings. After some days of no improvement Nettie takes her to see Dr Williams, who says *she is very ill, left lung affected. We are horrified and shocked.* Haddie records little else at this time but Bessy's health and the war news:

Feb 27 Joyful news! Kronje and his army have surrendered unconditionally to Lord Roberts at Paardeberg in the O.F. State! If only we could hear of the relief of Ladysmith, but the Boers are contesting every inch of the road.

Mar 1 Heard the joyful news that Ladysmith was relieved yesterday ... The public enthusiasm knows no bounds. Sir George White and his gallant garrison are free at last. We are so sad about dear Bessy that we can hardly realize and still less enjoy, this good news.

Mar 2 Leo and Nettie took Bessy again to see Dr Williams, who takes a bad view of her ... she is to go to bed at once ...

The news from South Africa continues to improve, but both Annie and Bessy are clearly very unwell, though Bessy causes the greater anxiety. She has to have her bedroom windows wide open whenever the weather is fine, has a bad cough and a high rise of temperature every night. She also has a very good appetite. A classic account of tuberculosis, we may assume. Dot comes up to commiserate, saying she has known many similar cases, and the two doctors do not quite agree, Dr Williams being always the gloomier. However, she surprises them both with her powers of recovery, and on April 2 they are told she will get perfectly well again. Gradually she begins to get up and come downstairs, then for little drives.

After much anxiety, Mafeking is relieved, amid tremendous country-wide rejoicing. But they hear from Harry, who has been in hospital at Fort Napier, where he has been quite ill. There is bad news from Ashanti where Bob is involved, and the Boxer rebellion in China also causes Haddie anxiety. Bessy, with Annie and Nana, goes to Folkestone for a restcure ... *We are very lonely without the young ones. No one knows how I miss my sweet Bessy, who is dearer than ever to me since her illness.* Although Annie and Haddie get on well, Nettie comments in a letter to Hal that it is accepted that he and Bessy are Haddie's favourites - "*quite lawful in an Aunt!*"

July 6 ... went down to Folkestone by train to spend some days with Bessy at 4 Priory Gardens. My companions in train were 2 Canadian soldiers, invalided home from S.Africa; I had much interesting conversation with them. I was much disappointed to find dear Bessy in bed, cause, an attack of shingles, accompanied by derangement of the stomach and heightened temperature.

Slowly, Bessy improves, and the family are able to go to Shedfield for the summer, on July 31. As usual, the health of both girls is radically altered by being in the country, though Bessy is not allowed to bicycle or play tennis. This must have been a dreadfully anxious year for the whole family, with Harry and Bob in Africa and the daughters ailing - in Bessy's case, with the most serious warnings about her state. Luckily Jack, though busy with courses and an exacting Gunnery Exam - in which he gets a First and comes 8th - gets home whenever he can and has an obviously cheering effect on them all. Their pleasant, sociable life at Shedfield goes on:

Aug 30 ....amongst others we called on Col. and Mrs Bower. He is over 90, and rides and hunts! An old Indian officer; they live in a house that belonged to Sir Harry Keppel and they are such old-world, old-fashioned people, but so kind.

Sept 1 ... Lord Roberts issued a Proclamation annexing the Transvaal to the British Crown.

Leo and Nettie go to London, where there are hopes of getting Bob home soon - invalided home, it appears. Leo has learned of the death of his second sister, Louisa Tipping, in New Zealand where she has been living with one of her daughters. On September 28 the rest of the party go to meet Bob at Botley station - *...It WAS a lovely meeting, and Bob looked so wonderfully well, but he was very ill with fever before leaving Africa. He seems to have grown taller, and is a little thin. Continued good news from South Africa; Lord Roberts says the Boer army has ceased to exist, and there are only lawless marauding bands about: still these are very annoying, and cost lives. Harry writes that he has been offered the post of Secretary to the new G.P.O at Pretoria. His Chief will be --- Bagot, and his salary £1,000 a year. This is most flattering to him, but of course we shall not see him for at least a year!*

Regretfully, they go back to London at the end of September.

Sept 26. Dr Evan Smith finds Bessy much improved and weighing close on 9 stone. She MUST go out of town early in Nov, as fog would be the worst thing for her. Bob, he says, looks tired, and is to take quinine daily to get the fever out of his system.

Oct 15 Annie hands over the secretaryship of SSAFA, South Kensington, to a Major Courtney. *She has indeed done good and hard work.*

After a good deal of leave-taking and the giving of a dinner party for the young, the family leaves town for Folkestone, there to spend the winter for Bessy's health. They arrive at 1 Trinity Crescent on 1 November, with Reeves and Watson the Cook, and two more servants go down next day with Leo and Nettie.

Leo and Nettie plan to spend some nights each week in London, but are often prevented by the usual colds. The weather at Folkestone is particularly bad for some weeks, and there is a hint of some depression. When Nettie goes to see her mother, Gaga, back in London in Cornwall Gardens, the latter refuses to see Leo! This is Haddie's first mention of ongoing family difficulties about money. We know from family letters that though Haddie was entitled to a good share of her father's money, her mother controls this and very little is forthcoming for her - Leo and Nettie meeting most of the bills; but Haddie's affairs are only one part of the disagreements. It is sad that, in her increasing age, Gaga no longer puts her faith in her Trustee, Leo, as in the past.

Dec 4 At last! A lovely fine sunny forenoon. Out walking and sitting on the Leas before lunch. Leo and N up to London by early train. Annie and I to Mrs Terrot's Tea, where we met several of our acquaintances here. A man sang some comic songs, and the young people played games. I do not know if they all cared much for them!

Dec 14 ... Bad news from S.Africa. General Clements surprised by large force of Boers - 4 companies of Northumberland Fusiliers had to surrender when all their ammunition was spent. De Wet has escaped again, and Cape Colony is very disloyal in parts, and some hundreds of Boers have invaded it. Martial law is being proclaimed by Lord Kitchener.

Dec 18 ... I was photographed, the first time for 20 years, and Annie came with me.

Dec 25 ...drank dear Hal's health, and Alick's and others. So happy to have Jack and Bob with us this Christmas. We all got charming presents and any amount of Xmas cards.

Haddie and Annette, Folkestone 1900

1901

This new century opens with the War in S.Africa not yet over! Guerilla warfare going on, chiefly led by De Wet on part of Boers. They are invading Cape Colony and trying to get the Dutch population there to rise. Kruger is in Holland, trying to get European powers to intervene. Lord Roberts in on his way home, to take up duties of Commander in Chief at home ... The Ashanti War is over, and Sir James Willcox is on his way home.

Harry is at Pretoria, where he is Secretary to the British Post Office in Transvaal... Jack is in H.M.S. Cambridge at Devonport as Gunnery Instructor on Junior Staff. Bob, who came back invalided from Ashanti is still on leave and with us. He is now quite well and fit. Annie is here, not very strong but quite on the mend. Bessy, thank God, is ever so much better, and constantly improving. How ill she was last winter and spring. We came here, on her account, to spend the winter, and this place seems to suit her. Leo is very well indeed. Nettie is fairly well, and resting after all the work and anxiety of last winter. I am very well. So is our Mother, at 29 Cornwall Gardens for the winter. Leo goes up to town nearly every Tuesday till Wed, to attend his Boards, and N goes too, to look after him. There is a caretaker at Athelstan Terrace and some of the rooms are open, so that L and N can go there.

Leo has taken this house, from Admiral Penrose Fitzgerald, from 1 Nov to 1 March, with power to continue. It is a comfortable, good-sized house, but not smart or pretty. Folkestone is cold in winter and spring. I shall be glad when we can return to town, but anything is worth doing that may restore dear Bessy completely, which we hope that the air here may do.

Jan 2 Bob and Annie arrived in London to see Lord Roberts' Procession. Today Lord R saw the Queen at Osborne, and she made him an Earl and gave him the Order of the Garter. Well-earned honours.

Jan 3 ... Better news from S.Africa, where some of the Boers are anxious for

Peace: but they are still invading Cape Colony, and sailors and naval guns are being landed to protect Cape Town - and this although we have about 200.000 troops in S.Africa!

Jan 19 ... Heard, first, that Bob is given a Brevet for Service in Ashanti, and then that darling Hal is dangerously ill at Pretoria - we are terribly anxious. Also that the Queen is not at all well at Osborne and that all her family have been telegraphed for.

Jan 21 ... such numbers of kind letters of sympathy about dear Hal. It keeps us all busy writing to answer them. This sad, trying suspense continues ... still worse news of the Queen, alas! the German Emperor has come over to Osborne.

Jan 22 ... at 6.30 [the Queen] passed peacefully away: the dearest, best loved and greatest sovereign that ever lived! she is a terrible loss to the whole Empire. Leo got a telegram from the War Office to say that our dear Hal was "slightly better" yesterday! This has cheered us, and given us fresh hope. Thank God!

Jan 27 All to Church. Harry was again prayed for. The Church was draped in black, and a sad and solemn service, and everyone in mourning, of course.

They receive a letter from Harry in hospital, dictated by a nurse, and later a telegram to say he is still dangerously ill. And Bob, from Fardross in Ireland, says he has been asked to give up the remainder of his Ashanti leave (to April) and go at once to S.Africa. Leo advises him to accept.

Feb 1 Better news of Hal, at last ...*Today, at 3 o'clock, the remains of our dear Queen leave Osborne in the Alberta, accompanied by all the Royal Family, and steam to Portsmouth through a double row of Men of War, saluting with their guns.*

News of Hal is slow to reach them, but it is clear from surviving letters that he was indeed very gravely ill, probably with enteric fever. All go to church to give thanks for his recovery.

Feb 2 ... this grandest and most touching Funeral [of the Queen] *ever seen took place, and the great Procession through London. Jack came from Plymouth with 2 other officers and 100 men, as a guard of honour at Victoria Station ... he and Bob dined together yesterday at their Club, ... I am so glad they have met before Bob goes to S.Africa. Bob marched in the great Procession, with Sir J.Willcocks and 20 other Ashanti officers. His going out again will be a fresh anxiety to us.*

Feb 15 ... Bob sailed for Capetown today in H.M Transport Ausonia. She takes out 900 recruits for Baden Powell's Police and about 500 Sappers and lots of officers, very full.

Feb 25 ... Such good news from S.Africa. De Wet fled across the Orange River out of Cape Colony, with but few followers, Plumer having taken his 2 guns, waggons and ammunition and 50 prisoners. We have no casualties. French is chasing 5000 other Boers before him.

March 2... [Back in London] *General Sir Redvers Buller has written to Lord Londonderry, Postmaster General, in the most flattering terms of dear Harry, praising him as much as it is possible to do, for his good and hard work in S.Africa. ...Colonel Thompson writes from G.P.O saying he heard from Pretoria to say Hal going on well: lying on sofa in garden and hopes to sail for England in about 3 weeks' time. Thank God, he is going on so well....*

March 23 ... went to see Gaga and had a most distressing scene with her and May about Leo and the Trusteeship. ... Paid visits with N and went to an At Home to meet Mrs Hamilton Campbell, nee Maitland Kirwan, which brought back so many memories of the Past! N and Annie to a musical Party at Mervyn Keating's, where the company was not select!

March 27 ... such a lot of people at the At Home, quite 60 ...When shall we hear that dear Harry is on his way home?

March 31 ... Several visitors, Mr Greenwell etc.

The first mention of Bernie for some time - he has been away, probably in South Africa. It is known he served in the Boer War, and gained the Queen's medal and 4 clasps. He comes next day, too, and undertakes to telegraph for Leo to the P/M.O. at Cape Town, to ask if Harry is to be sent home on sick leave. They hear later that this will not happen - but have to make the best of it as it must mean he has made a good and full recovery.

Bernard Greenwell, 1900

April 4 ... I visited H. Campbell, Miss Wilson ill in bed, and Gaga, where there was another scene! ...

April 5 Good Friday. All except Leo to 10 o'c service at St Jude's. Oriel and Ethel Skeffington to tea, also a Mr Moltens, 1st Lieut. of Jack's ship the Cambridge, a Dutch S.African and pro Boer! but nice. They all played pingpong.

April 20 A long list of honours out today for the S.African War. R. Lyle McClintock has a D.S.O, and we are getting congratulations for Bob! N and I called to see Mother and our sister Blanche, who, with her husband arrived yesterday from Ireland, but she was in bed with a bad cold. It is clear that they are trying to keep normal family relations going, but matters don't improve.

April 25 ... Charlie McClintock came to see Leo about this wretched business with our Mother!! It is too sad! and so wicked! - ... to Mrs Towers' At

Home, where I met Price Blackwood, whom I had not seen for many many years, and his nice wife.

April 26 ... N and I drove and left the two girls to spend the day at Ranelagh where they ate their lunch on the grass and played golf together. Mr Wynne [man of business from Ireland] *came to lunch. He is much shocked at the state of affairs!*

May 2 ... N and I to see our Mother and Blanche (who is better) Very distressing!

May 3 Long letters from Hal and Bob. Hal IS going to Bombay in charge of Boer Prisoners. We are so glad. He says he is practically well again except for swelled legs... Bob has finished his job at Captetown and will try all he can to get up to the front.

On 5 May Leo becomes ill; he rapidly gets worse, and on the 7th Jack is telegraphed for, *but the doctor fears he will be too late! alas!* Haddie mentions "alarming symptoms" though not saying what they are, and the doctor comes three times a day, and a trained nurse is got in for the nights. Nettie never leaves his side, and she and Haddie sleep by turns, in their clothes. By the 8th, however, they are greatly relieved to be told he will probably recover. He continues an invalid, with many kind enquiries from friends, while the rest of the family gradually take up their normal lives again.

May 15 ... went to say goodbye to Mother, who leaves today for Folkestone with May, Miss Renshaw and Daisy West ... Leo is so much better that the girls and I received at the At Home. 35 visitors, so kind and sympathetic.

May 18 Leo gaining strength and improving daily. He sat up in an armchair again today ... I took A and B to the Royal Academy. Mr B. Greenwell met us there.

May 24 ... Poor Nettie and Annie had to go off in haste to consult Mr Bircham (Solicitor) as Charlie McC and May are taking legal proceedings against Leo - notwithstanding his serious illness!!!!

June 1 Got a telegram from May to say Mother very ill. Annie and I down to Folkestone, but we missed our train and had a long wait. Alas, we found Mother quite unconscious, and breathing fast and loud, and no hope "whatever"! Daisy West was there, and Dot arrived after we left, before 7 o'c, and got home sad and tired before 11pm. Nettie met us at Victoria.

My dear Mother passed away painlessly at 11pm today, having been only a few hours seriously ill. She never regained consciousness after I saw her. Oh! what a shock this is!

June 2 Sunday. Only the girls to church. I feel much overcome in heart and body.

June 5 Jack arrived from Devonport, and left by night mail for Ireland to attend my Mother's funeral. He took our wreaths with him. It is impossible for Leo to go, and neither N nor I feel equal to the fatigue and

Anna E. Dunlop
in her later years

sorrow - and probable cold reception by Blanche and May.
June 6 Jack arrived at Townley Hall, where he dined and slept, and was hospitably entertained by Blayney Balfour. Jack went over to Monasterboice, where he was coldly and rudely received, alas!
June 7 My dear Mother was laid to rest today in the Vault at Mellisfont, by my Father, and dear Willie - till the glorious Resurrection!
May later puts up a memorial at Mellifont church for their parents. Family tradition says that May only is mentioned on it, as their daughter, but it has not been possible to confirm this.

.

Jack manages to call in at home on his way back to Devonport, *and his short visit has been such a comfort to us.*
June 11 Haddie sees all the others off to Margate for Leo's recuperation. She hopes herself to go to the Wests at Sacombe, *as I am feeling low and ailing, and want a change.*
As always, Dot is kind, taking Haddie for drives and letting her sit in the garden in lovely weather. But then Dot has to go to London to see sister Blanche, who has come over to consult a doctor for her son, Willie, who has been very ill at Woolwich. Later we hear that *Dr Philpot has a very bad opinion of the boy - consumption: and the only possible hope is the out-of-door treatment, which may cure, or help him. It is too sad!*
Blanche later takes him to Maudesley, near Cromer in Norfolk.

All back to London: Leo better, but still weak.
June 26 Would have been our Mother's 84th birthday. Henry West to lunch

and to talk over all our sad business.

June 29 N and I to see Maria Cole, and to tea with Kate Plunket and Mary Forster. They were much pained to hear what we had to tell them. These are all relations: Maria had been married to a McClintock cousin, clergyman "Father" Bob, after whom Bob had been named; when he died she married a Captain Cole and lived at Llys Meirchion, near Mold in Wales - a family favourite, it would appear. The Plunket sisters, Kate and Gertrude, live at Ballysmascanlan when in Ireland. Kate lives to be well over 100 and we have letters showing lively interest in all family affairs to the end of her life. *They were so dear and sympathetic*!

July 1 Shopping in sales, by bus and twice in carriage. Such a job to get nice black alpaca coats and skirts for the girls.

July 13 ... Bessy and I drove to St Swithun's Lane, Canon Street, to see Mr Powell. Who advised me to have nothing to say to Law with regard to Mother's Will. [It seems that a new Will, very much in favour of May, had been made not long before Mrs Dunlop's death].

July 16 ... We are still much worried with all this unpleasant business. May sent me one of Mother's rings, in exchange for a bracelet, but does not answer my letter, asking her what she is going to do for me!

July 31 ... Nettie's birthday. I have wished her a happier and brighter new year than the one which just closes on her - and yet, how good and merciful God has been! If only this wretched Trustee and Lawyer business were at an end; and we had Peace!

Aug 1 They all go to Shedfield again, and are glad to be back at Shirrel House. *It was decided only today that N should go over at once to Ireland, to see Mr Major, the family solicitor, about all this wretched business, and also to select those things she wishes to buy at the auction at Monasterboice. I fear she will be VERY tired, but it is better than fretting out her heart in inaction. She will stay with the Quins at Kingstown,* [their fifth sister, Dora] *and the Wynnes at Collon.*

Aug 3 ... A and B are taking great care of their Father, in N's absence ...

Aug 5 Leo off quite early, drove to Southampton, then in Trinity yacht to Cowes: on board the Antarctic ship Discovery, with Captain Scott, to meet the King & Queen, who came to inspect her; then to the Stella, Sir Alan Young's yacht, where he dined and slept.

Meanwhile ... *A to Monasterboice to meet Dora and Dick, and finally choose what she wishes to buy of what is left!! at the auction ...*

Aug 8 Nettie returns, very tired indeed., but she and Leo go to London a few days later, to look at possible houses among other things - they have been looking at houses for a few weeks; it is not clear why they need to move, but perhaps the lease is about to end. They go on with the pleasant social round of Shedfield, with parties and picnics, bicycle rides and tennis for the young ones, every day. Annie is keeping a diary too, over this period, and we have her account as well as Haddie's. Neither mention the family tensions in their diaries very much, but we know from family letters, in which they - and Bessy - express themselves much more freely, that Nettie is constantly fretting at the disagreements, and determined that Harry is not going to be done out of his share. Her daughters, though sympathetic, do not find Nettie easy to live with during these weeks.

Letter from Haddie to Harry, July 31, 1901. My darling Harry, I fear this will not reach you until after your Birthday, to wish you a very happy and prosperous New Year, and many such to follow. Indeed, no words can express what I feel and wish for my beloved Hal! ... Your dear Father is continually gaining ground, and very little more will make him quite himself again. I am so glad that you were spared all anxiety about him by not getting your Home letters at the time. You are quite right in the nice way you speak of poor Gaga. She was not a free agent: she would never of herself have disinherited all her other children, her grandchildren and even her servants in May's favour, if left to herself, as former Wills of hers prove. I would not be May even for all the money and valuables she has acquired as there must have been wrong doing in the matter, and as such she cannot have God's blessing on it.

When I am in the Country, where we hope to go tomorrow, I will write more to you on the subject. I am sure you are very sorry for the way I have been wronged, as it comes worse on me as an unmarried woman, without a Husband to support me, and I fear I shall not have much to live on if I am spared to old Age! But I pray God to provide for me. My love and fondest blessing. Your own loving Aunt Haddie.

It will be remembered that Haddie's father, Mr Dunlop, had wanted to make Harry, eldest grandson, his heir, having lost his only son Willie shortly after Harry's birth; but Leo and Nettie felt this would not be right, so it was agreed that the six Dunlop daughters and Harry should have one-seventh each of his estate. Of course, as the years passed, Blanche, Dot and Dora all had sons of their own so probably became less than happy with this arrangement. And, as we have just seen, Mrs Dunlop's Will was altered in favour of May shortly before her death. One must bear in mind that May had lived all her life with her Mother, and evidently had cared for her devotedly. May is 44 years old at this time.

News from Harry and Bob continues generally good, but Harry is tired of his Post Office work, and is looking out for a change.

Sep 16 Haddie records the death of President McKinley of the U.S.A, as a result of wounds suffered in an assassination attempt. *He is a great loss to his Country, and indeed to all the world.*

Sept 19 Sad news of the loss of H.M.S. Cobra, and about 60 lives. Next day there is bad news, too from S.Africa: *the Boers have taken 5 guns from us, and 17th Lancers have suffered severely - 3 officers killed and several wounded - thank God, Algy Skeffington is safe.*

Sept 21 [back in London] *Yesterday we were busy unpacking the furniture and china that N bought at Monasterboice! What a crowd of past memories they recall! Alas.*

Sept 24 ... Henry West to lunch and tea, and to talk over our sad business... Henry, Rector of Sacombe, is Dot's - Helen's - husband. He writes very long and rather pompous letters, many to Leo, over the years, about the disagreements, but generally tries to keep the peace, and we know that Haddie, for one, is very fond of him ... *Heard that Mr Hill Major, our family Solicitor in Dublin, had died suddenly! This is a sad loss to us, at the present juncture - as he was watching over our interests, and over Brodie's actions.* Brodie is lawyer to Charlie and Blanche, and to May.

Sept 30 ... Dear Bessy returned from the Fanshawes looking so well and sweet. Little Joy Markham (16 months) came with her nurse to see us. Joy, only daughter of Admiral and Lady (Dora) Markham, becomes a talented artist, but sadly dies aged 20.

Leo is ill again with a severe bronchial cold and cough, but, though they are anxious about him, does not become as seriously ill as before. He learns of the death of his sister Emily Crozier in Dublin, very suddenly during a Communion Service. He is much cast down by this news and the girls are unable to go on visits and to dances. They again hire a carriage for the winter season. The jobmaster can only provide a brougham at first, but is looking out for a suitable landau. They are busy househunting, too, and are outbid for several.

Bessy is sent down to Folkestone with Nana to get her away from the fog, which is so bad for her. Jack comes on leave and immediately Annie begins to have a great deal of fun, which is not possible when she has no one to go about with. He raises everyone's spirits noticeably, but has to go back to his ship before Christmas.

Nov 21 ...Harriet Campbell and I went to the Imperial Institute to see the vast collection of poor clothes made by the Princess of Wales and others - over 60,000 articles ...

Nov 22 ... Leo decided today to buy the freehold of 16 Queensberry Place. [The family were to own this house till after Nettie's death in 1920. It is still a very imposing house and has been for many years the headquarters of the Institute of Psychical Research.]

Annie and Bessy go down to Portnal for Christmas, but Leo, Nettie and Haddie stay in London, which H finds dull - but rejoices at a white frost in hopes that the girls will get some skating.

1902

Haddie gives none of her customary summing-up at the start of the year. It is very cold, and she comments that most friends are out of town. She is depressed at the dismantling of the house before the move, and her friend, Harriette Campbell has her to stay. In spite of the Whiteley's men being so *nice and civil*, there is a great deal of hard work and dirt, and they all get very tired. Bessy is sent off to Lamberhurst for a visit.

Jan 13 After Church I left H. Campbell and came to 16 Queensberry Place, Leo's own house. He and N came from the Plunkets, Annie from the Caves, and Bessy from the Morlands. Workmen still busy in the house, and everything at 6s and 7s!! We all, except the boys who are all absent, slept for the first time in this house Leo has bought - all well. May God give us His blessing!

Jan 15 ... Pleasant letters from both boys in S.Africa, still at Cape Town, but Hal thinks he may soon go back to Pretoria. They seem much more hopeful of peace now, in S Africa, where we have lately had several small successes.

Jan 21 ... N and Annie to a dance at Mrs Gardiner's. The ladies were all powdered.

Jan 22 ... This day last year, the Beloved Queen passed away - and we were all in sore anxiety about dear Hal, who was sick (dangerously) of Enteric at Pretoria.

A letter, from Bessy to Harry, gives a picture of the house move:

24 January 1902, 16 Queensberry Place, SW. My darling Hal ... we shall feel very desolate with all of you out of England, and long more than ever for you or Bob to come home. All this week we have been tremendously busy settling the house. The drawing-room is now habitable and we are to have tea in it today for the first time ... I do wish you could see the house and be able to think of us in it. We went yesterday over some of the rooms at no.8 and they are not prepossing [sic]*; the walls so dirty and marked. And they look like little boxes now that the furniture is out of them.*

... we have been doing nothing but the house for days and days past ... Mother remarks to Father every night at dinner, "I think we have got through a great deal today Leo," but when tomorrow comes there is always plenty more to do. With lots and lots of love, Your own sister, Bessy.

Jan 26 Bessy is tired out, and has been looking white and pinched, so she is to stay in bed for some days, and be crammed with food. ..... There is still a good deal of settling to be done in the house, and a carpenter is still working here all day.

Feb 5 ... Charlie McClintock and his son Tan called. Tan has just got into the Gordon Highlanders, and is soon going to S.Africa

This is the eldest son of Charlie and Blanche, Stanley Robert, known as Tan ... *Heard that Mr H. Dix, Leo's Brother- in-law, died this morning in Dublin. This prevents N and Annie going to Mrs Digby Pigott's dance this evening.*

Feb 8 ... after lunch, A and I to see Liberty's wonderful Exhibition of English silks, in New Bond St. Quite beautiful! Also lovely made up gowns, all of British make, and a model of a Peeress's Coronation robes.

Feb 17 ... still very cold; the girls skated on the Serpentine ... sent a corrected Copy of the R.N.Scripture Reader's Report to Colonel Farquharson, the Sec. Leo's eye troubles often require secretarial help from his daughters or sometimes, as we see here, from Haddie.

Feb 19 ... Leo worse in the night - Dr came at 4 am and also at 11o'c, and says it is a bilious attack. He must keep in bed today and have light food. It gave us a fright, after last spring's experience! 35 visitors at the At Home. N did not appear, as she was very tired after last night, so the girls and I did the honours. We had tea and coffee in the Square Hall.

Feb 20 ... Bessy and Leo still ailing. The Dr says they are both poisoned with a bad turkey we had last Saturday! Leo being the worst ... Annie went down with the Caves to skate at Wimbledon. I lunched with H.Campbell and then drove and fetched Ethel Skeffington and went to Mrs Allen Campbell, and the Kay Drummonds' Teas.

Aylmer Quin (Dora's son from Ireland) is staying; he is about to go to Woolwich. Haddie records that "Mr Greenwell" calls most Sundays (with others).

Feb 27 This day, 2 years ago, Cronje surrendered to Lord Roberts with his army at Paardeburg. We then thought the war was nearly over - and it still goes on, alas! Leo and N to Bath to spend a few days with the Jefferys. Leo is run down, and N has still got her cold, so I hope the change will do them good. ...The girls and I had a nice little dinner party. Cap. and Eleanor Cave, Lady Violet Powlett, Mrs Beckwith, Mrs Maxwell Lyte, Mr Butter (Colonial Office).

Feb 28 ... the girls had a tea at home, of girls, a good many ... Heard the extraordinary news that I am entitled to an Annuity of money under Uncle James Delap's Will! I cannot believe that it will come to anything - too good to be true! Uncle James is father of James Delap, Haddie's second cousin and possible sweetheart, long ago.

March 1 ... I took Emily Vesey Fitzgerald out driving, as she has had an accident. The girls and I to a Ping Pong tournament at Col. Jocelyn's. We had another little dinner, only 7 in all.

Mar 6 ... Harry de Salis came to stay 2 nights. The girls to tea at the

Greenwells ... I gave up my room to Harry de Salis ...

Mar 8 ... Reeves, the daily dressmaker, left today, having worked more than 5 years for us, and made all our gowns so well. She is a great loss.

Mar 10 ... Had a very nice letter from James Delap. Heard this evening that the Boers under Dela Rue, surprised Lord Methuen (dressed up like our men). He is wounded and a prisoner, along with a large number of our troops and 4 guns and stores. We have 40 killed and 80 wounded, a sad reverse! in Western Transvaal.

Mar 11 ... Mr Bevan most kindly came to see N and me about the Annuity in Col. Delap's Will. His father was one of his Trustees.

Mar 12 ... Another nice letter from James Delap, saying he believes my Annuity comes off the Coolfore Property, Monasterboice.

Mar 18 ... N and I to Reeves for N to fit on, and then to Somerset House, where we verified the extract from Col. Delap's Will, about the Annuity. The horse fell down, but was not hurt ... Heard from Mr Bevan that having searched the old ledgers of the Bank, he can find nothing that throws light on the Annuity. Heard also from James Delap on the subject - nothing encouraging.

Mar 19 ... Heard that the Legacy my Mother left me is nil, after paying all the expenses it was charged with: it is hard, and wrong! ...

Mar 21 ... N and I to Mr Randall's Studio to see a portrait of our Mother ... Pleasant letters from the 3 boys - Harry at Pretoria, Jack in Royal Sovereign cruising in the Mediterranean, and Bob at Capetown.

Mar 24 ... Leo took the Chair at one of Mr Finn's meetings for the Poor Jews ... My birthday!

Mar 30 Easter Sunday ... Leo and N in cab to St Jude's. I went to nearest church, St Augustine's, Queen's Gate, but did not like it, though the music was good.

April 6 Mr F Oldfield, lately back from S.Africa, called. He saw Harry and Bob at Cape Town. Mr Preece of the Post Office Corps called. Harry relieved him at Pretoria a month ago. He told us lots about him, so interesting; and maybe he does not like him, and praise him!!! This is transcribed exactly, but hard to fathom! However, we know that Harry's humour was sometimes of a sarcastic turn, as his Mother gently points out in at least one letter.

April 9 ... To Reeves to fit on ... Mr Wynne and his two girls, who are staying in London came. He advised me to employ a Dublin Solicitor, Mr P. Murphy about the Annuity... A new Cook, Warner, came. We hope she will be better than the one who has just left.

April 14 ... N and I to Lord Chamberlain's office, and heard that N would be asked to a Court on May 16th, and might present Bessy, and Mabel Vesey FitzGerald. After lunch, N and I paid visits, and to Mrs Rawlings' Tea, where we saw a Japanese painting fans etc.

April 16. ... Took dear Bessy to Waterloo and saw her off for Exmouth to stay with the Leopold McCs. After lunch drove and left Leo at Stafford House for a Committee about our Food Supply in time of war ...

April 18 ... Harry de Salis, May Drake and Dottie and Daisy to lunch. Charlie West has done splendidly having passed out Midshipman No. 4 out of the Britannia! N, Annie and I to tea at Harriet Campbell's to meet Crickie Cox and her two dear little children.

May 1 ... A and B down to Sheerness to stay with Adm. and Mrs Markham at Admiralty House for a Fancy Dress Dance. A goes as a poppy, and B as an Alsatian peasant ... Lady Rathdonnell to tea. She talked much about Hal and particularly Bob, whom she had known so well in South Africa.

May 10 ... Terrible news from West Indies; outbreak of Volcanoes and Earthquakes in Martinique and (less bad) in our own St Vincent. Great loss of life and property.

May 13 ... Good news from S.Africa. Over 800 Boers accounted for last week, but we know nothing further of the Peace Negotiations.

May 15 ... This day last year, I said goodbye to my Mother at her house in Cornwall Gardens. How little I thought that I should never see her again, except on her Death Bed!

May 16 Wet most of day. Dottie and Daisy to lunch; and spend afternoon to see Bessy. About 20 to 25 other friends to tea: rather a cockie-ollie party!! All sorts of people. Ethel S. dined here in her pink and silver Train. Mrs Vesey FitzGerald came in after dinner in red and white and they all went off to the Palace at 9 o'clock. It was a terrible crowd and thoroughly mismanaged. Bessy put on her Court Dress from 5 to 6.30 for friends to come and see her; and lovely she looked. Empire dress of white satin covered with Point d'Esprit net. Bodice of pearls, and white ostrich feathers round shoulders. Train of white brocade lined with white satin, with frill of Point d'Esprit.

Bessy in her Court Dress

They all go down to Portnall for a short visit - Haddie as usual revelling in her country surroundings.

May 24 ... From day to day, we are all waiting and hoping to hear that Peace has been concluded, as the Boer delegates are in conference at Pretoria, under a Safe Conduct from Lord Kitchener.

May 26 ... I had a letter from dear Hal written in pencil from Hospital at Pretoria. His cuts and bruises were better but he had a little fever ... Saturday's paper says he was discharged to duty, so we trust he is all right again [He had had quite a serious fall from his horse]

May 27 *Dear Annie is engaged to Bernard Greenwell, who has loved her for years!! God bless her! ... Bernie Greenwell dined here; he goes to Salisbury Plain tomorrow for a fortnight's training with his Yoeomanry and is very sorry for himself!*

Annie relates in her own diary that, while away staying with Georgie Hamilton, her mother writes that Bernard will be coming to visit her, obstacles to their engagement having been removed. His father had, till now, evidently felt Bernie could not yet support a wife, and he was still young, but now he had agreed to settle the Co. Durham property on him. So, on the 27th Annie records: *Bernie Greenwell came about 4 o'c and I have promised to marry him, and, as there are no longer any money difficulties, we can be really engaged. It does seem odd! I'm sure we shall be very happy. God grant we may. He took me off to 17 Portman Square in a hansome ...*

Letter from Haddie to Harry, May 30, 1902:

My darling Hal, You have given me so much pleasure by writing to me, for although I am allowed to read your letters to your Mother, it is charming to get one all to myself some times. We were anxious about your being hurt about the head ... I am sure it was not your Pony's fault, and so I bear her no grudge, and I hope you will have many more nice rides on her back ...

Your mother is writing to you about the great news of dear Annie, of course we have all known for a long time past that it was likely to come off. We all like Bernard so much. He is such a nice, good little fellow, and he has behaved so very well throughout in very trying circumstances. I think I never knew a case of greater love than his for Annie, and I think she has every prospect of happiness. And so has he, for he has drawn a great prize in Annie. She grows nicer and dearer and sweeter every day, and she will be a great loss in her home, for although she is not likely to go far away, it is never the same thing as living together in one house and could not be even were she to live next door. Poor Bessy will miss her sadly for they are inseparable companions, day and night.

Annie has got a lovely engagement ring of Diamonds and Sapphires. Another pleasant thing in this engagement is, that all the Greenwell family like Annie and will welcome her into their midst. We can talk and think of little else. Bernard is away soldiering on Salisbury Plain with his Yeomanry for a

fortnight. He is very sorry for himself!! ...
I took Bessy to her first London Dinner Party last night. She behaved as well and as demurely as if she were 30!!! And she looks 16, and so pretty! Fond love to my Own Hal from his loving Aunt Haddie.

June 1 Sunday. Fine and warm. B.Greenwell, Leo, N A and B to St Jude's and Holy Communion. A to lunch with the Greenwells, and back to tea. Bernard staid for supper and prayers. He goes back to Salisbury tomorrow early. PEACE SIGNED at Pretoria on Saturday night, May 31st. Thank God for the joyful news. Peace with Honour, no concessions on our part! We heard it this evening, but the Govt. knew it late last night. A good many visitors.
June 3 Dear Annie's Birthday, [29] *and the Announcement of her engagement appeared today in the Morning Post ...N, B and I drove to the Lady Mayoress' Reception at the Mansion Ho. and then to 4 other At Homes. Annie too tired to go on to face all the congratulations of friends. Mr Greenwell (snr.) and his daughter Kathleen called, and brought A a pretty pearl and sapphire bracelet ...*
June 5 Kate Plunket called to bring Annie her's and Gertrude's wedding present, a most lovely bracelet set with Pearls and Turquoises. This is the first wedding present she has received - Heaps of letters continue to come.
June 8 Sunday Thanksgiving Day for Peace All over the Empire this is the Day of Thanksgiving for Peace - the King, Queen and Royal Family to St Paul's.

Peace celebrations, Pretoria, 1902

June 10 ... Jack telegraphed his good wishes to Annie from Gibraltar where the Royal Sovereign is ...

June 14 .. A man came to show some telescopic photos. Leo and N drove and paid visits and saw Adm. Sir John Fisher, just come back from the Mediterranean Command. He praised our dear Jack most warmly. B.Greenwell, back from Salisbury, came here and had lunch and tea and dinner. A letter from Bob, with some excellent photos of himself, but nothing from Hal.

June 17 ... Today's paper gives Hal's name as one of the Officers in S.Africa recommended by Lord Roberts.

June 18 ... Bernie G took Annie off to dine at Portman Square and then took her by two Tubes to the City, to see the Coronation illuminations.

June 19 ...Leo, N and the two girls to a big dinner at Portman Square, where they had a conjuror after dinner. The two girls looked charming ...

June 21 ... Annie down to Marden Park with B.G. Bessy lunched with Mr and Mrs Mahon and went with them to Hurlingham where they saw the Americans beaten at Polo by the English. Harriet Campbell took me to an excellent "Coronation" Concert ...

June 22 ... All to St Jude's where the Bishop of London (Winington T ....) preached and unveiled a monument to the Parishioners who fell in the war. B.G. took Annie to lunch at Portman Square and to St Paul's at 3o'c to hear the Bishop of Stepney. Nearly all the sermons today have reference to the approaching Coronation.

But next day Haddie gives a solemn account of the King's worsening illness and a serious operation - the Coronation is postponed, to everyone's disappointment.

June 25 ... B.G. came and took Annie away to sleep at Portman Square and go down tomorrow to Mr G's yacht "Hersilia" till Monday. It was to have been for the Naval Review.

[The Greenwells'steam yacht Hersilia was used for minesweeping in the 1914-18 War, and was torpedoed to destruction then.]

Haddie's diary is filled with the latest bulletins as to the King's health, which gradually improves. Meanwhile they are all embarked on a hectic round of shopping, constant gaieties with the Greenwells (Bessy often included) and on July 18 they look at *a furnished flat for A and B.G - but it was quite too dirty.*

July 23 [In the coldest July known for ten years] ... *N, B and I to St Peter's Eaton Square to see the 2 McClintock girls, married to the 2 young Willies!* [identities unknown.Ed.]

July 26 [following a charming drive with Annie to Letitia Jeffreys at Wharton Cottage, Ascot] ... *So tired, I did not get up early. Leo, N and the two girls to Lord Strathcona's Garden Party at Knebworth. Last day of carriage, and Leo is not going to hire any longer from Offord, who has treated him in a mean, shabby way.* Twice the horse has fallen, and Haddie considers it dangerous. *A letter from Bob at Capetown. He is low about his prospects as promotion is so slow in the R.E.*

July 28 ... Ella Harman to dinner and she and I and the two girls to Mr Greenwell's Box at the Opera, where we saw Verdi's Rigoletto. Mme Melba was charming in every way, and Signor Caruso as the Duke a great success ... Such a delightful treat! I had so longed to go to an Opera: and now have gone for the first (and perhaps the last) time in my life! The generous and fun-loving Greenwells add to everyone's enjoyment.

July 31 They all go down to Shedfield, except for Annie, who goes to Marden. They take up again their pleasant life there, with travels in the donkey cart, and at the Curdridge Coronation Games Bessy wins a prize for tent-pegging on her bicycle.

Aug 5 ... Letters from Hal and Bob, both at Capetown. They hope, but are not sure, to be coming home soon! Too delightful!

Aug 7 Leo and N have been offered seats in the Abbey for the Coronation; but it comes too late, as we are in the country, and Leo would have to get K.C.B robes, and N has not got very suitable clothes for the occasion, as black is not allowed ... A letter from Annie, so happy at Marden and riding in the evenings with Bernard ...

Aug 8 ... Constance Skeffington cannot come here as asked, tomorrow or Monday. We are not sorry ... Hal is gazetted a Captain in the 24th Middlesex.

Aug 9 ... We all went to Church for the Coronation Service. Mrs Franklyn's son in the Durham Lt. Infantry came back from the War today, and was given an address and reception in this village, with triumphal arches, band etc. We went to look on. Today our King and Queen were crowned at Westminster Abbey with great pomp and I trust and believe, with very thankful hearts. How I would have liked to have seen it: Annie saw the procession with the Greenwells.

Aug 14 Leo, Henry West, B and I at 11 o'c left for Southsea. drove to Botley, then train and tram ... Got on board Excursion steamer, and steamed round and up and down the Fleet assembled for the Review next Saturday. The two Dupuis girls and their brother and a Mr Spenser joined us. Fortunately we had but little rain when on board and it was delightful. We saw several of Jack's former ships: ... and our own old "Northampton" ...

Aug 16 ... Leo, N and the 2 girls drove early into Gosport and thence on board Mr Greenwell's yacht Hersilia to see the Fleet (107 ships) reviewed by the King ... The evening turned very bad - lightning and a gale of wind and such torrents of rain that most of the crowds who went to see the Fleet illuminated, got soaked.

Aug 17 ... A letter from Bob, at Capetown, saying alas! (for us) that he has taken service under his present Chief, for surveying work in South Africa for 3 or 4 years, so adieu to the hope of having him at Annie's wedding ...

Aug 18 Pours of rain all day- was there ever such a summer? ... Dear Bessy's birthday! How vividly I remember this day 20 years ago at Halifax, and our joy at her birth, and she has been a joy to us ever since. A dull birthday for her, indoors all day in this wee house.

Aug 23 ... letters from all 3 boys. Harry hopes to be home rather early in October! It seems too good to be true! Bob expects to have a pleasant out-of-doors life for the next 3 years. God grant it, and spare us all to meet again. He is likely to go to the Transvaal, a pleasant change from Capetown.

Aug 26 ... N and the 2 girls to a garden Party, given by the Carpenter Garniers at their beautiful place, Rookesbury near Wickham ...

Sept 4 ... we had a good many people to tea and tennis. 3 Alexanders, 3 Carpenter-Garniers, 2 Dukes, 2 Gladstones, Miss A Farquahar, Mrs Phillimore and the curate Mr Egremont ...

Back in London, the Quin family comes for a few days' visit - Dora and her daughter Auriel stay in the house, while husband Dick and son Aylmer are at the Harrington Hotel. Henry and Dot West come up too, to see them. Haddie is sad that her great friend, Harriet Campbell is leaving for Australia. She goes for a little visit to Holbrook Hall, Sudbury, Suffolk staying with Mrs Mitchell and Miss Harmer, who send their carriage to meet her. ... *This Place and House are quite charming: the gardens and greenhouses lovely, and Mrs Mitchell so kind.*

They make several excursions - at Sudbury: *The old Church dates from early 17th century, or earlier. There are 4 large stone statues, of the 4 Evangelists, standing on the top of the Tower. Cromwell had their heads cut off, and there they remain, headless.*

A small collection of letters survive between Annie and Bernie during their engagement, when he was obliged to be off with his Yeomanry. Their relationship develops quickly, and one can sense his great devotion and her more cautious happiness. She shows some natural apprehension at the great change coming in her life, and though she summons all her energy to keep up with him, we know she is not robust; one note refers to anxiety he has shown on this score, though she asserts she is really perfectly strong. Gradually she becomes more relaxed and ready to tease him, though

MISS A. E. McCLINTOCK

MR. B. E. GREENWELL.

sounding alarmed when he admits he is considering buying a motorcar! Mr Greenwell, senior, is impatient at all the discussion about a date for the wedding and November is eventually decided upon. Annie at one stage wonders if he really approves of her as a daughter-in-law—but her doubts are set at rest by much kindness from both Bernie's parents, and a magnificent wedding-present.

Oct 13 ...Reeves comes to fit on bridesmaids' dresses and hats for Bessy and Ethel Skeffington.

Nov 1 ... Annie went to dine and sleep at Miss Macneill's, so as to be in St Jude's Parish, for the Calling of her Banns tomorrow.

Nov 5 ... Mr and Mrs Greenwell sent Annie a wedding gift of a beautiful diamond necklace.

Nov 7 ... Annie's wedding presents are now coming in fast. Most of them are so pretty ... I can scarcely realise the joy that awaits us tomorrow!

*Nov 8 ***********Dear Hal arrived ... early this morning at Southampton. Leo and N drove to meet him at Waterloo. He looks so well, and the marks of his accident are scarcely visible on his face.*

Nov 9 Sunday A beautiful day. All to St Jude's. Leo and N returned thanks in church, for dear Hal's safe return, and Annie's Banns were read for the 2nd time.

Nov 11 ...Fitting on and shopping. Dot and her two little twin girls to luncheon and tea.

*Nov 14 ... Shopping and fitting on as usual. N saw the Dr, who says it is chill and indigestion. Mrs F Colvin (*Isobel McC Bunbury*) called and spoke much of Bob who she had known so well at Capetown.*

Nov 15 ... N in bed all day. Girls and I shopping and fitting ... A slept at Miss MacNeill's for the last time. [In order to be married at St Jude's, Annie has to sleep in the actual parish a certain number of days.] *Such lots of presents keep coming in for Annie, and Bernie gets a good many, too.*

Nov 17 ... Fitting on my gown for wedding at Reeves. Shopping with Annie, N better, but very shaky... Gunters' men came into the house early to take away the furniture out of the sitting rooms in vans.

Nov 18 ... Bessy arranging the presents. We had a good many friends to tea and to see the presents, and numbers of old servants and their friends and tradespeople came later.

*Nov 19 ***A cold, dark dry day*** Dear Annie was married today at St Jude's at 2.30 by Bishop Montgomery and 2 other clergymen. She looked*

MISS ANNA E. McCLINTOCK,

Daughter of Admiral Sir L. McClintock, K.C.B., Married to Mr. B. Eyre Greenwell on November 19.
This Photograph Shows the Bride in her Wedding Dress.

GREENWELL—McCLINTOCK.

There was a pretty wedding at St. Jude's Church, South Kensington, S.W., on the 19th inst., the bride being Miss Anna Elizabeth McClintock, elder daughter of Admiral Sir Leopold and Lady McClintock, of 16, Queensberry Place, S.W., and the bridegroom Mr. Bernard Eyre Greenwell, eldest son of Mr. and Mrs. Walpole Greenwell, of Marden Park, Godstone, Surrey. The ceremony was performed by the Right Rev. Henry Montgomery, D.D., assisted by the Rev. F. Leveson-Gower (brother-in-law of the bridegroom) and the Rev. Prebendary Eardley Wilmot, Vicar of the Parish. Admiral Sir Leopold McClintock gave his daughter away. She wore a gown of white satin, trimmed with old lace, chiffon, and pearl passementerie, with a tulle veil covering a spray of orange-blossoms and jasmine, and she carried a large bouquet of choice white exotics, tied with white satin streamers. There were five bridesmaids—Miss Elisabeth McClintock (sister of the bride), the Misses Mildred and Aubrey Greenwell (sisters of the bridegroom), the Hon. Ethel Foster-Skeffington, and Miss Daisy West (cousin of the bride) who wore dresses of white crêpe de chine, trimmed with lace threaded with gold, and large black beaver hats, trimmed with black ostrich feathers and gold and green chiffon sashes. Each wore a green enamel and pearl brooch and carried a pretty bouquet of roses, tied with satin ribbon (the gifts of the bridegroom). Mr. Aynesley Greenwell (brother of the bridegroom) acted as best man. At the conclusion of the ceremony a large reception was held at 16, Queensberry Place, and later the bride and bridegroom left for Wales, where they are spending their honeymoon. The bride travelled in a smart costume of red cloth, trimmed with velvet to match and white passementerie. The coat had an old lace collar, and was finished off with paste buttons, while her large black moiré hat was trimmed with ostrich feathers. The presents were very numerous, and included, from Admiral Sir Leopold and Lady McClintock, a pearl and diamond ornament, a silver-mounted claret-jug, and a cheque; from Mr. and Mrs. Walpole Greenwell, a canteen of silver, a diamond necklace, and a pony-trap; and from the bride's sisters and brothers, a diamond star.

charming and her dress was lovely. 5 bridesmaids - Bessy, Ethel Skeffington, Daisy West and two Greenwells. Annie and Bernie left for Monmouthshire. Nearly 400 guests and over 400 presents.

Leo, N, B, Hal and I dined at the Vesey FitzGeralds. We were very tired and cold.

Nov 20 ... we are all so tired and flat, and the house is so upside down ...

Nov 25 ... Hal and Bessy by night mail to Ireland to stay with the Dix's in Dublin in the first place. How dull we 3 - Leo, N and I shall be!

Nov 26 ... Pleasant letters from Annie. She and Bernie seem to be very happy at Drybridge in Monmouthshire.

There has been news of Jack in hospital in Malta with possible diphtheria throat: it is decided not to tell the honeymooners, or Hal and Bessy, and luckily he soon is better. though he is away from his ship some time, and his letters have to be copied out, for fear of infection.

Dec 1 Nettie takes Nana and Anne the housemaid, to see all is well at Annie's new home, 14 Royal Avenue.

Dec 3 ... a telegram from Annie says their motor collapsed, and they will be in town at their house this evening. The first mention by Haddie of a motor car! In Ireland, Harry stays with the Fardells, and Bessy goes to Kingstown to stay with her Aunt Dora Quin.

Dec 11 Bessy, on returning from Ireland, goes with Nana to see Annie in her new house while Haddie goes to Derry & Toms to fit on a jacket. Bessy is somewhat ailing, and the Dr forbids her to go to a dance at Lady Bowden Smith's. As she could have gone with Harry, Haddie is disappointed for her and thinks it would have done her good to go!

Dec 20 A nice long letter from Chip [sometimes Bob's nickname] *He is to be quartered at Stellenbosch, about 30 miles from Capetown, with the Scots Greys and other nice regiments, to build temporary accommodation for the troops. This will keep him very busy for some months.*

Dec 24 All to Portnall for Christmas (including Nana). The party includes the Hamiltons and their little girl, Margot, also Cecil and Rachel de Salis and their three eldest boys.

Dec 29 ... There was an entertainment after dinner, in the Drawingroom, chiefly for the servants, etc. It was very well done by a man dressed up like a nigger. The entertainment man turned out to be a sort of gentleman, and dined with us.

1903

Jan 1 Dear Hal left us in the evening for a trip abroad. He goes to Paris, thence trains to Marseilles and then in a steamer to Athens. I do hope he will have fine weather and enjoy his tour. Jack arrived from Portsmouth, where his ship the Andromeda is paying off. He looks wonderfully well after his attack of Diphtheria. Later he joins the Jupiter at Chatham, as First and Gunnery Lieutenant.

Jan 6 N, Daisy (West), B and I to the R. de Salis Theatrical Entertainment in Victoria Street. Margery acted with other Professionals in the first piece - "Hook & Eye". Then Marvyn Keating sang. The second piece was excellent, "Ameliar" by 3 Professionals. The Electric Light went out twice.

There are a good many engagements for Bessy; though, on Jan 17 ... *Bessy and I were about to start for Lady Hope's afternoon partry, but the horse was lame and we could not go.*

Jan 20 Dot brings her daughter Jessie to stay for a few weeks and attend Miss Geach's school.

Annie suffers from a prolonged heavy cold. She and Bernie move to the north side of the Park - 49 Gloucester Terrace..

Feb 5 ... N and I went by Mrs Bright's kind invitation to a Box at Drury Lane Theatre to see a Pantomime, "Mother Goose" at a matinee ... I had never seen a Pantomime before and was quite delighted. It was so beautifully put on the stage. The Ballet was gorgeous and Dan Leno as Mother Goose quite capital!

Feb 11 ... House in the hands of carpenters etc. arranging for the Dance tomorrow, so no visitors admitted.

Feb 12 Nettie gave a dance this evening for Bessy, and it was a great success. Plenty of men, a good room and floor. About 140 guests. Gunter did the refreshments and service so well. All the furniture out of the drawingroom, doors off their hinges etc. I think the young people thoroughly enjoyed themselves. They danced for 5 hours! The music was excellent, by Mr Burgess, Piano and Violin, from 9.30 to 3 o'c.

Feb 14 ... Drove and shopped with Bessy and Jessie in open carriage. Mary the Parlourmaid ill, from overeating the night of the dance.

Feb 17 Leo, N, B and I to Kathleen Greenwell and Mr R. Johnson's wedding, at St Peter's Eaton Square ...

Feb 19 ... Out in carriage early for some business. Large Drawing Room Meeting, for the Ladies' League. Canon Fleming in the Chair. Lady Wimborne spoke so well, and we had some excellent music. Two friends of Antonia McClintock's played, violin and piano, and Rita Allanson Winn and Winifred Bowden-Smith sang so well. It was a most successful afternoon. About 90 people came ...

Feb 20 ... N was tired, so I took B and Ethel S to a dance at Greenwich. We drove down most comfortably in the carriage. We were Lieut D arrant 's guests, and he was most kind and attentive to us. The girls both looked so nice and they had lots of dancing. ... Annie came here to spend a few days, as Bernie goes to the Isle of Man on business. It feels like old times to have her back in the house again. So nice ...

Feb 25 ... Henry West and Alick to dinner here. Alick leaves tomorrow for Marseilles and India. Such a nice, handsome boy!

Haddie helps Annie shop for carpets and curtains for her new house (the first one had been ready-furnished) She records very strong winds, almost hurricanes, all over the British Isles, and especially in Ireland.

Mar 2 ... Bessy to a lecture on Dante at the Lubbocks. Anna McCreight to lunch. Poor thing, it is difficult to recognise in her, the pretty girl of 40 years ago!...

Mar 8 ... Ethel and Violet Skeffington to lunch. Poor girls, they are in great trouble with their Grandmother, Mrs Duncan.

This grandmother, with whom the girls seem to have lived when not in Ireland, has been mentioned before as being difficult. The widow of G.J. Whyte Melville, after his death she must have married Mr Duncan. We are told Ethel goes to the country, in the hope of seeing her brother, Algy, on business—no doubt to try to make some better plan for her life. Their parents are both alive at this time, but presumably in Ireland, or ill, or both. Their mother, Florence, was the only child of the writer, Whyte-Melville, who was well-known as a writer of several books, including "Market Harborough", 1861, about the Civil War, and many other novels, in which foxhunting generally featured He died in a hunting accident, in 1878.

Mar 16 ... Jessie back to Sacombe, where she is wanted, as both Dot and Daisy are ill in bed ...
Mar 18 ... heard Charlie Paget died, at Bournemouth [probably, son of Leo's sister, Caroline, by her first husband, once Leo's Captain]
Mar 19 ... N took Ethel to the Ladies' Shirt Co, and Mrs Biggs has engaged her for a week's trial. Poor child, I am so grieved for her ...
Mar 21 ... N and Bessy to Lord Cardigan and Sydney Madden's wedding, but there was no reception as they are in mourning.
Mar 23 ...Poor Ethel went for first time to Mrs Bigge's Shop ... in Sloane Square, to serve in the shop!
Mar 26 ... Leo, N and I drove to the Geographical Society and saw the Chart of Cap. Scott has done in the Antarctic - very good ... also the model of the "Discovery" Antarctic ship.
Mar 28. ... Annie came to spend a few days during the move to Gloucester Terrace. She came in a Bath Chair and Bernie carried her up stairs, and she went to bed at once in the Boudoir..

Harry also carries her to the Drawingroom for the next few days, and then she goes home to her new house, accompanied by Nana. Naturally Haddie does not spell it out, but Annie is expecting!

Ap 13 Easter Monday ... Ethel S called, just back from her short Easter holidays, to go back to the shop in Sloane Square tomorrow.
Ap 27 .. Leo, N, Hal and Bessy to a Geographical evening meeting to hear Sverdross' Paper (Arctic) read. Leo dined with the Geographers first.

May follows its usual course, with charity and social events, including two dances at the Hyde Park Hotel, one of which does not end till 7 am! Haddie sprains her ankle, and Annie goes for a drive most days with her mother.

June 1 This day, 2 years ago, my dear Mother passed away - and Annie and I had that dreadful and distressing visit to Folkestone!
June 10 A wet night and morning, indeed all day it poured!! Leo, N, Bessy, Hal and Jack to an Antarctic Geographical meeting. N, B and I to Mrs Ripley's Evening Party at the Institute of Water Colours in Picadilly.
June 13 ... Hal, Jack and B had intended going on the river, but the weather was quite too bad ... Bammie Ross and her two Skeffington girls spent some time in afternoon here. [Bammie or Blanche Ross has no children, but these two are probably her nieces Florence and Mabel, daughters of Sydney Skeffington. His widow Clementina had married again, James Craig. They are first-cousins to Oriel, Algy, Nora, Ethel, Constance, Winifred and Violet Skeffington. These seven are children of Lord Massereene and it must indeed have been unusual for one of the girls to be working in a shop, at that time and surely shows spirit on Ethel's part.]
June 22 ... the new "Baby Grand" Bechstein piano arrived today, and is simply charming.

Now the Season really begins to get under way and Bessy has balls, lunches, girls' tea parties, outings of all kinds, nearly every day and often accompanied by Hal. She seems to keep well at this time, thankfully. Annie is going about again, too, and we hear of her going to a wedding. Bernie often goes away on business, and she comes back to sleep at Queensberry Terrace on such occasions. Haddie makes a note to send in Coupon for payment to Schroder & Co. every so often and from this time she mentions an Income Tax claim for repayment every year - can this mean that the Annuity has come to something? Her friend Harriet Campbell is back from Australia, and they see each other often.

July 9 Home dinner of 10 - Ethel cannot come at the last moment and they rush about trying to find a spare girl - evidently, even numbers are very important.

July 10 Intensely hot. In bed till lunch, when I got up to take Flo (Skeffington) and B to Lords for the Eton & Harrow match. Oh! how hot it was! Leo and Hal to Trinity House Banquet where the Prince of Wales presided.

July 13 Leo and N and Flo Skeffington left for Ireland by night mail, to stay at Shankill with Leopold and Eva Dix (Leo's nephew and niece).

July 14 ...Bessy and I dined with Bernie and Annie at 49 Gloucester Terrace and Harry took B on to Mrs Vansittart's dance.

July 21 ... I fetched Annie and we drove and shopped, and she came to lunch to meet Letitia Jeffreys and Tizzy. After lunch we gave them a drive in the Park, and left them at their hotel ...Ethel, Hal and I dined with Harriet Campbell at Bailey's Hotel, and the night was so fine and mild that we walked there and back.

July 22 ... Ethel dined with Mrs Martin, her Chief at the Shop. Hal went to a Regimental dinner, in uniform and Ivy medals. Alas! this is the last day of the carriage! how I have enjoyed it! now I shall not be able to see so much of Annie.

July 23 ... Hal took Ethel and me to the Shaftesbury Theatre to see ... acted entirely by American Coloured People. It was unlike anything we had ever seen before. Some of the acting was very good, and the dancing towards the end in the "Cake Walk" quite wonderful.

July 30 The Cook out for the day, and came home having been in the room with a smallpox patient. Hal went to Mr Evan Smith about it, and he told us to send her back at once to Greenwich, whence she came.

July 31 ... The Dr. came and vaccinated us, Ethel too, and says we must not see Annie because of her condition, but may go among other friends. It is too annoying! Bessy, luckily, is away with the Wests, in seaside lodgings. Leo and Nettie, coming back from Ireland, go to stay with Annie at her house till quarantine is over. Haddie has a good deal of pain and trouble with her vaccinated arm. Ethel leaves them and takes possession of her lodging at 5 Royal Avenue - *she feels it very much, poor child.* Lodgings pronounced *neat and very clean, but SO small* a few days later.

It may have been the thought of the insecurity of a single woman's position that prompts Haddie to send a letter to May, of which a copy has come to light:

16 Queensberry Place, London SW August 10th, 03. My dear May, When I last wrote to you on this subject in the Summer of 1901 you replied that it was premature (and perhaps it was) as your affairs were still quite unsettled. Now that 2 years have elapsed, and that you have not communicated with me, I wish to remind you of what I wrote before - that I have not inherited one farthing from our Mother, and I am sure, that you know as well as I do, - that such was not her intention. Within the last 2 or 3 years of her life, she repeatedly told me, that she would provide for me comfortably; and you may imagine my surprise at being only left her money in Bank, by the Will that she signed, one month before her death, and whereby all her other children and grandchildren were [next five words crossed out] *disinherited in your favour. This small legacy, as you know, came absolutely to nothing, burdened as it was with payments! - I am* <u>*certain*</u>*, she did not understand this; - for she would never have mocked me with a sham bequest; little as it was, £514.14, she meant me to have it, and I am told on very good legal authority (not Mr Synnot's) that though I have no* <u>*legal*</u> *right to the Legacy, I have a very strong* <u>*moral*</u> *claim, and that whoever drew up our Mother's Will, was bound to make her clearly understand before she signed it, that in all probability, her bequest to me, would result in nothing. I hear that you have told people that our Mother divided her property between you and me!! - and that you are very poor. I know you are not what the world calls rich, but I should say, you are very comfortably off, and able to travel about to Rome, etc. etc. - As for me, I have only my share under our Father's Will - about £200 a year, I am told, though I have never as yet received so much. As long as Leo lives, he most generously gives me a home, free - but he is an old man now, and most of his income dies with him. What sort of a home do you think I could make on £200 a year? I, who am not strong, who am growing old? and who have always been accustomed to every comfort. (How would* <u>*you*</u> *like such a prospect?) Surely you will not allow this, but will* <u>*at any rate*</u>*, give me this small sum left by Mother at her Bank. I do not like having to ask you for anything. I did hope that you would have done it before now, of your own accord! I* <u>*always*</u> *loved you, from the time you were a little child, and you generally seemed to care a little bit for me - and I used to think you were generous. I leave it to you to act as you think right, and I hope soon to hear from you. No one knows that I am writing to you, so it is absolutely between you and me for the present.*

I was so sorry to hear you were laid up in Rome, but hope you are now quite well again. I do not forget that the 12th will be your Birthday and send you my good wishes. Your affect. sister,

Haddie C.A.Dunlop.

Aug 17 N and I by bus to Brompton Road to buy some real lace for N's birthday gift to Bessy tomorrow.
Aug 18 ... Dear Bessy's birthday! Dear child - the Baby!! is 21 today. God bless her.
This is the first time Bessy's birthday is not celebrated in the country - no doubt no one wants to leave Annie at this interesting time. But on Aug 21 Haddie goes down to Frinton to stay with Mrs Vesey FitzGerald and finds her alone, *with the two children. Heard that Annie had been unwell all night, and it is hoped that the Baby will soon appear. N went off to her after lunch.*
Aug 22 ... sat in the garden and on the Front,.. the air here is excellent, and it is a nice little place. A letter from N says that poor Annie is still in same state, pain and no sleep at night - but no Baby yet!!
Aug 23 ... Annie's first Baby, a little girl, was born at 5 am today ...so glad it is safely over!
Sept 3... B and I by bus to see Annie and her dear little Baby Girl, both doing so well...
Haddie then goes down to The Yews, Bengeo, near Hertford, to stay with her friends the Macleods, who give her a pleasant few days. On returning to London, she joins N and Leo and Bessy for a migration to Folkestone, where Mrs FitzGerald has lent her house for 3 weeks. *She has left her manservant and housemaid Julia, who was here when we were here almost 3 years ago. We have Hayes and the sewing maid, Nellie, and N sent her cook down yesterday, so we ought to be comfortable!*
Sept 23 ... Bernard, Annie and the Baby went to Marden. We hear the Baby "enjoyed" the train!!! only one month old today!!
They don't have good weather, but sit on the Leas and listen to the Band whenever they can.
Bessy and Hal are off to Ireland again. They go to stay at Drumcar, by now inhabited by the twin Miss McClintocks, Emily and Gertrude. [The house had passed to their brother, Frank, a bachelor and Dean of Armagh, and the two maiden ladies continued to live at Drumcar until their deaths. In 1931 the bulk of the estate, of over 1,000 acres, was acquired by the Land Commission for local distribution, and in 1940 the McClintock family sold the house.
In 1946 it was bought by the Brothers of St John of God for their Community and Home for handicapped people, now a well known institution.]

Oct 1 .... Sir Henry Irving called.
Oct 3......We all went back to town, leaving the sewing-maid, Nellie, behind for a few days, to oblige Mrs FitzGerald. Found the house so nice and clean.
Oct 9 ... Leo, N, Hal, Jack, Bessy Hayes and I down to Woldingham by train. Mr Greenwell met us at station and took us in his omnibus to Woldingham Church (reported to be the smallest in England). There Annie's sweet Babe was christened - Joyce Marjorie. Bessy held her as

Godmother, Mr Nicholson was godfather and Mrs Greenwell proxy for Mrs Crompton-Roberts, Bernie's sister. The Babe was so good and Sweet. Then we drove to Marden and had a champagne lunch. There was a beautiful christening cake, and the Baby came down to have her health drunk ... Annie does not look strong yet. It was a happy day.

Oct 10 ... B and Hal and Jack to tea at Ethel's lodgings to meet Oriel ... Elizabeth Lefroy and Kathleen and her intended, Capt. Lewis, came to lunch ... Leo back to the Aurist, and came back with his hearing much improved. If this only continues, how thankful we shall be! Dear Hal has been apponted Assistant Private Secretary to Lord Stanley, the new Postmaster-General, and it is evident ... that it is mainly due to his very good work in S/Africa. We are so happy!!

Oct 13 ... Annie and the dear Baby arrived. Annie went on in afternoon to join Bernie at Bexhill-on-sea, and left the Baby and Nurse here during her absence ... Little Joyce ...is a great delight to us: she is such a dear good baby - she has a very nice nurse, Blanche.

Oct 25 ... Annie walked in unexpectedly, having come up alone from the Leveson-Gowers' Rectory where she and Bernie were staying, because of the trouble in the breast. Mr Evan Smith saw her and said she must be steeped all through the night with hot water ...

she went home after supper and Hayes went with her. Annie continues unwell for some time, but gradually recovers her strength. Haddie has a bad spell herself:

Nov 11 ... As I continue so far from well I had to have Mr Evan Smith, who says I am suffering from severe cold all over, and it lies fallow chiefly on stomach and liver - Lady Tracey to lunch, 14 visitors; so sorry I could not be down to help N. She was at Kentish Town Hall in forenoon to help

Nov 16 ... Dunlin sent her Milliner to us, about Katie Shaw's hats, as I cannot go out. K.Shaw is the friend out in India for whom Haddie often does errands ... *Bessy has a cold I fear, in addition to the cough she has had for months. Saw Evan Smith again. I am better, but slow in mending, and still feel very unwell and weak. I am to keep warm and not go out, and take 4 tablespoons of Brandy a day.*

Nov 19 ... This day last year dear Annie was married. HOW cold it was! and how tired she, and we were!

Nov 27 ... N had a tea and sale of Lace, and Lecture on lace, for Mrs Whitfield, wife of an R.N Paymaster who is an Invalid. It was a great success, as we sold for nearly £50, and I do not think there were more than 50 or 60 people present ...Dear wee baby Joyce came here to stay for some days, while Bernie and Annie are paying country visits.

December has very bad fog, but Bessy is not sent away from London. She sees the Aurist about her cough and later develops "rheumatism" which keeps her indoors over Christmas. All the family seem to go to the theatre oftener than before, in which Haddie always takes an interest, whether she goes herself or not. Hal and Jack are home for Christmas, while Bernie, Annie and Joyce go to Marden. Ethel frequently spends nights with them - she is anxious about Norah Johnston, her eldest sister, ill with typhoid at Kirkcubbin.

1904

This opening New Year finds us in London. Leo, Nettie, Hal, Bessy and me. Jack has quite lately been here on leave, and is now on board the "Jupiter" at Chatham, where she is refitting. She is in the Channel Fleet. Bob is still in South Africa and does not know when he will come home. Bernie and Annie and Baby Joyce are spending Xmas at Marden Park, Mr Greenwell's Place. All quite well, thank God.

Jan1 ... in bed till dinner time with headache.... Leo, N and Bessy to the Albert Hall to hear the Messiah (in Mr Greenwell's Box, lent to N). They took some friends with them.

Jan 9 ... N took Bessy to see Dr Mitchell Bruce because of her constant cough. Mr Evan Smith went with them. It is all the effect of the serious illness she had 4 years ago.

Jan 14 ... I dined with the Tylers. A pleasant evening, only 8 people. Sir Henry Howorth most agreeable as usual.

Jan 16 ... Bessy and I to Mrs Heathcote's afternoon party, where Mrs Heathcote amused us, with Dramatic Recitals ...

Jan 22 Jack and Bessy down to Guildford to stay at the Tatton Browns for Mr Greenwell's High Sheriff Ball ... they greatly enjoyed themselves

Jan 27 ... Bessy met Henry and Helen West at St Pancras and went with them down to Bedford, to King(smill) Delap's wedding [Kingsmill is James Delap's son]

Leo has a spell of illness "nearly pneumonia" which wears Nettie out. A planned small dance has to be postponed.

Feb 6 Hal and B. to the Alexanders after dinner to play cards - "Progressive Hearts".

Feb 9 There is fear of war between Japan and Russia. *B over to Annie to meet Miss Bower, who is going to help Annie with modelling ... Baby was so good and so lovely! The War has begun, and the Japs have destroyed the Russians' finest battleship, and another ship, by torpedos at Port Arthur. Many other rumours .,.. Hal and B to a Reel Dance.*

Mar 1 ... B went to sit to Annie for her bust ... Heard of Ethel S's engagement to Mr Willis.

Mar 5 ... Ethel called and brought Mr Willis to introduce him - he looks very nice. Ethel subsequently comes to stay - no more shop for her!

Mar 13 ...Sunday Fine; to St Augustine's, the others to St Jude's, for the first time since his bad cold. Hal and B to lunch with the Greenwells; Leo, N and I by bus to lunch with the Leslies. He looks so ill! ...I went to tea with Mabel FitzGerald - I was so tired.

*Ethel out all day long with Mr Willis to Reading to see his horses, to Oxford to see Violet Skeffington (*her youngest sister*) - etc.!* A few days later she takes him to dine with her grandmother, and later still she leaves for Antrim Castle, no doubt to prepare for her wedding.

Mar 17 ... N and Bessy sold at Grosvenor House for the Irish Distressed Ladies ... Heard at 1.30 that the Duke of Cambridge had died this morning. N and B had to change their dresses (for the Sale) in all haste and put on mourning.

Mar 22 ...Walked to Mudie's and back (the Lending Library). N to Annie's to meet the Dr. He says she must keep quiet and not overdo. ... Ethel arrived here early from Ireland. She is to be married in April from Antrim Castle ...

Mar 23 ... Ethel left early for Halsnead Park, Mr Willis's place in Lancashire.

Halsnead Hall, Whiston, not long before its demolition

Picture courtesy of Knowsley Archives

[This was a large 17th-century mansion in parkland at Whiston, then an ancient village near Prescot, within a few miles of Liverpool. The Willis family had been principal landowners there since the 1600s. The house was sold in 1929 and demolished in 1932. Part of the park is now a static caravan site, and the M62 motorway thunders across it. But at the time, it must have been a welcome exchange for Mrs Bigge's shop!]...

Heard the sad news that Robert Leslie of Ballibay died this morning at 22 Cornwall Gardens. We have lost a good and true friend.

Mar 27 Sunday ... B walked across the Park to spend the day with Annie and help her with the Baby, to let Blanche the nurse go out.

Ap 1 Good Friday ... B and Jessie (West) to St Anne's Soho in afternoon to hear Bach's Passion Music. We dined at 6 and then all except Leo and N to the Greenwells' Box to hear The Messiah, a party of 10.

Ap 8. Poor Leo had a bad fall on the pavement, just outside this house. He was alone at the time. He cut his nose badly. The Dr came and said it would not signify, and that he is wonderful as he was neither sick nor faint nor giddy, not even a headache after it, and his pulse quite good, but he must not be left alone in future, as he is getting very blind.

Ap 13 ... Leo better, but not yet over the shock from the fall. The wonder is, he is not much worse ... Bessy and I drove down to Woolwich for a R.A. Dance. We went down in an hour and a half, but the Coachman lost his way coming back, and we drove for 3 hours, and got home at 5.30!! The Dance was a very pleasant one.

Ap 18 ... Leo's personal attendant Peters came today. I hope he will prove satisfactory.

Ap 20 ... N and Bessy to an excellent Concert at the Queen's Hall. Lord Hampton and Mr Cator were their hosts. Ethel Skeffington was married today to Mr Willis in the Private Chapel at Antrim Castle. I trust she will be very happy. Her two sisters and his little niece were Bridesmaids.

Ap 29. Dance in this house at 9.30 pm, about 120 people including several chaperones. It all went off splendidly, all done by Gunter. Carriages ordered for 3 o'c. Leo enjoyed it, but went to bed about 12 o'c. Bernie and Annie were here, she looking SO TIRED,

Ap 30 ... Poor dear Harriet Campbell is very ill at Bailey's Hotel. I went there and saw her maid, who is very anxious about her.

May 1 Sunday ... Leo to St Jude's for the first time since his accident. He is wonderfully better, thank God, and his attendant, Peters, is a great success.

Haddie visits H. Campbell to see her or enquire for her nearly every day, but on

May 8 ... Mrs Cecil Darley called to say that dear Harriette entered into rest today at 1.0 pm. Alas! I have lost a truly dear and good friend.

May 11 ... went to order a wreath for dear H.Campbell. Lunched with Leila Darley and we talked much about HER ...

May 12 ... N and I attended the Funeral service for dear Harriet, at St Mary Abbots. It was a touching, simple service. The Church was beautifully decorated with white flowers, for Ascension Day, a beautiful day for a funeral. There were many wreaths. They sang, "Peace, perfect Peace", which forcibly recalled those touching services at Westminster Abbey during the dark days of the War. Harriet's remains are to be cremated and sent to Sydney to be buried beside her Husband.

Annie and Bernie back to town to attend the Court tomorrow. Joyce was left in the country with Georgie Hamilton.

May 13 ... went to see Annie dressed for the Court. Mrs Greenwell will present her. She looked charming, all in white. Her satin gown all trimmed with the beautiful Maltese lace Jack gave her. She wore Bessy's brocade Train.

May 26 ... Little Joyce is perfectly charming, so sweet and good-humoured, and plays like a kitten. Annie and she are on a short visit while Bernie is with his Yeomanry in Hampshire.

June 3 ... My sister Blanche called. She and her husband are staying at the

Norfolk Hotel, close by.

June 4 ... Hal and B down to Ongar to the Whistlers to look at a Rectory which is to be let and may suit us.

June 7... Charlie and Blanche McC came in here after dinner. C to talk over the wretched family affairs with Leo and Hal.

June 15 ... Bernie and Annie dined here at 7.0 and they and Hal, Jack and Bessy to hear Faust at English Opera, Covent Garden. Tim Bunbury was expected, but could not come in time for dinner. He joined them at the Opera, and afterwards he and Hal and B to supper at the Carleton. Jack had to go on to a dance. He had been at Mr [Charles L.] *Maclean's (R.N, of the Jupiter) wedding in full dress uniform ...*

June 16 ... Leo, N and I drove and paid a good many visits, taking Peters to ring at the doors, a great luxury! ...

June 20 ...Leo, N, Bessy and I drove and we chose an evening gown for Bessy, after trying at several shops. She and Jack ran about town looking at bicycles all forenoon:: N, Hal and B to 3 dances - Davidsons, Bovilles and Lady Harriet Lindsay.

June 22 ... Annie and Baby to lunch, also Mr Willis and Ethel. We went to MrsWillis's afternoon party given for Ethel ... Leo, N and Jack to a Geographical Conversazione at the S.Kensington Museum ... Leo, N and

July 13 ... N and B to Lady Wimborne's afternoon party ... Hal and B to Mrs D'Avigdor's Dance, where it was very hot.

July 18 ... Annie came to lunch, but not the Bab Chick,[often Joyce's nickname] *as she does not go out in the heat of the day, as she is rather upset with teething.*

July 20 ... B and I drove with Leo, intending to go on to the Guildhall to see the Pictures, but the crowds in the street were so great, as Lord Curzon of Kedlestone, the Indian Viceroy, was receiving the Freedom of the City, that we had to give it up ... We are all greatly excited as to what the government is going to do - as one of the Russian Volunteer Fleet has passed the Dardanelles and captured OUR P & O steamer "Malacca" bound for Hong Kong with stores for that place - and made prisoners of our officers and men and put a Russian crew in her!!! and are taking her to a Russian port in the Baltic!!

July 26 ... Mr and Mrs Emory McClintock from America called and had tea. They seem very nice ...

July 29 ... Our difficulties with Russia seem to be somewhat quieting down: but her high- handed insolence is hard to bear.

Aug 2 ... Heard the sorrowful news that Mr Evan Smith, our family Dr, passed away last Sunday after a very short illness.

Aug 3 ... B, Hayes and the Cook met Annie and Joyce, her nurse and A's housemaid, at Liverpool St and went down to Kelvedon Hatch Rectory, near Ongar, which Leo and Nettie, in conjunction with Bernard

Greenwell, have taken for 7 weeks.

Aug 4 Very hot and close. Leo and N and Preece the Parlourmaid and Leo's man Peters down to Kelvedon Hatch to join the rest of the party there. I went down to stay with the Vesey FitzGeralds at Frinton ... found Mabel and the two children and Miss Leslie, of Bourdon House there.

Haddie hears that Bob hopes to sail from Capetown this month, at which she rejoices. She moves on from Frinton to Mrs Mitchell and Miss Hanmer at Holbrook Hall, near Sudbury. An entry with many *** records that Bob has arrived safely after 3 and a half years, and has gone to Kelvedon Hatch. *I am sorry not to be there to help welcome him.*

Aug 20 ... A large garden party here. Cap. and Mrs Kells among the guests, who most kindly asked me to stay with them on Monday, but I could not accept. They came in their 4 in hand. Beatrice Majendie, and a Lady Friend and her two little boys came to lunch and remained for the garden party; the eldest Majendie boy remained here.

Aug 22 ... Heard that poor Annie is laid up in Essex. N cannot have me at the Rectory until Friday, so I intended going to London for two nights, but Mrs Mitchell has most kindly asked me to stay on here until Friday.

Without self-pity on her part, we feel Haddie's position, as one who must always fit herself in with the plans of others.

Aug 23 Mrs Mitchell, Miss Hanmer, Robin Majendie and I in a victoria, and Miss Alice Hanmer and Lewis Majendie in a Waggonette, drove to Hedingham Castle. We had much rain by the way. Lunched there with the Majendies and Mr Temple, Governor of Upper Nigeria. Saw the old castle, date 1100. Very fine, walls 16ft. thick, with the widest Norman arch in the world. The modern castle is early Georgian ...

Aug 24 Fine and pleasant. Did not go beyond the place, as the horses had to be rested, after the long drive yesterday.

Aug 26 Left Sudbury at 12 o'c, changed at Chelmsford, waited there 40 mins, reached Brentwood about 3o'c, where dear Bob met me with a Fly, and we drove together 5 miles to this Rectory, where I found Leo, N and Bessy, and Annie and Joyce. Bernard and Hal came for the week end. Poor Annie is still in bed (from a Mishap) but she is much better and doing well. She has a very nice sick nurse. Joyce's nurse Blanche is away for her holiday, so Nana takes care of Joyce, and we all help. She is truly a dear, pretty little thing ... Bob looks so well and so handsome, and is, if possible, nicer than ever.

Aug 27 ... This is a charming house and grounds, but we are a large party, and the house is crammed. Bernard sleeps in dining room, and we have meals in the pretty hall.

Sept 11 Annie has progressed to walk a few steps and lie on a couch in the garden. A great deal of tennis is played by the others, though Bernie, Hal and Bob go regularly to London for work. A carriage is hired for Annie to take little drives - and Bernie also takes her in his motor. They return to London on Sept 21 *and found all so nice at No. 16.*

Sept 23 ... Annie's nurse came to tell what the Specialist said of Annie, that she must lead an Invalid life for 4 or 5 months, and that nature would right itself. Nothing serious.

Oct 1 ... Bob started early with Bernie in his Motor, and they went down all the way to Monmouth to stay with the Crompton-Roberts ...

Now it is Bob's turn to be ill - he has congestion of one lung and has to have fluid removed from it. The new doctor, Dr Jacques, attends, with Dr Hawkins from St Thomas's Hospital.

Oct 11 ... the three boys slept together under their Father's roof, for the first time [for nearly five years]

Oct 12 ... Bob's temperature diminishes very slowly, but still it is on the good side ... Dear wee Joyce paid us a short visit, looking so nice and pretty in very short petticoats. She stands, but does not walk yet ...

Oct 16 Sunday. Fine but cold; inclined to fog. Leo and N to Christ Church, Lancaster Gate, and then to see Annie. ... Cap. Scott (just home from Antarctic) called ... Dr Stokes paid his 20th visit to Bob, but progress is very slow ... Mrs Greenwell is ill with Neuritis and is to stay with Bernie and Annie. She has a Nurse, and Annie has given up her room to her, and gone a storey higher; not good for her, poor child.

Oct 24 ... Heard of this atrocious outrage committed on the night of the 21st by the Russian Baltic Fleet in the North Sea: There is indignation expressed by all civilized nations at this dastardly act!! and it is supposed the officers must have been drunk or mad.

Oct 29 Bob is slowly getting better, Mrs Greenwell also; Haddie reports that Mr Balfour has given the Russians an Ultimatum and Russia has apologised, *and given money indemnity, and promises to give orders to her Navies to prevent the recurrence of such crimes. ...Thank God, it is not War at present, but I trust it will be "Peace with honour."*

Nov 2 Affairs seem quieting down, but Mr Balfour and Lord Lansdowne have Allowed the whole Russian Baltic Fleet to go on its way rejoicing ... it looks bad, weak and spiritless!

Nov 7 ... we all went to the great Geographical Meeting at the Albert Hall, where Capt Scott gave a lecture on the Discovery's Antarctic Expedition, illustrated by Lime Light Pictures. The Hall was full and it was very interesting. Dr Stokes says that as long as Bob's temperature rises to 99 he must keep quiet and remain upstairs, and very soon he ought to go to Switzerland for 4 or 6 weeks. So the idea now is that he and Bessy should go to Montreux or Clarins or G... and that Hal should accompany them for his remaining fortnight of leave.

Nov 22 ... Dear Hal, Bessy and Bob left at 9 am for Paris via Newhaven on their way to Terretal. It is very cold, and we fear they will not have a very good passage. How very dull we shall be with no young life in the house!

Nov 26 ... A long, pleasant letter from Bessy. She and Hal and Bob are at the Hotel Bonivart, very comfortable, and Bob is better and stronger ...

Dec 1 I fainted quite suddenly at dinner alone with Leo, and fell flat on the ground. Dr Stokes said it is a seizure of influenza ...

Dec 2 ... Bernie and Annie left this morning for Southampton and embarked in the "Magdalena" Mail Steamer for Buenos Ayres. They felt much, parting with dear little Joyce. She and her nurse come to stay here, but of course I must not see her.

There follows a period of illness, as Leo gets influenza too, and has to have a night nurse. They have good reports from Territet, and gradually all get better, cheered by a visit from Jack on Dec 15. *Leo is better but so restless and unreasonable.* [Positively the first negative comment on her brother-in-law by Haddie.] Gradually the household returns to normal, the nurse departs, to Marden for Mrs Greenwell, Joyce leaves the dining room, which has been her nursery for two weeks, and goes into Bessy's room, where Nettie has been sleeping, and N goes back to her own room. Meanwhile, *Joyce DOES look blooming, dear Pet!*

Dec 25 ... Only Hal to church ... Joyce out in her Perambulator, which has at last come back from Harrods' with new India rubber tyres. This weather is sadly against us, poor victims of "flue" getting up our strength. Still, we are much better, in spite of it.

Dec 30 ... VERY high wind. We fear Bob and Bessy will have a tossing tomorrow ... Jack got a number of telegrams from brother officers congratulating him on his Promotion, and addressed to "Commander McClintock!!" We all hope this may prove true!

Dec 31 It IS true! Jack is promoted. Such good news, and he has entirely won it by his own hard work and merit, no interest having been used to get his promotion ...Dear Bob and Bessy arrived here ... so well and bright ... A happy ending to this year!

At the end of this diary we find a note about a new gown: *Total price of fawn Voile gown at Derry & Toms, lined throughout with silk, but untrimmed except with itself—£5.2.2.*

There is always a good deal of expenditure in June and July, reflecting the season's activities. This July listed: Blue velvet ribbon, 4 Hair Nets, 1 yard black glace silk, 2 gilt hat pins: 1 yard blue brilliante, 2 woven cotton bodices, 1 camisole, black crepe de chine blouse, 3 woven cotton combinations; cool stays, fancy pin for hair, roses and leaves, 2 pair black stockings, Ortis shields, 3 pr. Dress Preservers; cleaning stays, mending walking shoes, Dunlin altering Garden Hat, cleaning gloves—cleaning and colouring, charming lace fichu, black silk belt, recovering Umbrella, 1 yd orange ribbon—all amounting to £3.19.11.

Jack as Commander, R.N.

1905

Jan 1 Sunday. Very cold, frost and wind and a little snow All to St Jude's and Holy Communion except me, as my cough is too bad to go out in this very cold weather. I should dearly have liked to be at Church with all the dear members of this family (except Annie)...

Jan 3 Bessy in bed with rheumatism and a high temperature ...

Jan 6 Dr Stokes examined Bob today and\ says he has made a most complete recovery and that he does not think his late illness will ever Come against him. This IS good!

Jan 8 Dr Stokes saw Bessy again and said she has a return of the trouble in her left lung which she had 5 years ago. We are very much distressed!

Jan 9 ... A sad day, as Jack left to join the "Ramilies" at Chatham, and the sweet wee Joyce left us, to stay at Marden. How we shall miss the darling little child, and her loving and pretty ways! Bob went to the country, to dine and sleep with Colonel and Isabel Colvin. [A daughter of Lord Rathdonnell] *N and I called on the James Delaps, who were not at home.*

Jan 11.... Consultation about B between Dr Stokes and Dr Mitchell Bruce. A sad report: she must have open air treatment and probably go to S.Africa later on, and she can never be strong again! Alas! this darling, lovely child! We are very unhappy.

Jan 15 ... B drove and came down to lunch and supper but she looks ill today, and Dr Stokes saw her and says that the last analysis shows a good deal of Bacilli! which, of course, is bad.

Jan 26 ... I dined with Mrs Y. Burges, and we went on to a Concert at the Albert Hall, The Childhood of Christ, by Berlioz, and The Witch's Daughter. We did not care for either performance ...

Jan 31 ... Dr Stokes saw B and says her good progress is marvellous. She is gaining weight ... but she must go to Hindhead, and afterwards to S.Africa for a year - alas!

Feb 1 ... Hal had intended going down to Hindhead with Bessy tomorrow, to take care of her on the way, and then to go over to Ireland at night on business, to see Leopold Dix and Dick Quin. And Mr Synott and Mr Ryland, to try if anything can be done about our wretched family affairs, but he had to give it all up, as Mr Codrington, Lord Stanley's Chief Sec., has to go off to his dying Father, and Hal will be the only Sec. in the Office.

Feb 7 ... The Greenwells lent N their Box in the Albert Hall, to hear ... and Alexander, the American Preachers ... It was all earnest and reverent and unsensational, but not instructive, and on the whole, we were disappointed, and should not care to go again.

*Good accounts of dear Bessy from Hindhead (*where she is in lodgings, with Nana.) The news from Buenos Aires , however, has not all been good: Annie has been ill, and the doctor there said her *Pleurisy is of long standing in a sub-acute form.*

Feb 16 ... N and I to Algy Skeffington's wedding at St Margaret's, Westminster, and afterwards at 40 Grosvenor Gardens. The bride is tall, dark and handsome. [Miss Jean Ainsworth] *We saw many Skeffington relations.*

Feb 18 ... A telegram came from Edith Wilson at Charismata [South Africa] *to say "yes" to N's proposal for Bessy to go to her. This will make it all plain and comparatively easy.*

Feb 23 ... Hayes writes a very good account of Bessy, and Caroline Brady sends a pleasant description of Harrismith where she visited her sister Edith before the war ...

Feb 28 Letter from Bernie and Annie dated B.A Feb 3. She is a good deal better, but not out yet. She has had a bad time of it poor child.

Mar 1 ... We had 12 visitors, some of whom saw little Joyce and greatly liked her. She came to stay here 2 days sooner than we expected, as the Greenwells had not room for her after today. Another letter from Annie, having just heard of Bessy's illness, and naturally very much distressed. Jessie West went to stay with Bessy at Hindhead - I am so glad.

Bessy's passage for S.Africa is booked for Ap 29 *May God's Blessing rest on the decision!*

Mar 24 My birthday. How old I grow! [Haddie is 67]

Mar 28 A letter from Annie from the Country outside Buenos Aires. She is much better and can take walks. Bernie is in Chile.

*Ap 4 ... Edwy McClintock called (*son of Blanche and Charlie*). He has just been going through his Matriculation Exam for Trinity College, Cambridge. He seems a nice boy. Miss Dutton-Green came to lunch. Bessy knew her at the Hotel Bonivart at Territet last December. She comes from Australia and plays the Piano v. well.*

Ap 5 ... 15 visitors, George Richardson called, also Henry West, and James Delap. James had been asked to help buy a saddle for Bessy to take to South Africa, and a habit had been ordered; evidently riding is to be part of the cure. *Blanche (Joyce's nurse), Nellie the sewing maid, and the kitchenmaid, were Confirmed today, at St Paul's, Onslow Square.*

Ap 15 ... Hal down to Southampton to meet Bernie and Annie coming home from Buenos Aires. Leo and N drove to meet Annie at Waterloo and brought her home to Gloucester Terrace, where Bessy and I, and Nana and Blanche and Joyce were waiting for her. She looks so much better, and it was a happy homecoming: but WE lose the Babchick, and dear Bessy in a fortnight, which is far worse!

Bessy suffers another flare-up of her illness, which causes much doubt as to whether she will be fit to sail. Much heavy-hearted packing and shopping goes on.

Bessy and Joyce

Ap 27 Jack came back to us from Newcastle, in time to see Bessy off, and to cheer us after her departure. Bessy had a drive. It is quite wonderful how she stands the fatigue and excitement and emotion of preparing to leave us! Thank God... Lady Waldegrave writes that Lady Selborne cannot go to S.A on Saturday as intended, as one or two of her children have Scarlatina, so Bessy will not have her protection.

Ap 28 ... Our beloved Bessy and Nana left us at 10.30 am. Hal and Jack went with them to Southampton and left them very comfortable on board the Walmer Castle... Mr and Mrs John McClintock and Miss Lethbridge are on board and Bessy knows them. She has been given the use of a 2nd cabin for Hayes. She was so good and dear and brave to the last, and I trust and believe she will enjoy the voyage. May God bless it all to her good, and guard and protect her. Poor Leo, Nettie and I feel very forlorn; but so thankful that dear B has got off without a hitch .. this day has seemed longer than a week! We went to bed early, quite tired out.

May 3 ... a Wire from Bessy from Madeira, all well. Heard of Oriel Skeffington's death, at the Sanatorium (open air) in Scotland. Poor boy, what a sad life! [brother of Algy, Ethel etc.]

May 16 ... The afternoon papers announce that the "Walmer Castle" with Lord Selborne on board arrived this morning at Cape Town ...

Feeling in need of a change, Haddie takes herself off to Bexhill, where she is joined by Annie, with Joyce and her nurse. Bernie comes when he can, but has to go to Salisbury for his Yeomanry. Annie packs up her house, as it is now let for the rest of the season.

May 28 Sunday. A lovely warm, sunny day. Annie, Hal and I to Church. Blanche went to evening service and Annie put Joyce to bed. We were out all day long, only coming in for meals. Letter from Nettie to say she heard from Edith Wilson yesterday, saying that she will manage to take Hayes into her house, as well as Bessy. We are so thankful, as there was some difficulty about it.

The family are as usual, able to find cousins in their hour of need. Edith Wilson is one of the daughters of Dr Alfred McClintock, Leo's brother, and her husband is also a doctor. Her sister, Caroline Brady, is living in Africa, too.

June 3 ... Charming letter from dear Bessy, Bob and Nana from Cape Town. Bessy was so well ... we are so thankful ... I left for London and found all well there.

June 10 ..Joyce and nurse came up from Bexhill to stay here. Annie was to have come too, but Bernie said HE had been away from her for some time and must have a Honeymoon, so they went to stay at the Hotel Grand Central.

The Season is now in full swing and Harry is out every night at balls and parties.

June 17 ... N and I to Miss Ward's wedding. Annie, Bernie, Hal and Jack dined together at a Restaurant, also Jean Skeffington and then to the Play. Pleasant letter from B, Nana and Edith from Harrismith. Bessy and Nana like what they have seen of the place and the Wilsons ...

June 19 ... Auriel Quin [daughter of sister Dora] *arrived early from Ireland ...*

June 20 ... N took Auriel to the Westminster Flower Show, and I took her to Ranelagh in afternoon. We saw the Polo and had tea, but it was v. empty because of Ascot ... Joyce with her nurse left at 2 o'c for Bayford Cottage, Hertford, which Bernard has taken for the summer. We shall miss the sweet babe!

June 24 ... Auriel went to spend the weekend with Aylmer at Woolwich [her brother] ... *Hal down to Bayford Cottage to stay with Annie.*

June 25 ... We were made very happy by a visit from Dr Stokes, who has heard from Dr Wilson at Harrismith giving a most favourable and hopeful account of Bessy!

June 26 ... Massereene [Algy's Father and Haddie's first cousin] *died here in London this morning, at Hotel Windsor, Mayfair, from heart failure quite peacefully ... He had ... just returned from Madeira, with a nurse. None of his family were with him.... Jean Skeffington called here about all this sad business and was very nice.*

June 28 ... Jean Skeff. called early about family matters. Violet S to lunch and tea. Poor little thing, much distressed ...George Richardson came to see Leo ... [Leo's nephew, and a doctor.]

July 4 ... Harry took Auriel to Mrs Greenwell's dance. Bernard and Annie came up for the dance, and slept at Portman Square.

July 8 Leo's birthday. He is SO well in health, thank God; all but his sight ... Leo, N and I down to Bayford Cottage to spend the day with Annie, Bernie and little Joyce. On our way home, we went to look at a farm house, but it was too dirty and too dreadful for words, and could not be made to suit us!!...

Bayford Cottage (in 1934)

Haddie goes off on another jaunt, this time to St Helen's, Hastings, where Colonel Hilton meets her in his carriage. *Only he and Anna in the house. A young man to dinner from a neighbouring house. We play Billiards after dinner - Col. H and I won.*

July 31 Very fine and pleasant. Col. Hilton and I took a lovely drive to tea with some distant neighbours. He had to hire a horse, as his was lame. Anna in bed all day, but better. Anna Hilton is a first cousin.

Back to London next day to catch up with encouraging news from Bessy.

Aug 5 ... Found St Augustine's closed. Went to Christian Scientist Service in Queen's Gate Hall to see what it was like. The Service was almost entirely conducted by a Woman, helped by a man!

Aug 8 ... Went to Dr Stokes. He syringed my left ear which is so painful, and thinks I shall soon be better. At 2.0'c we all, ie Leo, N and I, Peters and two maids, started in an Omnibus from London Road Car Co and drove down to Miss Gribble's house, 5 The Grange, Wimbledon Common, which Leo has taken for a few weeks. She has left her Parlourmaid. The house seems comfortable, and has a small garden. at the back.

Aug 10 ... I have fought this cold for days, and now there is nothing for it, but to stay in bed, which I am doing ... We find there is a Plague of Black Beetles in this house, and a considerable absence of necessaries in the appointments.

Aug 11 ... Peters was sent into London to get some things badly wanted in this house. Hal and Jack arrived this evening to dine and sleep, in celebration of Hal's birthday, which is very nice of them...

Aug 12 ... A letter from Bob at Pretoria, and one from Bessy and from Nana. B so well, and had gone to an Officers' Dance at Harrismith, and was none the worse for it!

Aug 16 ... General Kent paid us a long visit, and was v. amusing ... Mr and Mrs Longstaff called. He gave £25,000 to the late Antarctic Expedition Fund. Annie sent some lovely flowers from Bayford Cottage.

Aug 18 ... Darling Bessy's Birthday. I miss her as much as ever! God bless her and bring her safely back to us! General Kent called and brought Capt. Hall, of his old Regiment, 77th. He is Staff Officer at Harrismith, home on leave, but returning in a fortnight. He is very nice.

Aug 19 ... Nice letters from Bessy. She and the Wilsons are going to Durban ... then B and Hayes hoped to go to Pretoria to stay with the Hildyards. He commands the Forces in S.A. Dr Wilson wishes B to go now, as later it would be too hot and relaxing for her at Pretoria, and just now she will escape the most dusty time at Harrismith, but that proves that she must be well!...

Aug 21 ... Leo, N, Eva Dix and I drove through the pretty little town of Maldon, and to Merton (close to this) where we went over Nelson's house, which is vacant. A fine old house, and charming walled garden. We believe that it was from here that he started for Portsmouth, just before Trafalgar ...

Haddie is off on a jaunt again, this time to Ireland, starting with her sister Dora Quin at Kingstown, her first visit to her homeland for many years. Hal sees her safely onto the boat train *A choppy sea, but I was not sick and got some sleep.*

Aug 23 V. fine morning. Dora's maid met me on board at 7.30 am. A warm and kind welcome from Dora, Dick and Auriel [at 9 Crosthwaite Park, Kingstown]..*dear little Joyce's birthday, 2 years old today.*

Aug 26 ... After lunch, Dick took Dora, Auriel and me out in his Motor, through Bray, to the Pass of the Glen where he had to turn back, as the Motor was stopping every now and then, and Dick feared that we might not get home. However we did all right, after an enjoyable drive of 27 or 28 miles, just as the rain was coming on!

This may be Haddie's first trip in a motor car.

Aug 29 ... We motored into Dublin ... I saw Merrion Square, Ely Place etc. etc. It all looked like an old past dream and it all looked so small and rather paltry.

Aug 30 Very overcast and dull, but we managed to see the eclipse of the sun quite well ... motored into Dublin, where we went into Brown & Thomas's

Shop in Grafton St, and then to the Pleasure Park, which I had never seen before ...Annie sends on a recent cheerful letter from Bessy, and tells her that Ethel [now Willis] has had a daughter, both well.

Sep 3 Sunday ... Dora, Auriel and I to the Marriners' Church for Holy Communion, in a cab ...

Sep 5 ... Went into 36 Upper Mount Street, by train to lunch with Bammie Ross. Flo Skeffington and her Major Laurie were there. Went with Bammie by train and cab to tea with the Miss Perrins at their charming place near ... beyond Rathmines. Remained to dinner with John and Bammie and the happy pair ...

Possibly Haddie's visit is chiefly to attend Florence's wedding.

Sep 6 ... Could not go out motoring with the others, as I had to go to tea with the Miss Griffiths. There I met the Rev. Charles Green, Rector of Clapham, and brother to Lady Stowell, and a very nice man.

Haddie reports much rain and heavy wind, which so often seems to follow an eclipse ... *Henry West to lunch. He, Dora, Dick, Auriel and I motored to Mrs Boosey's house to see Jessie West, who is staying there, and then on to Mr Alfred West's pretty place for tea. Such a charming house, opening into beautiful conservatories and full of such lovely things, china etc. Mrs A. West was so kind.*

Sep 8 ... In cab (as it was raining) to Sandycove to see Flo Alloway and Maud Bateman [the former is one of Leo's sisters]. *Poor things, they were so glad to see me.*

Sep 11 ... motored into Dublin, for Auriel to shop, and went to see the Doddie [?] who lives some way from here. Poor thing, she lives in 1 room, and seems miserably poor! [There is just one early reference to "The Doddie" in Haddie's youth—possibly a dressmaker?]

Sep 12 ... left for Rostrevor to spend a few days with Bammie. Found her, and Flo and Mabel, also Violet Skeffington there, and Miss Macdonnell, daughter of Sir Anthony, the Under Sec. for Ireland (unattractive, and a R.C.) It is much colder here than at Kingstown, but they have good fires.

Sep 13 ... looked at Flo's presents and trousseau, and walked in and near the village with her ...

The neighbours and, next day, the villagers, come to see the wedding-presents and to have tea.

Sep 16 ... Lunched at Fairy Hill with Eddy [Edmund Ross] and his daughter Kathleen and little Molly. Eddy showed me some of his pretty things, pictures, curios, china etc. Blanche and Charlie [McClintock] came to stay with him for the wedding after I left. John Ross of Bladenburg came from Dublin for the weekend.

Sep 19 ... Count & Countess Rochetta arrived ... I came to spend 3 nights with Mrs Hall at Moygannon , as Rostrevor Ho. will be quite full. Mrs H is so kind and hospitable. A nice Miss Bloomfield is staying here too.

Sep 20 ... went by train to Rostrevor Ho, where all the Relations, and a good many strangers assembled for tea. The Settlements were being signed, and the Bridesmaids and Page were given their presents. The young people went down to decorate the Church with flowers for tomorrow. Hal and Jack came to see me ... they are staying at the Hotel. The young Massereenes arrived, so all the wedding guests are assembled, some at Rostrevor Ho, some quartered on friends ...

Sep 21 Very fine and bright, but rather windy. The wedding was at 11 o'c in Rostrevor Church. None of the R.Cs were allowed even to be present at the ceremony!! [Bammie, the bride's Aunt, and some of her husband's family, the Ross's, had become Roman Catholics some years before] *Hal and Jack and I sat in a front pew as relations. Massereene gave Flo away. 3 bridesmaids ALL in blue - Mabel Skeff., Nellie Brodigan and Bessy Hall of Narrowater, and a Page in white satin. It all went off very well, except the Organ which was most lugubrious. I believe there were about 80 guests, several R.C Priests and one of their Bishops. The Happy Pair left at 1.30 for Dublin...*

Algy Skeffington, and his new wife Jean, have become Lord and Lady Massereene on the death of his father earlier in the year. [Jean dies in 1937; subsequently, in 1940, Algy marries his first cousin Florence Vere Laurie, the bride of this day's entry, both by then aged 67. George Laurie, bridegroom, Royal Irish Rifles, is killed in 1915.]

Charlie West was to have come to lunch, but is reported very ill with congestion of the lungs, at Portrush.

Sep 22 ... Left Moygannon at 2.30, and reached Dora's house before 7, a tiresome, fatiguing journey in 5 conveyances ... found a very kind welcome.

Sep 25 ... Heard that Nettie wants me back, so hope to cross Wed. night.

Sep 27 ... Left by 8.30 Mail Boat. Dick and Jessie West saw me off. A rough unpleasant passage (1st Class) and 2nd Class train.

Sep 28 ... Found Leo and Nettie well, thank God ... Mr Lawford, the oculist, says he can operate on Leo's left eye and will do so early next week.

Sep 29 ... Annie arrived at lunch time, to spend a few days, to shop and cheer her Father and Mother. She is by no means strong yet.

Sep 30 ... George Richardson called, and spoke so hopefully and cheerily about the operation to be performed on Leo's eyes ... Letters from Bessy, Bob and Nana ... Bessy has been given leave to ride and play tennis!

Oct 1 Sunday ... Bernie motored up from Bayford, and brought up dear little Joyce and her nurse for a few hours. J was quite delicious, and so amusing. She recognises us all, but was a little bewildered at first, and then got quite at home with us and the house. She chatters a lot! and is so good and obedient ...

Oct 3 The operation, for cataract, is performed by Mr Lawford; assistant, Dr Stokes, and George Richardson are all present. First results pronounced good.

Oct 5 ... Nettie took Annie to see Dr Stevens. He has found out the mischief, and says she will be perfectly well, shortly ...

Oct 7 ... there was some inflammation in Leo's eye, which is not good..... Such a long interesting letter from Bessy, telling all about her visit to Johannesburg with Bob, and her and Nana's day at Ladysmith

Oct 8 ... This afternoon, while Dr Stokes was visiting Leo, he saw light with the eye that has been operated on! Thank God.

Oct 9 ... Leo's eye much the same. He is restless and fidgetty. Peters has knocked up with water on the knee, so a 2nd nurse "Plunket T..." had to be got, for he can never be left alone night or day, as he is unreasonable, and WILL touch his eye!

Oct 12 ... Leo had a v.bad night... the nurse did not know what to do with him ... He spent most of this afternoon in my room and saw Adm. Cave who cheered him up. In subsequent days, Admirals Mann and Le Hunt Ward also come in to sit with Leo.

Oct 16 ... N and I by bus and tube to G.P.O, where Hal met us, and took us to excellent seats he had been given to see the King lay the foundation stone of the New P.O buildings, on the site of the old Blue Coat School. The Queen, the Prince and Princess of Wales and their two boys were there; it was a pretty sight, and went off well.

Oct 17 ... I saw Flo and Major Laurie who called here in forenoon ...

Oct 18 ... I stay with Leo whenever Nurse is out or busy, but he is so deaf, and I am so hoarse, that I can scarcely make him hear. [Both Haddie and Nettie have bad colds]

Oct 19 ... Mr Lawford and Dr Stokes saw Leo, and say he is extremely well, and they know of no reason why he should not see with his left eye, but they cannot know anything definitely for some time yet; so it is the old thing "Patience"! ...Out in forenoon about Bessy's Alpaca coat and skirt, which are all wrong!

Oct 22 Sunday ... Admirals Cave and Le Hunt Ward, Rodolph de Salis, Aylmer Quin and Mr Darley and his sailor son called, and saw Leo. I saw Charlotte Macartney in the Dining Room, as Leo does not like to see WOMEN yet! but two days later, his first lady visitor is his cousin's wife, Antonia McClintock!

Oct 23 ... Henry West goes over to Portrush this evening as his boy Charlie is very ill there with pneumonia - Jessie came to stay here, while her Father is away. Leila Darley came here, and she and I went to a 6 p.m service at St Paul's for Seafarers, the first of what is to be an annual affair, and St Paul's was full, and the hymn singing magnificent; and a beautiful sermon from Lang, Bishop of Stepney. It was a most moving service. [To this day, an annual event.]

Oct 28 ... Jessie back to Sacombe to keep house for her Father [presumably Helen is at Portrush nursing Charlie, still very ill.] *As if we had not trouble enough, Emily the Parlourmaid fell downstairs and dislocated her left shoulder!*

Oct 30 ... the last of the Nurses left today ... Mr Lawford and Dr Stokes saw Leo, and say his eye has made progress, and he ought now to go back to ordinary life. Nice pleasant letters from Bessy and Nana. Bessy wants some music to be sent her, also stays, and Dr Wilson wants a gold chain for Edith. B, thank God, is so well, and played 4 sets of tennis one day.

Nov 8 ... Hal, Jack and Mr Duff had a dinner party at the Junior Naval & Military Club. They 3, and Miss S de Pothonier, Miss Woulfe and Miss N. Cumberland - and me as Chaperone. We went on to Daly's Theatre to see the Little Minchins: and afterwards to supper at the Carleton - a v. dissipated, but pleasant evening; got home at 1.30.

Nov 10.... Russia is in a most terrible state! ... drove to Oxford St to look for some jewellery the boys want for Bessy. N and I drove in the Park from 3 to 4. I am anxious to take her out every day, for she is much tried by Leo's eye, and this last attack of illness.

Nov. 11 Leo no better. Dr S not satisfied. We are anxious

There continues great anxiety for some time - Leo has what Haddie describes as a haemorrhage in his stomach, which nearly killed him 4 years before. Dr says his illness is very grave, particularly at his advanced age, so it is mainly a question of his strength holding out. Annie and Hal are both constantly at the house, and they send a telegram to Dr Wilson in Harrismith to say "Bessy's Father seriously ill" to prepare her for even worse news. There is a very slow improvement, however; he is kept very quiet - even Nettie only sees him for a few minutes twice a day. On Nov 24 Haddie is allowed to see him, and *received his blessing.*

Gradually the family resume normal activities.

Nov 30 ... drove to see Mabel FitzGerald, who is having a rest cure and massage at 29 Wimpole St. Violet Skeffington to lunch. She and I to St Ermin's Hotel, Westminster, where we and some other friends had tea with Constance and [her husband] *Mr Sykes.* [Constance is sister to Violet and to Ethel and Algy].

Dec 12 Leo now is carried down to the drawingroom by two men in a chair. *Dear wee Joyce and her nurse came for 4 days while Bernie and Annie are paying a visit in Yorkshire. She is so engaging and intelligent, but talks almost too much "grownup"!!!*

Dec 18 ... Annie much struck by her father's improvement ... Hal dined out. He is appointed Under Sec. to Mr Sydney Buxton, the new Postmaster Gen. - and an outsider, the Hon. Richard Denman, 5 years his junior, is to be Sec. over him, and he is to teach him his duties! Truly marvellous!

Dec 19 ... dear wee Joyce left us ... how we shall miss Baby! she told me to be a good girl and not to cry!!

Dec 23 ... Ethel and Mr Willis and their charming baby girl to tea - she is a dear wee thing ...

[they are staying with Ethel's grandmother, friends again, no doubt.]

Dec 25 ... Hal, Jack and I to St Jude's. N. staid with Leo, and went for a little walk with Hal. Leo certainly better again. He talks much more, and takes an interest in everything. He walks a good deal, up and down the dining-room.

Dec 27 ... Ethel and Mr Willis dined here, and then Hal took them and Jack and me to the Aldwych to see "Blue Bell", such a v. pretty play or rather Pantomime - Mr Willis gave us supper at the Cavalry Club. A v. pleasant evening.

Dec 28 ... I drove to see Miss E. Lethbridge, who had been Bessy's companion going out to S.A. She quite appreciates her, and seems fond of her. The L's are very nice people ......Dr Stokes's Dr. [locum] *saw Leo and allowed him to walk up one flight of stairs, which he did quite easily and without fatigue.*

Dec 29 ... Sir James Stronge dined here. He is in town, looking after poor Mrs Burges' affairs. [Sir James was related by marriage to Leo's family; Mrs Burges had recently lost her husband, leaving her, in Wales, with four young children. She was possibly a niece of Sir James]

Dec 30 ... Hal played a concert for me on the Gramophone after dinner ... Leo going on well ... one nurse, and the water bed and carrying chair are gone!!

Dec 31 A beautiful pink sky in the morning, but very cold and frosty and east wind ... George Richardson and his sister Mrs Culwick called ... Leo's first visitors! This day last year Bob and dear Bessy came home from Switzerland, and we were so happy! - but on the 3rd Jan, she took ill, and all our sorrow and trouble began. This has indeed been a sad sad year, and I am not sorry it has come to an end! but I must not forget to thank God, for the many blessings still left to us! - Leo's recovery, and many lesser mercies. Heaven grant, the New Year may be happier.

Monasterboice House
An aerial view - 1960s

1906

The New Year finds Leo, N, Hal, Jack and me at home: dear Bessy and Bob in S.Africa. The past year has been a sad and trying one. Bessy's breakdown in January, and having to send her to S.A in April, and to bear the loss of her sweet company! Then the operation on Leo's eye early in Oct, and his subsequent severe illness. I pray that this New Year may have more happiness in store for us, but the old year has at its close, given us Leo's recovery, and excellent accounts of Bessy. Bernie, Annie and little Joyce are at Bayford Cottage, Herts.

Jan 2 ... Henry West came to lunch, and had a little celebration of Holy Communion in the drawing-room for Leo, N and me.

Jan 6 ...Letters from Bessy, Bob and Nana, all well. Poor Bessy had been suffering much from backache, but was much better. Bob does not know yet what the War Office is going to do with him.

Leo continues to improve, and is soon taking short drives. His last nurse (Macdonald) leaves, and on Jan 9, *Hal and Jack treated Peters & Nellie to seats at the Colliseum.*

Jan 12 The General Election begins, and Haddie is disgusted at the Radicals taking 14 seats from the Conservatives. Unionists, also, fare badly.

Jan 17 ... Leo, N and I drove early, and he voted for Lord Percy, our M.P in S.Kensington ... Leo lent the carriage for the Election after lunch ... Alas! the Elections going from bad to worse! John Burns is in for Battersea with an increased majority. SUCH a creature to be a Cabinet Minister!!!!!

Jan 19 ... nearly all the members of Mr Balfour's Cabinet are unseated.

Jan 23 ... Alas! the Elections are going on all wrong - scarcely a member of the late cabinet returned, and dozens of other seats lost: mainly by LIES about Chinese SLAVES in S.Africa, and calumnies; and there will be v. few GENTLEMEN in Parliament! Too sad for words.

Feb 3 ... Hal had a holiday and took me to Wyndham's Theatre where we saw "Captain Drew on Leave", Wyndham, and Mary Moore etc.

Feb 16 ... Great news from Bob and Bessy. The Wilsons will soon be breaking up house, as Edith is coming to England to put her boy to school; so they propose that Bessy and Nana should go to Pretoria and keep house for Bob! who has a house in his eye, and is looking out for a trap and two ponies. N. will telegraph to Bob to approve.

Feb 17 ... to Miss E. Lethbridge and Capt. Stapylton's wedding ... dear Bessy had been asked to be bridesmaid. It was such a nice wedding.

Feb 27 ... I went alone to Lil Fardell and Matt Toomis' wedding ... and afterwards at Sir G Fardell's house. V. nice, and I met many people I know. Poor Hal was knocked down by a carriage in the street this night, and bruised in the back and one leg - mercifully nothing worse.

Blankets, bedding - and a cookery book - are sent out to Bob and Bessy. John and Hal regularly attend Reels dances, known as "Macphersons". The usual round of social engagements proceed, though they are rarely At Home officially, as Leo is set back by influenza.

Mar 10 ... I went to Mrs Ferard's At Home in Montagu Square, where there was good professional music and reciting.

Mar 16 ... I went to a Ballard Concert at Queen's Hall, and heard Violet Clarke sing, under the name of Violette Louda ... N gave me the ticket ... Marie Hall played the Violin delightfully.

Mar 22 Haddie goes for a couple of days to stay with Annie at Bayford Cottage, and finds them all well and bright. Bernie has a holiday, and spends it *gardening and looking after the mess, building the addition to the cottage. Walked up to the Rectory to look at the house, as Leo is thinking of taking it in summer. I think it will suit very well.*

Mar 30 ... Robbie Quin came to dinner here, just back on a holiday from S.Africa, where he has been employed in a mine in the Transvaal ... Sent our S/Africa letters as usual - Bob's gun goes to him by private hand tomorrow.

Annie and Joyce stay a few days while the most trying part of the building work is done.

Joyce & Leo

Ap 3 ... Annie to lunch with the Greenwells. I took Joyce and Blanche there to tea, as Mrs G. had a gathering of her grandchildren.

Ap 7 ... little Joyce went to tea with Lady Normanton's 6 little girls! at Herbert House.

Ap 28 Delightful letters from Bessy and Nana, from 100 Devenish St, Sunnyside, Pretoria ... they like their new house, and dear Bessy is so well.

Ap 30 Leo is in perfect health, and his cough is nearly gone since the oil of mercury is put into his ears: but he is nervous and jumpy - and very much depressed, unfortunately. 4 servants, cook, kitchenmaid, Parlourmaid and housemaid left, and 4 others came! A great turn out ...

May 13 Sunday Warm and fine. All to St Jude's, Leo for the first time on Sunday, since last Sep. He and N went both ways in the carriage, and had a short drive in the Park afterwards.

Leo has another operation on his eye - said to be successful. All are made happy by good reports from a Pretoria doctor on Bessy's lung - she and Bob are very pleased with their house. One can imagine the fun they had, keeping house together.

May 31 Princess Ena of Battenburg was married today to King Alfonso of Spain at Madrid, with great pomp and rejoicing, but all was turned to horror and grief by a Bomb thrown at them, which killed several people close to them. Poor young things! SUCH a beginning.

June 1 Leo and N took me in carriage to the Greenwells' Office, to sign a Paper ... This day, 5 years ago, my Mother was taken to rest. Shall I ever forget that dreadful day, when Annie and I went down to Folkestone?

One wonders if Haddie's mysterious Delap bequest did come to something and was being invested for her.

June 3 Whit Sunday ... A few visitors, amongst others Sir Allen Young, v. pessimistic about the present govt. and the future of our country!

June 8 ... went to see Miss Goodall's water colour sketches of S.Africa. We saw Lord Roberts there ...pleasant letters again from Bob and Bessy ... she is driving and riding a lot, and learning to jump.

June 10 Sun. ... 7 visitors, amongst others Mr and Mrs Emory McClintock from New York.

June 11 ... Mr French and his son called. He is a Sydney Banker, and his son is engaged to Nina Jeffreys in Australia.

June 14 ... N and I drove and went to see the "weekend" Bungalows at Oetzmanns. They are very wonderful for the money.

June 16 ... Leo received his new glasses and can already see much better with them, but his eye must be trained to see properly and gauge distances... also they learn of a letter sent by Dr Saunders at Pretoria to Dr Wilson, *giving a most favourable and cheerful view of dear Bessy's state. How thankful we feel today about Leo and Bessy.*

June 27 Leo to London Assurance. Emily Harper to lunch. N and I to Mrs Crompton-Roberts, and to Prebendary Eardley Wilmot's tea, and made acquaintance with his intended - Miss Butcher. [The Prebendary is vicar at St Jude's]

July 2 ... Henry West gave a very bad account of poor Willie McC [first mention for some time, but he is known to be very ill with tuberculosis.]

July 7 ... Haddie by train to Shrewsbury, thence to Dorrington, where she was met by Mr Sykes in his Motor, to go on a visit to *Longhor Hall, a beautiful old house, where I found Constance and a girl, a Miss Ada Jenkins.* Constance Sykes is a sister of Algy, Ethel etc. The house is evidently rented, for the owners, Mr and Mrs Corbett, call. The party is joined by Lady Emily Chichester and her youngest daughter, Margaret. As usual, Haddie is so happy in the country, sitting in the garden or walking in the lanes.

July 13 ... Miss Jenkins ("Buntie") left. Her Father, Col. Jenkins, drove over to fetch her. She IS a funny girl!!

July 14 A lovely sunny day, and quite fresh. Constance's Mother-in-law had lunch here, and spent some hours. Sitting under the trees nearly all day, disturbed by some uninteresting visitors. Connie and I had a walk before dinner...

July 15 Sunday. A sad St Swithun's, with a good deal of rain. We all went to the little church in the Park. Mr -, the Vicar, is a trial! ...

July 17 ... Left Longnor at 12 o'c. By train from Dorrington to Shrewsbury. Drove to 3 Quarry Place, and saw Mrs Wanderford, and had lunch with her Companion. Missed the London train by 3 mins, and had to wait till 4.50. Reached Euston at 9 pm, and found dear Hal waiting on the platform for me! SO good of him ...

July 20 ... N and I packed and sent off a box to Bessy in time for her birthday, containing 2 white morning gowns, several blouses, a Seguin lace Bertha, ribbons etc. etc ...

July 26 ... Mr and Miss Gore Browne to lunch. He is Rector of Pretoria. It was so nice to see those, who had seen dear Bessy and Bob, and who gave such a nice account of them

Recent regular visitors are Mr and Mrs Alington. On August 2nd they all go to the Vicarage at Bayford, very near to Annie. The house is nice and comfortable, and the garden quite charming, full of lovely flowers. Eva Dix joins the party, Fitz Paget visits briefly, Bernie goes off for a few days with his family in Skye. The Vicar, is, of course, absent, but what Haddie calls the *Local* Tenens is a Mr Walham, a schoolmaster from Broxbourne, pronounced a nice little man. A crisis develops in the local water-supply.

Aug 19 ... Bernie himself, after hard work, managed to turn the water on again to Bayford (temporarily) but he was so tired after this and his long journey from Skye, that he had to go to bed ... Cook managed to cook our dinner but as the kitchen range can't be used, as the Boiler is dry, the servants' joint was cooked in the gardener's house.

Aug 20 ... Bernie is in bed, v. unwell and feverish. Nurse Wakelin arrived today, for Annie, but she has begun by looking after Bernie.

Aug 23 ... Still no water! we are in nigh despair! Dear little Joyce is three today: a sweet, pretty, graceful clever little girl - God preserve her.

Aug 24 ... Water coming in all right at last. We hope it may continue to do so. Joyce, Blanche, the servants and I to a big School Feast given by the Clinton Bakers at Bayfordbury. Leo would not go at the last so N had to stay with him ...

Aug 25 ...Bernie better. Heard that Flo Laurie had a son on 22nd ... Heard from Bessy that she had lost weight and saw the Dr. at Pretoria, who says her lung is all right, but she is anaemic and must take iron and cod liver oil, and not play tennis for a month. It is delightful to hear of her lung being so well.

Aug 26 ...Bernie better, and sitting up in his room, but he looks weak and pulled down. The Dr says he has had a narrow escape of congestion of the liver.

Aug 29 At 4.20 am, Annie gave birth to a 2nd little girl, a dear wee thing, so like Joyce. A boy was much wished for, of course! Annie and the Baby are as well as possible....N up to Bayford Cottage early. They there were all tired out with the night, and lying down ... I sent out 20 p.cs announcing the baby. Telegrams went too, one in Unicode to Bessy and Bob. *Leo, N and I to tea with the Miss Randolphs at Bayford House. Afterwards N and I had a peep of this Infant asleep in her bassinette. Joyce came to us early and announced that she had a "Baby Judy" at HER cottage!*

Sept 2 Intensely hot - much too hot! ... Annie going on so well, and allowed to see Leo, N, Jack and me. The Baby is a darling, but very tall and thin, 22 inches long, and weighed 6 lb.

Sep 7 A lovely pleasant day. Leo, N and I walked to a tennis party at the Manor Ho (the Berkeleys) ... Annie so well and the Baby much improved and filling out ...

Sep 26 ... the Dr will not allow Annie to sit or stand up for another week, but she is very well.[Baby now 4 weeks old!] In this very sociable neighbourhood there are visits and small social events every day, in fine weather. Edith Wilson arrives with her boys, to take the elder, Leo, to school at Marlborough.

On getting back to London, where they find the house clean, and repainted outside, they are sad to learn that Dr Stokes has died, in Ireland. They hear that Bessy's doctor recommends her coming home next spring, and remaining in Pretoria during the coming hot season. She asks for an evening gown to be sent out. Hal and Jack goodnaturedly take the younger Wilson boy, Ryves, to see the Diplodocus at the Kensington Museum.

Oct 2 ...Edith and Ryves, Hal, Jack and I to Court Theatre to see "John Bull's Other Island" - amusing.

Oct 9. Yet another operation on Leo's left eye - all said to go as well as possible.

Oct 17 ... N and Hal by train to Bayford for the Christening of Annie's Baby, Barbara Patience. Hal is godfather, Mildred Greenwell and Miss Clements godmothers ... I went to Reeves about Bessy's yellow satin evening gown. And this is sent off next day, with flowers, shoes, etc. to match.

Oct 21 Sun. Hal, Jack and I to St Augustine's ... Harry de Salis and Adm. Cave called - and Leo saw them!!!! [through the blue goggles he is required to wear, no doubt.]

Oct 24 ... Archdeacon Douglas-Hamilton, quite lately from Pretoria, called, and told us a good deal about "dear" Bessy. It WAS so nice to meet him.

They hear from S.Africa that Bob is away on a long trek, and Bessy and Nana had plans to join him for part of it, but after they got to Potchefstroom the rains came on so heavily that they could not keep dry, and in the end were forced to abandon the trip, with great disappointment.

Nov 5 ... we 3 to a British Israel meeting at Mrs Y. Bents - a Miss Cook spoke well, and Mr Reader-Harris gave a charming address. Not long ago he was an ardent follower of Bradleigh and used to give INFIDEL lectures!!

Nov 6 ... to Waterloo to meet Annie and Joyce, coming from Bournemouth to stay here for shopping. Annie looks so well and has grown quite fat and comely, weighs 10 st. 3 ...

Nov 16 ... Heard the good news that dear Hal is promoted to the 1st Class in Upper Div. P.O, over the heads of several senior to him. This compels him to give up his Assistant Secretaryship, but his pay is so much increased that he will get £60 p.a in excess of his present pay, and salary as Sec. combined.

Nov 17 ... Dr (now Whitcombe) saw me again and says I have Lumbago, and must put on linseed and mustard poultices and other remedies and remain in my room. What a bore! but in truth I do not feel fit for anything else ...Bob has sent for Bessy to join him again on the interrupted trek ...

Nov 18 ... Leo's sight is growing! Although he has not yet got his spectacles for near objects, he was able today to read some written addresses on envelopes, and also some LARGE print.

Nov 19 ... a wire from Bayford to say Bernie has a bad cold so he and Annie cannot come to stay here tomorrow ... they have been married 4 years today.

Nov 21 ... my back is more painful again. I came down stairs late as I cannot yet bear the pressure of a gown ...

Nov 24 ... Leo wrote a little note to Bessy, the 1st for a VV long time ... Bessy wrote from Pretoria, she and Nana having greatly enjoyed their trek, but she was grieved to find that her pet kitten Chinty had been killed by a dog while she was away.

Nov 28 ... Bernie, Annie, Jack, Hal and Nettie to the Garrick Theatre, to see "The Morals of Marcus"...

Dec 1 ... good letters from Bessy and Bob to Nettie, and from Nana to me. They had trekked for 12 days, and enjoyed it. Bessy is well but rather disappointed at the way Reeves has made her yellow evening gown, which she had just received. It IS annoying, for it ought to have been so pretty.

One suspects that this discouraging news came through Nana's letter rather than Bessy's!

Dec 5 ... Mrs McLachlan, just arrived from Pretoria ... made us oh! so happy by the splendid account of dear Bessy's health ... Mrs McL is charming and quite devoted to Bessy ...

Dec 10 ... Mr and Mrs Alington come to spend a few days, and Leo begins regular treatment by a Dr Hockinson, for reasons unspecified. Both Nellie, the sewing-maid, and Peters have been away on a fortnight's holiday recently, but now Nellie leaves - Dec 13 ... *she is an ungrateful girl* and, two days later, Peters leaves also, and is replaced by another soldier (Adams).

Dec 25 A subdued Christmas: Hal has gone to Marden to join Bernie, Annie and Joyce, who will be there too. Only Haddie is well enough to go to church, Leo having a bad cough which has kept Nettie up all night. This turns to influenza, and once again there are nurses in the house, and Haddie is moved out of her bedroom ...

Dec 31 So ends 1906 - a year to us of much anxiety and considerable trouble, mostly on Leo's account, and we have never once looked on sweet Bessy's face all this year! But we are cheered by the excellent accounts of her, and by the hope, all being well, of welcoming her home again, in the Spring. God has heard my prayers for her and for Leo - GOD IS GOOD!

Just heard that Jack is v. shortly to leave the Admiralty and join the Euryalus, Flagship of the 4th Cruiser Squadron, with Adm. Inglefield and Capt. Philpott. This is an excellent appointment for him, and he will be back from a cruise in the W.Indies, sometime in June, we hope. Of course, we lose him and his brightness and sympathy and help in the house, but we had him here in our times of need for almost 2 years, and it is right he should now go to sea; and, dear old Hal is still left to us.

Oriel Temple, Collon, c. 1910
Courtesy of Irish Architectural Archive

[Sadly, it has been impossible to identify these family members, though the gentleman is said to resemble Algy.]

1907

This opening year finds Leo, N and me here. (16 Queensberry Place) Also Harry, at the G.P.O, and Jack at the Admiralty since May 1905. Leo is at present laid up with influenza but is better and doing well. Bob still quartered at Pretoria, at Intelligence work, and Bessy and Nana with him since early last April ... we hope to have Bessy home in May. Nettie is a good deal used up by all the trouble and anxiety she has had. I am fairly well, but not v. flourishing. Annie and her 2 baby girls v. well.

Jan 1 Cold - Hal and Jack down to Georgie Hamilton's for Mrs Coode's dance. Leo ... has had a narrow escape from pneumonia, which would have been serious at his age. A Dull day for N and me. After dinner we 2 drank the Homeward Bound (Bob, Bessy & Nana) and the Outward Bound (Jack, who is going to sea).

Jan 2 ... Henry West and Dot, Jessie and Charlie [West] *to lunch. Poor Charlie has been inspected by a board of Naval doctors here, with the result that he is invalided out of the service. I am SO sorry for him, poor boy.*

Jan 12 ... letter from Bessy; she drove her trap with her pony Ginger in the Ladies' competition drive at the Pretoria Horse Show, and actually won the 2nd prize - there were 30 entries!

Jan 15 ... Leo's poor Nurse had to leave today to go and nurse her Mother at Brighton, who is v. ill with influenza. In any case she wd. have left tomorrow, as it is really ridiculous to sit up with Leo every night now.

Jan 19 ... Jack left us, after 20 months of his dear company ... he will leave a big hole behind him ...

Jan 23 Still colder, sharp frost. Up for lunch. Only a few visitors, Mrs Bromley, Mrs Ripley, and Mrs Jeffreys, wife of General Jeffreys, just home from Pretoria. She knew dear Bessy well - and how she DID praise that child! she is very nice ...

Feb 9 There has been an epidemic of Measles on board the Euryalus, and poor Jack succumbs: *after being two days in bed in his v. cold cabin (an iron box on deck, with no means of heating) was today moved to Haslar Hospital, I am thankful to say, where he has every care and comfort.*

Feb 13 ... 7 visitors, including Capt Amundsen, a Norwegian, who has taken his ship through the N.W. Passage in the Arctic ... Jack writes that the Measles are nearly well but he is still in hospital.

Feb 14 ... Auriel Quin and I to the Wallace Collection ... Hal took Auriel and me to the Court Theatre to see "You Never can Tell". A good and amusing play, well acted. We greatly enjoyed it.

Feb 18 ... Jack writes that he was out walking yesterday. He asks that eggs, marmalade, jam and cakes may be sent to him! A good sign! Auriel leaves by Mail for Kingstown, seen off by her brother Aylmer.

Feb 20 ... Jack expects to leave by Mail Steamer on 27th, to join Euryalus at Trinidad.

Mar 5 ... Leo, N and I drove early, to my Dentist, and to see Woollands' new fashions. After lunch, we drove again, Leo to Hoskinson for his treatment, and N and I to tea with Antonia McClintock.

Mar 7 ... Leo, N and I to meeting of National Church Society at a private house ...

Mar 9 ... Bessy wrote from Johannesburg where she was staying at an Anglican Convent with a Miss Robertson. Bob wrote from Pretoria, where he is trying to sell Bessy's pony Ginger, trap, piano etc. ...

Mar 16 ... Good letters from Pretoria: but Mr and Mrs Robertson are paying them a visitation of 17 days already!! Bessy and Nana turned out of their rooms, and scarcely any use of their horses, as the Robertsons monopolise them pretty nearly!! Too bad! the more so as the weather is v. hot there....

Mar 24 Sunday. Very fine and bright. My birthday. N gave me a little pendant, and Annie sent me last night a box of lovely violets. Leo, N, Hal and I to St Jude's in carriage. It seems when they have transport, they prefer this church to St Augustine's, which is much nearer. *Only Adm Le Hunt Ward and Mr and Mrs Alington called.*

Mar 29 Good Friday. Fine and sunny. Leo, N and I to St Jude's, later we had a nice drive in Richmond Park. Hal bicycled down to Bayford, to spend Easter with Annie.

Ap 2 Leo and N took me to Kings X Station on my way to spend a few days with Annie. Bernie met me in his Motor at Hertingfordbury. Found all so well at Bayford. Barbara is a splendid Baby of 7 months, and such a bright jolly little creature. Joyce has grown taller since last autumn: otherwise almost unchanged.

Ap 6 ... returned to London, to find that N's new Scotch Parlourmaid had run away! she was most inefficient ...

Ap 7 ... Kathleen Oldfield passed away today at her house in Clifton. She is much connected with Nettie's and my childhood. [Haddie's only first cousin on her father's side] *A good, simple woman.*

Ap 10 ... Today, we believe dear Bessy and Nana are leaving Cape Town for home, in the Armadale Castle. It seems too good to be true ...

Ap 12 ... Leo still goes daily to Hockansen for rather violent massage. We hope it may do his nerves good ... to tea with poor Vesey FitzGerald.

[This cousin has a wife, Mabel, who is apparently very ill. They have two young children and are frequently visitors or visited by N and Haddie].

Ap 15 ... sent in my claim for Income Tax ...

Ap 16 ... N down to Bayford for the day, to see the Babes, and enjoyed it, and thinks little Barbara a lovely child (which she IS, and quite charming.)

Ap 23 ... A wire came today from Bessy at Madeira - only one word - "Flourishing" - she could not possibly better that!

Ap 26 ...N and Hal left for Southampton to sleep there and, as we hope, to meet dear Bessy early tomorrow and bring her here!

*Ap 27 *********JOY!!********** Annie came here at 10.o am, also little Joyce with Blanche. At about 10.40 N. arrived with dear Bessy, quite well, thank God, but thin and burned brown, and v tired with the voyage and excitement and emotion. Hal came later with the luggage and Nana, who looks SO well and no older than when she left us.*

We had a happy day all together and, I trust, were thankful. Nana's brother and niece came here to tea with her. Bernie came and took Joyce back to Bayford.

Ap 28 Sunday Fine but quite cold. All to St Jude's, where we gave thanks as a family for great mercies vouchsafed.

May 3 N and General Donovan [described as *a nice little man*], P.M.O at Pretoria, take Bessy to see a Dr Wynter.

May 7 ... Bessy and Hal to Mrs Frank Gore Browne's Dance at Hyde Park Hotel. [Should have been] *Lord Strathcona's big Garden Party for the Colonial Premiers, but it was too wet to attempt it.*

May 9 Fine. We had a large afternoon party here to let Bessy's friends know she had come home. I do not know the exact number, but we must have had well over 100 people. Annie came up for the day, and Hal came home early to help us. Bessy with Cicy Macleod to the German Opera after dinner.

Bessy takes part in a busy social round, though the summer is rainy. Jack comes on a fortnight's leave, and her brothers take Bessy everywhere.

Jun 2 Sunday Chilly and rain off and on. Leo, N, Hal and I to Holy Communion at St Jude's, Bessy and Jack to St Augustine's and on to lunch with the Greenwells. Lady G took Bessy in her Motor to see Annie at Bayford.

[Bernie's father, Walpole Lloyd Greenwell, second son of Walpole Eyre Greenwell, had been created a Baronet in 1906.]

Jun 3 ... Hal, Jack and Bessy and their guests, Ella Harman and General Donovan to the Play "The Scarlet Pimpernel" and afterwards to supper at the Carlton, where others joined them....

Weather continues to be very cool, and wet.

Jun 18 Chilly and a good deal of rain here, and it POURED at Ascot, and the Gold Cup was stolen!

June 19. There is a scare when Nana detects Bessy's temperature has risen - *Dr Whitcombe says her cough and indisposition come all from her liver and not from the lung ... all there is to do is to keep well, and not let her overdo. She ought to go abroad this coming winter.*

June 22 ... Bessy down to Windsor Castle with Sir G and Lady Clarke for the King's Garden Party, but unfortunately he got in a fuss about the likelihood of rain coming on and hurried them back to town soon after reaching Windsor, so poor Bessy got no pleasure out of it! They got into an unpleasant crowd of racing men at Windson Station, and Sir G had his gold watch and chain stolen!

Jun 29 ... This is the 50th Anniversary of the Sailing of the "Fox", so we had a celebration of it, in the form of a lunch party of 12. Sir Allen Young, Sir Clements and Lady Markham, Sir Vesey and Miss Hamilton, and all of us, also Annie, who motored up for the occasion, bringing Joyce, and Jack came up from Portsmouth. It was, I think, quite a success, and we put the silver Fox on the lunch table, with a wreath of oak leaves, and white chiffon and silver cord round it. Friends sent us lots of lovely roses and other flowers.

The "Fox" escaping from the Pack Ice
drawn by Captain W.W.May, R.N, for Leo's book
"The Fate of Sir John Franklin, "1895

The "Fox" was the 177-ton yacht in which Leo, with a crew of 25, led the 1857 expedition to try to learn the fate of Sir John Franklin. Leo wrote a book about this arduous trip: "The Search for Sir John Franklin" 1859, which went into many editions. A sledge which he used during this epic is kept in the hall at the home of one of Leo's great-grandsons in Northern Ireland.]

Later Leo was sent a charming and flattering letter from the Geographical Society congratulating him on this anniversary - and this letter was also printed in the morning papers.

July 5 Weather rather better. N, Bessy and Hal to Their Majesties' Court - N presented Flo Laurie on her marriage, and Major Laurie went too. It was a fine night and everything went off beautifully. [Friends] *came in to see N and Bessy dressed. Bessy looked charming and lovely, in her white brocaded gauze Train lined with cloth of gold and trimmed with gold flowers, and gown of white net, trimmed gold. N was wondrously dressed in black brocade Train lined pale petunia silk and trimmed black lace and some gold - gown of black lace and wearing her lovely amethysts. Bessy wore turquoises.*

July 8 ... Dear Leo's birthday - 88 ! What a wretched cold summer this is. Temp. usually 10 to 15 degrees below the average for 50 years

July 11 ... Hal and Bessy had a dinner of 9 here - Mr and Mrs Spedding, Mr and Mrs L. Cator, Sapphire Gore Browne, Alick West, afterwards they all went on to the Greenwells' Dance, where they enjoyed themselves so much that they did not get home until after 4 next morning, in full daylight!

July 13 ... Leo and I drove and left Hal and B at Lords' ... Harrow won - but it was so exciting at the end, that they staid on, and did not get home till 8 pm. They enjoyed themselves well.

July 22 Dark and dull, and not warm. I went to the SSAFA Office, but found it closed. Such heavy rain came on that I got quite wet getting out of the carriage! Gen. Donovan lunched with us. Mr Marriott called to see N while we were out, to make an explication [what can this mean? Mr M has been recorded a few times as a visitor]

July 23 Same dark cool weather! Most extraordinary! Charlotte Leslie, Miss Grierson, Capt Lewin, Mr Walcote and Mr Wessells, S.Africa friends of Bessy's, to tea.

July 25. All go down to Bayford Vicarage again. Bessy is invited by Sir Walpole Greenwell to spend 3 days with them on their yacht, so she has to go out in a hurry to buy a white serge gown etc. They settle into the pleasant life of Bayford (though Barbara is teething, and the nurse, Blanche is away so Nana goes to spend nights at the Cottage.) Bernie has a business trip to the Isle of Man. Bob writes that Bessy's nice pony Ginger has been stolen out of his stable at Pretoria. Bernie gets stung on his wrist, which gives him a good deal of pain and trouble, and a planned motor tour in Scotland, leaving Bessy at Lincoln on the way, has to be abandoned.

Aug 18 Sunday. Mr G, the locum clergyman, as usual to lunch. He IS dull, and common! The babies came to see us and had tea - Barbara is SUCH a Duck!

Aug 21 ... Miss Constance Clements came to us for a day. We like her and very much hope she will be able to go abroad with Bessy in the winter. She is such an experienced traveller.

Aug 26 ... This day, 35 years ago, Nana came to us at Portsmouth, when Hal was one year old.
Aug 29 ... Little Barbara is 1 year old today. A dear, bright pretty little thing and a v. fine child. We kept her birthday here, and she had a tea, all decorated with white flowers. Bernie and Annie are still in Scotland. Bessy drove the donkey into Hertingfordbury to meet Leopold Dix who comes to us for a few days ...
Aug 31 Bessy and Leopold Dix to London early, and went down to Greenwich in Thames Steamer. They lunched at a Restaurant, where Hal joined them, and then to a matinee of the "Merry Widow" and back to Bayford, Jack joining them at Kings X so they all turned up together, which was charming.
Sep 12 ... Annie motored us into Hertingfordbury ... found the house [in London] *so nice and clean, and our beds so comfortable! I feel quite sad parting with dear little Joyce and Barbara, such sweet wee things! ...*
Sep 15 Sunday ... Freddie McClintock (Leo's nephew) and his little girl to lunch ...

Miss Clements, not being well, declines to be Bessy's escort abroad this winter, but after considering some others, they settle for Mary Jeffreys.
Oct 10 Annie, Joyce and little Barbara came in their Motor, on their way to Marden, and lunched here. Joyce was so sweet, and so was the Baby - it is her first peep of the world, as she has never yet been further than Hertford! ... After dinner, we went downstairs to shoot at a target with an air gun.
Oct 11 Hal took Jessie and me to Drury Lane to see "The Sins of Society" a splendid play, which we much enjoyed.
Oct 19 ... Dreadful rows in the house among the servants, resulting in the dismissal of Adams, Leo's man. N was fortunate in getting another (soldier) on the spot - named Lord.
Oct 21 ... The rows and anonymous letters among the servants continue! A detective came, but could throw no light on the subject.
Oct 26 ... Mr and Mrs Whistler are staying, while their little girl, Doreen, has an operation for squint ... the poor child very sick and wretched ... Hal and Bessy down to Marden for weekend ...
Oct 31 ... Dr Whitcombe saw Bessy as she has a bad pain in her back. He says it is akin to lumbago, muscular rheumatism from the liver. Her lung is doing splendidly and it will not be necessary for her to go abroad until early in January ... Mrs Whistler takes Doreen to Dr Lister's house [her eye soon gets better and they go home]
Nov 9 The Dr thinks Leo a little weak today, and he is to be fed up, and get extra stimulant and tonic. Nurse Wakelin came by chance to see us, and insisted on sitting up with him tonight to give N and Nana a night in, as

they are v. tired.

Nov 10 Though Leo is slightly better, he is v fidgetty and unmanageable, from his nerves! he did not seem so well towards evening and a night nurse was sent for, for he had a very bad restless night.

Nov 11 Very dark and dull, and a good deal of fog. N came out for a little drive with me. She is v. tired and sad, and so is Nana. Leo very ill all day. A 2nd nurse was got, and Dr came 3 times. He says it is failure of the vital power, the consequence of a chill, and that very little can be done for him beyond every care and watching, and food and stimulant and warmth, and that nature must do the rest. He has a very bad opinion of him, I grieve to say.

Bessy returns early from a visit to Bayford Hal has an announcement put in the papers about Leo's illness with the result that there are so many callers that Bessy has to put a Bulletin outside the halldoor, so the Inquiry cards are put in the letter box.

Nov 14 ... A telegram to N from the Prince of Wales enquiring for Leo. Hal wired to Jack at Malta, as he may wish to come home, if he can get here. Leo seems better in some ways, though still very ill indeed. Annie is in the house, and Bernie calls in, in the evenings.

Nov 16 A sad, anxious day. Dear Leo is certainly worse, and is sometimes unconscious. Dr saw him 3 times. Bessy and I out for various things required.

Nov 17 A very sad, long day, as Leo is evidently sinking; everything possible is being done to save his precious life. [Later] *Dear Leo entered into rest this evening, at 7.30, quite peacefully. Nettie and Hal were with him to the last. The Dr assures us, that he did not suffer pain, but his breathing was very laboured. He was one of the best men that ever lived, and a sad loss to us all.*

Nov 18 ... Poor N is very good and brave ...

Nov 19 ...Telegrams and letters of sympathy are now pouring in. Jack cannot get leave to come over from Malta. I do not know what we should do without Hal! so good and kind and thoughtful - and clever and tender. Bessy too, is admirable. Bernie comes here every day.

Nov 20 ... Hal is overwhelmed with business - and Bessy and I have plenty to do. Dear Nettie comes down among us. Dear Leo looks so beautiful and peaceful and happy. Numbers of handsome wreaths are arriving, as well as the letters and telegrams. Dear Leo is now lying in the Square Hall, surrounded with lovely flowers, and looking so beautiful.

Nov 22 Dear Leo was laid to rest - till Christ comes - in the Kensington Cemetery at Hanwell, near Ealing

Nov 23 Annie went back to Bayford. We are all very weary.

Nov 25 ... Bessy and I shopped in carriage. We have all such a lot of writing to do, and Hal is very, very busy.

Nov 26 ... Last day of the carriage, perhaps for ever - as N. must retrench all round. She is bearing up wonderfully, but needs much care. Nana sleeps with her in the workroom. Dr Whitcombe called, and says B is SO well, that it will be unneccessary to send her abroad!! HOW delightful. Perhaps she may go to Bournemouth in early spring. He says N is not ill in any way, but needs rest and care, and ought to go away soon for a change.

They are all busy all the time, answering condolence letters, having the furniture valued [for Probate?] Hal gets business advice from Bernie. A few visitors are gradually admitted, and bring comfort.

Dec 13 ... Nettie to Halsnead to spend a few days with Ethel, taking Nana with her. Poor dear, she did not like going, but did so as the Dr advised it, and we all wished her to do so - and I hope it will do her good.

Dec 25 Only Hal and I to Church, as N did not seem quite well. B and Nana stayed with her - but she soon got better and came downstairs. A sad and dull Xmas day. A wire from Bob at Canary ... due at Southampton on30th.

Bob gets home on 30th, followed by Jack *It IS delightful to have the 3 dear boys all at home together.*

The inscription on the Celtic cross erected on Leo's grave reads:

To the Glory of God
and in thankful memory of His Servants
Francis Leopold McClintock, K.C.B, Admiral
discoverer of the fate of Sir John Franklin
born in Dundalk 8 July 1819
his record is enshrined in Westminster Abbey
in the history of his country
and in many hearts which love and admire him
After he had served his own generation by the will of God
he fell asleep 17th November 1907
"so He bringeth them unto the haven where they would be."
"them also which sleep in Jesus will God bring with Him."

[see picture, September 1909.]

1908

Jan 2 ... N took Bessy to see Dr Whitcombe. I grieve to say, that she is not as well as she was - coughing, and some expectoration, but the Dr is not anxious.

Jan 4 ... Busy copying some old letters of Leo's, lent by friends.

Jan 5 Sunday ... no one to church. Bessy coughs a good deal still, and does not look well.

Jan 6 ... I took an eucalyptus bath, which did my lumbago good. Major Collins (RAMC) and Dr Whitcombe saw Bessy. Major C thinks she ought to winter abroad; Dr W thinks not.

[Dr Whitcombe is possibly out of his depth.]

Jan 9..... Hal and Jack took Bessy to see Dr Percy Kidd, who gives a cheerful account of her, and thinks she will soon surmount this little breakdown, which does not surprise him, considering all she has gone through of late. She must not tire herself or make any effort. He thinks London not the best place for her ...Hal and Jack down to Bournemouth to look for lodgings for her ...

Jan 10 ... Bessy is certainly better and coughs less - she went out walking. Hal and Jack ... have secured nice lodgings at Boscombe Valley. After dinner Hal and Jack went to Charing X to see Bernie off to S. America.

Jan 11 ... N out early, to get a Magistrate to witness her signature. She and the 3 boys by motor cab to Balham [Ealing, surely?] *to visit dear Leo's grave ...*

Jan 15 ... Bessy left us to spend some weeks at Bournemouth. Nana went with her, and Bob for 2 or 3 nights, to see her settled. Jack left ... to rejoin the Euryalus ... We have had him since Dec 31, and he has been a great joy and cheer to us, as ever...

Jan 18 ... I was busy shifting my things up to Bessy's room, to give mine to Annie, who we hope will come here on Monday with the Babies (unless they take the Measles, which are all around them at Bayford) ....Bob turned up and gave a pleasant acct. of Bessy ...

Her good Brothers have given her the use of a pony and trap which will be a great pleasure to her.

Jan 20 ... Annie, little Joyce and Barbara and 2 nurses arrived by Motor to stay here with us [while Bernie is abroad]... *it will be a great cheer. Annie is in my room, the Babies have N's large room and dressingroom, N is in the top Dressingroom, I in Bessy's, and Bob in the workroom. A great house full!*

Bessy gives fresh concern, and Nettie and Hal go down to see her. *Poor Bessy is quite broken down in body and nerve with all she has gone through since early in Nov, and she is v anaemic. Thank God, her lung has not suffered much. The Boscombe Dr wants her to keep in bed and have a good restcure - and for the present, the quieter she is, and the fewer people about her, the better.*

Jan 30 ... Jack took N to Westminster Abbey, to see the place where it is proposed to put up a tablet to Leo's memory.

Feb 1 Very sad! but Joyce, who has been ailing with a cold, has developed measles today, which she must have brought from Bayford with her.

Haddie takes some steps towards letting Queensberry Place, and also to sell some of Bessy's clothes - as she has been told to lead an invalid's life for the present.

Feb 11 ... N heard from Sir George Goldie and from the Dean & Canons of Westminster, that they have adopted her proposed inscription for the Tablet ... it is most gratifying ... Jessie West down to Bournemouth to stay with Bessy. I am so glad, as it must be dull and lonely for the child.

Feb 20 Alas! the Dr came and there is v. little doubt that Barbara has the measles! She has waited till the very last possible time of taking them from Joyce. This is sad for poor Bessy, as Annie and the children were soon to have gone down to her, and now they cannot do so for another 3 weeks. Much perturbed about two cheques for Bessy, lost in the post.

Bessy and Nana have moved their lodgings, as those they were in were found too expensive for a long term. Nana reports Bessy as being quite depressed, so Nettie makes preparations to go down to her - first disinfecting herself and all her clothes! Meanwhile, Barbara has quite a light attack of measles, and after due fumigation, goes on to join the rest, complete with Blanche and Mabel, the two nurses, and quantities of luggage and parcels!

Mar 15 Haddie is keeping house with Hal, still planning for it to be let. *Antonia and Emily McC. called, and told Hal and me, that poor Willie McC* [now aged 21] *is very ill with pneumonia at Tenerife and that Charlie and Blanche are going out to him. Poor Nana is not well yet, so Nettie cannot leave Boscombe, but writes that Bessy really seems better and the babies keep well.*

Letters from Annie to Bernie (in South America) give him loving accounts of the two convalescent little girls, and lively messages dictated by Joyce. She seeks to reassure his fears about them all sharing a house with Bessy—the house is large, she tells him; one can imagine that, with Bernie abroad, the sisters were much enjoying some time together, in spite of Bernie's very natural concern about infection from Bessy. One letter implies that Sir Walpole has apologised for keeping Bernie in South America longer than was planned—with an extra directorship bestowed on him as some consolation!

Mar 18 ... Poor Blanche and her boy Edwy sail today for Canary ...

Mar 24 [Haddie is 70!] *My birthday - how old I am, though I often do not feel so!! N and I to Westminster Abbey, to see the tablet erected to dear Leo's memory, by the Royal Society, the Geographical Soc and Trinity House.*

Ap 1 At Last! Hal has got a fortnight's leave from the G.P.O to attend to the Family business! but he has had to forego his pay, during the time!!! What he really wants is leave to spend out of London and get a much-needed change, but he cannot do that at present as there is too much urgent business to attend to.

On Ap 9 Bessy comes up from Boscombe to consult Dr Kidd again. *Alas! he does not give a cheerful opinion of our Darling, who must lead quite an Invalid life for some time to come! It is MOST disappointing, for Dr Horden at Boscombe was quite cheerful about her. WHAT is one to believe? All our plans for the present are changed, as B does not go back to Boscombe (she and I were to have gone down tomorrow), and Nana is to come home as soon as she can bring up things at the lodgings ...*

Ap 12 Sunday, N, Hal and I walked to St Peter's, Cranley Gardens and heard a good sermon from the Bishop of Stepney...

Ap 13 ... Hal saw Sir Clements Markham, just back from Portugal, and he gave him the rough copy of some of the 1st proposed chapters he has written for Leo's Biography.

Ap 26 Annie and the babies return to Bayford from Marden. .... *Yesterday, in a dreadful snow blizzard off the Isle of Wight, the American liner "St Paul" ran into HMS Gladiator and sank her - 1 officer and over 30 men lost, alas!*

Bessy and Nana to Bayford for a visit, and the doctor there - Dr Odell - agrees with Dr Kidd's opinion of her state, that she needs great care. *Antonia McClintock called, and gave a sad account of poor Willie McC, who is dying at Canary. Blanche and Edwy are with him.*

May 10 Alas! Winston Churchill has been returned yesterday, for Dundee, but with a reduced majority from 1906.

May 13 .... Heard that Willie McC died this morning at Canary. Poor Blanche; I do so feel for her, alone (with Edwy) far away in that rough place!

Jack comes on leave, and Bob is back at the Staff College after a trip to Alsace-Lorraine to see the battlefields of the Franco-Prussian War. Nettie comes back from Bayford with a good account of all there - *but what is to be done with poor Bessy and all of us, this coming winter?*

Jun 1 ... Jack came here for tea and dinner on his way from Bayford to Portsmouth and told me that all our nice plans are at an end, apparently, as Dr Odell wants Bessy to live out of doors, with a nurse, in some v. rural place. Poor, poor dear child. We had hoped to have gone v. soon to Camberley to be near Bob and make Bessy happy ...

Haddie has a few days at Bayford, delighted with Annie and the Babies, but less so with Bessy, who is naturally anxious about the future. On June 15 Bernie comes home from S. America, after 5 months away on business, well and sound. On many evenings, Nettie reads aloud the chapters of Leo's Biography as they are finished, which Haddie finds very interesting, and *so well-written.*

Jun 17 ... Disappointed by hearing that Lord Cranbrook, who we hoped might have taken this house for the remainder of the Parliamentary session - has just taken another. Also, the housemaid (Holmes) who was to have gone to Bessy in the country - will not go, annoying and troublesome.

Bessy is eventually settled at Horsenden Rectory, in the Chilterns, with a housemaid and Miss Bridges, a nurse/companion.

July 3 Heard from Bernie that Annie gave birth to another little girl at about 12 o'c last night. We had all much wished for a Boy! but it can't be helped, and Annie and Baby are well, which is the great thing.

July 7 ... N came up from Horsenden, and met me at Liverpool St Station ... and We travelled down to Frinton-on-Sea, ... drove to Inchierman, Vesey FitzGerald's Cottage, where we found only the little boy, Desmond, and his very nice governess, Miss Haberfield ... N left Bessy doing well, v comfortable at Horsenden, and she and Miss Bridges mutually like each other. Nana remains there, for the present at any rate.

July 8 ...N wired to Bayford for news of the new baby, who has been ill, and got a reassuring answer.

July 9 ... N had a letter from Annie (showing how well she is) to say that Baby had been so weak as to frighten them, but is now much better, and she herself very well.

July 14 ... N and I were much grieved by witnessing a terrible scene with poor little Desmond. His father has been back and forth, but his mother is ill, and not there.

[Back to London]

July 17... Nana came up from Horsenden to spend the night .. N back from Bayford, and brings an excellent account of Annie, who is to get up tomorrow. The wee Baby girl is now much better, and likely to do well; but she nearly died of weakness some days ago.
Nana reports well of Bessy on the whole, but there is no marked change in her. Her life is dull and lonely ... but she is so good and patient and never complains. Miss Bridger is quite a success.

July 20 ... N and I by tube to Gawthorpe in Long Acre, where we saw many specimens of Memorial tablets, in brass, bronze etc, some of them v. beautiful. We were much interested. ... Began my cure of Antigout Powders from Italy.

July 23 ... N, Bammie Ross and I down to Bayford ... where we found Bernie at home and Annie on the sofa, so nice and well. Joyce and Barbara sweet and flourishing, and the dear little Baby, coming on so nicely, and such a little duck - very like what her sisters were before her! She ought not to have been born before today!

July 25 ... Hal to Horsenden to see Bessy, and they had a sort of picnic at the White Cross about 2 miles from Horsenden ... she is going to get an old woman to teach her to make Buckinghamshire lace.

July 29 ... I went down to spend the day with Bessy ... dear B able to make herself content in her dull life; she bicycles a little, which is a pleasure to her. She likes Miss Bridger, who is really very nice, and I had a happy day, but was very tired indeed.

July 31 ... May, and a friend (not Renshaw) called here, and asked if the house was to be let; but would not come in beyond the Square Hall, and refused to give their names! Bob spied them, and recognised May!!!

It does not seem as if Haddie ever had any response to her touching letter to sister May in August, 1903.

Aug 1 ... Helen West [Dot] came here early: she is staying with May and Renshaw at Van Dyke Hotel in Cromwell Road. They have lately come over from Rome and are, I hear, going to Scotland ...

Aug 4 ... Left for Prescot in Lancs. to stay with Ethel Willis at Halsnead Hall ... found Mr Willis and Ethel and two children, Mabel Skeffington, Miss Hanbury and Mrs Lewis ... Left off the Antigout Powders for a few days, as they are lowering.

Aug 5 ... Miss Hanbury, Mabel and I in Motor to a Mrs Broadbent at Warrington to see a Pastoral Play "As you Like It" acted in the garden by about 20 girls (no men). It was very good. A cousin of Mr Willis, Miss Bradyll came to stay ... Ethel and Mr W very busy preparing for a great Fete tomorrow, in aid of a Charity ...

Aug 6 A lovely day which is good for the Fete, which went off splendidly. Entertainments of all kinds went on from 3.o'c to 8.30, kept up with incessant energy by Mr W and Ethel. There were hundreds of people of all sorts present, and it ended with dancing on the grass by moonlight.

Aug 7 ... I walked about the grounds with Mr Willis ...

Aug 8 ... The Annual School Feast took place in the grounds, and was a great success. Everyone (except me) danced on the grass till it was dark!

Aug 15 ... in Motor with Ethel and Mabel to a small croquet party at the Gladstones who live near Liverpool.

Aug 16 Sunday. A delicious day. All to Church. Walked and sat within the grounds the rest of the day.

Aug 17 ... Ethel and Mabel into Liverpool in forenoon. The Vicar, Mr Woods and his wife ...and her handsome sister Countess Blucher to tea. Mabel left for Ireland ... Mr Willis has caught a cold by sitting in a draught. He went to bed early, v. sorry for himself ... He had motored into Chester and back today...

Aug 18 ... Mr W and little Celia motored into Liverpool ... Darling Bessy's birthday. May God give her a happy new year, with renewed health and every possible blessing.

Aug 19 ... Mr W and Ethel left early in Motor for Shrewsbury Flower Show and to dine and sleep at Longnor with Connie Sykes ... [Ethel's sister]

Aug 21 ...Mr Horsley and Mr Curwen to dinner. We played cards afterwards, as indeed we do every night ... Hear that it would be rather inconvenient to Constance Sykes to have me, as intended on Monday, so have arranged to go to N and Bessy at Horsenden instead.

Aug 23 Sunday ... All to Church except Ethel, who staid to take care of her children. She went in the evening.

Aug 24 ... Left Halsnead Park at 9.30 Mr W [Dick]*took me in his Motor to the station, went from Prescot to Lime St, Liverpool, to Euston, thence by cab to Paddington, and on to Princes Risborough, where N and Bessy and Miss Bridger met me ...*

Aug 25 ... Not up till lunch time. Sat in a tent with Bessy and N a great part of the day.

Aug 28 Storm and a good deal of rain; v. unpleasant in this poor, badly furnished house, and dull for poor Bessy.

Aug 30 Sunday ...N, Bessy, Miss Bridger and I to tea with Mr and Mrs Conyngsby Disraeli at Horsenden House. We believed that there was a 3 o'c service at Horsenden Church, and intended attending it, but unfortunately we found we were mistaken, so none of us got to Church.

Aug 31 ... N to London to see Hal, and hear what Dr Horden at Bournemouth advises about Bessy [he says, without seeing her, it sounds as if she is doing as well as possible, which is what they all feel]

Sep 5 ... Grieved to hear that poor Annie is laid up at Bayford with Pleurisy, not a bad attack however, so far.

Sep 7 ... N and I and Bob to town ... found the house so nice and fresh and clean and pretty, after this grubby little place. Alas! that we cannot live in our home!

Sep 8 ... Bessy and Miss Bridger, Nana and the Kitchen maid came up from Horsenden ...

Sep 9 ... shopping for a coat and skirt for Bessy ... The French Naval Attache and his wife have been looking at this house, with a view to taking it; they seem nice people, but we do not know whether anything will come of it.

Sep 11 N, Bessy, the 3 boys, Nana and I down to Bayford for little Betty's Christening. [Elisabeth Kathleen, always known later as Betty] *Ethel Willis joined us at Kings X; so did Lady Greenwell and 2 daughters, and Mr Leveson Gower who was to perform the ceremony. We drove from Hertingfordbury in Bernie's motor, and a hired waggonette. All went off so well, except that poor Annie (although much better) cannot yet leave her room. We all had luncheon, and left by 2 motors for 3 o'c train back to London. Hal and Bob came home with us to tea, and then left to travel tonight to Ireland to stay with the Gledstanes at Fardross. ...*

Sept 13 Sunday ... the great Eucharistic R.C. Procession at Westminster was to have taken place, but at the last moment the Govt. stopped it, as illegal, so it was done in a v. modified way. N and Jack to St Peter's, Cranley Gardens.

Sept 15 Bessy, who has gained an encouraging amount of weight, leaves with Miss Bridger for Bournemouth. *For the 1st time for very long, Nana has not gone with her, and I fear she will miss her a good deal ... A good account of Annie, who was not overtired by seeing us all last Friday, as her temp. was normal next day, for 1st time.*

They negotiate to rent a house at Woking for the winter. Meanwhile, Hal and Bob, in Ireland, leave the Gledstanes and go to Drumcar to visit, and later to the Rathdonnells at Lisnavagh, Co. Carlow. ...

[Lisnavagh was built by William McClintock Bunbury, the cousin who first took Leopold to sea.]

Haddie is delighted that Bessy, with Miss Bridger, is going to Portsmouth by Excursion Steamer to spend the day with Jack in the Euryalus ... *Dear Bessy, HOW she will enjoy it!*

Sept 23 ... N and I by tube to Albemarle St to see Mr Hallam Murray about [Sir Clements Markham's] *Biography ... Mrs Whitfield called, and kindly looked over and named my Lace for me.* [Some of what may be Haddie's lace, labelled "*Believed very good*", is still in the family and is featured on the cover of this book.]

Oct 1 ... Jack and I to Mildred Greenwell's wedding to Mr Loynes at Holy Trinity, Sloane Street and 17 Portman Square...... Patience McClintock [eldest d. of Leopold McC, Leo's nephew] *called here. Such a sweet, pretty girl.*

Oct 3 N and Nana see another, preferred house at Woking ...Bob came up from Camberley, and he and Hal dined with Mrs Alexander, and took her and Dot Gledstanes to the Theatre, to see "The Flag Lieutenant"..

Oct 8... Very anxious about affairs in the Near East - looks so like War; please God, it may be averted ... N and I to Sth Audley St to see a miniature and an oil painting of Leo at Mr Hurst's Studio. People came to see this house but I do not think they will take it

Oct 16 ... Mrs Alington came to make arrangements with N about taking care of this house, if it does not let. Mrs Currey and her daughter called - she was a Brougham.

Oct 19 ... Mrs and Miss Disraeli called - we met them at Horsenden.

Nov 2 ... Major McMicking has taken this house for 6 months from the 5th, but only gives 5 and a half guineas a week, truly a poor rent - but better than nothing. It is a rush to get ready with so short notice Mr and Mrs Alington arrived early, and he went on to Ireland by night mail, she remaining here with us. They were to have staid here as Caretakers, if the house was not let, so they are rather disappointed.

Nov 3 ... Nana and I and the Cook and Between Maid left London and found Uplands, Hook Heath, Woking, very nice and fresh and clean.

Nov 4 ... Bessy and Miss Bridger arrived from Bournemouth ... Bessy still coughs a good deal, but is much better than she was a short time ago. She seems much pleased with this house.

Nov 5 ... Nettie and Long, the Parlour Maid, arrived from London .. Poor N very tired, as it was a job to get the house ready for the McMickings at such short notice.

Nov 7 Very cold indeed, with a N.E wind, and as all windows have to be kept open for Bessy, it is perishing: but if only the treatment does her real good - nothing else matters much.... Bessy drives the pony and trap, which belongs with this house. Poor Haddie is soon suffering from Neuralgia and Sciatica, perhaps not surprisingly.

Nov 20 ... Bessy went up to London by herself, on business - while B was away we were able to dispense with the bitter cold draughts in the rooms...

They do not know many people in the locality, but the Aynslie Greenwells live not far away, and Mrs Smyth, and later Mrs Phayre, come to call.

Dec 12 ... Bob spends the weekend with Lady Elphinstone, near Camberley … Bessy stays late in bed each day, but regularly drives the pony and trap to and from the station to meet and see off visitors. There is much dull, damp weather, and they have been through the first sad anniversary of Leo's death; Bessy has to come in from the verandah (where she presumably sleeps) because the cold and damp make her worse. They are glad when Bob comes, to cheer them all up. Nana leaves to spend the Xmas holidays with her brother in Putney.

Dec 23 ... Bob and Bessy drove in pony cart to Chobham and lunched with Lady Elphinstone and her daughters. I am so glad for B to have a little variety in her present v. dull life, which she is bearing so pluckily.

Dec 24 ... Poor Annie is laid up with influenza and a slight attack of Pleurisy - which is very trying, as she has just moved into their new house [Woodcock Lodge, Little Berkhampsted] ... *Bob and Bessy to Woking. They are v. busy over some mysterious business!*

Dec 25 The mystery has resolved itself into a charming little Xmas tree, all snowed and frosty with silver tinsel, which decorated our dinner table. All to morning service and Holy Communion, except B and Miss Bridger. All the young people had a long walk in afternoon.

Dec 26 SUCH a cold N.E wind. In bed with a heavy cold. I do so feel the hardship of having to live in rooms with doors and windows open in this weather! but it is for dear Bessy's sake SO - no matter! But HOW it can do her good is the puzzle. B and Miss Bridger, in the Pony cart, and Hal and Bob on foot, went to a meet of Beagles and enjoyed themselves.

1909

This opening New Year comes after a sad and anxious one, 1908. We came here on Nov 3 to continue the open-air treatment for dear Bessy through the winter, and to keep her quiet and out of the way of temptation in the form of invitations etc. in hopes (may God grant it) of restoring her to health; but it is unspeakably dull here; no one we care to know, and just this little house on the bare, brown heath - quite exposed, not even the shelter of a tree! and we are perished with cold, in an ill-built (otherwise nice) house, and having to keep all windows open, and a draught if possible, in the sitting-rooms, for Bessy's sake. If only it does her real good, it will be worth it all. N has a nice nurse companion for her, Miss Bridger, who has been with her since June, and is a great comfort. Hal comes down here every day, to dine, sleep and breakfast - and seems to like it. Bob completed his first year at the Staff College, and came to us on leave. How he does cheer us up, dear boy! Jack still Commander of the Euryalus, at present in the Mediterranean but soon coming home. Poor Annie is still an Invalid, not having yet recovered from an attack of Pleurisy, following Influenza. Her 3 baby girls are flourishing. They all moved into a new house, Woodcock Lodge, [Little Berkhamsted] *a few days ago.*

We have had a heavy fall of snow the last few days, and hard frost, in fact bitterly cold, 18 or 20 degrees below the average, and we have felt it all the more ...and most of us have taken cold and are more or less ailing.

Jan 1 ... Bessy in bed, as she certainly has a little cold. As she is not downstairs we have not to keep doors and windows open, so we are warm and comfortable. We have also put two large screens in the drawing-room, to keep off some of the draught.

Jan 2 ... Nana back from her visit - we are so glad to have her back again

Jan 6 ... Jack writes from Malta, just starting for Sicily after the terrible Earthquakes in Sicily and Calabria, where our Blue Jackets have been doing a magnificent work of mercy!

Jan 7 ... Henry West came over from Folly Court [near Wokingham, to where his family have moved, on leaving Sacombe Rectory after 20 years] - *sorry I could not see him* [in bed with cold] - *things not going on well!*

Jan 8 ... Jack writes again, back at Malta, after visiting disaster areas. He says it is appalling! His ship's Co. behaved splendidly and they distributed lots of food etc. and took on board a number of poor wounded people. Hal has seen Annie and babies and gives an excellent account of them all, but Annie is still in bed.

Jan 9 ... Still in my room; I dare not venture into rooms with doors and windows open! ... N and B to tea with the Pritchards [neighbours on the heath.].

Jan 11 ... N and B up to London and not back until 4 o'c, so I was able to spend that time in the drawing-room, without too much open air. My cold is better, but I want to get rid of it. N and B went to see the brass tablet that is to be put up in Drumcar Church to dear Leo's memory, and were greatly pleased with it ... we hear that poor Annie still has a temperature, still in bed! Sad!

Jan 14 ... N in bed all day, with general upset, and Nana was suddenly seized with Lumbago, which made her quite helpless, and she had to be put to bed, so the household is not v. flourishing.... Bessy and Bob made some peppermint sweets in the drawing- room - very good.

Jan 15 Nana somewhat better today, but still in bed. Miss Bridger is so kind to her, and nurses her beautifully. Charlie McClintock writes that a man is offering to take the farm, garden etc. at Monasterboice - all but the house.

Jan 18 Blowing again! This is SUCH an exposed situation! N and B called on Mrs Pritchard, to see her house, which she is offering us for April...

Jan 19 Gertrude Plunket and Miss Macnicoll came to lunch with friends near here, and they came on to pay us a visit. It was v. nice seeing some friends again.

Jan 20 ... I am suffering from face and earache - no wonder! ...

Jan 21 ... Bob brings a good account of all at Woodcock - Annie better, sitting up, and soon going to Bournemouth.

Jan 22 ... Bob left us to join at Chatham. What a dear boy he is, and how we shall miss him ... Mrs Pritchard has made N such a good offer for her house, Link View, for April, that it has been accepted. This will save N a lot of trouble and anxiety. We expected snow all day but it did not come - a black N.E wind instead.

Nettie goes for a night to Woodcock and reports Annie better, off to Bournemouth, and the three little girls very well and very sweet

Jan 28 ... weather as bad as yesterday, with thick fog. B cannot sit on the Verandah. She went out walking, and waved to Bernie and Annie, passing in the train near Woking, on their way to Bournemouth. Jack home on leave.

Jan 31 Sunday, N and the 3 boys to church ... delightful to have the 3 boys

Woodcock Lodge, from a painting by Annie

together,even for one night.

Feb 1 ... Bessy and Jack to London to order a coat and skirt, get a wedding present for Capt Duff, and lunch at the "Pot House on Incubator", Jack's club ...

Feb 16 ... saw by the Paper, that Jack has got the appointment he wished for - Flag Commander to the Admiral of the Home Fleet. His headquarters will be at Sheerness ...

Feb 19 Very fine and bright. Frosty. My cold better. B drove me to see Stoke Park, near Guildford, where Uncle James Delap used to live and where I used to stay, when a child ... AT LAST the Biography of dear Leo has come out, and N received from Mr Murray 10 copies of it. We do not like the binding at all, but the type and engravings are v. good

...[Sir Clements Markham: *Life of Sir Leopold McClintock*, London 1909]

It continues very cold, so that Haddie stays in her room to avoid the freezing downstairs rooms. Bessy and Miss Bridger get some good tobogganing. Hal gets influenza, in his lodgings in London and Nettie goes to look after him. He has been staying up during the week as he is very busy with Territorials.

March 8 ... Hal brought us bulbs some time ago, and we now have hyacinths, daffodils and tulips in bloom in the drawing-room, which is a great pleasure ...

March 13 ... Miss Abel Smith called and discussed her brother's (M.P for Herts) position with regard to Tariff Reform.

March 16 Quite fine and less cold. B and I up to town. She went off on her secret errand. I by tube ... shopped for B at Gorringes' and on to Buckingham Palace Hotel to see Kate and Gertrude Plunket who are staying there. B joined me, and we went to the Carlton where General Donovan gave us an excellent luncheon, and we came back ... It is so much milder in town, like another climate, and yet everyone there was complaining of the cold... B was none the worse for this little outing. She is going on so well, and the bad symptoms in the mornings have been markedly less the last few days - thank God.

March 27 Hal arrived from Bournemouth ... he is well again, but looks thin and rather weak. Nana arrived also at 7.30 pm, and reports Annie better and she has moved into other lodgings today. Joyce is with her, and little Barbara and the nursery-maid come on Monday ...

March 29 ... N Bessy and Hal drove in pony trap to have tea with Mr and Mrs Field, very agreeable people ...

Ap 6 ... We moved into Mrs Pritchard's house, Link Side ... and found it all very nice and pretty, a great improvement on Uplands ... We have spent 5 months and 3 days at Uplands, not at all what we liked doing - but I shall always feel grateful to the place, for the great improvement it has wrought in Bessy.

Ap 8 ... Tan (Stanley) McClintock came to spend a few days. He is Lieutenant in the Gordon Highlanders, at Aldershot, and is a nice and very LONG boy!! ...

Ap 9 Good Friday ... all to St John's church, except Bessy ... Jack arrived ... the young people all went for a walk after tea: they also played croquet.

Ap 10 What a pleasant party we are now, and in such a charming house and nice garden, and beautiful verandah and balcony. We ALL - a party of 8 - went in a hired carriage and on bicycles to Norlands' Corner a few miles off, and had tea on the grass - there was a good deal of mist which interfered with the fine view, but we much enjoyed ourselves. Billiards and dancing and fun after dinner.

Ap 11 Easter Sunday ALL to church and H.C. Jack and Bob bicycled over to the Elphinstones at Camberley, for lunch, tea and supper, and did not get back here until 11 pm. Spent all day out of doors.

Ap 12 Alas, our lovely weather is gone ... Tan and our 3 boys played hockey, leapfrog etc. on the croquet lawn in their bare feet! and we had billiards and dancing indoors. Tan left us after dinner to our regret, for he is a very nice young fellow and a pleasant and amusing companion.

Ap 13 ... Lady Elphinstone and her two nice girls motored over and had tea with us ...

Ap 14 ... Dear Jack and Bob left us for Sheerness and Chatham ... and so end these delightful happy days we have just spent. Days ever to be thankfully remembered.

Ap 21 Very fine and sunny ... N, Bessy and I in a hired motor to lunch with Lady Elphinstone and her youngest girl at their pretty place, Pine Wood, near Bagshot, then motored on to Portnall, where we found Harry de Salis and May Drake, Georgie Hamilton, Rodolph and Edith, Willie and Gloir, and Mary Balfour. Had tea there and Harry joined us from London, and we all motored back to Linkside, arriving at 6.pm after a most enjoyable afternoon.

Ap 23 ... N to tea with Miss Bowles (a dear little woman) at St John's. Mrs Aynslie Greenwell drove over and had tea with Bessy and me. Much annoyed at the exorbitant charges made for Damage Done by us at Uplands - most of which is not true.

Ap 25 Sunday ... Mr and Mrs Aynslie Greenwell motored over from their little place a few miles off, and took Bessy and Hal and me over to tea and brought us home again ...

Ap 26 ... Bessy, with Miss Bridger left for Bournemouth, and I left for Wokingham by motor car to Woking Station. Changed at Ascot. Dot met me at Wokingham, in her dog cart and we went on to Folly Court. Found all the family there (and well) except Charlie, who has just gone back to Cambridge. N went to 157 Cromwell Road to stay with Miss Macneill, Nana to Putney to her brother, and the servants have a holiday, so we are all scattered.

Ap 30 ... Mrs Dykes March (nee Macan) came to call on me, and staid for tea and dinner, after which Henry and Helen walked home with her. She is very nice.

May 1 ... Walked in the garden and drove with Daisy in "Taffy's Cart" (an old pony and governess cart).

May 2 Sunday. All to church except me as it is some way to walk. General Sir Arthur Wynne called on me and we had a talk about old times in Collon. Heard from Bessy, with the good news that Dr Horden is much pleased and she may make London her headquarters for the summer and pay country visits, and play tennis etc. - but not go out at night, or frequent crowded rooms ...

The Wests are much occupied with servant-hunting, evidently a great problem in their new home.

May 8 ... Helen and Daisy to Reading about servants. Henry took the other 3 girls to Aldershot for the R. E. Sports (Jessie and twins Aileen and Kathleen)

Haddie goes back to 16 Queensberry Terrace, where she found that *poor old no.16 has been left in an indescribable state of dirt and neglect by the Radical tenants, the MacMickings! Poor Nettie and the servants are in despair!*

May 10 ... Servants, charwoman and tradesmen hard at work trying to clean the house ...

May 11 ... Bessy and Miss Bridger arrived from Bournemouth ... Bessy looking wonderfully well and bright, and so glad to be back in town ...

May 14 ... Mr and Mrs Alington called and remained for lunch. They are in a pack of troubles, poor things.

May 15 Bessy got a wire from Bob, asking her to meet him today at the A & N Stores. We immediately guessed it was an engagement ring for Maidlie

Elphinstone [Mary] - *which was true! and afterwards Bob came and spent the evening here, and told us all about it, and how happy he was He went down to the Es at Bagshot for the weekend. ... Miss Bridger left us, after being nearly 11 months with Bessy. I do hope she will get on well without her!*

May 16 Sunday ... we are much excited about dear Bob, though we had quite seen it coming...

May 17 Bob came at 5 o'c, bringing Maidlie to dine and sleep here. He left at 11pm and went back to Chatham. This house is getting cleaner and more settled by degrees. N is doing up the Bathroom and putting in a new Bath. We are all much taken by Maidlie and think her such a nice dear simple, affectionate girl and consider that Bob has chosen most wisely. May God richly bless them both. We drank their health in champagne at dinner.

May 28 ... Hal and Bessy down to Pinewood, Lady Elphinstone's place at Bagshot, for Whitsuntide. I took Mrs Inglis to Madame Nordica's concert at Queen's Hall ... it was simply splendid. She is one of the most charming and finished singers I have ever heard (soon going to retire, alas!) and Mr John Coates, the only other Artiste, was excellent too. I greatly enjoyed it, and did so wish Bessy could have been there.

Jun 3 ... Lady Elphinstone and Maidlie, Tim Bunbury, Lady Wynne to tea. Expected Bammie Ross who did not come, and Lady Greenwell, who came later ...

Jun 9 Bessy spent the forenoon with the 2 Elphinstone girls at Mirette's the dressmaker about the Bridesmaids' frocks, but they have not yet quite settled about them! We had such a nice dinner here of 10 - Olive and Maidlie Elphinstone, Tim McC Bunbury, our own 3 dear boys, N, Bessy, Helen Crozier (who had been staying) and me ...

Jun 22 ... Annie's three babies, with two nurses, motored up from Herts and came here for early dinner. Then they went to be photographed, and N and Bessy took Joyce to the dressmaker to fit on her bridesmaid's frock ...

Jun 25 ... Bob came in time for lunch and afterwards went with N to a Lawyer about the Marriage Settlements...

June 28 ... Bessy and I by bus to Bishop of London's Garden Party at Fulham Palace, Helen C. came with us - Very dull. Hal and Bessy to Lieut. Shackleton's Lecture to the Royal Geographical Soc. at Albert Hall. They had v. bad seats in the orchestra, because they did not apply early enough for them. Dear Bessy DID so wish to go, that I am v. glad she was able to do so. This has been her 1st and only deviation from the rule of not going out at night!

Jun 29 ... It is rather less cold than it was a few days ago, but still so chilly that we have eiderdowns and hot water bags at night!! at the end of June!!

July 1 ... Mrs Scott, wife of the Antarctic Capt. Scott, called ... Bessy with the 3 Greenwell girls motored down to Woodcock Lodge, where they played tennis and had lunch, tea and dinner. Bessy back at 9 pm ... B saw Annie in her bed - but a good deal better. She has been more or less bed-bound since Betty's birth, one year ago.

July 2 General Sir Curzon Wyllie shot dead by an Indian at Imperial Institute this evening! Everyone is simply appalled!

July 3 Fine, and warmer. Bessy down to Hurlingham to lunch and see Polo. Helen Crozier went with her as Chaperone! They were General Donovan's guests and he fetched them in a Motor Car ... Bessy gave me two tickets for good private theatricals at Albert Hall in aid of "Dreadnought" Naval Hospital. I took Miss King with me, and we much enjoyed it.

July 6 ... Little Joyce motored up from Woodcock and lunched here, then Bessy and I took her in Bernie's car to fit on her bridesmaid's frock and hat, all pink chiffon! She looked like a lovely Xmas cracker, and was such a duck ...

July 8 ... Bessy and I to Sir George and Lady White's Garden Party at the Royal Hospital, Chelsea. It was refreshing to have a fine day! Bob and Maidlie and her sister Mrs Welch dined here and they and Hal went to a Theatre afterwards.

July 9 ... Bessy and I to the Eton & Harrow March at Lords. We had 3 teas at different friends' tables - Fardells, Nelsons and Greenwells....

July 12 ... Heard from Jack that he cannot possibly come to the wedding, as there will be still Manoeuvres and firing going on in his Fleet! We ARE disappointed.

July 14 A good deal of rain early, finer later. N and I and Nana by train down to Bagshot. Had lunch on the way. Drove to Pinewood, where we met all the Elphinstone family ... Saw the presents, which were charming and so nicely arranged... Went in Lady E's Brougham to Stone Hill where we are to be Lady Grant's guests for 2 days... nothing can exceed Lady Grant's kindness and hospitality. Rain at night - what will it be tomorrow?

July 15 A lovely, genial day! So glad! To St Anne's, Bagshot, for the wedding. They were married by Bishop Montgomery and Henry West and a Mr Hill. 4 bridesmaids - Olive Elphinstone, Bessy, Miss Cole and Miss Vivian, in grey and pink, and two children, Joyce, and Norma Cowie, in pink chiffon. Bob, and his best man Capt Jackson, and Hal and Capt Cowie in uniform, and the aisle lined with NCO Sappers.
The flower decorations done by the Duke of Connaught. Lady E. gave Maidlie away.

[Her father, Sir Howard Elphinstone, had died some years before, being lost overboard off Usshant, on a holiday voyage with his wife. As a young man he had lost the sight of one eye, winning the V.C when he rescued 20 wounded

Bob & Maidlie's Wedding

men at the Siege of Sevastapol.. He had been Comptroller to the young Duke of Connaught, and much valued by Queen Victoria.]

It was a BEAUTIFUL wedding! Maidlie looked charming, and Bob SO nice and so handsome. Many of our friends and relations could not come because of the distance and the unsettled weather we have had of late. The reception at Pinewood was held mostly in the garden, where the R.E band from Aldershot played. Bob and Maidlie had a great send-off and the Sappers cheered. They motored to Oxford to spend 2 nights there ... everything went off splendidly, without a hitch. We are v. thankful for dear Bob, for we are sure he is going to be happy. Two days later, they appear briefly to re-pack before going off to Norway for the rest of their honeymoon looking *so well and bright and happy.*

July 22 Fine, but not much sunshine. N down to Falmouth to stay with the Quins. I went down to spend the day with Annie at Woodcock Lodge... I had not seen Annie since last Sept - she has grown very stout and red sunburned. I could scarcely recognise her. She is very much better, at LAST, and hopes to get on pretty fast now, but is still quite an invalid, not allowed to walk more than a few steps, lies in bed or on a sofa nearly all day, in the open air. Goes a little in a Bath chair in the garden. The 3 babies so well and sweet. I only saw Bernie for a few minutes ... High wind, which greatly blew me about in the motor car!

July 24 ... Jessie West turned up at 9.30 pm having missed her train to Wokingham. I wanted to keep her for the night, but she so feared her Mother would be frightened, that she left by a late train, to reach home after midnight. Hal down to Jack at Sheerness for weekend, so I am quite alone.

July 29 ... Freddy McClintock [one of Leo's nephews, son of Alfred] *came in after dinner, and brought his nice little boy Geoffrey to see us ...*

July 30 ... Mr Yates, the artist, called, and took down his portraits of Leo and Nettie, and washed and rehanged them.

July 31 ... Hal came .. to pack and put on his uniform, and then went down to Salisbury Plain, to spend a fortnight under canvas with his regiment, the Post Office Rifles, or 118th Battalion, City of London Territorials. He is now a Major ... I shall now have a v. quiet time of it all alone for a week ...

Aug 4 ... Ambrose Gledstanes called ... he is to be married on the 18th, to Miss Webber, in Wales ...

Aug 9 ... Bob and Maidlie arrived here from Norway, where they have had a good time, all but the weather in general. They both look well and happy ... left for their new home at Chatham, where I hope they will be blessed.

Aug 11 ... Nettie left here for Kingstown by day Mail. She is going first to Eva Dix at Ferndale....Disappointed to hear from Bessy, at Halsnead, that the house there is full, and Ethel cannot have me on the 13th, as I had hoped ...

Aug 17 ... Hal down to Mold, in Wales, to be Best man at Ambrose Gledstanes' wedding ...

Bessy crosses to Ireland, to meet her mother in Dublin and go down to Drumcar together.

Aug 18 Haddie makes the long journey to Huyton, then by fly to Halsnead Park, where she finds Dick and Ethel and their two children, old Mrs Willis and four other guests.

Aug 20 ... I watched the party here playing Bridge after dinner, and we did not go to bed until quite late.

Aug 24 Haddie spends much time watching croquet, meanwhile recording that Bessy is attending the Dublin Horse Show with Henry West and Jessie. The weather is fine so she can sit out. From the 30th, poor Haddie spends much time wiring various friends and relations, as she cannot stay at Halsnead when Ethel goes away, and the workmen are in at No 16! *... we play Bridge EVERY evening, which I don't much appreciate!*

Sep 4 ... Back to London, and found the house so nice and fresh after all the staircases, doors etc being painted, and no smell left. Haddie never relishes being by herself, wistfully recording the progress of Nettie and Bessie in Ireland - and then hearing that Bessy is going to Annie on her way back - *I am glad for her sake, but a little sorry for myself!*

But, to her delight, she is invited down to Chatham by Bob and Maidlie.

Sep 9 ... Down to Chatham, where Maidlie met me. Their house is so nice and pretty. Bob took M and me after tea to the R.E Brompton Barracks and showed us the Mess Rooms etc, which greatly interested me, and refreshed my memory of when I saw them before, when Leo, Nettie and I were staying at Chatham with General and Mrs Gordon in 18 ?? and were present at an R.E dance in the beautiful large Mess Room. I also thought of my dear Brother, who spent some years there long, long ago.

Sep 11 ... I have greatly enjoyed my little visit here. Bob and Maidlie so kind and hospitable, and it is delightful to see how perfectly happy they are, dear young things ...all to Victoria, and they went on to Woodcock for the weekend, where Annie and Maidlie will meet for the first time!

Sep 14 Haddie joins Bessy at Woodcock. *Annie is much better, and beginning to move about a little, and the 3 children are well and charming.*

Sep 15 ... Bernie comes back every day from London, in time for a late tea. Annie in Bathchair to Bayford to call on some friends there. Her nurse and Bessy walked with her ...

Sep 17 ... Mabel, the nurserymaid left, and Joyce cried a lot, poor child. Bessy left for Bovinger Rectory to spend a few days with the Whistlers. We shall miss her much; the children love her so, and no wonder ... a new head nurse arrived for the children, who, we hope, will prove satisfactory.

Sep 19 Sunday. Bernie and Joyce to church. I did not go as it was rather too long a walk for me ... to the Trotters (very nice people) for tea, and ... they gave us a strange (but v. good) kind of jam they had brought from Sweden, with gold-coloured aromatic raspberries.

Sep 26 Sunday.[back in London] *I went to Brompton Church. Hal took Bessy to see dear Leo's grave. Nettie (very tired after her journey from Ireland) came down at lunchtime.*

Sep 27 ... Bessy and I to a show of live Models at Harrods. Mrs Inglis gave the tickets.

Oct 3 ... N and Dottie [sister Helen West, who is staying] *to morning Service at Westminster Abbey, which they much enjoyed ... Aylmer Quin lunched with us: he is now working in a stockbroker's office in London.*

Oct 7 ... We expected General Donovan and his intended, Mrs Morell to tea, but she has a bad cold, and they could not come ... Much disappointed and surprised to hear that Annie's Dr Odell will not allow Bessy to spend the winter with Annie at Bournemouth as intended! and says "it would be bad for both of them!!" (Stuff and nonsense!)

But Dr Odell seems to be managing Annie's illness more successfully than Bessy's doctors are with hers. Dr Odell subsequently becomes a great feature and friend in the Greenwell family: his word is law and Betty, third daughter, in her memoirs, recalls how fond they all were of him, and how kindly he removed her tonsils, on the nursery table! He is evidently ahead of some other doctors in perceiving the contagious nature of communicable tuberculosis, and Annie's children recall, with cheerful resignation, that their Mother never was able to cuddle and kiss them. She seems to have compensated for this, however, as all speak of her with much love and affection., and many of her wonderful letters to them in later life have been carefully kept. They also had a most affectionate father in Bernie, who always stoutly denied any disappointment in the birth of daughters.

Oct 12 ...Heard that Winifred Skeffington died last Sunday at the nursing home just after her sisters had gone home, believing that the worst was over. She had had a dreadful operation. [A sister of Ethel Willis, Violet Radford, Constance Sykes, and Algy Massereene.]

Oct 14 Dr Horden, Bessy's doctor at Bournemouth, being up in London, very kindly came here to see her, and has made us oh! so happy, by his excellent opinion of B - who is so very much better in every way, that we must try and keep her so. She may stay in town until the new year, and then go somewhere in England till about the end of April. What a relief this is! and we have plenty of time to look about us, etc.

They do have a tenant for No. 16 - the Capels, from 5 December, but have trouble finding somewhere suitable for themselves: many changes of plan. Haddie also gets a bad cold, but stays upstairs, partly so as not to give it to Bessy, but also to avoid the open windows downstairs!

Nov 3 ... Miss Hawkes, Lady-in-waiting to Princess Louise of Schleswig Holstein, called to arrange with N about a Drawing-room Meeting for the R.N Scripture Readers.

Nov 11 ... Hayes did not seem very well, and lost her memory for about two hours, after which it came back all right. Dr Schacht came, and thinks it was due to indigestion. She was kept in bed, and soon seemed absolutely well ...

Nov 17 ... Carrie Macnaghten called, and gave us an interesting account of her work among poor London boys. Went with Bessy to Mrs Hickson in .... Square and was much interested and touched ... [Mr and Mrs Hickson are Spiritual Healers, and Bessy has been seeking help from them for some time] *...very busy writing invitations for the Drawing-room Meeting*. Further tremendous preparations go on.

Nov 25 We had a Drawing-room Meeting here at 4.30. Nearly 800 cards have been sent out: and I think we had quite 100 people. Princess Marie Louise came with her l-in-w, Miss Hawkes, and Canon Sheppard, Dean of the Chapels Royal was in the chair, supported by the Chaplain of the Fleet, Sir Robert Hart, the Bishop of Kensington, Adm. Sir E. Fremantle, Adm. Holland etc. ... The Princess said a few charming words, and Hal proposed a vote of thanks in a few well-chosen words - his maiden speech! Afterwards, there was tea. The Princess and a small party had it in the Boudoir.

Nov 30 ... This night took place the great Division in the House of Lords, who referred the Budget to the Constituencies by a majority of 350 to 75! Well done, the Lords!

Dec 1 ... Bernie called here at tea time. His youngest brother, Geoffrey, [about 15] *was with him. They had a Memorial Service today at Marden, for poor Mildred Loynes - Hal and Bessy were asked to it, but could not go.* This is Bernie's third sister, married just over a year, aged about 29. She died in India, leaving a baby, Godfrey. *Bessy is recovering from a cold, which fortunately did no lasting harm.*

At the last minute, Nettie manages to find a little house at Camberley, Eversley, to which they migrate, with Nana, Cook, the new Between-maid and the Parlourmaid, on 7 December. They are quite near to the Elphinstones, and to Elizabeth Lefroy (a great-niece of Leo's) so a modest social life springs up.

Dec 18 ... Olive Elphinstone, in her motor car "George" came to lunch ...

Dec 19 Sunday Frost and cold wind, frequent heavy showers. N and I to St George's Church, Camberley. Heard a good sermon on the State of the Blessed Dead. Bessy out more than once, but was driven in by the rain. I'm afraid we are all a little dull and depressed!

Dec 20 ... N, B and I in a hired Brougham to tea with Col. and Mrs Percival, where we met a nice Mrs Ashe, an American married to Admiral Ashe.

Dec 24 Frosty, and fine and bright. N, Bessy and I drove over to Pinewood (3 miles) in a hired Landau for a Xmas tree and tea. Found Maidlie there, also Capt and Mrs Welch (Irene) and their dear little girl. Bob arrived from Chatham, and Hal and Jack from Switzerland, all so well. Some Mummers turned up - rather grotesque!

Dec 28 ... Helen West and Jessie came over from Wokingham, and had tea here. General Owen called - he lives next door to us here. Jack and Bessy played golf, and had tea with the Bolds ... Hal up to town early, to find that this is a holiday at the GPO, and he need not have gone. Hard luck!

Dec 30 Annie's Dr at Bournemouth and Bernie are quite satisfied with her progress. Joyce quite recovered from her v. mild attack of whooping cough, and Barbara and Betty are expected at Bournemouth today.

Dec 31 .. N, Jack, Bessy and I spent the day with the Wests at Folly Court, by bus to Blackwater, then train to Wokingham, where Helen's carriage met us. Found all at home, except Daisy and Charlie, who are in Switzerland, and Alick in India ... Quite a big tea party, Col, Mrs and Miss Buchanan Dunlop, Sir Arthur and Lady Wynne, Anne Macan and Mrs Dykes Marsh, and several others. Everything was so nice and we enjoyed ourselves ..

1910

This New Year finds us at Camberley in this nice little house - Eversley— Nettie has taken for the winter, so as to do the very best possible thing for Bessy who, thank God is so wonderfully better and stronger, and able now to enjoy her life in many ways. Hal and Jack arrived from Montana, Switzerland, on Dec 24 and came to us here. Hal back to his P.O work and Jack back to Sheerness on Jan 2. Bob and Maidlie spent Xmas with her people at Bagshot, only 3 miles from us, so we saw them.
Annie and her children are at Bournemouth. The Drs say that Annie is making good progress and is v. much better, but we cannot see the progress. She seems well and SO fat but is not allowed to do almost anything! N and I are well and so far are having a very much brighter and pleasanter winter than last one was, on that dreary common near Woking, which was dull, and cold, beyond words.

Jan 1 ... Bessy and Jack played golf with Mr and Miss Bold, and brought them back to tea.

Jan 2 Sunday. Dull early, v. fine and sunny later. N, Hal and I to St George's Church, where we heard a good sermon.... Today registers a somewhat higher temp. than we had for 3 or 4 days last June!!

Bessy plays golf most days with the Bold girls, and goes for a golf lesson.

Jan 11 ... N and I to tea with General Owen, next door. He is a nice old man, and showed us his sketches done in the Crimean War, and elsewhere.

Jan 14 ... two new visitors called today. Bessy was asked to a dance near here at Adm. Johnstone's, but she is not going out at night.

Jan 15 ... This is the first day of the most important General Election we have had for many years! HOW will it go?

Jan 16 Sunday ...We got The Observer to see the results of yesterday's Poll. Fairly satisfactory, but not as good as we had hoped - 15 Unionist gains, and 3 Radical gains!

Jan 17 ... Elections today went well, several gains for us - but we are not SWEEPING the country. It is feared there will be but a narrow majority for whichever side wins, which is always a bad thing.
Jan 20 Fine, and wind gong down a good deal. Mr and Mrs Buchanan Dunlop, who live near Reading, came over to lunch here and we had a great talk about our Pedigrees, to our satisfaction ...
Jan 23 Snow lying this morning ... There is a wonderful new Comet, visible most evenings, but we have not yet managed to see it here. This is of course Halley's Comet, observed in our skies about every 76 years - last seen in 1986.
Jan 24 ... Jessie West came, bringing a Bicycle to lend to Bessy ... Elections better today.
Jan 26 ... Here we are in Chertsey Electoral Division, and they are polling in Camberley. We walked into the town.. All was very quiet. The L.U. Candidate, Mr MacMaster, won the seat from a Rad. by 4600 votes.
Jan 27 ... There are the most dreadful floods in Paris: it looks as though most of the town may be destroyed.
Jan 28 ... Several more Unionist Gains - but alas, we have no chance of beating the Coalition of Rads, Labour, Socialists and Nationalists - truly a weird combination of Mr Asquith's!
Jan 29 Fine, cold, frosty and sunny. I walked to the town. N to a Lecture on Faith Healing with Mrs French ... We saw the "Daylight" Comet this evening: but it was very faint, and not much worth seeing.
Feb 1 ... Miss Coddington and her sister Mrs Cunningham came from Windsor and lunched with us ... They are nice women ... Lady Elphinstone, Olive and little Norma Cowie, also Kathleen Lewis, came to tea. Bessy still in bed, but her cold is much better. Olive Elphinstone paid her a visit in her room ... Heard of the death of James Hilton - poor fellow, he had cancer of the throat. [Colonel James Hilton, Seaforth Highlanders, husband of Haddie's cousin Anna.]

Bessy goes to London regularly every Wednesday, for a Music lesson and to see Mrs Hickson. A period of heavy rain sets in.
Feb 8 Shrove Tuesday. B across the road to tea with the Abbot Andersons. Miss Bold called, to say that Golf is impossible at present, as the Links are under water! B to Holy Communion at St George's Church in Camberley. B lost a pretty enamel brooch. It was searched for everywhere, and notice of it given to the Police, and in several shops in Camberley, and at last, was found in Nettie's bed!!!!
Feb 10 ... Harry de Salis drove over (8 miles) from Portnall to lunch. We expected May Drake too, but as the R.N College at Osborne is being broken up, on account of illness, and they expect Willie De Salis's boy Tony to arrive today, May remained there to receive and look after him.

Harry De S is anxious about Georgie, who is v. unwell.
Feb 12 ... Col (Mud Major) and Mrs McClintock to lunch. Hal and Jack arrived from London.
Feb 14 ... Col. and Mrs Ruxton to tea. He is a son of Major Ruxton of Rohanna [Haddie's first home, at Ardee, Co. Louth.]
Feb 17 ... No one can tell what Mr Asquith and the Govt. will do, with their very mixed friends (?and supporters?)...
Feb 18 ...B and I to Concert for National Service League at Camberley Drill Hall. A v. good Orchestra, and two solo singers. We walked there, and came back in a Fly as it looked like rain ...
Feb 19 Blowing hard ...rain later and tremendous wind. Adm. and Mrs Ashe to tea. She is an American (Boston) and very nice.
Feb 20 Sunday. H, N and I to Church. SUCH a gale of wind! Hal and Bessy to lunch at Pine Wood - walked there with not much rain, and Lady Elphinstone sent them home in her pony trap in pours of rain. A good deal of lightning in the evening - WHAT bad, wild weather!
Feb 21 ... Today, the King opened Parliament in state. What is going to happen? This Govt. is surely doomed. Will it last for days, or weeks or months?
Feb 23 ... N and B to town early. They went to Mrs Hickson, and the Luard Beans, and wrote their names at Buckingham Palace ... B to Queens Gate and had her Piano lesson and lunch, then visited Josephine Singleton, [widow or daughter of "Siggenny", the family's very old friend] *who drove her to the Buckingham Palace Hotel to join N, who had lunched there with Kate and Gertrude Plunket....*
Mar 7 A lovely sunny day. Out walking. B to lunch with the Mrs Abbot Anderson, to meet Mrs Gove, a S.African friend. Elizabeth LeFroy had tea with us. Received 10 days treatment and loan of instrument. Paid 3/6 [not clear what this is for - possibly backache or headache].
Mar 8 ... Train to Bagshot, where Lady Elphinstone's Brougham met us, and took us to Pine Wood, where we had tea with her and Olive, Mrs Welch and her little girl, Varvara ... Lady E sent us back all the way in her Brougham.
Mar 9 ... N and I by Omnibus to Blackwater, then on by train to Reading, where Col. Buchanan Dunlop met us in his carriage and took us to his nice old home, where were Mrs D and their youngest girl, Rhoda ... we spent a pleasant day.
Mar 16 ... Bessy to stay with the Welch's at Norfolk Farm. N and I, and Nana, left for Sunningdale, where H. De Salis's carriage met us and took us to Portnall, where we shall be alone until tomorrow, as he and May Drake are staying in London. SO kind of him to let us come under these circumstances.
May 17 ... Willie De Salis (Capt, RN) came for the night. His ship, the

"Russell" is at Devonport ... he is VERY nice.

Mar 18 ... Mr Snowden, Rector of Sunninghill and his wife and daughter, and Major and Mrs Dupree to dinner. She was a Thornhill. We had music, singing and violin and pianola in the evening. Dear old Harry De S sang, so wonderfully, for a man of his age.

Mar 21 ... N and I and Nana back to 16 Queensberry Place. Found the house clean; very different to the state the tenants left it, last year.

Mar 24 Fine, but dull, dark and misty. My Birthday - Feel so depressed Why? [written later] *I know, - but will not say.*

Bob and Maidlie leave for a fortnight in Ireland. This may have been her first visit. Family tradition says that she later developed a great dislike of Ireland and things Irish.

Ap 5 ... Bob and Maidlie arrived early from Ireland, having been v. sick at sea, and quite tired and knocked up. Bob left for Chatham ... Maidlie remains here to rest, shop and get a cook.

Ap 7 ... Bessy down to Salisbury to stay with the Chetwynd Stapletons. Maidlie went to her Mother ... We felt so dull and quiet when both dear girls were gone!

Ap 15 ... Heard that Georgie Hamilton passed away yesterday at Cranbourne Rectory. [she is much the same age as Annie and leaves at least one child, Margot] *I went out early to order a cross, for N to send for Georgie.*

Ap 18 ... N, Hal and Bessy in a hired Motor Car to Cranbourne to attend Georgie Hamilton's Funeral. They took luncheon with them, and were home about 3 o'c.

Ap 22 ... Unfortunately, we are going to lose Long, the excellent Parlourmaid, who has been here for two and a half years, as she is not strong and finds the stair work too much. [later pencil note] *Afterwards she changed her mind, and remains on with us.*

Ap 23 ... Miss E. Cole called, also Rodolph De Salis, who is much pleased at Margery's engagement to Dr Bayley ...

Annie sends a present of some lovely daffodils, so she must now be back at Woodcock - and Nettie goes to visit her there.

Ap 28 ... N came back from Woodcock in Bernie's motor car, and brought dear little Joyce to spend the day ...

Ap 29 ... N went to see the Irish Primate who is in a nursing home ...

May 1 Sunday. N, Jack and I to St Peter's, Cranley Gardens ... a v. good sermon from the Vicar, Mr Swayne.

May 4 ... Margery De Salis brought her intended, Dr Bayley, to tea .. Hal and Bessy to Albert Hall for Peary's Arctic Lecture.

May 6 ... The King is reported v. ill with Bronchitis ... alas! each bulletin is worse than the last. So anxious all day ... Bessy wrote names at Marlborough Ho. and Buckingham Palace, where it took her 50 minutes to walk up in the string of people! At 11 pm Princess Marie Louise's l-in-w, Miss Hawkes sent N a line to say the King was unconscious ...

May 7 ... Alas, our beloved King Edward passed away before midnight last night. WHAT a loss to us and whole world. Bessy out shopping and so was I ... It is remarked that there is not a smile to be seen on any face in the streets.

May 9 ... N, B and Hal left for Oberammergau, via Folkestone and Boulogne. I went to N. Bond St to take up the character of a Nurse for Annie's children. V. satisfactory.

May 13 ... Jack walked in and slept here. He had been busy all day at the Admiralty and War Office, arranging for the Bluejackets who are to line the streets (along with the soldiers) for the King's funeral.

May 14 ... I left for Dover, where the Lauries' carriage met me and took me to 10 Victoria Park, a v. nice situation, with gardens all round and a lovely view. My train was v. late and crowded with Whitsuntide trippers. Flo Laurie is not at all strong and spends a good deal of the day in her room, and Major L is away nearly all day on duty with his Regt (Royal Irish Rifles) They have a fine little boy (Hal) and a wee girl, who has just had the Mumps, and now very swelled glands.

May 15 Whit Sunday. A lovely warm sunny day. With Major Laurie to St Mary the Virgin, a fine old Church.

May 16 ... Walking and sitting in the gardens, and Flo and I drove to the sea front. There are 5 large RN ships in the harbour, one being the "Prince of Wales", Flagship of Prince Louis of Battenberg. I am thinking much of our three travellers, who are today, I believe, witnessing the Passion Play at Oberammergau.

May 17 ... Drove with Flo. Her poor little girl has an abscess on one side of her glands ...

May 19 Flo and I drove and walked on the Pier ... For the last 3 days the remains of our beloved King Edward have been lying in state in Westminster Hall, and hundreds of thousands of people have passed through it, after standing for hours, a queue in the streets.

May 20 ... Today took place the Funeral of the great King, and I believe such a sight was never before seen in the world! I DO regret not seeing it! Flo and I attempted to attend the service at St Mary's, but were misinformed of the hour, and so arrived too late, and found the church crammed, and crowds trying to force their way in! so we took a drive instead. Major Laurie took me up to the Castle, but it was such a fatiguing climb that I was v.v. tired.

May 21 ... another thunderstorm at bedtime, then fog: and guns firing, bells ringing and syrens hooting, rather disturbing.

May 25 ...Left Dover, and reached home after 6. Train late. Found dear Bessy - and my sister Blanche, who came to tea. She and Charlie are staying at an Hotel in town ... N down to Chatham to spend a few days with Bob and Maidlie.

Jun 1 ... N, Hal and Bessy dined with John Leslie. B looked charming in her new black evening gown, and black velvet in her hair ...

Jun 6 ... Bernie gave Bessy the use of Lady Greenwell's Box for the Opera tonight. She tried in vain to get various people to go with her, and at last she and I and Hal, and Mr C Inglis and his sister-in-law Mrs Inglis, went and saw La Traviata with ?Tetraggini as Violetta. She has a splendid voice, wonderfully trained....

Jun 7 ... N, B and I to Mrs Mayne's afternoon party, where we heard some v. good Violincello playing . A trying, hot, oppressive day.

Jun 11 ... B had a music lesson from Mr Bradley. She and N lunched with Mrs Severne in Eaton Place to meet the Rathdonnells, and then paid visits ...

Jun 18 ... Bessy to Hurlingham with the Donovans to see the great Polo Match between England and Ireland. N and I in Lady Greenwell's Box at Albert Hall for the Melba Concert. She sang quite deliciously, and I never heard anything to equal Backhaus's splendid pianoforte playing. Then we went to tea with the Miss Nepeans in Eccleston Square ...

Jun 22 Oppressive, resulting in a thunderstorm ...a poor woman in the Mews, just at the back of this house, was struck by the lightning today, and died two days afterwards.Heard that Agnes Bradford died at Margate, llth inst.

Jun 25 ... Hal and Bessy down to Oxford for 3 nights, to sleep at the Mitre Hotel and spend the days with the Fraser-Millers, friends of Hal's ...

Jun 26 Sunday. N, Jack and I to St Peter's. Carrie Macnaghton to lunch, and her son came to tea, as did also Tan McC and Aylmer. Two daughters of Charlie Garnett called. They are living in London, and working for their maintenance, poor girls!...

Jun 29 ...Bessy and I by Bus to Mrs Dunbar-Buller's Tea in Grosvenor St, and also to Mrs Hanbury Tracy ...

The Season continues with a very busy social life - no wonder Haddie and Nettie are often tired and take days in bed!

Jul 4 N went to 2 meetings of Conference about Spiritual Healing at Kensington Town Hall, and Bessy and I went to the afternoon one, and were much interested (about gifts of Healing in the Church)... Alick West called. He has quite recovered from his serious illness, and is on leave from India...

Jul 7 ... Bessy and I busy trying to arrange her gown for tomorrow, which has been v. badly done, and left unfinished by a bad workwoman - I think we succeeded rather well!

Jul 8 Dull and still chilly. Maidlie came up ... and she and Bessy went to Lords, for the Eton & Harrow March, looking v. smart. Rachel De Salis came here to lunch ...

Jul 12 ... I had a motor drive with Mrs Inglis and we went to a Sweet Pea Show at the Horticultural Hall. Such LOVELY flowers!

Jul 15 ...For some reason or other, both N and I lay awake most of last night, and then had breakfast in bed! The two Miss Merritts from Toronto came to lunch and as ever, were most agreeable. Bessy dined with the Allhusens and went with them to the Theatre - a party of 10 girls and ONE man!!

Jul 20 ... N and I, in Mrs Inglis's motor car, which she lent us, paid several distant visits, going as far as Hampstead ... Hal and B to a small impromptu Dance at the Allhusens' in Eaton Place, which they much enjoyed. B looked so pretty in black with paste ornaments. Very few people in town are yet in colours, but much white and grey and mauve are worn, as well as black ...

Jul 21 ... Kathleen and Eileen West (twins) ... came to lunch and then N, Bessy I and they went by underground to Hurlingham, where we saw a Polo match - nothing v. particular, a scratch one, but we quite enjoyed it, and had no rain ...

Jul 28 At last, a nice bright summer day! ...Hal down to Woodcock this evening, and he, Bessy and Bernie, and Sybil Greenwell, went to a dance given by the Clinton Bakers at Bayfordbury...

Jul 31 N born at Monasterboice, 70 years ago!

Aug 3 Bessy indoors, washing my hair etc......she and N left at 7.30 for Ireland by the Mail for Ireland. They had a good journey and were not ill at sea, tho' it was not very smooth. They went as far as Dundalk together, and then N to Ballymascanlon,[home of the Plunket sisters] *and B to Drumcar. They met May in the train and boat, who came up and spoke to them!!*

Nana goes down to Shedfield and poor Haddie gets bad lumbago and has to cancel her own trip to stay at Cley with Cicy Macleod.

Aug 6 ... In bed all day, my back bad enough. The Cook, Funnell, is away but Long, the Parlourmaid, cooks nicely for me and the little housemaid, Alice, does all she can for me, brings me up my meals and rubbing my back etc. I wish Nana was not away. It IS dull!

Aug 8 ... Pleasant accounts from N. She met Bessy at a Garden Party at Stephenstown on Friday, looking so pretty in a lovely pink frock ...

Nettie has had lumbago, too, and had to give up her visit to Lisnavagh (Bessy having gone there alone).

Aug 13 Heard that Bernie, Annie, the 3 babies and all their household have been v. ill, with bad throats and high temp. - poisoned, it is supposed by bad water. They are better now.

Haddie, still in some pain, gets herself packed and off to Falmouth to stay there with the Quins, who give her a kind welcome. They have retired there from Ireland.

Aug 17 ... We all sat in the garden. This seems a v. nice place, and the house very nice, too.

Aug 18 ... Dick and Dora and Auriel went to the Dance at 9.30. Dora had not been to a party for years, and naturally much enjoyed seeing Auriel dancing and amusing herself ... Dear Bessy's birthday - 28 today; she is, I believe, at Rostrevor ...

Aug 24 Such a nice, fine day. Dick took Dora and me a lovely motor drive to two charming country places, at one of which we had tea. The other was quite lovely, SUCH vegetation, almost tropical and SUCH a view. Truly this is a charming neighbourhood.

Aug 27 ... All in motor car to an afternoon party at Col and Mrs Faulkner Browne's . It rained on the way back, but we were well-protected. Very high wind and heavy rain at night - very disturbing. I believe that N and Bessy go today to Glendaragh for about 3 days [home of Charlie and Blanche McClintock].

Sep 1 ... Dick saw me off. Had v. uncomfortable lunch in the Restaurant car ... and so home. Found Hal, and also Nana. Very, very tired!

Sep 2 ... I believe Annie and the 3 babies are going to Sheringham today, for change, after the poisoning at Woodcock.

Haddie has two days at Chatham with Bob and Maidlie. Katie Shaw, the friend in India for whom she did so many errands, is now in London.

Sep 10 I dined with the Shaws at their beautiful flat, 38 Hyde Park Gate. Lily Campbell was there and her son Willie, and his intended, Miss Pilkington, and a Mr Verschoyle, a cousin of Katie's. I went both ways in a taxi-cab. N and Bessy go to the Palace, Armagh today.

Sep 21 ... Hal took me to see "Priscilla Runs Away" - amusing, but almost too much of a farce at times. We arrived half an hour too early and went to the "Carlton" close by, and sat there listening to the Band, and Hal had coffee and a cigar. I greatly enjoyed myself. It was a beautiful clear night, and we came home in a Four-wheeler. Bessy left Eva Dix, at Ferndale, and came home by Irish night mail, and had a v. smooth passage.

Sep 25 Jessie West to tea and supper. She is spending 3 months in a lodging near Regents Park, and attends classes to learn Massage and Mannheim treatment, and Electric baths etc.

Oct 4 ... N back, from Ireland and from Halsnead (Ethel Willis) ... N has been just 2 calendar months away - a long time!

Oct 5 ... Heard that there is a Revolution in Lisbon, fighting in the streets and a Republic proclaimed! It seems doubtful what has become of the poor young King Manoel.

Oct 8 ... a RN friend of Jack's, Mr Lake and his wife dined here, and so did

Jessie West, and then went to His Majesty's Theatre to see Henry VIII (with Beerbohm Tree) and afterwards had supper at the Carlton. Poor Jack could not go to this, his own party, being in bed with what seems to be a chill on his liver; such a pity! Jessie was telephoned to, to take his place, and if she could not have come, I was to have gone, which I should SO have enjoyed!

Oct 17 Went down to Potters Bar, where Annie and Joyce met me in motor car. She seems now quite well again. The 3 babies are charming. It blew and rained hard - and chilly, but plenty of fires at Woodcock Lodge.

Oct 20 ... Annie out walking ... Gwendoline Greenwell, Bernie's sister came this evening to spend a few days. Bernie went after dinner to a popular entertainment in the village, and played his gramophone there. Hal left today for Portofino on a visit to Lady Elphinstone. She has been lent Agnes Browne's Castello there.

Oct 21 ... Annie out walking and motoring, hunting for servants, and is much worried by them.

Oct 23 Sunday ... Annie is tired by all the trouble she is having about servants, and did not do much today. This evening in London, it was discovered that the fires next door, at No. 14, were nearly burning through the partition wall, and grave danger of fire. N and B got Firemen in, and a salvage man spent the night in the house at No. 16.

Oct 24 I came home ... the whole nursery came with me in the motor car to see me off at Potters Bar. Found N and Bessy well, but much put out by the alarm of fire, and all the work it entailed, with Fire Insurance, architects, builders, workmen etc. Left Annie in bed, v. tired, but not ill, fortunately.

Oct 30 Sunday ... N, Jack and Jessie to St Peter's. I went to Brompton Church. Jessie to see May at Kensington Hotel ... Jack was so amusing!

Maidlie's sisters, Mrs Welch and Olive, come and go. Olive is said to be househunting at Camberley with Capt. Jackson - so he must be her intended!

Nov 7 ...Dr Horden, from Bournemouth, came to see Bessy, and advises us to go out of town again this winter - and we had SO hoped to stay at home!

Nov 15 ... N and Nana spent the day househunting at Camberley, with no result ... it is so difficult to get a large enough house, for all the servants N has to keep! ... Edwy McClintock came here ... on his way to St Alban's to be examined there by the Bishop. He is to be Ordained.

Nov 23 ... Miss Bold, who we knew at Camberley, came to offer N her mother's house there, and it sounds most promising! ...

Dec 1 ... N and B lunched with Antonia to meet B.McC [sister Blanche.]
I went to 2 S.Eaton Place to help Flo Fardell at Election work, but found I had to go on by bus to the P.L.Offices by Victoria St, where I did a lot of writing along with many other women. I was foolish enough to

come home on foot and by train, instead of a cab, and was wet, and quite tired out.

As winter draws on, Bessy is frequently ill and in bed with a bad cold, though Dr Horden does not seem unduly worried - he says she needs rest and care. They continue to see many friends every day, but Haddie's concern for Bessy is obvious.

Dec 21 A v. wet day, but not cold. N, Hal, Bessy, Nana and I to Olive Elphinstone's wedding at Bagshot. Dear Bob and Maidlie there, he and Capt. Welch, Capt. Cowie and the bridegroom Capt Jackson, and best man Capt. Ommanney, in uniform, but it was a dull wedding, and we all felt for Lady Elphinstone, losing her last daughter. We had a very slow train and nasty wet journey, and did not get home till 7.30 ...

Christmas is marred by the news that Maidlie has been seized with appendicitis - she has the operation and all goes on well, but they have some anxious days.

Dec 28 Bessy goes to the Carol Service at Westminster Abbey, and hears it from the organ loft with Sir F. Bridge the organist, and his daughter who is a former school friend of hers. *She much enjoyed it.*

Dec 30. They begin the packing-up to leave London for Camberley.

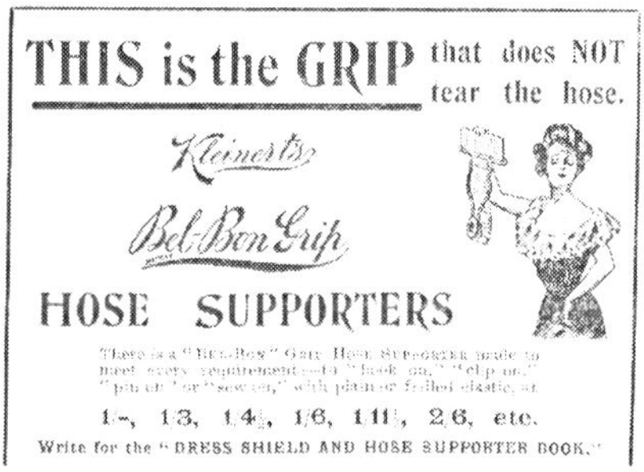

1911

For the first time, Haddie records a few telephone numbers in the front of her diary. Bernie and Annie, for instance, are "Hatfield 17"!

Jan 1 ... Several people called to say goodbye. Bob came, and brought an excellent account of Maidlie, who is making splendid progress towards recovery. He looks so happy and thankful, dear Boy.

Jan 2 ... At 12 o'c Bessy, Nana and I, and the Cook and Between Maid left for Camberley, and reached Ridgeway House ... and found everything comfortable for a beginning. Poor Bessy is coughing much due, we believe, to the Tuberal she is taking. We hope the change of air will invigorate her.

Haddie is soon back in London, though, for a visit to Katie Shaw at 38 Hyde Park Gate. They see "Is Matrimony a Failure?" at the Criterion *(most amusing)* and take a young godchild to "The Piper at St James's - *only moderately good, and too much spun out.* She goes back to Camberley, to find *Bessy still v. ailing, and N much depressed. B in carriage to Pine Wood for tea, to see Maidlie, who is now down in drawing-room and getting on first rate.*

Jan 19 Helen West and Kathleen rode over here but could not stay for lunch. Bessy drove the pony in the trap, taking the Coachman with her, to show her how to manage the pony.

Jan 21 Same dull, dark weather, not even a peep of the sun for about a week... B went with Lady Elphinstone to an afternoon party at Lord and Lady Ellenborough's ...

Jan 28 A lovely sunny day, after a frost last night. B and Jack drove in Pony Cart. N and I, in Brougham, to Farnborough to return Miss FitzRoy Somerset's call ...Bessy looks better. This fine day is so good for her.

Haddie struggles with a cold, desperate not to give it to Bessy - she misses a visit to Portnall because of it. Bessy goes about a good deal, driving in the pony trap most days, but they are anxious about her.

Feb 15 All up to town. I went to Holborn Viaduct Station to see Bernie, Annie and Joyce on their way to Arosa in Switzerland. Annie seems much better, and is travelling in every luxury that money can buy ...

Feb 21 ... The Bishop of Derry and his bride, Mrs Chadwick, arrived here from London ...

Feb 22 ...N sent the Chadwicks in Brougham to see the Napoleon tombs at Farnborough ... Elizabeth Lefroy and her daughter Kathleen Lewis came to luncheon...

Feb 28 ... Nearly constantly wet all day! N, B and I in brougham to lunch with Adm and Mrs Johnstone, a party of 12 - dull, but V good food. We had intended going on to a tea at Mrs Trench's - but it was so wet, that we forebore.

Mar 4 .. to tea with Eliz. Lefroy and the Lewises at Green Lodge, Frimley, where we met Col. and Mrs Skeffington Wynne; he is a son of late Capt Wynne of Collon - and we were playmates together as children ...

Mar 7 ... to tea with Miss Cave, and met a Mrs Miles, widow of Capt Miles, who was ADC to Sir Patrick Macdougall, when we were at Halifax ...

Mar 12 Sunday ... Jack back to Sheerness. This is the last time we shall see him as his job with Adm. Neville comes to an end ... and he is then likely to go on half pay, and then we are likely to have him for a bit.

Bessy still goes to town every Wednesday (which has cheaper fares) to see Mrs Hickson, and usually to have lunch with Mrs Inglis. As the time comes to leave Camberley, her fever returns and, obviously anxious herself, she wants to go ahead to Bournemouth to see Dr Horden with Hal as escort. However they cannot get the lodgings they want, so end by going down all together on Mar 21, to 3 St John's Road, Boscombe. Dr Horden calls, and on the whole is reassuring: progress this winter has been disappointing, but no real cause for anxiety. This of course, is Haddie's interpretation of what he says, or rather, of what other people have reported to her. There is no hint that she is ever present at any of the consultations. Carrie Macnaghton, Annie Macan and members of the Paget family - Mrs C Paget and her daughters, and Charlie Paget - are nearby and callers come thick and fast, and Hal and Jack come for the weekend.

Mar 29 ... N, B, Jack, Nana and I by train to Christchurch, where we saw the beautiful old Minster. We had not much of a "showman" - he seemed more bent on making rather bad jokes than on giving much interesting information. Dr Horden came again, and says there is a decided improvement, and she feels better herself ...

Mar 31 ... Jack and Bernie left London for Paris to meet Annie and Joyce there ...

April 9 Sunday ... B had a wire from Bob at Bagshot: "Son and Maidlie doing well" - This is good news indeed! ... No wonder there was extra anxiety over the appendicitis! ... *the Census was taken all over the Kingdom tonight.* They go back to London next day, and find No. 16 painted white, with a red front door.

Ap10 ... Bob came to dinner ... he looks so well and happy and gives an excellent account of Maidlie, who is nursing the wee Boy, who has "a pink face and a red nose" We had a happy dinner all together, and drank the baby's health in champagne ...

Ap 13 Maundy Thursday ...B and Jack to church together, to St Peter's ...

Ap 17 ... Hal and Jack spent afternoon at Brooklands to see the Flying and Motoring ...

[First mention of flying by Haddie]

Ap 21 ... N and Nana to Pine Wood to see Bob's baby Boy ...

Ap 28 ... I drove to Debenham & Freebody's to meet Annie, who was fitting on coats and skirts. .. she looks v. well ... House dinner of 12 - Adm Sir George Egerton (2nd Sea Lord) and Lady E, Mrs Maclachlan, Gen. and Mrs Donovan, Winifred Bowden-Smith, Tim McClintock Bunbury, Capt Staveley RN, Nettie, Bessy, Hal & Jack - I dined in study. A pleasant evening. Equality of numbers/sexes is de rigeur, still.

Ap 30 Sunday N and I by Motor Bus to the Middle Temple, by Mr Digby's invitation. A charming service, and beautiful music; then we were shown all the historic things and rooms, and then had an excellent cold luncheon, and were waited upon by Judges, K.Cs, Benchmen etc. as they had no servants in the room ... a most enjoyable time ...

May 2 ... Annie and Joyce and Nurse Rowling came here to luncheon, on their way to Marden. The first mention of Rowley, who becomes a feature of the Greenwell family life for many years.

May 3 ...Dr Horden and Dr Rhodes came to see B - and Hal came to meet them. It is easy to understand that Bessy would be glad of her brother's presence at consultations; less emotional, no doubt, than her Mother or Aunt.

May 6 ... Dr Rhodes again saw Bessy, and has made us v. sad by his opinion of her; and he recommends most unpleasant treatment, which I do not think can be carried out with any advantage.

May 11 ... Helen Brownlow came to spend 2 or 3 nights here ... Dear B still very unwell and in bed. Dr Rhodes saw her twice. He quite thinks she will get better, but alas! has not a good opinion of her case.

May 13 ...A perfect day. N, Hal, Jack and I down to Pine Wood where we met large Elphinstone Party - lunched and went to Little Jo's christening. He was v. good and nice, then back to Pine Wood for tea. Sat in the lovely garden, and back to town in time for dinner, and found poor Bessy v. miserable, with a sharp liver attack and temperature. [next day] *B was a good deal better this morning: but of course could not go to the christening, which was a great disappointment to her, and quite spoiled our pleasure ... Maidlie is wonderfully well, and Bob so bright and happy.*

May 17 ... I drove early shopping mostly about things for Bessy. In afternoon N and I drove and shopped and got into thick blocks of vehicles in Piccadilly. N lost her purse, which fortunately was returned to her by a lady who picked it up in the street ...

May 18 ... The Dr thinks B decidedly better in every way today, and only came once. Annie came here on her way to Beaulieu for Bernie's Yeomanry training ... Annie is not to see Bessy for fear of any excitement ...

Mrs Hickson comes several times to see Bessy. On May 22 N and Haddie attend Mrs Hickson's Prayer Meeting, where Bessy is prayed for, though not by name.

May 24 ... N to a Committee meeting, and she and I to Mrs Wethered's and Miss Vansittart's Afternoon. Maidlie and Nurse and Baby Jo came up from Chatham. They sleep at the Naval & Military Hotel close by. Maidlie has her meals here and nurses little Jo, who is a darling.... It is beginning to dawn on the family and doctors that Bessy had better not be with small children if possible.

May 25 ... Maidlie had the carriage, and 2 ladies, relations of hers, came here to lunch. Bob up from Chatham, then N, Bob and Maidlie to their Majesties' Court, looking so nice, and it all went off so well ... Bessy saw Bob and Maidlie for a few minutes, but not the baby. Poor child, it IS a disappointment to her not to be able to go with them, and she has such a pretty gown and train, all yellow, gold and white.

May 27 ... N and I to the Greenwell Box at Albert Hall for Melba's Coronation Concert. Lovely singing, and Backhaus played piano splendidly ...

May 28 Sunday ... I went to St Stephen's, Gloucester Road ... B going on the same. Dr Rhodes sees her every morning, and N telephones to him every evening to report symptoms etc.

May 29 ... B much the same, but improving- the Dr says - and so good and patient. Annie, Barbara, and A's nurse to lunch, also Bammie Ross. B saw Annie for a few minutes.

May 31 ... Dr delighted with Bessy's condition and feels quite hopeful of her ultimate recovery if she will do exactly what is best for her, for some time to come.

June 1 ... My sister Blanche and her Edwy to lunch. ... Hal and Jack after dinner, to see Charlie McClintock on business, at the Bruces', where the McCs are staying...

Jun 3 ... Hal and Jack left for Dieppe to spend the few Whitsun holidays bicycling in Normandy and Britanny. Do hope they will have a good time. ... Dr says B is going on excellently well, and unless something happens he will not see her tomorrow, and she need not now take her temp in the morning, but only in the evening. Poor child, she looks pale and depressed, and feels the best in bed.

The weather is now very hot, much felt by Bessy, and an electric fan which helps her greatly, cannot be mended till after Whitsun. Many friends visit, and often take N and H out for little drives, etc. showing their kind concern. Bob comes up to spend some hours with them, bringing flowers which Maidlie has sent for Bessy.

Jun 15... Patience McC came to lunch and spent the day, and saw Bessy. N took P to the Victoria and Albert Museum ....We went to Gunters and ate ices and saw the monster Coronation cake! Ambrose Gledstanes and his wife dined here, so we were a party of 7. Played "Bombardo" - but nothing is really a pleasure without dear B.

Jun 16 ... Bessie and Mary Gray, from Bermuda, came to lunch. They had never been out of Bermuda, and are delighted with England, and London. We had not seen them since 1882!!!...

Jun 22 The Coronation Day of our beloved King George V and his Queen! Chilly and some showers, but not a bad day. Up before 5 am ; N and Jack drove to Admiralty Stand, and Hal and I to War Office Stand with Bob's tickets. Bob and Maidlie to seats at Clarence House given by the Duke of Connaught. We had only a short distance to walk and saw v. well, and it was worth seeing! We took some food with us.

Jun 23 Up again at 5 am and with Jack to the Senior Utd. Services Club, where we had nice seats, and afterwards an excellent luncheon. It was the finest sight I have ever seen (much finer than yesterday) and the enthusiasm was wonderful, and the troops splendid. Bob and Maidlie had seats at the Bank of England, of which her uncle, Mr Cole is Governor. They also saw the Illuminations. N gave seats at Charing X to Nana and her niece, and she staid with Bessy. Poor Darling, I am so sorry for her, out of it all, and going on so slowly ...

Jun 26 ... N heard that Mrs Richardson is dead. [Rosa] *She was the last of Leo's sisters...*

June 27 Some rain and very dull and chilly forenoon; cleared into a lovely day, so fortunate for the King and Queen's Garden Party, to which N did not go...

Jun 28 ... Dr Rhodes has sent in a nurse here, because the constant strain, night and day, is becoming too much for Nana, who is so devoted to Bessy. She is still sick, but in a rather less degree, but it is v. weakening. Jack here for a few hours, and to the Admiralty, and back again to his friends in Sussex. Dr Rhodes ... later in the day brought in Dr Byrne, in consultation. He fears this will be a long and trying business, but as some similar patients pull through, he hopes she will. Dr Rhodes is more sanguine, but alas! all doctors fear she can never be but v. delicate, poor child. May God in His mercy raise her up - for she is unspeakably dear to us all.

Jun 29 ... I went with Julia Jeffreys to Ranelagh this afternoon. A Gymkhana by Indian Chiefs - and polo, Indians v. Wanderers. N kindly lent us her carriage...

July 4 ... Mr Farr, a Dentist, saw B about her teeth which, alas, are getting loose, and poison from her germs is swallowed, and is v. bad for her. Mr Hickson came to see her. She has still to be kept as quiet as possible, and we can each be but a very short time with her. She is as good and patient as ever ... Jack down to Windsor to see the King inspecting 35000 boy scouts, which interested him much. He has heard from the Admiralty that he is appointed to the "Diadem" at Portsmouth, and is to join on Monday.

July 5 ... we drove to St Martin's Lane to see a shop where they have a lending Library of Jig-saw puzzles, which may be nice for B when she is better ... B weak and depressed and had to be kept v. quiet. I did not even behold her! She was a little sick which the Dr much regretted. He now fears this comes chiefly from her teeth. The Donovans sent her lovely roses and peaches, and Annie some sweet peas.

Nettie and Haddie make the most of the carriage for the time they still have it, making many calls. There is some improvement for Bessy, who now lies for a short time each day on a special couch in her room and can do a little needlework, which helps to pass the time. Jack joins his ship, but comes up when he can - his visits are very cheering to all of them and especially to Bessy.

July 20 Bessy does not like the new nurse, and nor do any of us. She is ponderous and rather rough and ready. N spoke to Dr Rhodes about her and he will do all he can to get another, but as this is their holiday season, they are very scarce.

They have a long heatwave, and drought, all feeling the strain.

July 24 ... May Drake called. She and Harry De Salis go tomorrow to see Charlie consecrated at St Paul's. Hal up at 3 am and went with Mr Cator to see the Flying at Hendon ... Tremendous scene in the House of Commons where Mr Asquith was refused a hearing, with cries of "Traitor" (wh. he is) and Who killed King Edward? The Speaker had to adjourn the House. What IS going to happen?

July 26 A thunderstorm early this morning, followed by much rain, hot and sunny later. Nurse ... left, and until we get another, Nana will nurse Bessy ... Great political excitement, as Lord Lansdowne and Mr Balfour have decided to let the iniquitous Parliament Bill pass, and thus avoid Mr Asquith's creating some hundreds of bogus Peers! The Morocco question is anxious, too, and the King cannot go to Goodwood.

Sister Dora Quin has been ill at Falmouth, apparently with heart trouble, but Haddie's reports of her are scant - now said to be much better. A new nurse, Nurse Crease from New Zealand, is installed and Bessy likes her. Haddie finds her *rather rough and noisy, and very colonial, but she is not bad.*

Aug 3 ... Annie's Nurse Rowling came here, with flowers, grapes and tomatoes, and a bowl of sweet lavender, and good news of all at Woodcock, except that the chauffeur, Noble, and children have whooping cough.

Aug 8 ... In this v. hot weather, we generally have ices for sweets at luncheon, as B likes them so much. The cook makes them v. good at home.

Mr Balfour's Vote of Censure on the Govt. was defeated in the House of Commons, but carried in the Lords by a large majority.

Aug 9 ... Nana to the A & N Stores to get a wire pillow for B as she finds the down ones so warm in this weather ... temp ran up to 97 in the shade! Quite too hot ...

Aug 10 ... There is a large and v. serious Strike going on among Dock workers and carters, and food cannot be delivered in town, from ships, or by carts, and is going up in price.

Aug 11 Dear Hal's 40th Birthday - God bless him, he IS good ... Miss Robertson, who Bessy knew in S/Africa, came to tea, and gave us a dreadful account of the natives there ...

Aug 14 Strikes - very bad and violent in most English and Scottish towns. It is really dreadful, and our miserable Govt. seem either unable or unwilling to cope with the disorder, amounting to Revolution.

Aug 15 The Strike is better in London, but dreadful in Liverpool and other places. The troops had to fire some shots, and charge with the Bayonet! ... The Dentist, Mr Farr, came to see Bessy, to fit a mechanism in her mouth, which he hopes may do good to her gums ... Her room was cleaned out today, and she was carried into the next room during the process.

Aug 17 It is greatly feared that a General Strike, of all the Railway men is coming, which would be dreadful. Thousands of troops are told off to be ready to go off to keep order at any place where they are wanted. All this is mainly due to this wretched Govt. who have brought us to the verge of Revolution.

Aug 18 Dear B's birthday, and she seems much better and brighter today ... she had several presents and letters ... All are v. excited about the Strike - thousands of troops have arrived in London, and are under canvas in the Parks.

Aug 19 ...Hal and Jack reached London without any incident ... This dreadful Strike, with all its deeds of violence, is still going on, but here we do not feel it, and can get everything we want so far.

Aug 20 Sunday. Hal to Euston, where he saw Bernie and Annie on their way to Scotland (Duart Castle, Mull) to stay with his people. The strikes being better, they hope to travel through.

Aug 21 Bob and Maidlie turn up from Norway, Bob having been summoned home from their holiday there. *M on her way to Pine Wood to fetch Jo ..*

Aug 30 Dr Rhodes, back from his holiday, finds Bessy very much better, and they all feel more cheerful. Haddie goes to Norfolk, to stay with Cicy Macleod at The Knoll, Cley-next-the-sea. Olivia Monument also is nearby.

Sep 1 ... Cicy and I went over the splendid old Church, St Margaret's at Cley (end of 12th Century). It is greatly out of repair. After dinner we walked to the Town Hall at Cley, where we had a v. nice concert in aid of some local charity, performed by residents and visitors, violin, cello, singing, reciting and dialogues and solo piano by Olivia Monument.

Sep 2 Quite hot again, and fine ... we drove to Bayfield, where Sir Alfred and Lady Jane Jodrell live; a magnificent house full of china, pictures etc. and such a fine place. They were so kind and hospitable. He spends large sums on restoring the fine old churches in his neighbourhood.

Sep 3 Sunday ... Cicy and I to St Margaret's ... after tea, we went in to Olivia, and sat in her Verandah. She played the piano for us.

Sep 5 Hot again. Cicy and I drove and called on some people in Cley. We also visited Blakeney Church, v. old and restored. Olivia came over after dinner, so we could not go to bed quite as early as intended, for we were v. tired.

Sep 6 ... Back to London and found all well at home - Bessy going on satisfactorily ...

Sep 8 ...Annie motored over for lunch and tea here, looking so well. Her children are at Sheringham.

Sep 10 Sunday. Pleasant, bright and breezy. N, Hal and I to 10o'c service and Holy Communion at Westminster Abbey. A good sermon from Canon Beeching.

Sep 11 ... Dr Rhodes ... quite delighted with the progress B has made. He is going to try the Spirone treatment with her, in addition to what she is already having.

Sep 12 ... Archbishop Alexander, late Primate of Ireland, passed away this afternoon at Torquay aged 87. He was a very gifted and charming man ...

Sep 16 ... Jack arrived early, having travelled all night from Oban. How dear B is enjoying having Jack with her. Her present life is so dull and monotonous, but she never complains.

Sep 22 ... Good news from Canada; as in yesterday's elections they have thrown out Laurier's Radical Govt. and the Reciprocity Bill with America!

Sep 24 Sunday ... N and Jack to Westminster Abbey and Hal and I to St Mary Abbots ... It is hoped and believed that the Morocco question is settled between France and Germany! Thus we are saved from War, for we must have stood by France ...

Sep 26 ...Very fine and bright. N and I by bus to Agnes Dupuis' marriage to Lieut. Gregory, RN at Brompton Church, where the music and flowers were beautiful, and afterwards at the Rembrandt Hotel, just opposite church, new and quite nice. ... Mr Hickson saw B - he now charges fees ...

Sep 27 ... Bob and Maidlie came - he looks splendid and she looks stronger [she seems to have been slightly unwell but details are not recorded] *Dear B had a happy day, seeing them and we think it did her good ... A fresh political difficulty has arisen between Italy and Turkey, about Tripoli.*

Sep 28 Hal took Maidlie to the Colisseum to see Sarah Bernhardt.

Sep 30 Cold, with rain and hail ... N, Hal and I to the "New" Theatre to see "Romeo and Juliet". Miss Phyllis Neilson-Terry acted the latter v. well. It was all good, and well worth seeing.

Oct 2 ... The Italians are now at war with Turkey, about Tripoli, which they covet! But there are such conflicting accounts about it all in the papers, that it is impossible to know the truth.

Oct 3 ... Fitz Paget lunched here, looking well, and v. nice, as ever. Hal came to meet him. Mrs J. Alexander to tea. She told us much about the Primate's last days.

Oct 6 ... Mr Whistler came at 12o'c, and he, and N, Hal, Nana and I had a nice Service of Holy Communion in B's room. [A clergyman, old friend and a connection of Maidlie's]. *Mr W staid for lunch, and then sat and chatted with Bessy ...*

Oct 12 ... Wars, and rumours of War, and disturbance and discontent nearly all over the world! WHAT is coming?

Oct 19 ... Gen. Wynne called. He is now Keeper of the Jewels at the Tower.

Oct 24 ... This is the anniversary of Balaclava - and of Agincourt.... The Dr says B must not move until her Temp. has been well sub-normal for several days! it may be weeks - or perhaps months!

Oct 25 ... N and I to St Paul's at 6 o'c for the Service for Seafarers. Most interesting - the Church crowded. The hymns sung with a WILL! Bishop

Welldon (late of Colchester) preached. First day of the carriage ...

Oct 26 ...Bob came unexpectedly to lunch. His lumbago is v. much better, but he looks a little thin and pulled down ... Maidlie is still in Scotland with Princess Louise ...

Oct 30 ... Very wet afternoon so N and I did not go to Mr Hickson's Prayer Meeting as intended, and only paid 2 visits (Lady Egerton and Miss Vansittart's) not to keep the man and horse out long in the heavy rain.

Nov 1 ... heard that Mrs Chadwick (Helen Crozier) wife of the Bishop of Derry has just died in Dublin, after an operation. She had only been 9 months married ... Nurse Creese (from N. Zealand) left today. She is rather rough and noisy ... Dr Rhodes has sent Nurse Tyndall in her place. She seems v. nice and gentle and I hope B will find her a pleasant nurse ...

Nov 4 ... 6000 taxi cabs have struck, and the streets are so nice and quiet in consequence! and a good many Hansoms and 4-wheelers have turned out, and as town is not v. full, I think London will get on all right without these taxis!

Nov 5 Sunday N. Hal, Jack and I to Brompton Church ... The French and Germans have come to terms about Morocco and the Congo, so that war is averted: but there is the Italian and Turkish war going on, the Rebellion in China, and Guerillas in Portugal and a Frontier Campaign in India! Truly, enough fighting!

Nov 7 ... Dr Rhodes is simply delighted with B's condition. Her temp. has gone down steadily ... I am sure v. much due to nice Nurse Tyndal, and we hear to our horror that she must leave us in a month! This is really intolerable...

Nov 11... The King and Queen start for India, in the "Medina" with a splendid escort of Battleships, but at Portsmouth there was much fog and rain!...

Nov 15 ... Sister Helen comes for the night on her way home from staying with Dora at Falmouth; both are now well, and her visit is enjoyed. Bessy sits up in a chair for a short time each day. The Dr now speaks more cheerfully of her than ever before, but they are cast down by the departure of Nurse Tyndal, whose Matron will not allow her to stay more than four weeks with any patient: a possible successor is rejected as she is R.C! Helen returns to town with Eileen to consult Dr Rhodes. Nettie pays a flying visit to Chatham, and *returns delighted with baby Jo. Nurse Cattell is installed.*

Dec 2 ... N, Hal and I to Hilda Woulfe's wedding at St Paul's Knightsbridge, and 58 Grosvenor St, a beautiful lent house. She married Mr (Cecil) Goodden, a Barrister. It was not a v. smart affair. We called on the Egertons, as he is being turned out of the Admiralty (2nd Sea Lord) by Winston Churchill, the new First Lord.

Dec 5 ... I left Kings X for Hatfield, where Annie met me in her motor car. Found A and her 3 small girls v. well, and Bernie away from home.

Dec 7 ... Bernie back (from shooting in Yorkshire) in the middle of the night ...
Dec 9 ... Hal down, and he, Annie and I motored to Edwy McC's little house and had tea with him and his Mother ...
Dec 11 ... Neither Annie nor I come down to breakfast, as it is at 8.30 to suit Bernie's going into town every morning. The children's nurse is away for a day's holiday, so we saw a great deal of them, and they were all down for luncheon.
Dec 13 ..to Kings X, where N's carriage met me. Dear B seems, if anything, better. Long the Parlourmaid is laid up with rheumatism and anaemia and can do no work. I have had quite a pleasant week at Woodcock Lodge - so quiet and restful, and the house nice and warm. The 3 children so nice and sweet, and Betty, aged 3 and a half, simply delicious. And it is so nice to see Annie so much better, though still needing care.
Dec 21 We are trying to finish our Christmas shopping, though it seems never-ending!! ... N, Jack, Nana and I drove to Waterloo Station to see Maidlie and little Jo on their way through London. Jo is a fine, big boy, with a beautiful face, v. like what Bob was at his age.
Dec 23 ... Bessy is getting many nice Xmas boxes. So her friends do not forget her, though she has been shut up so long.
Dec 25 ... Nana has gone to Putney to spend Xmas with her people. N and I, Hal and Jack to Westminster Abbey ... Sir Allen Young paid us a long visit. Dear Bessy was sad and low this morning, then bright again. Hal lighted a pretty little Xmas tree in her room, and she had lots of presents, which she much enjoyed.

List of *"Xmas Boxes I gave": N - violet scent*
Bessy - photo frame
Hal & Jack - pen wipers
Maidlie - boots for Jo
Bob - large Xmas card
Annie - South Kensington Box
Helen - book of texts Dora - large Xmas card
Greenwell children - Xmas stockings
C. Macleod - large Xmas card
Nana - book of texts Cook (Funnell) - tie
Long - lace collar Housemaid (Florence) - needle-case
Girl (Christie) - work basket

Dec 26 ... Dr Rhodes ... is sorry that B is making so little progress this last month; but he is not anxious and regards it just as a "retardation" ...
Dec 28 ... I have a cold, and feel rather miserable. Drove to see Katie Shaw, who is not well.
Dec 29 ... N, Hal, Jack and I to Haymarket Theatre. A clever little Curtain-raiser and then an amusing Comedy "Beauty pulls the Strings" and we had good seats in Dress Circle, and N's carriage each way.

Joyce Betty

Lottie Nanny Pratt
Barbara

[About 1912]

1912

Queensberry Place now has a telephone - 5130 Western!

Jan 2 Long the Parlourmaid's Mother and brother slept here. [She had been ill] ... *Annie and her Nurse (Miss Rowley) motored up and took N down to Woodcock Lodge for a few days' change. I am so glad for she badly needs it, after all her anxiety about B - and she has not slept one night out of this house since last April! Dr Rhodes is immensely pleased with dear B and confidently expects good results if only this treatment of rest and food is persevered in!*

Nettie soon comes home, however, and Bessy seems to make little or no progress. Haddie is unwell, too. The Dr orders Bessy back to complete bed rest - for about a month, he says, and then see how she is - *very trying ...*

Jan 23 ... Hal off to Switzerland, to Grand Hotel, Arosa, with Annie and Bernie and some of the Greenwells. He has got a fortnight's leave, and I do hope he will have a good time, which he much needs, out of our depressing atmosphere and circumstances, but we shall miss him much.

Jan 24 Dark and foggy. N and I visited poor old Chapman [who used to do sewing for them] *and then to tea at the Dyson Lauries where Flo is staying. Heard that Agnes Bradford left me £200. She died in June 1910 - a long time ago!*

Jan 25 ... Great excitement about affairs in Belfast, where the Ulster men are determined not to let Winston Churchill speak in Ulster Hall on Feb 8!!

Jan 30 Cold and frosty. N drove down to Chiswick to an afternoon party given by Bishop and Mrs Montgomery on the eve of their daughter Una's marriage. Dr Rhodes says B feels this cold weather, and it gives her a little bronchitis - he is satisfied on the whole, but will be glad when her temp. is lower.

Jan 31 ... I drove to Bank and went to Buckingham Palace and Marlborough House to write names

Feb 1 ... N and I paid visits, amongst others to Hylda Goodden (nee Woulfe) a bride.

Feb 3 Oh! it is snowing and freezing and SO cold! ... Jack came as usual at 5.30 but he appears much saddened by the disaster to Submarine A3, with loss of 4 officers and 10 men, yesterday off the Isle of Wight.

Feb 5 Very cold. N and Nana took poor old Chapman to the A & N Stores to get an Anti- rheumatic ring for her; and they saw the King and Queen etc. drive past on their way home from India - splendidly received.

Feb 7 ... Maidlie looked in for a short time. She is staying in town with her Aunt, and v. busy hanging her Pictures for her Exhibition this week.

[This is the first mention, by Haddie, of what we know of Maidlie, that she was a serious professional painter, trained at the Slade, and never ceased to carry on with her work. The family still has many examples, and her work is very individual and of the period, edging towards Art Nouveau. She also later wrote books - one, about her Father, "The Queen thanks Sir Howard" - which were well-received.]

"Cinerarias at Marden 1934"
by Maidlie McClintock

Patience McClintock called, and brought her Intended, Mr Wilson. They are to be married in April. She looks so happy!

Feb 9 ... N to the Grafton Galleries early and she and I there in afternoon to see Maidlie's charming 50 water colour pictures done in Norway, Italy and Scotland. She sold 10 of them today, which WAS good. We met many people we knew there. Bob came to see Bessy.

Feb 13 ... Bernie dined here, to talk about business. Annie is still at Arosa ..
Feb 14 ... Helen West and Jessie came to lunch and tea, and N drove them to see Maidlie's pictures ... B was so glad to see Jessie ... The King and Queen opened Parliament today - What IS going to happen?
Feb 15 ... N and I to tea at the Australia Club in Dover St with Leila Darley, who I am sorry to say, leaves tomorrow for Australia with Mr D and Constance; and they MAY remain there altogether. They learn that George Richardson, Leo's nephew, has died, in a private hospital.
Feb 17 ... N and I lunched with Mrs and Miss Maitland in Montagu Square, a party of 8 women, rather pleasant. Then we called for Mrs Culwick at poor George Richardson's lodging, and brought her here for tea and dinner. May Drake called and saw Bessy ...
Feb 23 ... Maidlie is staying for 2 or 3 nights. *N, Maidlie Hal and I went to the Scala to see the "Kinemacolor" - the most wonderful reproduction of the King and Queen's visit to India and the Durbar and great review of 50,000 men at Delhi. We were much interested and pleased. It is a great pleasure to dear B to have Maidlie staying here.*
Feb 25 Sunday ... N, Jack and I to Brompton Church. The Dean of St Paul's preached, but we were in the Gallery, and I cd. not hear!
Feb 28 ... Hal dined with John Leslie, and then went with Tissy Jeffreys to an Anti Women's Suffrage meeting at the Albert Hall.
Feb 29 ...Hal with the Greenwells to Olympia to see "The Miracle" ... Alas! the big Coal Strike has begun in earnest! It had been hoped that possibly it might have been averted, but no! the men WILL have it so!
Mar 1 ... Those dreadful Suffragette women turned out this evening, and smashed the plate glass windows in v. many of the big shops in Bond St, Piccadilly and Regent St - with stones and hammers.
Mar 2 ... We drove to see the devastation wrought in the West End shops. We feared that the Strike would interfere with the train services to Portsmouth, but Jack was able to come, by a later train than usual.
Mar 4 ... B has again taken an infinitesimal dose of Tuberculin and in consequence feels depressed and miserable - poor child. The Suffragettes smashed windows in Kensington today and the British Museum had to be closed as it was feared they might attack it. Many other places are closed too - Natural History Museum, Painted Hall at Greenwich, etc.
Mar 5 ... N and I drove to St Paul's Cathedral, chiefly to see the Duke of Wellington's monument, which has only just been completed, by putting a large equestrian figure on the top. It is very imposing.
Mar 6 ... N and I to a Musical Afternoon given by Antonia McClintock - good professionals.
Mar 8 ... Cicy Macleod came to tea. The Coal Strike and Suffragette troubles still continue, but the latter are being given sentences with hard labour, which they don't at all like! I have no fire, because of this horrid strike.

Mar 9 ... N and I to a Meeting of the League of Mercy at Lady Naylor-Leyland's house in Knightsbridge. Princess Louise was there, and the American Consul-General spoke very well ... Dr R says B has made good progress in the 10 months she has been in her room - but it seems a long time to us!

Mar 10 Sunday ... The vicar preached on the sad state of unrest all over the country - which indeed is sad, and this miserable govt. seems to be doing nothing for it, beyond talking platitudes. Hundreds of thousands of men in all trades are out of work, and if the strike is not soon ended, there will be piteous distress ...

Mar 11 ...paid visits, and to tea with Mrs J.H.Buxton, where we met Edwy and his intended, Margaret Buxton ... I much like what I have seen of the Buxtons.

Mar 12 ... Annie and Miss Rowley came ... Annie looks quite well, and thinks B looking much better. She brought her honey and lovely flowers

Mar 13 ... it is a blessing that it is generally mild, as we have so few fires going, and those generally poor ones, because of the strike.

Mar 14 ... May Drake lunched here. She and Elsie De Salis and her husband, and Ursula her girl are going tonight to the Court at Buckingham Palace. John Leslie is going with them. N and I to the Chapel Royal for a special service for the R.N.Scripture Readers Soc.

Mar 15 ... N and I to tea with Mrs Phillimore, and then to Mrs Willis to see Ethel and Mrs Vernon dressed for the King's Court tonight. Ethel looked charming in a lovely blue gown and train, embroidered with gold and patte.

Mar 17 Sunday ... N, Hal, Jack and I to Brompton. It is a day of Humiliation and Prayer for the sad and sinful state of unrest in the country, and there were special lessons, Psalms, Litany and Prayers. The Bishop of Stepney preached on "Your Country is desolate - may God hear our Prayers".

Mar 19 ... N and I to A & N Stores to choose Spring Mantles ... Mr Asquith today introduced a Coal Mine Bill, which he hopes will cope with the dreadful state of affairs, but one fears that he is incapable of drafting a wise or just one! ...We had expected Ethel [Willis] *at 12 o'c to see B, but she did not turn up, and poor B was so excited and tired looking out for her, that when she did come, she could not see her. Mr Asquith's Coal Bill pleases no one, and though it is all in favour of the Miners, they say it is not good enough for them, and so the impasse continues, and no one knows what is going to happen. Tom Mann, the Socialist, has been arrested for preaching Rebellion to the soldiers against their officers - What next?*

Mar 24 Sunday ... Aylmer Quin called. I'm sorry to say, he can give but a v. indifferent account of Dora's health.

Mar 25 ... Auriel Quin wrote me a bad account of Dora, I'm sorry to say ... We hear that a good many coal miners are coming back to work here and there, but the distress is great.

Mar 26 ... Cicy Macleod and her brother, Roddy, came to see us; he is doing good work for the Unionist Cause. Mr Asquith is forcing his Miners' Bill through Parliament, but it does not please either Masters or Men ... Dr Rhodes came again [after a spell of illness] *and gives a cheerful account of Bessy, tho' of course he could wish that her temp. were lower than it has been ...*

Mar 30 ... Antonia McC lent N her Motor Car, and she and Hal drove down to Woodcock Lodge, had luncheon there, and on to Easney, the Buxtons' place, where there was an afternoon party, and where they met Edwy and Margaret again ...

Ap 4 ... N and I drove to Gorringe's where we met Bob, Maidlie and Jo, on their way from Pine Wood. Jo is certainly a v. fine and handsome little fellow. Bob made a short visit to B, and it has been a great pleasure to her to see him, but I am sure she must feel sad at not being allowed to see Jo.

Ap 7 Easter Sunday. A glorious sunny Easter Day! Thank God, the coal strike is officially over, and many men returning to work. What a blessing the mild weather has been!

Ap 8 ... Josephine Singleton, the Luard-Beans and Miss Colthurst to tea, which we had in the Square Hall to save Josephine the stairs, as she is so stiff from rheumatism ...

Ap 16 ... I took Louisa Luard to the Scala to see the Kinemacolor of the Indian Durbar which is excellent. I never saw anybody enjoy herself as much as she did - just like a child!

We heard the dreadful news of the wreck of the new huge White Star Liner "Titanic" from collision with icebergs, off Newfoundland, with over 2000 on board, most of whom are lost!!!!

Ap 18 Hal took me to the Palace Theatre to see the Russians dance. Anna Pavlova was wonderful, and so graceful and pretty.

Ap 21 Sunday ... N, Hal, Jack and I to Brompton church, where there was a special service and sermon for the Titanic - very moving.

Ap 23 ... N and I ... enquired at the Dyer Edwardes house and heard that they had the joy of hearing that their daughter, Lady Rothes, is safe and well with her husband at New York. She helped to row one of the Titanic's boats, and was so plucky.

Ap 25 ... N, Hal and I to wedding of Sybil Greenwell and Mr Geoffrey Strutt at St Peter's, Eaton Square, and 17 Portman Square. A great crowd at the latter.

Ap 30 [This account is written much later] *After having felt v. unwell for a good many weeks past, I was seized with serious illness this afternoon. Septic Pneumonia, bronchitis and pressure of blood on the brain. N found me lying unconscious on the floor of my room. I remember nothing at all for several days, SO ill. Dr Rhodes brought Sir Lander Brunton to see me but neither he nor anyone else thought I could possibly recover, but as a last chance, I was repeatedly inoculated with* [blank space] *and it is thought that this, and my v. good constitution saved my life. I had to have nurses day and night, and was given lots of oxygen. Poor dear N had a bad time of it, with all the illness and Drs and nurses in the house!*

I can't understand why God spared such a useless life as mine. Oh! I wish I could have gone thro' the golden gates when I was on the very threshold! but God MUST do what is right.

There are no further diary entries till Saturday, 24 August, 1912, in rather shaky writing, a short note. It seems that Bessy, meanwhile, has improved a good deal and has been staying in a flat of her own, at Hornton Street.

Aug 29 To Mr Hosford, 12 o'c. I had to wait an hour, as he was called off to a consultation in Harley St. He is quite pleased with my progress and need not see me again for 3 weeks, unless something goes wrong with my eyes.

Aug 30 ...Fine. N, B and I drove. The floods are dreadful at Norwich, and other parts of the country, quite devastating.

Sep 10 Dear B came home from the Flat in Hornton St, where she has been since June 27th. She is very much better, thank God. Her nice Nurse Cattell is still with her, also Nana.

Sep 14 ... N, B and Nurse Cattell drove to get a carrying chair for B - the workmen have nearly finished the lift.

Haddie is receiving regular massage treatments. Annie is reported as looking well and strong.

Sep 25... Dr Rhodes saw both B and me, and inoculated her again, but much more mildly. I must persevere in all remedies, and some Petroleum oil he has added. Bob, Maidlie and little Jo came here at 4o'c on their way to Scotland to stay with her Mother in a house near Roseneath lent by Princess Louise. They left us after dinner to travel all night. Jo is a charming and splendid wee boy, of about 18 months.

Sep 27 Saw Dr Rhodes again. I have bitten my tongue badly in my sleep, from the bad pain in my head and eyes. It is v. annoying to have this in addition to all my other ailments, and the remedies are so tiresome.

Sep 28 This is called "Ulster Day" as the loyal Ulstermen today sign a Solemn Covenant, a loyal Protest against Home Rule. We have a large Union Jack flying on the balcony, and are all wearing badges of small ones. The Loyalists made a wonderful grand demonstration in various parts of Ireland, and kept perfect order...

Oct 1 ...Crickie Cox, dear Harriet Campbell's step daughter, just come from Australia, came to tea. We had not seen her for years. She is VERY nice.

Oct 3 ... 8th Massage - it is certainly doing me good in several respects, and I like Nurse Kirk, my Masseuse.

Oct 4 ... N to Frinton to spend weekend with Vesey FitzGerald ...

Oct 7 ... A little impromptu dinner of 8 got up by Hal and Jack - Adm, Lady and Miss Bowden-Smith, Ella Harman and Major Menzies ... I did not feel fit to appear, but had dinner with Nurse Catell in the study.

Oct 12 ... Poor N in a pack of Household troubles - the Cook, Scott, is leaving; the Between-Maid is not much use, the Housemaid Nellie leaves today, and poor Long, the Parlourmaid is ill with bad rheumatism in her foot and can do nothing, and has gone off to a friend's house to be nursed. N spent hours looking for a temporary Parlourmaid, and at last found an elderly one, rather crippled with rheumatism in hands, who came in at once for a few days.

Nettie spends a few days at Shedfield, with Mrs Franklyn. A new cook is found, Long is visited by N, H and by Nana and slowly gets better. A very good temporary parlourmaid, Hazel, comes. Bessy has a slightly raised temperature, which puzzles her doctor. Little Jo comes with his nurse on a visit, on his way home from Scotland. The three little Greenwell girls come up with their nurse and Rowley, to see him. *Dear Bessy came down to drawing-room to see the 4 children, carried down and up again - and was none the worse for it.*

Nov 3 Sunday ... Mr Willis and Ethel called just before lunch. They are up in town because of the death of her Grandmother, Mrs Duncan. Later Louisa Luard, Miss E. Cole, Mr Cator, Sir Arthur Wynne and Sir Allen Young called. Great excitement about the war in the Balkans!

Nov 6 B drove out in forenoon with little Jo and his nurse. Bob and Maidlie came to lunch and tea; little Jo is to remain here for a few days longer. ... Bessy lunched downstairs and spent some time in drawing-room besides driving out ... The cistern in my cupboard leaked again, and wetted many of my things - very troublesome.

Nov 8 Dr Rhodes wants me to go to a Dentist and have 3 large teeth extracted! I do not see it at all! ... I am to go on with the massage - so expensive! Fire in my room for massage, and also to dry my things that have been wetted by the leaking cistern.

Nov 9 ... N went to Great Ormond St Hospital to see little Bella, child of Bernie's Chauffeur [Noble]...

Nov 12 ... Henry West and Daisy came to lunch, and he administered the Holy Communion to N, Bessy, Nana and me in B's room ... Bob and Maidlie fetched little Jo home. We shall miss the dear little child greatly. He has endeared himself to us. N took Daisy to Ella Delap's 2nd Concert at the

Bechstein Hall and liked it very well.

Nov 14 ... N took Mrs Warde to the Savoy Chapel, to be married to Mr Pollard, RN. Jack was Best Man to this, his great friend. The reception was at Morley's Hotel. N was given a lovely white bouquet ... Miss Rowling brought Joyce Greenwell to go with N to the wedding, and then Bernie came to fetch her. He saw Bessy in her room.

Nov 15 ... Poor N is in servant trouble again: Cook and Housemaid going, and Between-maid no use, and none seem inclined to do any work!!

Nov 16 Poor B is a good deal upset because her nice Nurse Cattell, who has been almost a year with her, is leaving today for a restful holiday, as she is not well and suffering from insomnia. Her successor is Nurse Fuller, who we hope may prove a success.... I am certainly feeling better in many ways, and less pain the last few days - thank God.

Nov 17 Sunday ... Dr R. saw B, and spoke comfortably to us, for we were rather low as B's illness drags on so long. He confidently anticipates a happy ending to it, though he cannot say WHEN ... The new nurse, Fuller, we only like so-so - v. inferior to Nurse Cattell.

Nov 18 Dull. I drove early to get flowers and fruit. Annie came up for a dinner of 12 - Annie and Bernie, Bob and Maidlie, Capt and Mrs Montgomery, Tim McC Bunbury and his Intended, Miss Ievers, Antonia McC, Nettie, Hal and Jack. I did not feel equal to appear so had some bread and milk in my room. The cook, Mrs G... is so uncertain that N had to get in a good job cook to cook the dinner!!

Nov 19 ... Annie remains here and sleeps. It is so nice to have her, for we so seldom see her. Miss Macneill and Rose Cave to tea. Other friends of Annie's were asked, but could not come.

Nov 25 ...Frank McC, Dean of Armagh, [and a brother of Charlie, Blanche's husband] *arrived here this evening from Ireland, to marry Tim McC Bunbury tomorrow ... B keeps very quiet, I have not seen her for 2 or 3 days as I have a cold, and fear to give it to her. It is a good thing that we have good Nurse Wood with B, as we would have felt anxious if that careless Nurse Fuller had had charge of her, the last few days.*

Nov 26 ... Tim McC Bunbury was married today to Miss Ethel Ievers, at St Mary Abbotts, and N and the Dean, Hal and Jack, went to the wedding, which went off very well, and they met numbers of friends and relations...

Nov 28 ... I drove early to enquire for Sir Edward Henry, the head of the London Police, who yesterday was shot at at his own Hall Door! Fortunately the wound is not serious, but it is a horrible thing! The Dean left for Ireland - he is very nice. Lady Rathdonnell and Miss Bruen, called. [Bridegroom's mother and aunt]

Jack has several days' illness, and telegraphs Admiralty: "Laid up, but not dead". Emily and Gertrude McClintock, the two ladies who inhabit Drumcar, come to dinner. Haddie does visit a dentist, but to her relief he does not think

she needs any extractions. Nessie finds and engages a cook, Mabel Daysh, from Shedfield. Nurse Cattell comes back, *and that Terror, Mrs G....., left!*
Dec 24 Jack goes off to spend Christmas with Mrs and Miss Cordes at Sillwood Park, Sunningdale, so they have a very quiet Christmas Day, Bessy very pleased with all her cards and presents.

Dec 25 Dr R. sent B a funny mechanical toy of a Rabbit, and she played a lot with it, and a squeaking dog which Leopold Dix sent her! Nana spent the day and night at Putney with her brother.

Dec 28 Dr R finds that B does not yet seem fit for the Tuberculin injections, so he will leave them off for the present; and instead she is to eat a good deal of raw garlic, which is believed to be a poison for microbes!...

The year ends without any summing-up.

1913

Jan 1 Poor B had a rather miserable and uncomfortable day - and sick from all the garlic she has had to eat; on the other hand, it has lowered her temp. and much diminished her cough. but it is all v. slow and trying; and she is so good and patient.

Jan 2 ... Patience Wilson (nee McClintock) came to luncheon. Her husband is a Master at Charterhouse ...

Jan 7 ... A home dinner of 10 - Capt. Duff (Jack's chief at the Admiralty) and his daughter, Capt and Mrs Larken, Betty Rhodes and her husband, Silvie Ross (nee Ruxton), N Hal and Jack. I had dinner in the Study with Nurse Catell. The new Cook, Dayshe, did v. well. Dr R came, and says he is v. sorry for B, but if the Inoculations did not affect her unpleasantly they wd. do her no good! She remains in bed ... she received some lovely Xmas roses from Portnall.

Jan 13 ... Carrie Macnaghten to lunch, and then went up to see Bessy and teach her to paint flowers.

Jan 15 ... Henry West came ... and gave us a nice little service in B's room. Poor Henry is losing his sight, but is so good and plucky about it, and is learning to read the Braille type. B remains altogether in bed now ... but nearly always busy, latterly making pretty lampshades.

Jan 18 ... We went to see the picture of our Grandfather, Ferrard, which Hal has bought from one of the Fosters, and had restored and mended and framed - V well done, indeed.

Hal, we know, was deeply interested in family history, and we largely have him to thank for the wealth of papers and letters still in existence.

Jan 21 ... Dr Rhodes again; as B's temperature is persistently too high, he wishes her to keep perfectly quiet in bed for some days ... she may read, but not write or paint or needlework. This will be dull for her, poor child, but she is always good and submissive.

Jan 28 ... I did not go up to see B, because of my cold. Dr R cheered us somewhat today, and says we must not be too downhearted about these setbacks, but there is some mischief going on in her right lung! alas. He wants to have a consultation, with Dr Riviere.

Jan 29 Poor B is not allowed to use her arms or hands for anything - not even to play Patience. So she is v. depressed today - partly boredom, and also the v. bad, dark weather...

Jan 31 Dr R brought in Dr Riviere in consultation for N - as he begins to fear that he sees B too often, and has got too near his subject. Dr Riviere is quite sanguine about her ultimate recovery. She is to keep quite still, for another week, and go on with the vaccine in a v. mild form, and also with the garlic.

Feb 1 N had intended going to Annie today, as Bernie left yesterday for S.America, but it is feared her children have whooping cough, and one could not run the most remote chance even of conveying it to B, who has not had it.

Feb 3 ... Henry West is lying very ill at Folly Court, and is not likely to recover

Henry, born 1842, now 70 years of age.

Feb 4 ... Dear Henry West passed away this evening. A truly good kind man to all, and v. much so to me, as my Brother-in-law. Dr says today, that B is now almost recovered from the setback she has had ... She is still in bed. He wants her to go to Switzerland in June, if all is well enough.

Feb 5 Ash Weds. N to Church. I drove to get a bonnet at Dunlin's for my mourning. Carrie Macnaghten spent the afternoon here; it is just possible that she may take B to Switzerland, which would be delightful, but of course, nothing can yet be settled.

Fardells called, but we did not admit visitors.

Feb 8 Lovely sunny weather. N, Hal and Jack down to Folly Court for poor Henry's Funeral. He was laid in the beautiful Cemetery at Bearswood a few miles off. A good kind man goes from among us!...

Feb 13 ... Very sad news! After reaching the S. Pole, Capt Scott and his party all perished in a cyclone, it is believed! His poor wife had gone out to New Zealand to meet him ...

Feb 17 ... Poor darling B is v. ill - having taken influenza from Nurse Catell - who ought to have known better than to conceal the fact that she had the Flue, and not to have continued attending B. A night nurse is necessary, and fortunately a good one was got, a little Scotchwoman, Nurse Caird.

Feb 24 ... Dear B very ill and suffering ... Dr R came twice, and is v. anxious about her, but not hopeless!

Feb 25 ... Hal to a Fancy Dress Dance in a Windsor uniform. He loves B DEARLY, but does not and will not realise how ill she is. She is just barely holding her own ... This is a dreadful time of trial and suspense for all who love her, and v. v. trying and suffering to the poor child herself.

Feb 26 ... Poor B suffering much, from excessive flatulence pressing hard upon her heart, and from breathlessness and sleeplessness. Her dear face looks sadly changed, but so sweet and bright, and plucky!

Feb 27... Dr R brought Dr Riviere to consult as to the desirability of drawing off the water from the lung, but they decided against it, and she was so disappointed, as she thought it would have given her some relief ...

Mar 1 ... Dr R came 7 times to see dear B. We are terribly anxious. Everything possible is being done for her, but all is in God's hands.

Mar 2 Darling B is evidently worse, and the Dr, even so hopeful as he is, has at last given up hope. Alas, and he even thought she was passing away while he was in the room. She suffered much, from spasms and pressure on the heart, and gasping, following by unconsciousness.

Mar 3 Our beloved Bessy entered into rest at 12.15 today. We were all around her. She was unconscious for some hours, and so felt no pain or discomfort, for which we praise God. So happy and peaceful was she, anxious to go: and said she was not in the least afraid to die, but mortal afraid to live! Darling child, it is all well and glorious with her, but alas! for us all, who so dearly loved and valued her. What will life be without her? She has left us a most beautiful example of Godliness, Patience, Peace, Love, and cheerful content and resignation. May we be enabled to follow in her dear footsteps.

Maidlie spent much of the day here, and we have the 3 dear boys to comfort and strengthen us.

Mar 4 Jack went down to see and comfort poor Annie, for whom I feel greatly, as she cannot come up here because of the whooping cough - and now, because it might be too much for her, in her present condition.

Mar 5 Darling Bessy looks so lovely lying amid flowers, with that wondrous look of peace and happiness on her sweet face. But oh! it is heartbreaking to think that never again in this world can we have her beloved presence among us, or hear her dear voice! May God help and comfort us. He gave - and He has seen fit to take away - and it is all right and happy for her. How sweetly and patiently she has born these years of ill health. Never a murmur, and just trusting in God - and quite cheerful.

Mar 7 A sad, sorrowful day. Our precious Bessy was laid to rest in Hanwell Cemetery, close beside, or rather, just over where her dear Father lies. There was a beautiful service at Brompton Church, where we all were. Bishop Montgomery and Mr Whistler (her great friend) read the Service and she had the same hymns dear Leo had. The boys would not let Nettie or Maidlie or me go on to the Cemetery, as they thought it would be too much for us.

A letter from Bob to Annie dated 6 March shows his understanding of what it must mean to her to be unable to join them all at this time. Bernie, too is abroad and it is indeed hard for her.

Bessy's inscription, on the left side of Leo's Celtic cross, reads:

Here also lies
in God's holy keeping
Elizabeth Florence Mary
much loved youngest child of
Admiral Sir Leopold McClintock
she joyfully entered into rest
on the 3rd of March 1913
aged 30
"death is swallowed up in Victory"

Mar 10 ... I went down to Folly Court, hoping it may do me good, and also because Nettie and Nana go to Annie on Weds, and Hal and Jack hope to go out of town for a few days at Easter. They really need a change, dear boys. Dear Bessy's very nice little Scotch Nurse Caird, who Nettie has kept on for a few days, came down to Folly Court to take care of me, and then returned to town. HOW kind every one is - but the terrible heartache goes on.

Mar 11 Dot kept me in bed all day, I was so done up and miserable. It will be remembered, Dot had only lost her husband, Henry, on Feb 4.

Mar 13 A lovely mild, sunny day. I am better (less weary) and came down at tea time to meet Mary Jeffreys, who came all the way from Crowthorne to see and sympathise with me.

Mar 14 ... Down to tea again. Mrs Dykes March and her sister Lena Macan came. Alick West came this evening from Dorsetshire, where he has been having some good hunting with a friend. Dottie and her three girls Daisy, Kathleen and Eileen are so kind me, and letters of sympathy are still coming in, but oh! the aching void and longing. God help me and the other dear ones.

Mar 17 ... Still feeling v. tired and shakey and constant headache, but certainly better for the rest and kind care of all here.

Mar 18 ... Left Folly Court ... N arranged that her nice Parlourmaid, Long, should meet me at Waterloo and look after me, and so she did, and dear Hal and Jack were there too, so I was well cared for. So dear of them. Cicy Macleod came to spend a few days with me at Queensberry Place, so that I may not be too sad and lonely by myself, as the boys go to Portnall for Easter. I am glad, as they much need a change after all they have gone through. Their tender goodness to me is unspeakable, and the greatest blessing and comfort possible. But oh! to come back to this house without HER - and yet I love it, chiefly because she did, dear child.

Mar 22 Devastating gales, all over the country. Dr Rhodes gave me some soothing and sleep-inducing remedies ... I hear from Nettie that she and

Nana are better.

Mar 24 My birthday. Very sad. Cicy out in carriage. Olivia Monument came to see me.

Mar 25 Easter Tuesday. Went alone to Holy Communion at Brompton, but v. little comfort yet!

Mar 26 ... Cicy left for her little house at Cley. She has been a great help to me during this sad week. N and Nana back from Woodcock, and both look better.

Mar 31 ... Lady Page Wood called. She was v. kind to dear Bessy in S/Africa and is v. fond of her. Her husband died some months ago ... This sad, sad month is ended.

Ap 2 ... The clearing and sorting of all dear Bessy's little belongings goes on, and the room she so loved looks empty and desolate. Sad, sad work.

Ap 8 ... Frederick McC died this evening [Brother to Charlie and Dean Francis] *Hal and Jack went to enquire for Antonia. So many people we know have died within the last few weeks. I drove to see Josephine Singleton ... She was so nice and sympathetic. She really loved dear Bessy, and feels what a terrible loss we have.*

Ap 9 ... My sister Blanche spent most of the afternoon here. She and Charlie are staying at the Naval & Military Hotel close by ...

Ap 10 ... Blanche called in ... This is our Father's birthday, born in 1809.

Ap 12 ... Maidlie came up unexpectedly and cheered us much - I was SO glad, for N and I were v much down.

Ap 14 ... N and Nana to Islington to get a carpet for dear Bessy's room, now a spare room. We have now lived 6 weeks without our precious Bessy.

Ap 15 ... I am feeling much better and stronger, but my eyes do not seem to improve, and I cannot help feeling anxious about them sometimes ... N and I drove out to see a supposed portrait of dear Leo which a dealer has for sale - but it is not he, most certainly.

Ap 20 Sunday. Louisa Luard called, and insisted on my going for a little drive with her in her 4-wheel cab, as Agnes was not with her and she could not bear to be alone!

Ap 23 ... Nana and I to A & N Stores to fetch a Canary bird Hal has bought. Then we had a charming drive in the Park. Alick West had tea ... He starts for India on Monday next. He is a very nice young fellow.

Ap 24 ... Nana down to Bognor to spend some days with Annie's children, as their governess has been called away by the death of her Mother. They are at Bognor for change after whooping cough. N and I to Lafayette's to see the beginning of a miniature of dear Bessy, which looks promising. Miss Douglas-Hamilton called. She knew dear B at Pretoria and appreciated her ...

Ap 26 ... Hal bought a Hen Canary to keep the other company ...

Ap 27 Sunday. N and Hal to church ... Miss Dutton Green called - she is a v.

nice Australian and dear B made her acquaintance in Switzerland when she was there with Bob. A most extraordinary thing has happened - the Chinese Republic are reorganising their House of Parliament and have asked all Christian Churches to pray for them today! This is being done all over England, I believe - certainly in London.

Ap 30 ... N drove to Victoria to meet Nana coming back from Bognor, where she had an accident falling in the street, and her nose badly cut by the wire rims of her spectacles ... now nearly healed. She left the three children v. well, and their governess coming back to them.

N and Nana go to spend a week with Annie, who is awaiting Bernie's return and keeping very well. Bob is Bessy's Executor and writes to Annie about the Will—Bessy added a note the day before she died saying that something of hers should be chosen for Joyce. Bob says Annie will be glad to get Bernie back, as a week without Maidlie is the most he can stand. He says no doubt she is very much hoping for a boy this time, but reminds her that Maidlie was a fourth daughter, and he is very glad indeed that she was not a boy!

May 4 Sunday ... Sir Allen Young paid me a long visit. He offers to take N to the great Antarctic Geographical Meeting at Albert Hall, but I doubt if she could face it yet.

May 6 ... I am feeling miserably ill, but had to come down to look after Blanche and Daisy... but later had to call the doctor, who found my temp 100, bad pulse and violent diarrhoea and sickness ... I AM so sorry to be ill and troublesome again.

May 13 ... Dr R called again and was so kind and sympathetic. He wants me to have some more massage, which is an expense and troublesome, but I would do anything to get strong again.

May 16 Much disappointed to hear this morning that Annie had a fourth girl at 1.20 am. We had so hoped it might have been the Boy so longed for! She and the baby are well, and Annie was not ill for long...[This is Anna Margaret, always known as Peggy].

May 17 ... Very good accounts of Annie and her baby. A letter from Hal who seems to be enjoying his days in Ireland ... at Drumcar, fishing etc, and he sent some lovely white roses from poor old Monasterboice.

May 21 ... Kathleen and Eileen (the West twins) came here early, and I took them for a long drive in Hyde Park and Regents Park to see the flowering shrubs, but unfortunately, they are poor this year, blighted, it is thought, by the inclement weather ...Jack dined with Mrs Upton Ruxton, and went with her to the Great Geographical Meeting at Albert Hall, where Captain Evans, one of the surviving Antarctic officers, read a paper.

May 24 Empire Day ... N, Jack and Nana drove to Hyde Park to see Lord Roberts reviewing Scouts, Reservists, Church Lads' Brigade, Gordon Boys etc. Many thousands of them, and great enthusiasm....

May 26 ... N to a Meeting of Sailors & Soldiers Families to prepare a great scheme in case of war, which Heaven forfend! Maidlie brought little Jo here to be taken care of while she and Bob go to Norway in a few days time ...

May 29 ... Admiral Sir Lewis Beaumont dined here to choose some MSS and Arctic relics of dear Leo's, which Hal is going to lend for Exhibition to the R. Geographical Soc. In their new premises close by us, at Lowther Lodge. Little Jo is staying at this time, but Haddie does not see as much of him as she would once have done.

May 31 Much cooler, and fine. Dr Rhodes came to see me, and to my horror, says I must go AT ONCE into a Nursing Home, for an operation to remove a growth on my chest! I must say, I dread it - but I will try to be as brave as I can...

Sadly, there are no further entries in the 1913 Diary. The Nursing Home was at 24 Chapel Street. Some poignant items in her Cash record at the back -

Altering and stretching fitted shoes of dear B's to fit me, at American Shoe Co - 2s.6d. Black tea gown £1.1.0

1914

Although there is a full-size diary for 1914, it is unused. Instead, Haddie reverts to a very small one - two inches wide, and her entries are mostly in pencil. For the first time, they are difficult to read. But though clearly not well, Haddie's urge to record events is still strong and, as we would expect, she becomes increasingly anxious about, first, events in Ireland, and then the gathering menace of World War I.

The diary begins with little else but appointments for "X-rays" which are clearly Radium treatments. Haddie is left with troublesome scars. The Dr recommends a Mrs Beall who makes "stays" and there are frequent fittings for these. Haddie sleeps badly, but records when she has "help" with sleeping - presumably opiates. Her handwriting remains strong, on the whole, and though almost overwhelmed at times with physical discomforts, she remains interested in world events, the doings of the Government (bad), the Suffragettes (very bad), and, of course, the comings and goings of her beloved family. Dr Rhodes and the Masseuse are still prominent in her life. Nana and Haddie both get influenza, but Nettie, on the other hand, seems to be quite well, goes about and entertains a little.

Feb 22 Sunday ...N and Hal to Westminster Abbey at 7 to hear Charlie De Salis preach ...
Feb 26 ... Daisy and Eileen West to lunch and tea. N took them to see Maidlie's pictures [possibly another exhibition]. The young Mr and Mrs Tim McClintock Bunbury are often at the house, especially when Bob is around. Bob hears he is to go to Woolwich, which does not please him.
Mar 3 Sad anniversary. Drove with N. Did me no good, increased cough etc. We moved down to Dining-room and Square Hall, as Drawing-rooms are to be painted and papered.
Mar 24 My birthday. Drove with Nettie. Shameful revelations about the Govt. - but the Army has saved the country!
Mar 25 ... Drove to see Maidlie's two pictures and tapestry at Surrey House ...
Mar 26 ... Drove to Brompton Church for Holy Communion at 11 o'c. This mid-week service is the first time Haddie has recorded church attendance for a long time. *Looked over my clothes with Nana.*
Mar 29 ... All v. indignant at conduct of Govt.
Mar 30 Saw Dr Rhodes, said I must see Mr Legge alas!
Ap 1 ... to Harley Street to consult Mr Legg and Dr Rhodes about scars; so kind they were, and reassuring.... Maidlie and Jo and nurse staying ... V. tired and upset about Mr Legg.
Ap 6 ... Poor Rowland v. ill in St George's - N and I saw her. This is Rowley, Annie's nurse; her illness must have caused consternation, as Annie is expecting again.
Ap 7 Haddie undergoes further X-ray treatment at the Temperance Hospital - Nana goes with her.
Ap 29 ... Joyce and Bernie and governess to lunch. N went back with them to Woodcock.
May 4 ... Maidlie to lunch and tea and paint at Museum. N and I drove and to tea with Antonia. Blanche and Mrs Carew there ... Dear Jack saved from capsized boat in Channel. Boat's crew also.
May 11 ... Drove to Bank, St George's etc. [As well as Rowley in hospital, they were visiting brother-in-law Charlie, who had trouble with his eyes] *Much disturbed by pain in leg and foot.*
May 19 ... N and I to Chelsea Flower Show. Lost each other and saw but little (of) flowers. I came home in taxi, very v. tired ...
May 20 ... Blanche McC came to stay, as Charlie's eye is not yet well.

May 23 ... with Nana to XRay ... Heard birth A's Son, great joy - Both well. Great Unionist victory at Ipswich.
May 24 Sunday ... Maria Cole, M. Jeffreys and Alingtons called. Hal to Woodcock in afternoon - all well there. Eiderdown and hot water bag

again!

May 25 ... Drove with N. Hal and Blanche to Court Theatre for Lady Roden's Theatricals.

May 27 ... N out early looking for a French maid for Annie....To Mr Wethered's big Tea. Good account of Annie and Charlie McC. He and Blanche to St Ermin's Hotel.

May 28 ... N read to C. McC at St Eermin's Hotel. I paid him visit, he's going on well ... v.good reports of Annie and Son ...

May 29 ... Maidlie slept here; played cards after dinner.

Jun 1 ... N lent carriage for Rowling. She and I drove later, saw Procession in Park ... Feeling better today. Looked out clothes. Hal to Arundel and Littlehampton to see Greenwell children. This day year, operation. Thank God, past.

Jun 3 ... Drove and shopped High St with Nana. N. lunched with Flo Laurie at Mrs Athelstone Riley's, and to Royal Academy. I saw Miss J. King about a French maid for Annie.

Jun 5 ... N, Nana and I in Mrs Inglis's car at 11.00 to Woodcock. Lost our way. Found Annie well, in bed, and Baby Boy, and lovely wee Peggy. [The new baby is Peter, born barely a year after Peggy.] *Had lunch and tea. A v. pleasant, happy day. V. tired.*

Jun 11 ... Heard Dora dangerously ill.... Received money from Mr Freke + income tax. To Brompton Church - Holy Communion.

Jun 13 ... Long (came) with me to Hospital ... Saw Dr Rhodes at hospital... [Haddie is undergoing X-rays once a week at this time]

Jun 15 ... N and I drove shopping, got a moire coat & skirt. Fit on at Miss Macpherson's. N and I to tea at the Miss Chichesters' ...

Jun 16 ... N lent carriage to Nana to take Rowling to station and down to Woodcock. Nana back in evening.

Jun 20 ... To XRay at 11.30 with Nana for last time - 12th and last. Have had 26 in all. N, Blanche and Hal to Lambeth. Dora not so well. Charlie's eye better.

Though the news of Dora continues bad, Haddie gradually feels stronger, and is sleeping better, often without "help"

Jul 5 ... N and I, Hal, Jack and Nana in Mrs Inglis's car down to Woodcock for Christening of Peter [Peter McClintock Greenwell]. *Everything and everybody so nice. Back for dinner.*

Jul 8 ... Blanche McC left us, and she and Charlie down to Toll [House, Buxted, Sussex] to stay with May.

Although Haddie's first mention of May, in several years, gives news surprising to the reader, it is clear that May must have been back in the country, and within the family, for some little time. She is living at Buxted with one or perhaps, two Miss Dons. Haddie's warm heart must have rejoiced at such a rapprochement, especially at this time of great anxiety about Dora.

Jul 12 Sunday   V. hot. Some heavy rain. N and Jack to church. Feeling v. unwell today. Sat much on balcony. Gladys Allhusen called. R. Macleod to supper and spent evening. V. anxious about Ireland. Hal back for supper.

Jul 13   V. hot and fine. Dr R early to see me. Annie and Joyce motored up to lunch, and on to Marden for Garden Party. N, Nana and I drove after tea in Park etc.... Telegram from Dick. Dora gone today. Dora Quin must have been barely 60 years of age. *Not much sleep. Began Bromide and Chloroform at night.*

July 14 ... Dr R early. Radium. Still feeling very unwell. N and Hal (did not go) to Marden. N and I drove late to Putney, Roehampton etc - v. refreshing.

July 16 ... Bob and M turned up, just back from Ireland, Belfast, Antrim etc, also Annie & Joyce going home from Marden. Lovely surprise!

July 17 ... Too shaky to go to Dentist as intended ... Feeling rather better as day goes on. Dora's Funeral at Falmouth.

July 18 ... Great political excitement ... Review of the great Fleet at Spithead ...

July 23 ... Nettie and Mrs Tim in Mrs Inglis's car to spend day at Woodcock ... I went to Mr Farr to get a tooth drawn, but he wd. only stop it for the 3rd or 4th time. To Holy Communion at Brompton Church at 11 ...

July 24 ...I went to a RNSR meeting at Mrs Browning's; N too tired ... The King's Conference at Buckingham Palace ended - no good.

Jul 27 ... 1st Fighting near Dublin! ...

Jul 28 ... Busy in my room. Nora helped with furs ... Heard War declared, and our 1st Fleet to North Sea...

Jul 29... Jack early for a few hours, left for Sheerness ... Bob & Maidlie to tea, they and Hal dined (with) Tissie and to Theatre ... Busy in my room. Better, but v. tired ... Professor McClintock and his daughter from

Chicago to tea ...

July 30 ... Busy packing etc. House being dismantled. War rumours worse than ever ...

Jul 31 ... N and Nana left for Penoyre [to Antonia McC, who had inherited this large house in Brecon from her family, the Cleasbys] *at 11o'c and I for Buxted.* [Sussex] *Long saw me off. Great crowds and a long wait at Victoria. Mrs Orchard met me at Buxted. So tired out, went to bed, and could not see Dot, Eileen and May, who called.*

We have not heard of Mrs Orchard before - evidently she and her husband run a Retirement or Nursing Home, or a caring Boarding House, at Oaklands, Buxted, Sussex, quite near Toll House, where May is living; it seems certain it is chosen for its nearness to May.

Aug 1 So v. tired, in bed all day.Dot and May called. Dreadful news in Papers.

Aug 2 Sunday ... May fetched me in car to The Toll, to have lunch and tea with her, Dot, Eileen and Miss Donne. [Actually, Don.] *All so kind and house lovely. Back in fly, v. tired but better than yesterday. Hal with his P.O Rifles to camp at Beachy Head. War broken out, by Germany.*

Aug 3 Fine, high winds. Out in garden after tea when wind lessened. Dot came to see me. Report that Germans have fired on our ships. Felt much upset and shaken. Hal and his Territorials back to London to mobilise - had a letter from him.

Aug 4 Dot came for goodbye. Do not feel well enough to spend this afternoon with May, as asked, but I am less weary. Heard from Nettie about her tiresome journey Friday.
Alas! we are at War! ...

Aug 5 ... Out a good deal in garden. V anxious and excited about War. Germany violated Belgium, Luxembourg and Switzerland. A LOVELY letter from Jack, at Portland with HMS Lord Nelson.

Aug 7 ... May called early. War news very alarming. Our "Amphitrite" sunk by mine. A nice long letter from Annie ...

Aug 8 ... A letter from Nettie. Very anxious and uneasy. Called on Miss Darby in the house. Belgians wonderful at Liege ...

Aug 10 ... Not able to leave my room except to see Miss Donne who called. May has a bad cold. A p.c. from Nettie.

Aug 12 Too hot to go out in midday, v. pleasant at other times. May offered me a car drive but have too much pain and headache. Hear that N and Nana are to travel home from Wales today. Feel v. anxious about them! Hear that Bob has joined the British Force for foreign active service, but we do not know where he is. Kitchener's Silence [?] is splendid, it is said.

Aug 13 Great battle raging in Belgium! Austria declared war against us! Russians not yet come up. Dreadfully anxious! Out much in garden ...

Aug 14 May fetched me in car to lunch and have tea with her and Miss Donne and her sister. Rested for an hour after lunch, then lay out in garden. After that a long drive in car. Beautiful - but overtiring for me ... Had nice news from N and Jack, which gave me a better night than I cd. have expected...

Aug 15 ... May called late with an evening paper. No special new news.

Aug 16 ... A nice long letter from Nettie - Bob still in England. Jack (2nd Fleet) believed to be in Channel protecting ships taking our troops across to France ...

Aug 18 ... Grand news. British army landed SAFELY in France ... Letters from Hal and Maria Cole.

Aug 19 ... In garden early. May called with two Miss Donnes and took me for lovely drive to Crowborough etc. To tea at The Toll, asked to stay for dinner - too tired. Great battle going on near Brussels - our troops not engaged. A good night (Whiskey!)

Aug 21 Fine, soft wind. Solar eclipse at 12 o'c. Out in garden. Prayer for our troops all day long in Church. Names given in early this morning.

Aug 22 ... May called in car to take Mrs Orchard and me to tea, and drove to Uckfield. V. pleasant but oh! so tired. Letters from N at Woodcock, and from Jack "at sea" somewhere.

Aug 23 Sunday ... War news much the same - small successes on each side, but much the best for the Allies. Germans horrible, cruel. Heard Bob left for front Friday night. Hal seconded for work at home. Doesn't like it!

Aug 29 A lovely day. May called in car with Miss Donne, her sister and niece and took me a lovely drive and then to tea at the Toll. Both sides in war reported worn out with constant fighting for many days. Our troops splendid against v. great odds of Germans. They have burned and sacked Malines and other towns and villages in Belgium, and beautiful Louvain.

Aug 31 ... Mrs Griffiths called on me, also May and the two Miss Donnes.

Sep 1 ... Report that large numbers of Russians passed through London from Northern Scotland and embarked for France at Newhaven and Folkestone; great excitement; can it be true?

Sep 2 May and Miss Donne motored to Newhaven hoping to see the Russians, but were told by a sentry there that thousands of them had arrived there by train yesterday, and embarked at once for France. Lots of troops at Newhaven, and four Men of War.

Sep 4 Very fine and less hot. May and two Miss Donnes took me for a lovely drive, and afterwards to tea with them. Quite overtired. The Orchards' big dog, Mick, was poisoned with strychnine by Suffragettes [surely not?] *and had to be destroyed...*

Sep 8 Fine and pleasantly warm. Out in garden afternoon. Better but v.shaky. Wrote to Mr Lawson about securities. Indifferent sleep.

Sep 12 ... May came, and also Miss De la Torre. Good news from Front. Hard fighting, but Allies driving Germans before them, in retreat, we hope.

Sep 14 May fetched me for lunch and tea. Lay down between ... Drove in car to Uckfield for papers and to see a Camp of Artillery. Convincing account of Russian troops in France, and favourable news all round, but terrible fighting. ...

Sep 16 ... May took me lovely drive to Lewes; LOTS of recruits blocking streets and roads. Miss Donne and a friend, Miss Bridge, also in car ...

Sep 17 ...May called - and Miss Darby (in the house) came to see me.

Sep 18 ... May and Miss Donne drove me to Crowborough, where we had tea in a nice Inn. Feeling better after a good night.

Sep 20 ... In bed all day with chill. May lent me an eiderdown - great comfort.

Sep 22 ... Letter from N. Furious battle on the Aisne raging since Sep 12. Allies slight advantage, and holding their own. Mr Orchard left for home service, but sent back after tea ...reported officially that 3 of our cruiser ships have been sunk in North Sea ...

Sep 26 ... May, Miss D and Norah fetched me in car; had a nice drive and returned 2 calls, and had tea ... saw Aylmer Quin at Maresfield Camp ...

Sep 27 Sunday ... May called late, also Aylmer, to say goodbye. Got commission in R.F.A and going to Front almost at once, SO happy.

Sep 29 ... May called, also Auriel Quin, and Miss Griffith, the Vicar's daughter.

Oct 2 ... Lunch at the Toll with May, Dick Quin, Auriel, Miss Donne. Long letter from N. Mr Orchard back from Camp near Bexhill, on leave for weekend.

Oct 3 ...The terrible battle on the Aisne still going on - 21st day. It is hoped we are getting the best of it, but so wearing and trying.

Oct 4 Too windy to stay out long. May sent me a Picture Newspaper. Terrible war pictures.

Oct 6 ... Tried sitting out a little but it was too cold. P.c. from N, and Nana sent me some butter cloth I wanted. May and Miss Donne are up in town.

Oct 10 ... Heard of the Fall of Antwerp, alas!

Oct 13 ... May called, and Miss Donne, also Mrs Griffith and Miss Darby (in this house)... Heard from N that Charlie West is interned in Holland with his men! Poor young fellow...

Oct 14 ... Heard from N that Charlie is safe in England with 1st Naval Brigade. Germans taken Ghent and Lille, and marching towards Ostend!! ...

Oct 16 ... May called, but I did not feel v. able to have a drive. Miss Darby and Miss De la Torre, lodging here, left for a house they have taken near by.

Oct 17.... May called. Mr O came back for good from Camp, as he is physically unfit for the work...

Oct 23 ... The Vicar called on me. May did not call today.

Oct 24 ... May lent me her car after lunch. Mrs O and I drove to Uckfield and Crowborough, and to Maresfield Camp to see Aylmer. Drive rather too long for me ...

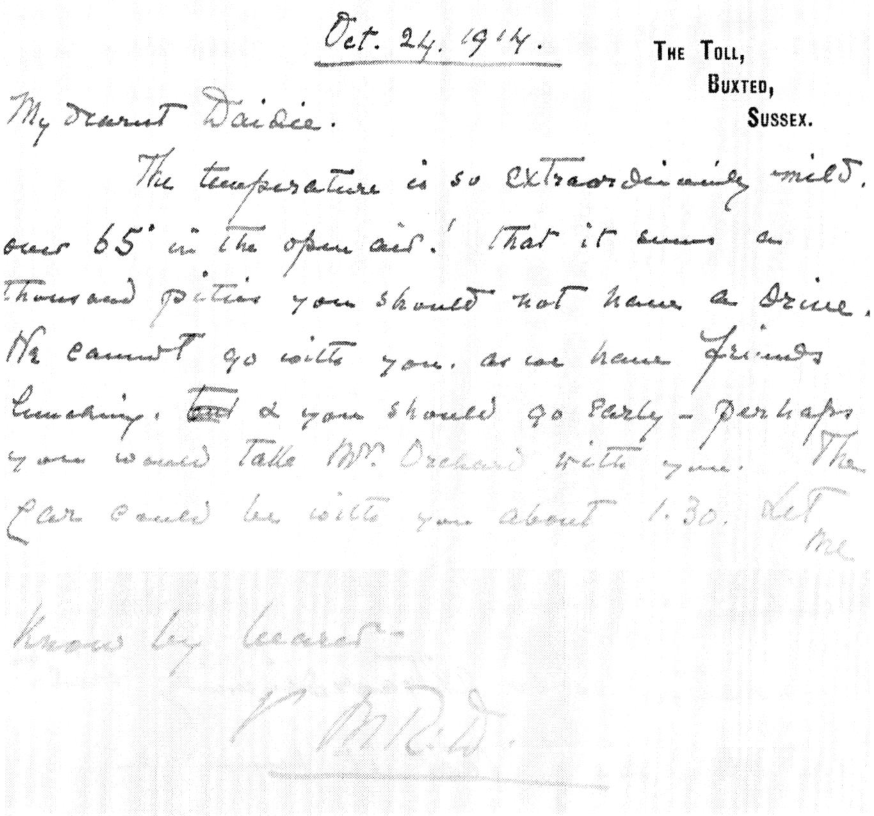
Oct. 24. 1914.

THE TOLL,
BUXTED,
SUSSEX.

My dearest Daidie.

The temperature is so extraordinarily mild, over 65° in the open air! That it seems a thousand pities you should not have a drive. We cannot go with you, as we have friends lunching, & you should go early – perhaps you would take Mrs Orchard with you. The car could be with you about 1.30. Let me know by bearer –

M.R.D.

In the pocket of the unused, larger diary for 1914 was found this note to Haddie from May :

My dearest Daidie [a childhood corruption?] *The Temperature is so extraordinarily mild, over 65 in the open air! that it seems a thousand pities you should not have a drive. We cannot go with you, as we have friends lunching, and you should go early - perhaps you would take Mrs Orchard with you. The car could be with you about 1.30.*

Let me know by bearer. M.R.D.

[The distinctive handwriting is an interesting study.]

Oct 25 Sunday ... Terrible fighting going on near Calais. So far good for us. Our ships shot the Germans from the sea.

Oct 27 Fine, sun, less mild. Sat in garden after lunch ... Terrible fighting still for Calais. Allies making good resistance.

Oct 31 ... Not out. Better than yesterday. May sent me a beautiful Pear. Daisy and Kathleen West called.

Nov 2 ... No visitors. Nettie begins carriage in London. War news good - but slow! May sent me some grapes ...Fires in both rooms. A bad night.

Nov 14 ... Sat at open window a short time. No visitors. 3 RAMC officers to be billeted in this house on Tuesday.

Nov 15 ... Alas! dear old Lord Roberts died yesterday in France, where he had gone to encourage the troops, and to see the Indian soldiers.

Nov 18 ... Heard from Nettie, and Nana, with warm underclothing ...Billeted soldiers not yet come.

Nov 21 ... May came and fetched me in car, to spend a few days. A pleasant change ...

Nov 24 ... Fainted in my room, and knew nothing till I found myself in bed and Dr Pearse standing looking at me, and May. They sent for a charming Nurse Darby, who sat up all night with me, as I was v. ill all night from a weak heart and pulse.

Nov 26 ... Feel much the same. In bed, and Nurse D with me all night and most of day. SUCH care and kindness I have never had.

Nov 28 ... Dr. again. Feeling rather better, but must not move.

Nov 30 Great storm of wind and rain. Mrs Orchard came to look after me while Nurse was out and resting. Dr called ...V good war news.

Dec 2 ... Dr hopes to let me up in a few days but must continue the absolute rest and quiet. May's chauffeur left to enlist. A great loss to her. May spent most of afternoon with me as nurse was out ... A nice letter from Nettie.

Dec 6 Sunday ... Dr Pearse again. Wishes me to take a little Brandy twice a day ... Very stormy evening and night and chimney smoked badly nearly all night ...

In the next few days, Haddie says she is better but her writing is very feeble - though she manages to write a letter and a p.c.

Dec 11 ... Nettie came from London and spent the night. Still so weak, could only see her for a short time ...

Dec 12 ... Saw Dr Pearse early - he and Dr Rhodes saw me. Much pulled about roughly by Dr R. He went back to London and so did Nettie. Miss Donne's nephew came for night.

Hal

Dec 13 ... Mr Donne left; he came to see me in my room - a nice boy.

[V.G.Don, Queen's Own Regiment, died at Loos aged 20, in 1915.]

Dec 14 ... I got up for half an hour ... Miss Donne went in car to meet Dot at Edenbridge; saw her for a short time.

It seems likely that Haddie's remaining sisters had been sent for, to see her and say goodbye.

Dec 19 ... Somewhat stronger; Dot left for Folly Court ...

Dec 23 Too cold to get up. Dr Pearse came. Dear Hal came to see me for 20 minutes (karchi) [sic] *So*

unexpected and delightful, exciting. Very tired afterwards.
Dec 25 Christmas Day. No Dr. Got up for half an hour. Slept in afternoon, watched by May. Had champagne at dinner. A very good night.
Dec 27 Poor dear little Nurse Dudley was ill all night and Dr fears appendix. Had to go home to bed ... Mrs Orchard came to spend the night with me.
May and Miss Don develop colds - the nurse comes back, but is not well and May sends her home in the car [having found a new chauffeur]. Once or twice Haddie records *"War news good"* - perhaps they were sparing her.
Dec 31 - in very shaky writing ... *I believe Dr. came.*

There are no more Diaries.

Haddie died on 1st February 1915. She died at Oaklands, so they must have moved her back from The Toll. Her death was registered by Mrs Orchard, who was "present at the death." Causes of death were given, by Dr Pearse, as Arterio Sclerosis (5 years), haemorrhage of brain (2 and a half months) and hypostatic pneumonia (17 days). Haddie would have been 77 in March.

Haddie was buried in the same plot with Leo and Bessy, at the Kensington & Chelsea cemetery at Uxbridge Road, Hanwell, Middlesex. It must have been hard to make all the arrangements, with the War worsening and all the young men in uniform, but it is surely in accordance with her wishes. Her inscription, on the right-hand side of the Celtic cross, reads:

Here also lies among those
dearest to her as sister and as aunt
Harriet Catherine Anna
eldest daughter of Robert Foster Dunlop Esq.
of Monasterboice House, Co. Louth, Ireland
born 24 March 1838 died 1 February 1915
"in thy presence there is fullness of joy."

Haddie's Will is dated 5 March 1913. It seems likely that she re-wrote her Will following Bessy's death, having originally left everything to her beloved younger niece. Now it is left to Annette, asking her to divide all between her three nephews. "... To my dear niece Annie E. Greenwell I do not leave anything as I know she is well provided for by her marriage except my love and one little personal keepsake if she wishes for it. To all this dear good family I leave my blessing and fondest love and may God reward them for all

their goodness and love to me."
There is an added Codicil appointing Annette as residuary legatee, naming Hal as Executor and " ... I do absolutely trust my three dear nephews H.F.McClintock, J.W.L.McClintock and R.S.McClintock that if after my death they see fit to do so they are at liberty to apportion the legacies I leave them in a somewhat different way to what I have willed always provided that neither shares investments jewellery or anything of mine shall go to anyone except the direct descendants of my dear late brother in law Adl Sir Leopold McClintock I think my niece Mrs Annie Greenwell is not likely ever to want any of the small money I have to leave and she has already got most of my little jewellery bequeathed to her by her late sister E.F.M.McClintock to whom I had given it during her lifetime so it is not from lack of affection that I do not name her in my will. I hope my little legacies will not be squandered on lawyers surely all the above is simple enough to understand without their intervention ..."

This sounds like the authentic voice of Haddie, as we have come to know her. Harry was duly granted Probate, the net value of her estate being £6,028.4.8, so it would seem that at least some of her inheritance had finally come to her.

Afterword Readers may like to know a little of what became of some of Haddie's beloved family who have featured in the Diaries. Nettie died, 14 May 1920, having seen all her sons survive the 1914-18 war. She is of course also buried at Hanwell, with her name and dates at the front base of the Celtic cross. The grave is near to the cemetery chapel, by the south-eastern corner.

Annie preserved a letter written to her on her mother's death from Mrs Gledstanes :

"... From my childhood, my first memory of Nettie when staying at my house in 1857, when I was six and she was 17 or 18 - a lovely girl, such hair and skin, all in white and blue; it is as clear as yesterday, and she has been so good and true to me all the last year. And I have many letters telling me how she valued our unfailing friendship all these long years ..."

Hal married his early sweetheart and kinswoman, Marion Gledstanes, daughter of the above, in 1930. Children were out of the question by then, but they lived very happily and hospitably at The Red House, Ardee, a house which Haddie knew well from birth. He continued to be interested in family and Irish history, and became quite a Fenian sympathiser. A niece, Annette, remembers standing with him on a bridge over the River Boyne while he explained to her, at some length, the justice of parts of the Fenian cause. Though slow of speech and inclined to "hold forth" he was much loved by his nephews and nieces, and made Bob and Maidlie's second son his heir.

Jack became a Rear-Admiral, C.B., D.S.O, and married Hon. Rose O'Neill, of an ancient Irish family. They had a son and two daughters;, but their years together were cut short by Jack's death at the age of 56. They made their home in Co.Antrim, in the house now lived in by their grandson.

Jack's wedding—1920. Barbara, Joyce and (?) Betty are bridesmaids and Jo is the pageboy on the right. Harry is best man.

Bob's eldest child, Jo, joined the Royal Navy, and was killed in World War II, in H.M.S "Pintail", in 1941. Bob (awarded the D.S.O. in W.W.1) and Maidlie had another son and two daughters. For a long time, after leaving the Army, Bob acted as Agent for his brother-in-law, Bernie, at Marden. Maidlie continued to paint and write throughout her life. She died in 1966 and Bob married again, Diana Clements, nee Lenox Conyngham, and made his home in Ireland, which had never appealed to Maidlie. He died aged 92, a handsome man to the last.

Annie, as we know, had four daughters, then a son, Peter, and finally a fifth daughter, Ruth. Dr Odell must have laid down a good regime for her in her illness, for she was able to lead an active life in many ways, though never robust. No chances were taken with Peter, who slept in a small tent in the garden at Marden all his childhood. But all six children lived full lives in good health. Bernie died in 1939, a generous and loving husband, father and head of his extended family. Senior partner of the old stockbroking firm, W. Greenwell & Co, he had other business interests in the electricity supply

Marden Park in the late 20s. Note Peter's tent

industry and in engineering. But he was a countryman at heart, and took great interest in his breeding of Shire horses and cattle, and later extended his farming into Suffolk, where he reclaimed land into a good state of cultivation; ahead of his time, he did pioneer work in inducing London boroughs to handle household refuse so as to make it useful on the land. Marden was requisitioned in the War, while Peter was a prisoner of war, and was subsequently sold, when Peter and his family settled in Suffolk.

Annie, 1910

Peter c.1924

Annie died at the age of 84, living, by then, with her daughter Peggy. She and Bernie had 20 grandchildren, 54 great-grandchildren, and, so far, more than 70 great-great-grandchildren. Part of a tribute to her in the local parish magazine, 1957, reads " *In spite of bad health ... she never allowed her interest in her surroundings to be cramped, and her time was spent in controlling her large household, training her children in Christian living, and in keeping in*

touch by correspondence with a very wide circle of friends ... As a wife, as a sister, as a mother and as a friend, there were few to equal her ..."

Annie's fourth daughter
Peggy
2006

Mary Hayes - Nana and later "Grand-Nans", stayed with Nettie and survived a little while longer, looked after at Marden, with a nurse of her own.

Mary Hayes

Margaret and Edwy

Blanche's eldest son, Stanley Robert, known in the family as Tan, won a DSO and bar in WW1. He married, late in life, Nellie Brodigan, and they lived at her house— near to Drumcar, which Stanley had inherited from his uncle Frank, a bachelor and Dean of Armagh. His two aunts, Gertrude and Emily, lived on at Drumcar till their deaths. Blanche and Charlie's youngest son, Edward L.L.McClintock (Edwy) was ordained and his first curacy was at Stanstead Abbots, Herts, where he met and married the squire's daughter—

Margaret Buxton. They went to live at Jesmond, Newcastle, where WW1's only bombardment destroyed all their wedding presents in store. His first parishes were Haltwhistle, Northumberland, and Frinton-on-sea. He then worked for a while for C.M.S. and furthered his interest in mission, especially in East Africa.
As WWII began they were at Hayes, Kent, near the Greenwells at Marden, which became "bomb alley" in the blitz and occupied them both in social work. His last parish was Platt, Kent, and they moved back to Hertfordshire to retire. Edwy and Maggie had a son and four daughters; the son became the distinguished botanist, David McClintock.

Helen or Dot, whose sweet nature is plain, died in 1933. Of her family, Charlie West (DSC) was killed in 1917. His brother Alick survived WWI and received the DSO and Bar. He married Harriet Chichester in 1915 but had no children. Jessie, Daisy and twins Kathleen and Eileen lived a good span but are believed to have died unmarried.

So far, it has not been possible to trace Aylmer, Auriel or Robbie Quin, though we know that Aylmer survived the War and had at least one son, Cormac.

Haddie's youngest sister, May, who had reappeared in her life as a surprise (to us) at the very end, lived on at The Toll, Buxted, till her death on 18 February 1924, presumably with Miss Don (to whom, we are informed in a note of Bob's, many remaining contents of Monasterboice were bequeathed.)

May has a handsome grave in Buxted churchyard - a large Celtic cross inscribed:

Mary Rachel Dunlop,
youngest daughter of Robert Foster Dunlop, Monasterboice, Co. Louth.
"Blest are the Pure in Heart, for they shall see God."

The End

INDEX

* denotes shown in Family Trees

Abel Smith, Miss 204
Alexander, Bishop of Derry 101, 106,124 231
Alexander Mrs Cecil F. 69, 95, 116
Alington, Mr & Mrs, 182, 187, 200, 205, 249
*Alloway, Dr & Mrs 35, 174
Amundsen, Captain Roald, 186
Anderson, Dr Mary Garrett, 73
Asquith, H. H. 215,229, 238

Baker, Lady 124, 126
Balfour of Townley Hall, Mr 10
Balfour, Blayney 139
Balfour of Fairyhill, Lady F. 3, 14
Balfour, A.J., Prime Minister 91, 166, 229
Barth, pianist 37
Beauford, Maurice 40, 50, 61, 102
Bellingham, Mabel 30
Bernard, Mea 30
Bernhardt, Sarah 231
*Birchall, Ruth 259
*Bogle, Mary Anne 21
Borthwick, Sir Algernon 57, 58, 59, 63 105
Bower, Col. & Mrs 133
Bridge, Sir F. 223
*Bruen of Oak Park family 66, 115, 241
Buffalo Bill 69
Burges, Mrs Y. 103 168, 178
Buxton, Mr & Mrs J.H. 237
*Buxton, Margaret—see McClintock
Buxton, Lady Victoria 87, 99

Campbell, Harriet 137, 142-144,146, 149, 151, 157, 163
Carnwarth, Lady 54, 70
Carpenter-Garnier family 151
Caruso, Enrico 150
*Casement, Elisabeth K (Betty) 196, 199, 233 *234*
Casement, Rear Adml. J.M & Mrs 109
*Chadwick, Bishop of Derry & Mrs Helen 224, 232
Churchill, Lady Randolph 74
Churchill, Winston 196, 232, 235
Clanwilliam, Earl of 38, 52, 67, 72, 73
Clarke, Sir G. & Lady 189
Clements, Francis 6
Clements, Miss 183
Clinton-Baker family 182, 220
Cole, Maria, 54, 89, 93, 99, 140, 147, 249, 253
*Colquhoun, Ruth, see Birchall
*Colvin, Mrs Isabel 152
Conybeare family 25, 81
Cottenham 55, 60, 61
Craig, Clementina 27, 53
Crompton-Roberts, Joan 180
*Crozier, Constance Dillon 58
*Crozier, Emily 57, 80, 142
*Crozier, Helen, 45, 208
Culme Seymour, Lady, 52, 128
Curzon of Kedlestone, Lord 164

Daniell, Aubrey 153
Darley, Leila 161, 176
*Delap, see also Dunlop
*Delap, Ella 240
*Delap of Monellan, James Bogle 15, 16, 23, 25, 33, 144, 145, 161, 167
*Delap, Kingsmill, 161
*Delap, Rev. Robert 54
Denison, Lady, 97, 98
De Salis of Lisrenny, Col. 11
De Salis, Cecil 94, 154, 218
De Salis, Charlie 59, 115, 249
De Salis, Edith 59, 176
De Salis, Elsie 237
De Salis, Mr & Mrs Fane 59, 115
De Salis, Georgie, see Hamilton
De Salis, Rev. Harry 335, 52, 66, 101, 126, 127, 144, 184, 205, 215, 22
De Salis, Lady Mary 115
De Salis, Margery 94, 217
De Salis, Minnie, 101, 126
De Salis, Rodolph, 90, 99, 105, 176, 205
De Salis, Tony 215
De Salis, Willie, 85, 215, 216
De Salis, Ursula, 237

Dilke, Sir C. 63
Disraeli, Mr & Mrs Coningsby 199
*Dix, Emma 100. 106
*Dix, Eva, 101, 124, 157, 173, 182 210
*Dix, Leopold, 99, 116, 156, 167, 189, 191, 242
Don, Miss 252, passim to 256
Don, Norah, 254
Don, V.G. 256
Donovan, Gen. 188, 190, 204, 208, 212, 219, 225, 227
Drake, May 71, 127, 125, 204, 227, 236
*Dufferin, Lady 5,11,15, 40
Duncan, Mrs 155, 178, 240
*DUNLOP, Hon. Mrs Anna *1*, passim to *16*
letters 29
loss of husband 29
gives H.D brooch 99
very strong 118
illness, estrangement 122
scenes with 134, 137
death 138, *139*
*Dunlop, Annette, see McClintock
*Dunlop, Blanche, see McClintock
Dunlop, Col and Mrs Buchanan 214, 215
*Dunlop, Dora, see Quin
*DUNLOP, Harriet C.A.
Birth date 1, enjoys riding 3
Confirmation 9
travels on Continent 12, 1
sewing 28
facsimile diary *55*
Primrose League 57
moves house 75, money 76
injures hand 79
diet 111, "treatments" 117
"favourites" 133
letter to Hal 147
first opera 150
letter to May 158
Ireland again 173
opinion of suffragettes 236
serious illness 238
cancer 248
death 257
*Dunlop, Helen (Dot) see West
*DUNLOP, Mary R (May)
birth, christening 10
bad eyes 29
interest in nursing *40*
Miss Renshaw 68
Parnell trial 77
exhausted, 111
legal proceedings? 138
Mother's Will 141
letter from H.D. 158. 198, 220
returns 250, passim to *255*, 257
note 262
*Dunlop, Mary, (Grandmama) 1,8,9,22,35,40
*DUNLOP, Robert F *1*, 4, passim to *16* ,
death , 27
*DUNLOP, William D 1, 75th birthday 5
new road 14
Annette's memories of
injures leg and death 21
*DUNLOP, William J.S. 2, *3*
to school 11, *13*
to Winslow, 14
to Switzerland 19
Royal Artillery 18
death on railway 19
inquest 20
birthday, 51, 104, 211
Dyer Edwardes, 64, 238
Dykes March, Mrs 205, 214, 245

Eardley Wilmot, Rev. 102, 113, 122, 181
Edward VII, King 124, 150, 190, 217, 218
Elphinstone, Sir Howard, 54, 208
Elphinstone, Irene, see Welch
Elphinstone, Lady 201, 207, 222, 224, 225
*Elphinstone, Mary, see McClintock
Elphinstone, Olive, see Jackson
Evan Smith, Dr 118, 132, 157, 160, 164
Evans, Captain E 247

Fardell family, 119, 121, 123, 124, 153, 179, 208, 222, 243
*Ferrard, Viscount 1, 22, 242
Filgate of Tulleykirk family, 11
*FitzGerald, Dorcas 3, 8, 12, 13, 32, 37
FitzGerald, Penrose 135
*FitzGerald, Percy 32
FitzGerald, Purefoy 117

Fisher, Adml of the Fleet Lord, 42, 70, 79
85, 149
*Fleury, Archdeacon 49
*Foster, Judge Anthony 1
*Foster, Bishop of Clogher 1
Filgate, Harriet and T.W. 4,5, 11, 14, 15
Folkestone, Lady 57
Franklin, Lady 18, 87, 189
Franklyn, Mrs 150, 160, 240

*Gardiner, Caroline 20, 91, 98
Garnett, Charles, Wade and Anne 14
Garnett, Ella & children 25, 74, 219
Gervers, Francis T. 109
Gladstone, W.E. 43, 52, 62, 84, *95*, 99,
100, 106, 123
George V, King 100, 227, 231, 232, 237
Gledstanes of Fardross, Ambrose 119, 122
210, 227
Gledstanes, Helen , Mrs M., 23, 35, 80,
94, 117,258
*Gledstanes, Marion, see McClintock
Glyn, Lady Mary 62, 70, 74, 77, 99
Goodden, Cecil & Hylda, 232 ,234
Gordon, Gen. 52, 53
Gordon, Gen. & Mrs, 81, 82, 87. 211 146
Gore Sankey, Mary, see Dunlop
Green, Pericles 57
*GREENWELL, Anna E.
birth 22, *31, 52*
schools 65,73
Confirmation 77
health 85
meets B.G 90
no Switzerland? 94
classes 98
Greenwells' Ball 111
court dress, health concerns 118
to Ireland 130
engagement 146
marriage *151*
to S.America 166, home 168
travelling 223
grief 243
afterword 259 *260*
*Greenwell, Anna Margaret, see Wilks
Greenwell, Aubrey see Daniell
Greenwell, Aynsley 201
*Greenwell, Barbara, see William-Powlett
*GREENWELL, Bernard, 2nd Bt.
90, 111, *137*
engagement 146
wedding 151
to S. America 193
as father 212
afterword 258
Greenwell, Cecil, see Leveson-Gower
*Greenwell, Elisabeth K see Casement
Greenwell, Geoffrey 111, 212
Greenwell, Joan, see Crompton-Roberts
*Greenwell, Joyce, see Miles
Greenwell, Kathleen see Johnson
Greenwell, Mildred, see Loynes
*Greenwell, Peter 250, *260*
*Greenwell, Ruth, see Birchall
Greenwell, Sybil, see Strutt
Greenwell, Sir Walpole L. 120, 188
& Lady Greenwell 124, 148, 150
151, 179, 187, 194
Greenwell, Winifred see Crompton-
Roberts
Grocers, Worshipful Co. of 29, 49, 54
Gull, Sir William 67

Hamilton, Georgie 52, 66, 72, 73, 147,
153, 184, 214, 216
Harcourt, Vernon 71
Hardcastle, 49, 58
Hare, Mrs Marcus 107, 119, 121
Harman, Ella, 150, 188, 240
Harman, M. 73, 85
Harris, Miss 2
Harris, Ellen, 19, 23, 41
HAYES, Mary (Nana) 27, 35, 41, 62, 65,
78,
unwell, 85, 121
to S.Africa 170
returns unchanged 188
Xmas with her family 233
injures nose 247
note *261*
Heneage, 81, 82
*Henderson Stewart, see Wilks
Hickson, Mr & Mrs 212, 215, 216, 224,
226, 228, 231, 232

*Hilton, Anna &
*Hilton, Colonel James, 172, 215
Hood, Lady 54, 71, 77, 88, 102
Horden, Dr 196, 199, 206, 212, 224, 225
Horstman, 5, 6

HOUSES & PLACES
Antrim Castle 3, 12, 162, 163
Arundel Castle 78
Ballybay, 116
Bayford, Herts 172, 182
Bettshanger, 38
Bramshill Park 65
Castlebellingham 16, 18
Clandeboyes Castle 11, 14
Craigdarragh 14
Dover Castle 39
Drumcar 9, 11, 32, 41, 47, *116*, 159, 203, 210, 220 247, 261
Elm Park, 9, 10
Favour Royal l35
Glassonbury Park 56
Glendaragh 11, 75
Glyde Court *9*
Grantham Hall E.Sussex 54
Groomsport House 14, 15
Halsnead Hall, Lancs 162, 192, 198 221
Hedingham Castle 165
Hillsborough Castle 12
Knole 55
Lamberhurst 56
Ladysmith, Relief of 129, 131, 132
Lambay, wreck at 2
Lisnavagh, Carlow *200,* 220
Marden Park 120, 191, 213, 251, 259, *260*
Mellifont Church 9, 12, 46, 108, 139
Monasterboice 1, 22, *21,* 46, 97, 140, 142, 145, *178,* 246
Moygannon 174
Mulrose Castle 96
Northaw House, Potters Bar 62
Oriel Temple 7, 8, 9, 13, 34, 42, *185*
Ouseley Lodge 72, 94
Portnall Park 35, 52, 59,*72,* 73, 84, 99, 102, 107, 127, 146, 154
Red House, Ardee, 14, *17,* 26, 257
Rohanna, Ardee 1, 11
Scotney Castle 50
Shane's Castle, 3, 12
Stoke Park, Guildford 20
Townley Hall, 3, 5, 10, 29, 30, 35, 42, 139
Uplands Park, Fareham 82
Wellington College 64
Woodcock Lodge 200, *204*
Huguenots 49, 50, 61

Ievers, Ethel , see Rathdonnell
Inglefield, Sir E 68
Inglis, Mrs, 205207, 211, 220, 249-251
Irish Distressed Ladies 73, 87

James, Rev, & son Philip 57, 58
Jeffreys, Julia, 1, 26, 54, 92. 100, 228
Jeffreys, Mary 191, 245, 250
Jeffreys, Nina 181, 186
Jeffreys, Tissy, 100, 149, 157, 180, 227, 236
Jessell, Sir G & Lady 56
Jodrell, Sir Alfred and Lady Jane, 30
Jolly, Miss 44, 46, 70
Johnson, Kathleen 148 154
*Johnston, Hon. Nora 119
Johnstone, Capt. and Mrs 64

Kelly, Dr. 19, 21, 24, 47, 48
Kerr, Lady Louisa 2, 6, 13
Kimball Cook's School 51
Kirwan, Agnes 72
Kirwan family 13, 14
Kirwan, Mary 3, 10
Kitchener, Lord 120, 131, 132, 134, 147,

Lang, Bishop Cosmo Gordon 176
Larken, Capt & Mrs 131, 139, 242
*Laurie, Major George 174, 176, 190, 218
*Laurie, Mrs Florence, see Massereene
*Laurie, Hal 218
Law of Kilbarrack, Capt & family 24, 26, 35, 63
*Lefroy, Elizabeth 24, 39, 101, 160, 213,

216, 224
Le Hunt Ward, Admiral 176, 186
Leitrim, Earl of 37
Leslie of Ballybay, Robert 116, 129, 162
Leveson-Gower, Rev.F.A.G. & Cecil 160
Locker-King, Mr & Mrs 48
Louise, Princess Marie– 74, 76, 112, 113, 213, 218, 232, 237, 239
Loynes, Mildred 119, 153, 182, 212
Luard family 68, 97
Luard, Louisa 238, 249, 246
Luard-Bean 216, 237

Majendie, the Misses 64, 99, 165
Mann, Admiral 176
Markham, Adm. Sir Albert 59, 81, 102, 109
Markham, Clements 25, 102, 122, 146, 189, 196, 200, 204
Markham, Lady [Dora] *109*
Markham, Joy 142, 145
Mary of Teck, Princess 91, 100, 103, 143
*Massereene, Algernon, 12th Visct. 26, 142, 155, 169, 170, 175
*Massereene, Clotworthy, 11th Visct. 3, 8, 12, 13, 26, 156, 171
*Massereene, Florence, wife of 11th Visct. 26, 30, 47, 88
*Massereene, Florence, formerly Laurie, 2nd w. of 12th Vsct. 50, 90, 175, 176, 183, 218, 250
*Massereene, Harriet, 9th Vsctess 1
May, Captain W.W. 69, *189*
Melba, Dame Nellie 150, 219, 226
*Miles, Joyce 159, 162, 164, 166, 167, *170*, 173, 177, *180*, *234*, *259*
Montgomery, Bishop 152 208, 235, 244
Montgomery, Capt & Mrs 241
Montgomery, Sir R & Lady 25, 29, 53, 58, 60, 62, 69, 70, 104, 110
Montgomery, Una 235
Monument, Olivia 230, 246
Mowat, Clara 22, 37
Murphy, David 23

Macan, Lena, Anne 225, 245
McCausland family 11, 1
McClaggan, Jessie 25, 33, 46
*McClintock, Dr Alfred 19, 24, 35, 38, 41, 84
*McClintock, Anna E. see Greenwell
*McCLINTOCK,Annette *1* , 2, 18, *22*
memories 21
30, *31*,*44*, 85, 94
at Halifax *44*
silver wedding *112*, 113
2 months away 221
to Wales 252
last visit to H.D 256, 258
*McClintock, Antonia, 33, 155, 157, 176. 187, 195, 196, 222, 236, 238, 241 246, 249, 252
*McClintock, Blanche 2, 29, 31, 33, 39, 41, 46, 69, 75, 87, 94, 111, 122, 162, 138, 174, 195, 196
*McClintock, Charles E., 33, 46, 69, 137, 163, 249
*McClintock, Edith, see Wilson
*McClintock, Edward L.L. 117, 123, 125, 169, 195, 222, 227, 233, 237, *261*
*McCLINTOCK, Elizabeth F.M. (Bessy)
birth, babyhood 45
serious unwellness 67
scarlatina 90
Bournemouth 93
Miss Wyatt's School 96
music exam 107
Miss McDowall's 113
Miss Geach's 114
French play 121
Confirmation 124
visits Sacombe 126
serious health warnings 132
letter to Harry 143
presented at Court *146*
21st birthday 159
to Switzerland 166
serious fears 168
leaves for S.Africa *170*
keeps house with Bob 179
returns 188
bedrest 235
death 245
*McClintock, Emily 60, 159
McClintock, Mr & Mrs Emory 164, 181 250

*McCLINTOCK, Sir F.Leopold
marries Annette *18*
Adml. Supert. Dockyard 19
W.Indies Command 41
retires as Vice-Adm. 50
Flag Officer & Good Service Pension 68
moves house 75
K.C.B. 87, *88*
Silver wedding *112*
very ill 138
eye operation 175
photo with Joyce *180*
anniversary of the "Fox" *189*
death 192
*McClintock, Frank, Dean of Armagh 33, 60, 159, 241
*McClintock, Fredk. F 191, 210
*McClintock, Fredk. Robt. 33, 152, 189, 209, 245
*McClintock, Geoffrey, 204
*McClintock, Gertrude 241
*McClintock, Henry, b. 1783 11
*McCLINTOCK, Henry Foster
born 19, *31*, 32
letter from 44
starts at Winchester 56
Confirmation 73
prize for Nat. Science 77
goes to New College Oxford 83
comes down—career 96
Post Office Corps 109
joins P.O. dept. of Army 124
leaves for Transvaal 128
very ill in S.Africa 136
home 152
last visit to H.D. *256*
marriage 258
*McClintock, John L.E 226, 233, 239, 240 248 *259*
*McCLINTOCK, John W.L.
born 24, 28, *31*, *32*
to Mr Littlejohn's 64
passes into Navy6 70
joins "Britannia" 72
Confirmation 77
to sea 79
"Royal Sovereign" 94
dinner with Queen 111
to Gaga's Funeral 139
promoted Cdr. 167, *168*
earthquakes in Med *202*
Channel Fleet, *253*
wedding 258, *259*
*McClintock, Margaret 237, *261*
*McClintock, Marion (Dot, Cecilia) 20, 200, 258
*McClintock, Mary (Maidlie) 206, 207, *209*, 211, 217, 223, 225, 226, 230, 233, *235*, 239, 244
*McClintock, Patience, see Wilson
*McCLINTOCK, Robert S.
born 30, *40*
school at Brighton 51
school at Crowthorne 68
school at East Sheen 75
scholarship to Charterhouse 78
to Woolwich 87
Bisley 88
Confirmation 93
Royal Engineers 111, *121*
Captain, R.E 125
home 133
Brevet & back to Africa 136
home 165
engaged to Maidlie 207
wedding *209*
letter to Annie 247
leaves for Front 253, 258, 259
*McClintock, Hon. Rose *259*
*McClintock, Stanley b. 1812, 33, 89
*McClintock, Stanley Rbt. 46, 75, 94, 102, 108, 122, 127, 144, 205
*McClintock, William 107, 121, 122, 139, 180, 193, 195
*McClintock Bunbury, Tim, see Rathdonnell
*McClintock Bunbury, William 200
McCreight, Margaret 9, 11
McCreight, Anna 155
Maclean, Charles L 164
Macleod, Cecily & Olivia, 79, 83, 85, 93, 98, 104, 125, 129, 159, 188, 220, 230, 236, 238, 245
Macnaghten, Carrie 242, 243
Macnaghten, Cissie 27, 32, 212 218

Nansen, Fridtjof 97
Neilson-Terry, Phyllis 231
Nelson, Lord 173
Nepean, the Misses 88, 219
Noble (Chauffeur) 229, 240
Normanton, Lady 180
Notting Hill High School 65

Odell, Dr 196, 212, 259
*O'Kelly, Major Arthur D.D 111
*O'Kelly, Henrietta 111
*Oldfield, Allan 126
*Oldfield, Frank, 145
*Oldfield, Katherine 24, 29, 94, 187
O'Neill, Lord 3, 37, 69, 88, 115
*O'Neill, Hon. Rose, see McClintock
Orchard, Mrs K.E 252, 256, 258

Paddington Baths 65
*Paget, Captain Chas 20, 72
*Paget, Charles 20, 111, 114, 156
*Paget, Charlie, 71, 72
*Paget, FitzClarence 33, 35, 42, 68, 71, 72, 99, 111,114, 155, 224, 182, 231
Parnell, Charles S 60, 76, 84
Phillimore family 128, 151, 237
Plunket, Gertrude, Kate, 52, 54, 61, 69, 87, 88, 91, 95, 97, 99, 101, 105, 140, 143, 148, 150, 203, 204, 216, 220
*Poë, Rear Adml. Edmund 42, 84
*Poë, Hon. Elizabeth 8, 9, 11, 12, 14, 16, 17, 22, 35, 37, 38.
*Poë, Hutchinson 60, 83
*Poë, William 90
Primrose League 57, 62, 68, 77, 79, 93

*Quin, Auriel 151, 171, 173, 174, 186, 221, 237, 254, 262
*Quin, Aylmer 46, 96, 102, 171, 176, 187, 211, 219, 237, 254, 262
*Quin, Dora 2, 19, 27, 31, 42, 46, 140, 151 153, 173, 175, 221, 229, 237, 251
*Quin, Richard 42, 47, 96, 140, 151, 108, 173, 175, 209, 221, 254
*Quin, Robert 46, 111, 102, 162, 180, 262

*Rathdonnell, John 1st Lord 41, 60
*Rathdonnell, Ethel, Lady 241
*Rathdonnell, Lady 60, 146, 241
*Rathdonnell, Thomas, 2nd Lord 131, 145
*Rathdonnell, Thomas (Tim) 3rd Lord 164, 200, 207, 219, 225, 241, 249
Reader-Harris, Mr 184
Renshaw, Lucy 68, 69, 74, 76, 84, 92, 95, 101, 111, 117, 125, 130, 138, 198
Rhodes, Dr, 226, passim to 249, 256
Richardson of Prospect 5
*Richardson, Dr. 95, 169, 172, 175, 236
*Richardson, George 99
*Richardson, Rosa, 228
R.N.College, Greenwich 65, 106
R.N.Scripture Readers Soc. 120, 237
Roberts, Lord 13 0, 131, 132, 135, 144, 149, 181, 256
*Ross, Blanche (Bammie) 14, 29, 37, 40, 45, 48, 57, 72, 74, 75, 156, 174, 175, 197, 205, 227
*Ross, Eddie and Nina 38, 45, 63, 96, 173
*Ross, Harriet (Titi) 45, 63
*Ross, Hon. Harriett 5, 19, 47, 49
*Ross, John, 37, 45, 72, 115,174
Rothes, Countess of 238
Rothes, Earl of 116, 123
Rowland, Nurse (Rowley) 225, 229, 240, 249, 248
Royal Alfred Home for Sailors, 67, 74
Ruskin, John 63
Russell, Sir Charles 66
Ruxton, Admiral & Mrs 39, 67, 68, 71, 79, 88, 105, 124
Ruxton, Col. & Mrs 216

Salisbury, 3rd Marquess of 60, 63, 68, 91, 93, *95,* 100
Sangers Circus 39
Scott, Robert F. 140, 156, 166
Scott, Mrs R.F. 207 243
Shaw, Katie, 61, 65, 111, 117, 120, 221, 224, 233
SHIPS of the Royal Navy
"Active" 96 facing p.*262*
"Alert" 25
"Amphritite" 252
"Andromache" 127
"Anson" 78, facing p.*262*

"Aurora" 72
"Bellerephon" 40
"Cambridge" 135
"Camperdown" 82
"Discovery" 25, 32, 156
"Diadem" 228
"Euryalus"185
"Eurydice" 37, 39
"Excellent" 128
"Fox" *189*
"Galatea" 50, 53, 74, 82
"Gladiator" 196
"Howe" 82
"Immortality" 113
"Jupiter" 154, 161, 164
"Northampton" *42,* 150
"Philomel" 129
"Pintail" 258
"Powerful" 129
"Prince of Wales" 218
"Royal Sovereign" 94, *110*
"Serpent" 83
"Victoria" *102*
"Victoria & Albert" *119*
Singleton of Collon family 3, 27, 29, 30, 32, 216, 238, 246
*Skeffington, Agnes Foster– 38, 65, 106
*Skeffington, Hon. Anna Foster– see Dunlop
*Skeffington, Blanche (Bammie)see Ross
*Skeffington, Hon. Chichester 13, 25, 111
*Skeffington, Hon Constance see Sykes
*Skeffington, Hon Dorcas see FitGerald
*Skeffington, Hon. Ethel F– see Willis
*Skeffington, Florence, see Laurie
*Skeffington, Hungerford 3, 22, 31
*Skeffington, Mabel 174, 175, 198
*Skeffington, Hon. Oriel 26, 92, 119, 123, 137, 166, 170
*Skeffington, Hon Violet 123
*Skeffington, Hon Winifred 123
Smith, Richard 48
Smyly, Dr. 22, 24
Somerset, Mrs & Miss FitzRoy 64, 24
S.S.A.F.A. 71, 126, 130, 134
Stapylton, Capt & Mrs 179
Stawell, Letitia 2, 14, 251
Stokes, Dr 165, 167, *passim* to 175, 183
Stronge, Sir James 178
*Sykes Hon Constance 177, 182 198
*Sykes, H.R. 177

Tatton-Brown family 92, 109, 161
Temple Grove School 75
Thesiger family 85, 89, 119, 121, 128
Thistlethwaite family 23
"Titanic" 238
Trinity House 50
Tyler, Mr & Mrs 54, 70, l81, 82, 93, 96, 100, 105, 161

Upcher Family, 120, 126

Van Kaughuick, Capt. 53, 57, 72, 90
Vansittart, Mrs, Miss 68, 73, 89, 101, 157, 225, 232
Verschoyle, Helen, see Gledstanes
Verschoyle, Helen 23, 38, 94, 111, 116
Verschoyle, John, 61
Vesey-FitzGerald family 6, 195, 131, 144, 146, 153, 159, 165, 176, 187, 240
Victoria, Queen 28, 62, 68, 73, 93, 111, 119, 135

Welch, Irene, 208
Welch, Varvara 216
*West, Alexander 36, 57, 76, 111, 113, 121, 130, 134, 155, 219, 241, 246 262
*West, Alfred, of White Park 174
*West, Charlie 145, 176, 186, 254, 262
*West, Daisy 47, 78, 114, 195, 221, 254, 262
*WEST, Helen (Dot) 2, 26
marries 23, son born 25
at Longford 27,
writes to Leo 31
twins born, 36, 49
terrible year 86
twins born 89
98, 117, 119, 125, 129, 139, 206, 245, 252, 255, 262
*WEST, Henry
marries Helen 23

curacy at Longford 27
talks business 77, 142
Rector at Sacombe 86
at Fleet Review 150
139, 150, 155, 169, 186
in Ireland 174
retires to Folly Court 202
Bob's wedding 208
Dublin Horse Show 210
pastoral visits 179, 240
illness 25
death 243
*West, Jessie 46, 49, 121, 138, 154, 186, 206, 210, 215, 222, 236, 262
*West, Henry Erskine 41, 86
*West, Kathleen & Eileen 89, 117, 129, 220, 245, 247, 252, 262
*West, William Robert 66, 86
Whistler, Rev. & Mrs 164, 191, 211, 231, 244
Whyte-Melville, Florence, see Massereene
Whyte-Melville, G.J. 155
*Wilks, Mrs A.M (Peggy) 247, 250
*William-Powlett, Barbara Lady 182, 183, 187, 188, 190, 191, *234, 259*
*Willis, Hon. Mrs Richard (Ethel) 119, 122, 153, 156, 157, 160, 161, 162, 177, 178, 192, 198, 210, 237, 240
*Wilson, Mrs Edith 48, 169, 171, 177,183
*Wilson, Patience 121, 125, 200, 227, 255
Wolseley, Sir Garnet 23
Woulfe, Hylda, see Goodden
Wynne, Mr 29, 35, 47, 52, 140, 142, 147
Wynne, Gen. Sir Arthur204, 213, 230, 265
Wynne, Col. & Mrs Skeffington 223

Young, Sir Allen 81, 181, 189, 223, 247

Annette at
Halifax, Nova Scotia c.1882

- Robert Delap, 6th in descent from Hugh Delap of Irvine, Ayrshire who settled in Ireland soon after 1600 = Mary Anne Bogle
  - Samuel (e.s.) Delap of Monellan & Lillingstone Lovell Dorset = Susan Bennett
    - Rev. Robert Delap d. 1886 = Miss Galbraith
      - James Bogle = Minnie Frothero Smith
        - Kingsmill = Audrey Davison
          - Hugh Delap
          - David
        - Ella
      - Susan
  - J. B. Delap
  - William D. Delap 1780-1873 = (1) Catherine Foster d. 1842 d. of Rt. Rev. W. Foster (2) Mary Gore Sankey
    - Mary Anne = David Ross of Bladensburg ¶ [see FOSTER tree]
      - Kathleen = Col. F. Oldfield
        - 8 children
    - Robert F. Dunlop 1809-1875 = Hon. Anna E. Foster Skeffington 1817-1901 yst. d. of Visct. Ferrard & Visctess Massereene
      - May 1856-1924 d.s.p.
      - Dora -1914 = Richd. Quin
        - Aylmer Quin
          - Cormac B. Quin
        - Robert
        - Auriel
      - Helen (Dot) -1933 = Rev. Henry West -1913
        - Wm. Robt
        - Alick West = Harriet Chichester
        - Daisy
        - Harry d. 1891
        - Jessie
        - Kathleen
        - Eileen
        - Charles k.a. 1917
      - Blanche -1925 = Chas. E. McClintock 1844- ** [see McCLINTOCK tree]
        - Stanley R. 1882- = Nellie Brodigan
        - Edward 1886-1961 = Margaret Buxton 1885-1974
          - David C. McC. 1913-2001 = Anne Dawson
          - Margaret 1912-86 = R. M. Gambles
          - Kathleen 1914-2005 = C. Kinahan
          - Rachel 1917-80 = J. C. Croft
          - Monica 1922-05 = W. D. Kerr
          - Rhoda 1925- = D. W. Witcomb
        - William 1883-1908
      - William J. S. Dunlop 1847-71 d.s.p.
      - Annette Eliz. 1840-1920 = Adm. Sir F. Leopold McClintock * 1819-1907 [see McCLINTOCK tree]
        - Bessy 1882-1913 d.s.p.
        - Col. Robert S. 1876-1968 = (1) Maudie Elphinstone (2) Diana Clements
          - John 190 -1941 k.a.
          - Nicholas 1916-2001 = Pamela Mansel
          - Araby -1997 = G. Carter
          - Patsy = J. Cyriax
        - Vice Adm. John W. L. 1874-1929 = Hon. Rose O'Neill 1884-
          - John 1925-2006 = Monica Blyth
          - Annette = R. Firth
          - Ethne 1922-34
        - Anna E. 1873-1957 = Bernard Greenwell 2nd Bt. 1874-1939
          - Joyce 1903-95 = David Miles
          - Barbara 1906- = (1) N. William Powlett (2) Sir P. William Powlett
          - Betty 1908-'02 = R. Casement
          - Peggy 1913- = (1) Sir J. Henderson Stewart (2) G. Wilks
          - Peter Greenwell 3rd Bt. 1914-78 = Henrietta Haig
          - Ruth 1916-'04 = (1) R. Colquhoun (2) P. Birchall
        - Henry F. 1871-1959 = Marion Gledstanes d.s.p.
      - Harriet C. A. Dunlop 1838-1915 d.s.p.

- Rt. Rev. W. Foster D.D. 1744-1797 Bishop of Clogher = Catherine Leslie of Ballybay [s. of Anthony Foster of Collon & Eliz. de Burgh]
  - (1) Catherine Foster (see above)
  - other children of the Bishop include de Salis, Gledstanes, Stawell, North, Vesey Fitz-Gerald, Jeffreys

[John McC was nephew of Alexander McClintock of Drumcar 1692-1775 = Rebecca Sampson]

- **John McClintock of Drumcar** (s.3) 1744-1799 = Patience Foster 1746-1830 [d. of Wm. Foster 1710-1783 of Rosy Park & niece to Anthony Foster of Collon]
  - **Henry** (s.4) McClintock 1783-1843 = Eliz. Melesina Fleury 1790-1853 d. of Archd. Fleury of Waterford
    - Chas. F. McC 1836-1907 = Ann Horace
    - Emily 1833-1901 = Geo. Crozier
      - Constance = Dillon
      - Alfred d. 1890
      - Helen
    - Emma 1830-1894 = H.T. Dix
      - Eva
      - Leopold Dix
    - T. Ernest 1829-1900 = Ann Holden
    - Florence 1826 = Geo. Alloway M.D.
    - Rosamund 1823 = G.W. Richardson
      - Geo. Richardson M.D. = ? d. Mrs Culwick
        - George
        - Sarah
        - Georgina
        - Florence
    - Alfred McC, M.D. 1821-1881 = Fanny Cuppidge
      - Fred K. F. 1859 = Clara Adams
        - Alfred McC. = Marg. Thompson
        - Geoffrey
        - Melesina
        - Fanny
      - Leopold A. McC = (1) (2) 1853 Jane
        - Patience = Wilson
        - Jane
      - Caroline = Sir G. Brady
        - 1d.
      - Edith = Wilson, M.D.
        - Ryves
        - Leo
      - Elizabeth = C.J.M. LeFroy
    - F. Leopold 1819-1907 * [see DUNLOP tree]
    - Caroline 1817-1893 = 1. Capt. Ch. Paget 2. Col. Gardiner
      - Edward
      - Fitzclarence
      - Charles = Mary Matchett
        - Charles
        - Louisa =
        - Dorothy
    - Louisa 1814 = F. Tipping
      - 5d. 1s.
    - Marianne 1812 1. T. Battersby 2 E. S. Dix
    - Louis 1810 d. Trinidad
  - 4d.
  - **William McC.** 1777 = Mary Holden
  - **Rev. Alex** = Ann Pratt
  - **John McC.** 1769-1855 = (1) Jane Bunbury (2) Lady Eliz. Trench
    - George McC (s.7) 1822 = Catherine Stronge
      - Arthur G.F. McC of Rathvinden 1866 = Susan Haywood Collins
        - Jane = Bruen
        - Ronald McC d. 1922
        - Edward Stanley = (3)
          - Susan = 1. Edwards Jones
          - Alan McC
          - Nigel k.a. 1942
        - Robt.
        - John Heywood
        - Arthur G. McC.
      - 4d.
    - Stanley (s.6) 1812 = Gertrude La Touche
      - Fredk. Rbt. 1842 d.s.p = Antonia Cleasby
      - Chas. E. McC * see DUNLOP tree *
      - Francis McC Dean of Armagh
      - Emily
      - Gertrude
    - (2) Fredk. W.P. d. 1834 in Strangford Loch
    - William 1800-1848 of Lisnavagh = Patience Stronge d. of Sir Chas. Stronge of Tynan Abbey
      - Thomas McC Bunbury 1848-1929 2nd Lord Rathdonnell = Kath. Bruen of Oak Park
        - Wm. (Billy) k.a. 1900
        - Thomas (Tim) McC. Bunbury 1881-1937 3rd Lord Rathdonnell = Ethel Ievers
          - William R McC. B. 1914-1959 4th Ld. Rathdonnell = Pamela Drew
        - Isabel = F. Colvin
        - Mamie = Bramwell
        - Pauline = Dalgety
    - (1) John McC. 1798-1879 1st Lord Rathdonnell = Anne LeFroy

- John Foster 1740-1848 Baron Oriel [s. of Anthony Foster of Collon d. 1776 Judge & Chief Baron of the Exchequer] = his 1st cousin Margaret Burgh of Birt Viscountess Ferrard
  - Thomas H. Foster d. 1843 2nd Ld. Oriel Visct. Ferrard = Harriet d. 1831 Viscountess Massereene [descendant of Sir John Skeffington 5th Bt. d. 1695]
    - Hon. Anna E. Skeffington [see DUNLOP tree]
    - Hon. Elizabeth = Wm. Poë as wife (2) [Stepsons: Adn. Sir Edw. Poë, Col. Hutchinson Poë]
    - Hon. Harriet d. 1883 = as wife (2) David Ross of Bladensburg
      - Edmund Ross = Nina Lindsay
        - Mary
        - Kathleen
        - Olive
        - Angela
      - Harriet (Titi) = Wm. Ross later a Nun
      - Sir John Ross of Bladensburg = Hon. Blanche Skeffington b. 1844
    - John Skeffington Foster 1812-1863 10th Visct. Massereene & Ferrard = Olivia O'Grady d. 1912 = (2) Duncan
      - Hon. Blanche Skeffington b. 1844
      - Hon. Hungerford 1845-1870 d.s.p = Louisa M.D. Grady
      - Hon. Sydney 1849-1876 = Clementina Dennistoun = (2) James Craig
        - Mabel
        - Florence 1873-1978 = (1) Maj. G.B. Laurie (2) 12th Visct. Massereene
          - Eleanor 1907 = A.W. Johnstone
          - Sydney
          - Geo. Haliburton Laurie = (1) (2)
      - Hon. Reginald 1850
      - Hon. Florence 1841
      - Hon. Olivia 1840
      - Hon. Dorcas 1838-1876 = Percy FitzGerald
      - Clotworthy 1842-1905 11th Visct. Massereene = Florence Whyte-Melville d. 1929
        - Hon. Violet 1879 = C.A.E. Radford
          - Mary 1910
        - Hon. Constance 1877-1965 = H.R. Sykes
          - Hugh
          - Arthur
          - Robin Sykes
        - Hon. Ethel 1876 = Richd. Willis
          - Winifred 1910 = Peter de Salis
          - Charles Willis = Ursula Kearsley
          - Cecilia 1905 = Chas. Johnston
        - Hon. Nora = Chas. Johnston
          - Algernon 1899-1949 = Eileen Kearney
          - John 1902-58 = G. Zoëthout
        - Hon. Winifred 1878-1909
        - Algernon 1873-1956 12th Visct. Massereene = (1) Jean Ainsworth (2) Florence Vere Laurie
          - John 1914-92 13th Visct. Massereene = Annabelle Lewis
        - Hon. Oriel 1871-1905
    - Hon. Chichester F.S. 1813-1880 = Amelia Blennerhasset d. 1887
      - Ada = R. Harman
      - Anna L. = Col. Jas. Hilton
      - Flora G = Lord Muskerry
      - Henrietta = Maj. A.D.D. Kelly "The O'Kelly"
      - 4 s.
      - 2 d.
    - Rev. Hon. Thomas F. Skeffington 1820-1862 = Henrietta Blackwood
      - Hungerford 1850-1881 = Grace Ruttinger
        - Hungerford 1879
        - Agnes 1880
      - Agnes 1857
  - Anna D Foster d.s.p. = Lord Dufferin

drawings from the

Midshipman's Journal of

John Moore Casement
(later Rear-Admiral)

Sept 1895-March 1897